P9-BBT-603

ALSO BY GORE VIDAL

NOVELS
Williwaw
In a Yellow Wood
The City and the Pillar
The Season of Comfort
A Search for the King
The Judgement of Paris
Messiah
Julian
Washington, D.C.
Myra Breckinridge
Two Sisters
Burr
Myron
1876
Kalki
Creation
Duluth
Lincoln
Myra Breckinridge and Myron
Empire
Hollywood
Live from Golgotha

SHORT STORIES
A Thirsty Evil

PLAYS
An Evening with Richard Nixon
Weekend
Romulus
The Best Man
Visit to a Small Planet

ESSAYS
Rocking the Boat
Reflections Upon a Sinking Ship
Homage to Daniel Shays
Matters of Fact and Fiction
The Second American Revolution
Armageddon?
A View from the Diner's Club
Screening History
United States

PALIMPSEST

GORE VIDAL

PALIMPSEST

A MEMOIR

ANDRE DEUTSCH
LONDON

*Grateful acknowledgment is made to the following for
permission to reprint previously published material:*

PETER OWEN LTD: PUBLISHERS: Excerpts from *The Diary of Anaïs Nin
1944–1947.* Copyright © 1971 by Anaïs Nin. Reprinted by
permission of Peter Owen Ltd: Publishers, London.

WYLIE, AITKEN & STONE, INC.: Excerpts from *The Letters of William S.
Burroughs 1945–1959.* Copyright © 1993 by William S. Burroughs.
Reprinted by permission of Wylie, Aitken & Stone, Inc.

Manufactured in the United States of America
on acid free paper

ISBN 0 233 98891 2

Book design by Carole Lowenstein

Photo research by Ann Schneider

First published in Great Britain in 1995 by
André Deutsch Limited
106 Great Russell Street
London WC1B 3LJ

Contents

PALIMPSEST

The memoirist in 1992.
I am about to start writing this book
in Ravello, aided by the white cat.

Palimpsest

A Tissue of Lies? Could there be a more persuasively apt title for a memoir? Particularly if the rememberer of his past is referring not so much to his own lies but to those of others, and, if I may immodestly boast, I have gone *mano a mano* with some of the truly great liars of our time. But then I was a novelist in an era when the line between fiction and fact pretty much broke down as, in coldest blood, the "novelist" felt free to make up things for actual people to do on the page. I have also been engaged in politics, theater, and movies, three worlds where no one is ever on oath–until indicted, of course–in which case he who takes the fall gets to write the definitive tissue of lies, often more than once, like the incomparable R. M. Nixon.

I am writing this on August 26, 1994–glumly, avoiding a tempting lie of convenience; since I usually like to keep the present in the present tense, I wanted to note that *today,* after the hottest summer ever in southern Italy, the heat wave broke. But it was not today but yesterday that the weather changed. From our house here in Ravello, on a cliff above the Gulf of Salerno, there was a lightning storm to the west and another to the east, and a sudden gale that has filled the house with dried leaves.

I am now cool for the first time in two months and able to contemplate what I've been writing for the last two years, a description of the first thirty-nine years of my life as viewed from twenty-nine years later.

I have just noted in this Tissue—no, no! this record of eternal truths and verities, as William Faulkner so famously and typically put it—that last summer the heat broke on August 21, five days earlier than this year.

The room where I work is a white cube with an arched ceiling and a window to my left that looks across the Gulf of Salerno toward Paestum. At the moment: metallic-gray sea and a white haze that obscures our ever more hostile sun. Robert Frost thought that between fire and ice the world would end in ice. Plainly, it is going to be fire this time around.

The room is a mess since Carmela, who looks after the house, has not come to work. She is young and we have always known that we would lose her to marriage, but now it looks as if gravity will get her first. She has fallen, yet again, off her bicycle.

On the long chestnut-wood table where I write, the collected works of Hazlitt. I wanted to write about him two years ago. But did not. *The Spirit of the Age, 1825* has a reproachful look. Several volumes of Mark Twain are piled on a nearby table. I am about to write a preface to his anti-imperial writings. Also—shall I or shall I not?—review the first-person narrations of the two principal "spin masters" in the last presidential election? *He* told lies for Clinton; *she* for Bush. Then they got married. Is there a moral? Next to their Joint Tissue, a bowl of green figs just in from the garden. There is either too much of everything here or nothing at all. Almonds have just come and gone. Since a Norwegian writer and his new wife are due to arrive this evening, Carmela has just rung up to say that she will be coming this afternoon, ready to dust with martyr's smile.

I have always been curious to know where writers are physically situated when they write memoirs. Their placement in works of the imagination is less interesting because the true geography of a novel is all in the mind. But a memoir is set off by a thousand associations, often by objects in a given room. So—opposite me there is a large gray tufa-stone fireplace with elaborate green-yellow-blue tiles. On a console to its right, a photograph of Tennessee Williams with Maria St. Just. She died a few months ago, and her daughter has been staying here. Tennessee looks away from Maria, who looks at him. This was long ago. In Key West.

On the other side of the fireplace, a photograph of me with the president who did us the most harm, Harry S Truman—more on him later. Truman has come to Poughkeepsie to speak for me in my race for

Congress. It is the year 1960. I gaze fawningly upon him while, all about us, the flower of Tammany Hall stare straight ahead. Then a photograph of me, welcoming Jack Kennedy to Dutchess County. He has just been nominated for president. We are both very young, to state the obvious.

By the door, two framed documents: my honorary citizenship of Ravello and my honorary citizenship of Los Angeles, the one and the other of my–home?–towns. A week ago, in the gardens of the Villa Cimbrone, just above our place, the town had planned an homage to the films that I have written. Characteristically, they began with *Bob Roberts,* a film in which I only act. Since the writer-star-director Tim Robbins and his friend Susan Sarandon were staying with us, it ended up as an homage to Tim, which was just as well, though Italy's latest minister of culture, Vittorio Sgarbi, a colorful art historian and television "personality," was still able to continue his long public debate with me on who makes the movies. This is a subject which everyone knows all about except those of us who have actually made a film.

Recently, a television interviewer quoted me as having said, "I seem to have met everyone, but I know no one." Grinning like a tiger in anticipation of antelope, she leaned forward, gently salivating, eager to hear a tragic sigh, see a tear of self-pity. Plainly, due to my high and solitary place in the world–am I not the Living Buddha (or is that Richard Gere?)–and to my cold nature and to my refusal to conform to warm mature family values, I am doomed to be the eternal outsider, the black sheep among those great good white flocks of folks who graze contentedly in the amber fields of the Republic.

I told her briskly that I had never wanted to meet most of the people that I had met and the fact that I never got to know most of them took dedication and steadfastness on my part. By choice and luck, my life has been spent reading other people's books and making sentences for my own. More to the point, if you have known one person you have known them all. Of course, I am not so sure that I have known even one person well, but, as the Greeks sensibly believed, should you get to know yourself, you will have penetrated as much of the human mystery as anyone need ever know.

A memoir is how one remembers one's own life, while an autobiography is history, requiring research, dates, facts double-checked. I've taken the memoir route on the ground that even an idling memory is apt to get right what matters most. I used to say, proudly, that I would never write a memoir, since "I am not my own subject." Now I'm not so sure. After all, one's recollected life is just about all that's left at the end of the day when the work is done and gone, property now of others.

I may not have known well any of the characters in this drama, but I was certainly more interested in my view of them than I was in any view of myself, unlike so many diarists, memoirists, and self-invented fabulists. Yet, reading their records, true or false, my own memory is stirred in a nonsequential way, which explains why I'm not going to start at the traditional beginning: I was born . . . In fact, I give away "Rosebud" in the next few pages, unlike *Citizen Kane,* where revelation comes at the end. I also record daily life so that it can trigger memory, in the hope that the resulting narratives, impressions, sentences should make a pattern not visible to me now.

Title: *Palimpsest.* For years I've used this obscure word incorrectly. Worse, I've always mispronounced it, not sounding the second *s.* I had thought that the word was applicable only to architecture, like the wall of San Marco at Venice with its fragments of bas-reliefs, bits of porphyry, shards of ceramic, all set in plaster to form a palimpsest.

I have just now looked up the earliest meaning of *palimpsest.* It is even more apt than I thought: "Paper, parchment, etc., prepared for writing on and wiping out again, like a slate" and "a parchment, etc., which has been written upon twice; the original writing having been rubbed out." This is pretty much what my kind of writer does anyway. Starts with life; makes a text; then a *re*-vision–literally, a second seeing, an afterthought, erasing some but not all of the original while writing something new over the first layer of text. Finally, in a memoir, there are many rubbings-out and puttings-in or, as I once observed to Dwight Macdonald, who had found me disappointingly conventional on some point, "I have nothing to say, only to add."

These memories were recorded during 1993 and 1994 and completed–or abandoned–in March of 1995. I go back and forth between the present (now already past) to people and places that I knew long ago, duly noting along the way a number of familiar selves, some more real than others.

Palimpsest: discrete archeological layers of a life to be excavated like the different levels of old Troy, where, at some point beneath those cities upon cities, one hopes to find Achilles and his beloved Patroclus, and all that wrath with which our world began.

The
Small Bedroom
at Merrywood

I N JUNE OF THE YEAR 1957, my half sister, Nina (known hence-
forward as Nini) Gore Auchincloss, married Newton Steers in St.
John's Church, "the church of the presidents," in Washington, D.C.
For over a century presidents, of a Sunday, would wander across the
avenue that separates White House from Lafayette Square and its odd
little church, whose chaste Puritan tower is topped by an unlikely gold
Byzantine dome–metaphor?

Newt Steers was a businessman-professor, twenty years older than
the bride. I was among the groomsmen or ushers ("An *endless* parade,"
moaned the ancient Senator Greene of Rhode Island), who, one by one,
in our cutaways, proceeded down the aisle. Among our crowlike number were Senator John F. Kennedy and Senator-to-be John Warner.
Bridesmaids were headed by Mrs. John F. Kennedy, Nini's stepsister
and matron of honor.

Later that day, in a bathroom at Merrywood, the Virginia house
where we had all served time as stepchildren or children of Hugh Dudley Auchincloss, Jr. (known as Hughdie or, more often, poor Hughdie),
Jackie hitched up her gown and showed the innocent Nini how to
douche post-sex, one foot in the bathtub and the other on the white tiled
floor. Although the bidet was known in those days, no proper house
contained one.

*I was one of the groomsmen at the wedding
of my half sister, Nina Gore Auchincloss,
and Newton Steers in 1957. At the far right is
Nina's stepbrother-in-law, Senator John F.
Kennedy; behind me stands my sister's next
husband, Michael Whitney Straight. As
family tradition required,
both marriages failed.*

To the consternation of Nini's stepmother, Janet Lee Bouvier Auchincloss ("of the *Virginia* Lees," she used to boast until the real Lees ordered her to shut up), Nini was not only a virgin on her wedding day– something of an anomaly at Merrywood–but, despite a passionate girlhood astride horses, she had been obliged to undergo last-minute minor surgery. Janet regarded all of this as a sign of Nini's essential tiresomeness and, perhaps, depravity. After all, if she was technically a virgin at nineteen, what on earth had she really *done*?

In the church sat the mother of the bride, Nina Gore Vidal Auchincloss Olds. Our joint mother was uncommonly sober. There were a number of oldtime Washington gents on hand, and they were most delighted to gaze yet again on what had been, twenty years earlier, the town's reigning beauty and mistress of numerous revels at the ill-named Merrywood. Nina was a bit puffy by this time, but the thick high-arched brows and large hazel eyes–gift of a Creole grandmother–still commanded attention. One purple-faced old man, elegantly turned out in frock coat and gray waistcoat, leaned over to whisper in her ear, "How are you, sweetie?" Nina was not doing too badly. Like so many ladies of limited means but luxurious tastes, she had retreated, first to Los Angeles, to the Beverly Hills Hotel (bungalow number one), where she had a good–that is to say fun–war, then on to Southampton and, finally, when her income no longer matched inflationary costs and unchanging tastes, she withdrew to Cuernavaca, in Mexico. Here servants were plentiful and cheap, and raddled bridge partners grew like so many alligator pears on the local trees. Another resident of Cuernavaca, the writer Carlos Fuentes, told me that she was known as "the American empress. She would be up at dawn, ordering the police to clean the street in front of her house, carry things for her, run errands– no one dreamed of disobeying her."

Palimpsest time: I am now writing over the half-rubbed-out account of Nini's wedding, dull as all weddings. It is 1946. I am twenty years old, riding in a taxi down Park Avenue on my way to the publisher E. P. Dutton. My first novel, *Williwaw*, is about to appear. In the left-over-from-the-war khakis that we all wore, skinny, yellow-faced Jack Kennedy is wandering down the west side of the avenue. In a blaze of publicity, he is now running for Congress. Our fathers are friends, but we've never met. As I watch him, I wonder, Have I made a mistake? Instead of the book that I am currently writing, shouldn't I have followed my grandfather Senator Gore's plan and set out for Congress instead?

Next glimpse, 1956. Kennedy house in Georgetown. Jack is in a bathrobe. Nothing under it. Face swollen. Impacted wisdom tooth. "How can I speak tonight in Baltimore, looking like this?"

"Isn't he vain," Jackie purrs.

AFTER THE SERVICE at Nini's wedding in 1957, Jack and I were driving across the Potomac River for the reception at Merrywood on the Potomac palisades. Jack had almost won the vice-presidential nomination in 1956–a narrow escape, I had remarked at the time. He had come to agree with me. He was running now for the presidential nomination.

Meanwhile, I had been offered the Democratic nomination for Congress in upstate New York's Twenty-ninth District, something of a kamikaze mission in a Republican district, but apt to be useful if I should ever want to pick up that conventional political career which I had abandoned before it had ever properly begun. But then, as Ronald Reagan blithely observed to fellow actor William Holden, "Politics is a wonderful second career. You ought to try it." So if politics could not be for me, as of the forties and fifties, the first career that I had always wanted, why not a second one in the sixties?

In the back of the limousine, Jack and I waved to nonexistent multitudes, using the British royal salute, in which the fingers of one hand unscrew, as it were, an invisible upside-down jar of marmalade. Jack thought that Nini had made a mistake in not marrying his brother Teddy. I had no view on the matter. Absently, he tapped his large white front teeth with the nail of his forefinger, click, click, click–a nervous tic.

ALL OF MERRYWOOD'S downstairs French windows were open onto the lawn and the woods beyond the lawn and the milk-chocolate-brown Potomac River far below. The view was at its poison-ivied best on that spring day. We were greeted, if that is the word, by the stepmother of the bride, Janet Auchincloss; she was a small woman, with a large pouterpigeon bust that neatly balanced large low-slung buttocks set atop sandpiper legs. The sallow face was all great curved nose-beak set between small, fierce dark eyes. With me, she was her usual rude self while I, too, was equally rude but with an awful, studied graciousness: What a wonderful stepmother you have been to my half sister! What a superb job you have done in making Merrywood look like a proto–Ralph Lauren dream of upwardly mobile gentility!–or something along those lines.

A year earlier, when a play of mine was on tour at the National Theater in Washington, Nini had insisted that I come to lunch at the house where I had grown up. Since there was a special children's table in the dining room, Janet assigned me to that, and so the much-sought-after (by Washington hostesses, anyway) author of *Visit to a Small Planet* had a splendid time, with the children. At least Janet had not the cruelty to put me on her right.

Janet and I exchanged insults in the main drawing room. "Nini always hated you," she said, thoughtfully, "until you became a great success in the theater."

I replied with what I hoped was appropriate sweetness. "Why should she be any different from the rest of you?"

Jackie came to my rescue. I wanted to see my old room on the second floor. Originally, I had been quartered beneath the eaves, along with my mother's two small children by Hughdie, and my stepbrother Yusha . . .

INTERESTING MAIL has just arrived this morning, December 8, 1994, so I shall palimpsest–that is, scribble over Janet and even Jackie. They will be back: Janet, inadvertently a laugh a minute, and Jackie, whose boyish beauty and life-enhancing malice were a great joy to me. Now, for an instant, frozen in time, I shall leave Jackie and me at the foot of the stairs on whose first landing was a small bedroom that had first been mine then hers and the geographic locus where our love lives had crossed. Now I shall go further back in time to explain how we came to share the same small bedroom.

RAVELLO. Province of Salerno. Italy. Twenty-two years ago, at this table and in this room, I wrote the last sentence of the novel *Burr*. December 8 is the day of the Immaculate Conception, an Italian holiday. I also made it the day on which the book concludes: "At sundown I was on the terrace, wondering how to capture in words the exact way the sea below looks in winter light; the way the gradations of milky blue and green father darkest sapphire . . ." Deliberately eccentric choice of verb. My narrator's father was on his mind in those last pages, as mine is— suddenly—now. A half brother has just sent me the letters that I wrote my father. I am touched that Gene, my father, kept them, but then in the forty-three years that we knew each other, we never agreed on much of anything and never once quarreled. Gene's older sister used to complain, "You aren't like father and son, you're like two brothers, off together, making fun of the rest of us," which was just about right.

Eugene L. Vidal was born April 13, 1895, in Madison, South Dakota. At the University of South Dakota he was so formidable a football player that he was acquired by—that is, appointed to—the U.S. Military Academy at West Point. Despite his training as an engineer at West Point, he had a divergent mind. In 1917 he went into the newly constituted air corps as a pilot, a glamorous thing to be in those days. Then, with Charles Lindbergh and Amelia Earhart, he helped found three airlines, TWA, Eastern, and Northeast. He liked creating things. He had no interest in making money, and he made no fortune.

My letters are strewn across a table; there are several copies of Gene's replies to me, neatly typed on crumbling brown paper. There are also several pages of what looks to be a transcribed interview with him on the early days of aviation. As President Roosevelt's director of air commerce in the thirties, Gene got to know Orville Wright, the surviving brother of the two inventors of the airplane. Orville and Wilbur Wright were lifelong bachelors, as *Time* magazine used to write when eager to suggest uranism. At random I pick up a page from Gene's recollections:

"I often visited Orville Wright at his home and we talked a great deal about their early problems. I asked him what was their most serious problem in developing the first powered airplane. To my surprise, he said the design of the propeller. He said there were almost no books or papers on the subject.

"A year or so after the first flight, he and Wilbur discussed the matter of sitting up while in flight, and decided to try it. He told me it was some time later that they got the idea of using wheels for takeoff, landing and handling the machine on the ground.

"Years went by, perhaps twenty, before airplanes had brakes; yet automobiles had brakes from the beginning."

It was my father's dream to be the Henry Ford of aviation. He wanted to develop a cheap plane that anyone who could afford a car could own and was simple enough for even a child to fly. Thus I was made famous for an instant in my tenth year when, together, we drove out to Bolling Field, where the so-called Hammond flivver plane was on the tarmac, as well as a newsreel crew from Pathé news.

Gene was a superb salesman. He knew that I was so used to flying with him that taking off and landing a boy-proof plane was no problem for me, but my not-so-secret dream of being a movie star could now be consummated, he told me, in the newsreels. I flew the plane; made a bumpy landing; then, overcome by stage fright, I froze before the camera as I was supposed to say (against my will) that the flight had been just as easy as riding a bicycle. I still watch this old newsreel and wonder how that blond boy was ever me or that astonishingly handsome stranger my father.

The year before my newsreel debut, my life had changed drastically. Gene and Nina were divorced, and Nina and I settled into a two-room flat in Washington, D.C.'s Wardman Park Hotel. I slept on a sofa in an alcove off the living room and made my own breakfast in a small kitchen while Nina worked her way through the stations of the cross of her homely morning hangover. Later, a bus would take me to my school, St. Albans.

On my tenth birthday, Gene paid us a call and presented me with a signet ring. Then I went off to bed while Gene and Nina, on rather better terms since the divorce than before, discussed me. I listened smugly as Nina confided, "I think I've done a pretty good job." I felt very complacent indeed as Nina congratulated herself on her success as a single parent while Gene politely agreed with her. Then they discussed money, an urgent subject, always, with her, and one of no interest to him or me. I fell asleep. I gather now that what they had really discussed was the necessity of her marriage to Hugh D. Auchincloss.

One month later, Nina and Hughdie were married in the hotel; then, later that night, she and I moved into Merrywood, where I knew no one except for my new stepfather. I was quite used to being very much the only child at my grandparents' house in Rock Creek Park, and so I did not crave the company of other little folk, particularly my new stepbrother, Yusha.

In due course, I moved myself out of the attic and into the small bedroom at the head of the stairs on the second floor. Nina's bedroom was at one end of the landing; next to it, ominously as it turned out, was Hughdie's. Nina had made an informal prenuptial agreement with Hughdie. She would marry him in order to bring glamour–he had a passion for senators–into his life and to be a good stepmother to his forlorn child, but since she did not care for him "that way," theirs would be a *mariage blanc*. Crafty Hughdie agreed; then he made a *formal* prenuptial agreement that she be given a fixed income for life, and never anything more. Apparently, he had had to pay too much to Nina's predecessor, a colorful Russian lady who had been accidentally scalped by an airplane propeller. Delirious, in the hospital, she spoke of the true love of her life, whose name was not Hughdie. When she recovered, Hughdie divorced her and she married her true lover and lived happily ever after; something poor Hughdie did not.

Obsessively, Hughdie had fixed his gaze upon my mother, who was otherwise engaged, or so she believed. The ill-matched, wealthy Mr. and Mrs. John Hay Whitney–Jock and Liz–and the star-crossed, fortuneless Mr. and Mrs. Eugene Luther Vidal had been, as they say at dances, double-cutting for some time. Everyone assumed that once the unhappy couples broke up, Nina would marry Jock and Liz would marry Gene.

I went with Nina to the TH Ranch outside Reno, Nevada, where phase one, divorce, was to take place. Suddenly there was Hughdie, looking out of place in his banker's suit. Some years earlier, his mother had bought him a brokerage house.

Nina asked me if I'd like him for a stepfather. I said no, largely on aesthetic grounds. After my father, the large, cumbersome, stammering Hughdie was simply neither plausible nor decorative. Even if I had entirely grasped the necessity of a fortune for feckless Nina, I don't think that I would have been impressed. If it was to be big money, I preferred Jock's.

After we came back to Washington, Nina still expected to marry Mr. John Hay Whitney, while Mrs. John Hay Whitney still expected to marry my father. As it turned out my father said no to the glamorous Liz–to my sorrow. Liz was a celebrated horsewoman; looked like an Indian princess; made a screen test to play Scarlett O'Hara in *Gone With the Wind*, which would eventually be produced by Jock's movie partner, David O. Selznick. Jock said no to Nina, leaving her high if never entirely dry. Since her father, Senator Thomas Pryor Gore, was facing a difficult primary in Oklahoma and had no money to spare, my mother was obliged to say yes to the persistent Hughdie. Nina would be poor no more. Best of all, it was understood from the beginning that there would be no sex.

So, in the dark of night, we were whisked across the river to the unfinished Merrywood, a mock-Georgian brick house set among some forty acres of woods on the high Potomac palisades. From terraced lawns, there was a steep rocky drop to the river, down which it was dangerous to walk, much less run, and so, of course, I often ran this hazardous course, leaping from rock to rock. To this day I still dream of making that descent to the swift mud-brown, swirling river–going faster and faster, ecstatically unable to stop until dream's end.

I also recall the sharp smell of new paint inside the house and the rich supper prepared by a Russian chef from the czar's Winter Palace. Where else?–all Russian cooks of that day were so billed. For the first time I saw gold spun sugar. We were served by an amiable Russian butler, named Affranasi, who taught me to count to ten in Russian, which was just about as long as it took my mother to get rid of him and the other relics of her predecessor's regime.

NOW I AM BACK at Merrywood with Jackie. Janet has rejoined the wedding party on the lawn and I can hear her voice, in the distance, harassing the guests.

As Jackie and I went up the stairs, I paused on the first landing and showed her the spot where, at about six in the morning of the day after my mother's marriage to Hughdie, I found Nina seated on the steps, wearing a dark gray silk dressing gown with a burgundy stripe–I, who never notice what anyone wears, often have a good visual recall of crucial scenes. Not long ago I described that dressing gown to a lady knowledgeable in such things: "Bergdorf Goodman 1935"; thus, briskly, the picture was captioned.

Years later Nina told me that the "white" marriage she had agreed to had turned very black indeed the first night. I should note that the only advantage for a child in having an alcoholic parent is that you acquire, prematurely, quite a bit of valuable data. Apparently, there was going to be Sex whether Nina liked it or not. She did not like it. But then no woman could have liked Hughdie's importunate fumblings. He ejaculated normally but without that precedent erection which women require as, if nothing else, totemic symbol of a man's true love, not to mention a homely source of hedonistic friction. Since Hughdie wanted children, Nina was obliged, in some fashion that she, on several occasions in her admittedly never-long-empty cups, vividly described to me and I would promptly erase from memory. I *think* she inserted–with a spoon?–what she called "the bugs" in order to create my demi-siblings.

I told Jackie some of this on the landing. She knew exactly what I meant. But she did not know–and I never told her–that Nina had engineered her mother's marriage to Hughdie. Nina had first known Janet when she was a saleswoman at a New York City department store. A financially desperate "social climber" with two small daughters to raise, Janet was eager to marry someone just like . . . just like poor Hughdie, which Nina suggested that she do, shortly before she herself surfed on a wave of Scotch whiskey into True Love's arms, becomingly attached to an air corps officer called Robert Olds. Nina's wit about herself was often appealing. When asked why, after the death of General Olds, she had not married again, she replied, "My first husband had three balls, my second two, my third one. Even I know enough not to press my luck."

As is well known and too often noted, time shrinks the houses and rooms of one's early days. Jackie and I entered our old bedroom, not much larger than a closet. To the right, twin beds. To the left, the door to a small bathroom with a white tile floor, unchanged since the thirties. Directly ahead, a single large window with a view of lawn, woods, river–Nini's wedding party.

Jackie said, "When I first moved in here, I found some old shirts of yours. With name tags. I used to wear them, riding. Then Jack and I stayed in here, after the honeymoon. I must say he suffered quite a lot in this house, from Mother." She left me, standing at my old window.

I LOOKED DOWN at the wedding party. On the lawn, Jack was charming not girls but politicians. I noted, as always, the odd curve to his back below the neck–"that spavined hunchback," as Lyndon Johnson, unaffectionately, called him.

I knew, even then, that Jack was going to be elected president. When I told my omniscient Hudson River valley neighbor the journalist

Richard Rovere, he was delighted by my political innocence. Patiently, he explained to me how Jack's election was not possible, ever. Patiently, I explained to him how the family political machine worked, as well as the unusual appeal of its candidate, whom I had got to know through Jackie. As it turned out, Dick was the innocent–even gullible–one.

At the window, I started to free-associate, all the while looking down on the lawn where my imaginary characters in the novel *Washington, D.C.* would one day have their being. I saw a number of figures from my childhood; they had continued to know Hughdie and the third wife, something of an alien in our city, but then so was Hughdie, a New Yorker who was drawn to senators the way that some men are to women or to Meissen china. In a short autobiography that he composed for a family album, he noted that he had had the high distinction of being twice related through marriage to U.S. senators: "as son-in-law to Thomas Gore of Oklahoma and stepfather-in-law to Senator John F. Kennedy of Massachusetts."

On the lawn, below the window, the bride and groom, Nini and Newt. "At last," said Jackie, later, in her smiling toast to the newlyweds, "a couple in the family whose names are as alliterative as Jack and Jackie." Teddy Kennedy, standing next to me, raised high his champagne glass and then poured its contents over his handsome youthful head. The marriage of Nini and Newt was, of course, a disaster. Family tradition must be observed.

EVEN IF MY MOTHER had been invited, she would not have come to the wedding reception. There had been an ever-increasing tidal wave of bad blood between her and Hughdie over the usual, money. Impulsively, in 1940, she had left him in order to marry her off-and-on lover, Olds. Hughdie's mother, Emma, a formidable old lady awash in Standard Oil money, begged her to stay. Emma spoke of increased revenues for Nina; spoke candidly of Hughdie's sexual problems, which she attributed to excessive masturbation in youth. Although Emma had sent Hughdie to a number of psychiatrists, the Grail–a full erection–was never more than a tantalizing vision. He had, incidentally, a superb collection of pornographic books that Nina obliged him to drown like kittens in the Potomac River, to protect the innocence of the two growing boys in the house. Fortunately, he had held back a few, which I found.

As Nina was temperamentally incapable of sensible action, she turned old Mrs. Auchincloss down. Then Hughdie offered to increase her monthly stipend. "But I want all or nothing," he said. Since limpness was all, it was to be nothing, or so Nina said she said, though what she actually said, when repeated over the years, was not always reliable. In fact, much of her time was spent revising, often drastically, the scenarios of her life in order to show how she had always been "the fall guy"; like Garbo, she often referred to herself in the third-person masculine. I suspect that if Nina had been literate—as opposed to articulate (she could have out-argued Clarence Darrow in any court any day)—she would have written much like Anaïs Nin, the next woman to come seriously my way. Each believed that she gave all of herself to others only to receive, as recompense, a token serpent's tooth in the mail.

Nina's favorite phrase, left over from the twenties, was "Let's face it." This usually preceded a soliloquy on what a "good guy" she had been while others had let her down. She *hated* selfishness in others, and saw it everywhere, especially in me. Ominously, I would be warned "to turn over a new leaf"—this usually preceded my being sent off to yet another school, even farther from "home" than the last. "From here on out," Nina would announce, at regular intervals for the rest of her life, "I'm looking out for number one." Like most dedicated drinkers, she could not spare the time to go to the movies, but she was quick to appropriate argot. At the TH Ranch, she had been all girl-cowhand. "Stop beefing!" she would roar at any complaint that I might make. "You're always bellyaching!" A man's woman, no doubt about that.

The fact that Nina had not wanted to come to Nini's wedding reception spared her the humiliation undergone by Jackie's father, known as Black Jack. He was a charming alcoholic gentleman with whom Cole Porter had had a "flirtation," whatever that might mean, since, according to legend, Black Jack was as notorious and as busy a womanizer as an alcoholic can be.

For the earlier wedding, that of Jack and Jackie, Black Jack came to Newport, Rhode Island, to give away the bride. He was on his best behavior. But, inspired by who knows what furies, Janet decided that although she could not bar him from the church, she could disinvite him from the reception, which, as it turned out, the Kennedys were to take over as a sound-and-light spectacle, celebrating the triumph of the Boston Irish over that old Protestant patricate which had scorned

Jack's father, Joe Kennedy, not because he was Irish and Catholic, as he would have it, but because he was so exuberantly and successfully a crook.

Janet's younger daughter, Lee, was married to an uncommonly charming and decent youth named Mike Canfield, somewhat out of place in our wild world of bloody tooth and claw. Janet ordered Mike to go to Black Jack and tell him that he was not to come to the wedding reception. Mike later wrote a short story about all this and gave it to me to read. The denouement was predictable. Black Jack went straight to the bar. I suppose that the essential difference between Janet and Nina was that while Janet *made* trouble, Nina *was* trouble.

In due course, Lee, in her lifelong search for the higher solvency, divorced Mike to marry one "Stas" (pronounced "Stash") Radziwill. Mike was always surprisingly mild about his ex-wife. "There were times when . . ." Mike stammered on *w*'s. So did Hughdie and so did I until I took up debating at Exeter. "When what?" I was helpful. "Wh . . . when I think she went perhaps too far, you know? Like going to bed with Jack in the room next to mine in the south of France and then b . . ." There was a problem with *b*'s, too. ". . . boasting about it."

STILL IN THE SMALL BEDROOM. I brood now on what truly mattered to me. I look at the twin beds where Jackie and Jack had slept and where, earlier, a classmate from St. Albans, Jimmie Trimble, and I had slept.

From below, I hear the cawing of Janet's voice, like that of some dark crow. Poor Jack, I think, a loveless marriage and a hateful mother-in-law. But then he had told a mutual woman friend that he had never loved anyone. Had I?

Since I don't really know what other people mean by *love*, I avoid the word. None of us brought up in a world of such crude publicness tends to trust much of anyone, while those who mean to prevail soon learn the art of distancing the self from dangerous involvements. In a recent biography of Jack, *Reckless Youth*, I was struck by the similarities between my youthful self and his, particularly in sexual matters. Neither was much interested in giving pleasure to his partner. Each wanted nothing more than orgasm with as many attractive partners as possible. I remember that he liked sex in a hot bath, with the woman on top, favoring his bad back. Once, with an actress I know, he suddenly pushed her backward until her head was under water, causing a vaginal spasm for her and orgasm for him. She hates him still.

On this point, Jack and I are unalike. All men—women, too?—have a streak of sadism. But mine was plainly narrower than Jack's. Also, the small bedroom reminds me that, unlike Jack, I had once been (in this very room—and ever since?) in love.

The Desire
and the
Successful Pursuit
of the Whole

R ECENTLY, I LECTURED AT HARVARD on how we are shaped
by the movies we see while growing up. In preparation for the
lectures, I watched *The Prince and the Pauper* for the first time
since 1937. Like most of the movies that impress themselves on a child,
the story is simple, but the subtexts are disturbingly complex if one is
the right age to be affected by them. The prince and the pauper were
played by Bobby and Billy Mauch, identical twins who were the same
age as I—twelve. So there was I, in surrogate, on the screen not once but
twice, not only prince but pauper, and the two of them—of us?—were so
alike as to be interchangeable as well.

I do not know if a desire to be a twin is a common one or if such a
longing might run in families, psychically as well as genetically. My
grandmother Gore lost *her* twin at birth, and it required no uncanny
knowledge of the human heart for the family to figure out that when
she took over the task of being not only wife but eyes to a blind husband, she had found in him her long-lost twin. On the other hand, I was
quite pleased to be an only child. Later, I acquired various step- and half
brothers and sisters, but I never really knew any of them, since I was
gone for good at seventeen—into the army and to all those other worlds
elsewhere.

When I watched *The Prince and the Pauper* the first time, I wanted to
be not one but two. Lonely children often have imaginary playmates,

Jimmie Trimble as he looked the last time
I saw him, when we were seventeen, in 1942.
What I was not, he was,
and the other way around.

but I was never lonely–I was solitary, and wanted no company at all other than books and movies, and my own imagination.

A childhood desire to be a twin does not seem to me to be narcissistic in the vulgar Freudian sense. After all, one is oneself; and the other, other. It is the sort of likeness that makes for wholeness, and is it not that search for likeness, that desire and pursuit of the whole–as Plato has Aristophanes remark–that is the basis of all love? As no one has ever actually found perfect wholeness in another human being, no matter of what sex, the twin is the closest that one can ever come toward human wholeness with another; and–dare one invoke biology and the origin of our species?–back of us mammals doomed to die once we have procreated, there is always our sexless ancestor the amoeba, which never dies as it does not reproduce sexually but merely–serenely?– breaks in two and identically replicates.

Anyway, I thought Billy and Bobby Mauch were cute as a pair of bug's ears, and I wished I were either one of them–one of them, mind you. I certainly did not want to be two of *me*, as one seemed more than enough to go around even in so exaggerated a family. Yet doubleness has always fascinated me, as mirrors do, as filmed images do. I have read that a recurring theme in my work is doubleness or duplicity. If this is the case, I see now where it might have–unconsciously, at least–begun.

In any case, it was after I saw the film that I saw my other half in Jimmie Trimble. It was thought best by Nina that I board during the week at St. Albans, an all-boys' school near Washington's cathedral. I was allowed to come "home" on weekends. At midterm, Jimmie became a boarder. We were friends immediately. I was one week older than he. We were the same height and weight. He had pale blue eyes; mine were pale brown. He had the hunter-athlete's farsightedness; I had the writer-reader's myopic vision. I was blond, with straight hair. He was blond, with curly hair. His sweat smelled of honey, like that of Alexander the Great. At seventeen, when he graduated from St. Albans (I was doing the same at Exeter), he was offered contracts to play professional baseball with both the New York Giants and the Washington Senators; each club would have sent him to college and kept him out of the war. Loyal to his native city, he chose the Senators.

I had lunch with Jimmie's mother in Washington not long ago, our first meeting in fifty-five years. At ninety, Ruth Trimble Sewell is like a woman of fifty; she is alert, straight-backed, with blue eyes like Jimmie's, only just beginning to fade. Over lunch, we brought him back to life, briefly, each for his own purpose. She had been disturbed by the revelation in a magazine that the "JT" to whom I had dedicated *The City and the Pillar* (about one boy's love for another) was Jimmie Trimble; and the journalist made it as clear as he could, with no corroboration from me, that we had been schoolboy lovers. Of Jimmie's death at nineteen, on Iwo Jima, the journalist quoted me as saying, "He was the unfinished business of my life." A response as cryptic as it was accurate.

"Kind friends"–Mrs. Sewell emphasized the adjective in her Washington-Kentucky accent–"wrote me from all over to say how upset I must be. Perhaps I overreacted." She had given Jimmie's letters to a master at St. Albans, who was aware of my interest in . . . what? bringing him to life again? in order to . . . again, what? Discover who he was? As if I hadn't once known him as well as I knew myself. But since we had been separated by geography the last years of his short life, I suppose that I wanted–now–to fill in the details. "I shall but love thee better after death," as Mrs. Browning so stonily put it.

"Yes, perhaps I overreacted." She ordered a single vodka martini. She had been born in Washington, a belle of the town, one year older than my mother, whom she remembered. "So good-looking," she said tactfully.

Ruth told me of Jimmie's first report home after a weekend in the great house in Virginia where I was prince, he pauper. Of course, we were interchangeable, as I was not really prince but only living for a time as princes do. Upon my mother's divorce from Hughdie, when I was sixteen, I, too, became pauper.

I had a very nice dog, Jimmie had reported, a toy Scottie named Wiggles. But my mother would not let the dog in the house, so while I was away during the week at boarding school, a thirty-minute drive from Merrywood, Wiggles was exiled to a fenced-in area beside the garage, itself set over a squash court, where Hughdie never played but Jimmie and I used to roller-skate, ruining the wood floor.

The dog was one of a thousand sore points between Nina and me. My father had brought me the puppy, a present from Liz Whitney, whose numerous dogs roamed her eighteenth-century Virginia house, Llangollen. Litters were constantly being produced beneath Chippendale consoles and allowed to grow up on the spot. I often wished that Liz were my mother.

Nina promptly took the dog and said that Liz had given it to her. This was followed by a flaming row of the sort that punctuated her life with me and, indeed, with anyone that she knew well. In later, more reflective years, she blamed her behavior on an agonizing menopause. But as of 1935 she was all set to have two more children–ladled into her by silver spoon?–so she was also obliged to note, for those who might be counting, that her periods had also been more excruciating than those of any other woman in medical history.

At the beginning, Wiggles had slept in Nina's Art Deco bedroom. A fashionable word in those days was *neurasthenic*, which could mean practically anything. In Nina's case, it meant fearful hangovers combined with a morphine habit. Once or twice a week one Dr. Huffman, wearing a Prince Albert, would arrive to administer a shot; then, if the company was not too grand, he would be asked for lunch. "I am *upper*-middle-class," the drunken Auden kept repeating at our last meeting, "my father was a *doctor*." To which I finally replied, "Well, he would never have made the grade in my day, in my city." But with or without the humble Dr. Huffman's drugs, the sound of the dog's claws at night on the bedroom floor gave Nina the jitters and so Wiggles was banished from the house.

On those weekends that I was allowed to come home–usually when Mr. and Mrs. Auchincloss were on safari in Hobe Sound or places even more dangerous and farther to the south–Jimmie and I would join Wiggles in the enclosure and tell her how sorry we were about her exile. Jimmie's mother had been much struck by details of life in the great house: " 'They also have silk sheets,' Jimmie said to me, 'and the butler asks you at night what you want for breakfast.' " Mrs. Sewell was beginning to remember a lot. So was–am–I.

I tried to recall, as I looked into what proved to be Jimmie's eyes across the table from me, what it was that we had talked about when alone together. He was an athlete; I played nothing except erratic tennis. I read everything that I could; he read as little as possible. But I am intrigued by a letter he wrote his mother from Guam, in the South Pacific. Would she send him Whitman's *Leaves of Grass*? This set off a tremor. He and I had certainly lived out the Calamus idyll. Now someone–a lover?–had suggested that he read Whitman. Is this to be a mystery story? Who was he, after all? Will I ever know now?

I remember him mostly in flashes. I'd go with him to hear Benny Goodman at the Capitol Theater. He loved jazz, swing; played saxophone. I liked "classical" music; played nothing. What we had entirely in common, aside from each other, was the fact that each was already what he would be when grown-up. He was professional athlete; I was writer. That was that. Neither was uncertain about what to do in the future because each was already doing it. This completeness set us off from our contemporaries. As a result, neither was much of a success as a schoolboy. Little of what we were offered in class was of the slightest use to either him or to me. I wanted to know far more history and literature than any school would ever have taught, while all he needed was a playing field to dominate. So, haphazardly, I educated myself, all the while resentful of the dullness and irrelevance of the classroom. Since learning then was mostly by rote, I developed a block against memorizing so great that now, when I occasionally act in films, dialogue must be glued to the backs of chairs or written on cards held out of camera range. Today, schools–for the rich, that is, there is nothing much for the rest–know better *how* to teach; their only problem is *what* to teach.

The differences between Jimmie and me were sometimes polar. I detested my mother; he adored his. I said as much to Mrs. Sewell. She smiled. "I remember when he was first brought to me, at the hospital. I had so much wanted a brunette, and there he was, all blond already. I must admit I was a little disappointed, to have two blonds, Jimmie and his sister." The smile vanished. "Tell me, did he ever talk to you about his father?"

I said that I couldn't remember. I had always assumed that his father was dead. I did know that there was a stepfather whom he disliked. She frowned. "Well, *he* and I were not married long. Then I married Mr. Sewell, and we lived happily ever after until last year, when he died. So you see," she said with no dramatic emphasis, "I am bereft."

I had been in her apartment earlier that morning. Over the mantel was a painting of Jimmie made in 1937. He is holding a model sailboat. Though he smiled a lot in life, in almost all his pictures he looks grave, eyes usually turned from painter or camera lens. I have a life-size reproduction of the painting on the wall beside my bed. Jimmie is looking to his right, to the west, to the approaching end, I morbidly think. Jimmie used to be excused from class so that he could go sit for his portrait. He was also excused, from time to time, for surgical enlargement of his urethra. I never knew what this condition was called medically, and I was not about to mention it to Mrs. Sewell. Jimmie said that it was a remarkably painful, slow business.

Mrs. Sewell described his first serious girlfriend, "She was absolutely beautiful, but she wasn't really. . . . Well, once I asked her to help with the punch bowl, to fill cups, you know? and she refused. She was . . ." But the word *common* did not pass her lips because, "I always tried to love anyone he loved. Then he met Chris White that last year and wanted to marry her."

"You mean Chris White the actress?"

She was surprised. "You know who she is? Yes, she *was* an actress on television, a long time ago." In the fifties, Chris White was a successful television actress who almost invariably got the parts that my friend Joanne Woodward wanted. When Joanne received the Academy Award, I wired her, "Where is Chris White tonight?" So here was Chris White yet again: Jimmie's final love except, perhaps, for whoever it was who got him to read Whitman.

"When they sent me Jimmie's footlocker, I burned all the letters to him from girls–hers too." But Chris, a Washington girl, continued to see Mrs. Sewell after the war. Then, some years ago, she dropped from view.

Mrs. Sewell laughed. "I remember Jimmie asked me, once, 'Did you ever tell a man that he was *beautiful*?' " Jimmie had been shocked at such a word applied to himself by a girl. But then, in those days before Tennessee Williams and Marlon Brando, males were taught to think of themselves as coarse and brutish Calibans, on a lower level of evolution than the fragile Ariels of the other sex.

Jimmie overflowed with animal energy, not to mention magnetism for both sexes. Even so, at twelve or thirteen, I was delighted to be able to report to him that I had had sex–if that is quite the phrase–with a girl before Jimmie did. He was riveted; wanted details. The event had taken place in the game room at Merrywood, an airless chamber in the cellar where game was hung and aged–game never shot by Hughdie, but often sent him by friends. I was showing a girl that I'd known for some time this scary room–scary because on the inside of the heavy metal door there was a rusty round knob that one had to push in order to open the door; if it failed to work, you would suffocate, unheard by anyone, since the room was soundproofed. On the floor, the girl and I fumbled about, and I was almost as interested in what I was going to tell Jimmie about the great mystery that I had at last–barely–penetrated as I was in the earthshaking event itself.

Rousseau thought that Montaigne should have told us more about his sex life. I think Montaigne told quite enough. But then I have never had much interest in the sexual lives of real people. I suspect that I was the only boy of that era to have read Frank Harris, skipping the sex parts in order to get to the political and literary anecdotes. I do like pornography, but only when it is clearly fiction.

Mrs. Sewell picked at her elaborate lobster dish. The dining room at Willards, as we used to call the hotel, was half full. The hotel is not very like the original Willards, where Lincoln stayed; it was entirely rebuilt at the beginning of the century and, lately, rather well redone. I am at home with the result. Across Pennsylvania Avenue from the hotel is the Commerce Department, and from the windows of my room I can look into what had been my father's second-floor office when he was director of air commerce–a corner office at the west end of the building, with windows shaded by a row of pillars set in a ledge, already darkened, even then, by the excrement of those multitudinous pigeons who were–and are–almost as numerous as civil servants in our now imperial capital city. Together, from the ledge, we watched Roosevelt's second inaugural parade, in which Gene took no part, since he was resigning his post.

"Before my children were born, I took a course in nutrition. I always made the bread, and just about everything else, from scratch."

"Did they like it?"

"I never gave them any choice." She was serene. I wondered if her diet explained Jimmie's odorless sweat. Anaïs Nin also prided herself on having no odor, as I have just read in her latest posthumously published journal, *Incest.* I remember otherwise. Yet too little is made of the importance of human odor when it comes to sexual attraction. But then–is it the smell of a particular person whom we already like that attracts us? Or does a liking for a certain smell draw us, bee to flower's pistil, to its owner?

Mrs. Sewell was a strong character. When the war turned bad for us, Jimmie had wanted to enlist in the marines. He was seventeen, an age when one needed parental consent. I got mine readily, but Ruth had refused to give hers and so he had stayed at Duke University on a scholarship paid for by the Washington Senators. But then, when he came of age at eighteen, he enlisted. The last letters that he wrote to her are more those of husband to wife than son to mother. I had also not realized how much of an artist an athlete is until I read, again and again, about "my arm," the pitcher's arm which he guarded with the same single-mindedness that a dancer does his legs. Toward the end, he knows that he is not going to survive and he tells her what to do about insurance and his effects, and Chris. He is plainly in a rage at being killed before he could have his life.

"I think I'd like to make a little book about Jimmie, photographs, letters, what people remember . . ."

Mrs. Sewell was on her guard, as well she should be after that magazine article. I told her of a similar book about Hobe Baker, a Princeton athlete much admired by Scott Fitzgerald's generation. "Of course," she said, "I wouldn't want anything said about his father and *his* problems." Jimmie's father had left Washington under a series of clouds. He was thought to be dead until he did indeed die, years later, in California. I said that I had no interest in the father; after all, the subject never came up between Jimmie and me. But then he was a boy who could keep secrets, as I was about to learn.

I assured her that the book would be largely based on his letters to her. Copies of several of them had been shown me by the master at St. Albans, who, that morning, before my lunch with Mrs. Sewell, had also given me a tour of the school. The gray Gothic-style stone of the original buildings still harmonizes agreeably with the now-finished cathedral on its hill, separated from the school by a green herb garden and tall trees. The Lower School dormitory of my day, with its flimsy partitions and linoleum floor, has been replaced by a row of small cell-like rooms. So all of our ghosts are gone. I did push open the swinging door to the shower room to find that our communal spartan shower was now modestly compartmentalized.

Boarders in the Lower School were divided between the aristocrats, who had pubic hair, and the plebes, who did not. I was part of the aristocracy. When Jimmie arrived, at midterm, he was much discussed. Did he or didn't he have pubic hair? He went for a shower, and I joined him: aristocratic, with bright gold curls. As I looked at him, he gave me a big grin and so it began, likeness drawn to likeness, soon to be made whole by desire minus the obligatory pursuit.

When I came to read the *Symposium*, I was amazed at how precisely Plato had anticipated two boys twenty-three hundred years later. The classical scholar M. I. Finley once told me that it was not he but one of his students who first noticed that Plato never speaks in his own voice at that famous dinner party; rather, he gives to others viewpoints that he may or may not have shared. So it is Aristophanes—not Plato—who explains to his dinner companions the nature of sexual desire.

To begin with, there were three sexes, each shaped like a globe—male, female, hermaphrodite. The three globes behaved offensively to the king of the gods, who chose to discipline them by slicing each in half. "Just as you or I might chop up sour apples for pickling," remarks Aristophanes, "or slice an egg with a hair." Apollo was then called in to tidy up the six creatures that had once been three. "Now when the work of bisection was complete it left each half with a desperate yearning for the other, and they ran together and flung their arms around each other's necks, and asked for nothing better than to be rolled into one."

This explains, according to Aristophanes, how the male half of the hermaphrodite is attracted to his female half, while the half of the woman sphere is drawn to woman and man to man. "And so when this boy-lover—or any lover, for that matter—is fortunate enough to meet his other half, they are both so intoxicated with affection, with friendship, and with love that they cannot bear to let each other out of sight for a single instant . . . although they may be hard put to say what they really want with one another, and indeed the purely sexual pleasure of their friendship could hardly account for the huge delight they take in one another's company. The fact is that both their souls are longing for something else—a something to which they can neither of them put a name. . . . And so all this to-do is a relic of that original state of ours, when we were whole . . ."

Parenthetically, I have just been reading Kenneth Dover's wonderfully self-confident memoirs. The author of *Greek Homosexuality* asks, "Why did Plato make Aristophanes the mouthpiece of the 'other half' doctrine? My own answer was (and is) that Plato recognizes it as a vulgar, unedu-cated idea, and therefore appropriate to a writer of comedies which are undeniably vulgar and populist." Dover then celebrates "those of us who are happily married . . ." One is pleased, of course, for the Dovers; even so, there are other equally successful unions. But I am hardly disinterested as I, too, have written vulgar and populist comedies.

I cannot think just how or why my coming together with Jimmie happened to take place on the white tile floor of the bathroom at Merrywood. I suppose that the butler was on the prowl at the time. But there we were, belly to belly, in the act of becoming one. As it turned out, Jimmie had been involved with another boy, while I, despite wet dreams, had never even masturbated. As it was, mutual masturbation was impossible with Jimmie—too painful for me because his large callused hands gripped a cock like a baseball bat. So we simply came together, reconstituting the original male that Zeus had split in two. Yet "sexual pleasure could hardly account for the huge delight we took in one another's company." There was no guilt, no sense of taboo. But then we were in Arcadia, not diabolic Eden.

Suddenly, Mrs. Sewell turned to me. "I want to ask you a question," she said: our roles reversed. "What did Jimmie tell you about his stepfather?"

"He said he didn't get on with him, and that was why he moved into the dormitory." Jimmie had not said much more than that. "I suppose they disliked each other."

"No, my husband didn't dislike Jimmie. I'm afraid he liked him altogether too much."

I could not believe what she was telling me. "He was German. A fine decorator, a great horseman. Master of the Warrenton Hunt. A popular man, but he wanted to adopt Jimmie, and change his name, which I couldn't allow—I mean, the Trimbles would have been horrified. Jimmie was James Trimble the *third*." Then she looked very grim. "One day I found a letter written to my husband from a man who was . . . like *him,* in *green* ink," she added, the smoking gun, as it were, "and that was the end for me. We were divorced. Funny, I've only told two other people this story, the real story."

So Jimmie had become a boarder in order to escape from his stepfather. I am still startled by all the implications. Had anything happened between them? If so, what? As I replay the ancient tapes of memory, I begin to see the story from quite a new angle. I had always thought that I had been the seducer, as I was to prove to be for the rest of my life, and so it had never occurred to me that it might have been the other way around. Like me, Jimmie would have found repellent the idea of a sexual act with a grown man. But with another boy, an equal other half, it is the most natural business there is. Yet if *he* had made the first move . . .

If it were possible, I would like to reedit all the tapes, but they are now so fragile with age that they would probably turn to dust, as Jimmie has, in a box at Rock Creek Cemetery near the statue of the mysterious veiled youth that Henry Adams commissioned Saint-Gaudens to make as a memorial to his wife, Clover, and to—who knows what else?

Now there is a second startling mystery, along with the first one that I found in his letters to his mother.

I move to safer ground. "Did Jimmie go to Mrs. Shippen's?"

Ruth laughed. "Well, I used to aim him there, but I can't say if he ever arrived. He thought the girls were a bit on the plain side." The upper-class youth of small-town Washington were sent to one of two dancing classes, Mrs. Shippen's or Miss Hawkes's. Boys and girls were taught not only to dance but to deport themselves in such a way that in due course they would either marry someone from the dancing class or someone very like someone from the dancing class, and settle down to a decorous life.

The last time I saw Jimmie was at one of these dances, held at the Sulgrave Club during the Christmas holiday of 1942, a year after the Japanese had attacked us at Pearl Harbor. I had not seen Jimmie since the fall of 1939, when I had been shipped off to the Los Alamos Ranch School in New Mexico, where one lived the vigorous life, much of it on horseback; the next year I moved on to Exeter. Nina wanted to keep me as far away from her field of operations as possible, and for once, we were in accord. The deterioration of her marriage with Hughdie was disagreeable for everyone.

Since Gene had remarried by then and moved to New York, I saw him only in the summers and so, as always, it was the Gores in Rock Creek Park who represented home during my exile, a life at whose emotional center was not my family but Jimmie; yet we never wrote each other. Of course, boys don't write boys, more or less on manly principle; even so, since I thought so much about him, I am surprised that I was so unenterprising. We had last seen each other as fourteen-year-old boys. Now we were seventeen-year-old men. Would we take up where we had left off in the spring of 1939, on a May day, in the woods above the Potomac River?

We met awkwardly in the ballroom. We wore "tuxedos"; girls wore long dresses. An orchestra played such novelties as "The Lambeth Walk" and "The Big Apple." Also slow fox-trots. "Night and Day." I could only turn right.

NOW I ERASE a bit of Jimmie as Rosalind appears, demanding, if not equal, fair time. I had brought Rosalind to the dance. She was tall and dark and exuberant. We had known each other all our lives. We had been "a couple" for several years. We were used to each other in a low-key, comfortable way. Then the war came and everything changed. The desultory boy-girl relationship of our old life suddenly became urgent: The boy might soon be killed. We experienced what so many did in our time and place. We decided to get married between my graduation from Exeter in June and my enlistment in the army in July (a special army program for high school graduates was the army's siren song). Our announcement galvanized my usually casual family. My grandfather, Senator Gore ("I *never* give advice"), was suddenly Polonius; he also changed his usual line from "Never have children, only grandchildren" to "Be *not* fruitful, do *not* multiply." Certainly, his son and daughter had always been annoying to him and of little consequence to anyone else, while I, who read to him gladly, had been a treasure. But treasure no longer, since I seemed to be following both son and daughter into premature marriage, to be followed by certain failure in life's great adventure. Nina was concerned about the alcoholism in Rosalind's family.

Even my amiably offhand father came down to Washington to ask a significant question: "How much do you think you'll need to live on?" I said about five hundred dollars a month. Gene wondered where this would come from; an army private makes considerably less. I already knew that there would be nothing from my family, ever. It was a close contest who was meaner, T. P. Gore or Gene Vidal, two self-made men who had no intention of contributing one penny to the making of any other man, beyond the grim obligation to pay for a son's Education.

Education was the key to everything, as my uneducated mother knew when she approached Mr. True, head of the Lower School at St. Albans. My grades must improve "because," she said, "he is living in the lap of luxury now, but he's never going to inherit anything! And he doesn't understand the *value of money* [a favorite refrain]." Mr. True said that my grades would probably improve if I could be persuaded to do more homework. She confessed defeat: "He locks himself in his room," she said sadly, "and *writes.*"

As it turned out, I did not go to college after the war, while my income during my first year of civilian life was about five hundred dollars a month. I could very easily have married and, conforming to every last one of the rules of the game, followed my grandfather into the Senate. Happily, life was to be more interesting than that. Unhappily, Rosalind, whom I did not marry, became an alcoholic–not on my account. Happily, in later life, Rosalind pulled herself together to become a commercial artist in London, where she had an affair with Churchill's attorney-general, John Foster, a large bearlike man of marvelous wit. I last saw the two of them in 1970 at the airport in Katmandu, where, on the tarmac, John gave a superb imitation of the judge in the Margaret Argyle divorce case. This featured a compromising Polaroid of the duchess sucking the cock of a man whose head is not visible in the Polaroid and whose pubic hair was not straight like the duke's (the valet's solemn testimony) but curly like–like an adulterer's.

"You are a jeweler, sir, by trade," said the judge. "I pray you, sir, note the ring on the hand that is holding the penis. Disregard the penis. Disregard the hand. Disregard the headless man. Concentrate your attention, sir, solely upon the ring. Is that your handiwork?"

BUT ALL THIS was far in the future that evening when I told Jimmie that I was going to marry Rosalind after I graduated from Exeter. "You're crazy," he said.

We went downstairs to the men's room with its tall marble urinals and large cubicles. I wondered what, if anything, he felt. After all, men are not boys. Fortunately, our bodies still fitted perfectly together, as we promptly discovered inside one of the cubicles, standing up, belly to belly, talking of girls and marriage and coming simultaneously.

Thus, we were whole for what proved to be the last time for the two of us–and for me, if not for him, for good. I not only never again encountered the other half, but by the time I was twenty-five, I had given up all pursuit, settling for a thousand brief anonymous adhesions, as Walt Whitman would put it, where wholeness *seems,* for an instant, to be achieved. Quite enough, I think, if the real thing has happened. At least, in Platonic terms, I had completed myself once. Jack Kennedy–a half of the hermaphrodite rather than the male–by his own admission never came close. I am lucky. He was not.

Why did Jimmie ask his mother to send him Whitman? Why am I jealous of a ghost–*two* ghosts? Did he find a lover in the marines, someone of a literary nature, who wanted him to read . . . I "knew too well the sick, sick dread lest the one he lov'd might secretly be indifferent to him . . ." So Whitman now resounds in these late, late reveries.

Two vivid images of Jimmie. One came back to me while I was smoking ganja in Katmandu, not an easy thing for a nonsmoker to do. But as I gasped my way into a sort of trance, Jimmie materialized beside me on the bed. He wore blue pajamas. He was asleep. He was completely present, as he had been in the bedroom at Merrywood. I tickled his foot. The callused sole was like sandpaper. It was a shock to touch him again. The simulacrum opened its blue eyes and smiled and yawned and put his hand alongside my neck; he was, for an instant, real in a hotel room in Katmandu. But only for an instant. Then he rejoined Achilles and all the other shadowy dead in war.

My second memory: I am lying on top of him, after sex, eyes shut; then I open them and see his eyes staring up into mine. The expression is like that of his sad-looking photographs rather than of the actual smiling boy whom I recall, or think that I do. In his last photographs, the marine private of nineteen looks to be a powerfully built man of thirty, in a rage because he knows that what's next is nothing.

After our final encounter at the Sulgrave, I knew that we would go on together until our business had finished itself in a natural way. I certainly never wanted to grow old with him. I just wanted to grow up with him. Each would marry in time; find wholeness elsewhere, if lucky. And so we went back to the dance upstairs, he as happy as I at being, if only briefly, rejoined.

In the light of all this it is puzzling to me now that I did not write him after he finally joined the marines in 1944, the worst year of the war. Of course, I was already in the army, and concerned with my own fate. So I left Jimmie to time and chance, as I left everything else. But then I hadn't much choice, while, a year later, he had none at all. I was stoic since, forever after, I was to be the surviving half of what had once been whole.

I realize that according to the School of Vienna (the Riding School), I should have become a lifelong pederast. But that did not happen. Naturally, like most men, I am attracted to adolescent males–this is, by the way, one of the best kept secrets of the male lodge, revealed in a study called *The Boys of Boise,* where most of the male establishment of that heartland Idaho city (each a *mature* married man) were revealed to be lovers of the high school football team. But I did not go prowling for fourteen-year-old athletes. After all, if the ideal is the other self, then that self would have had to age along with me, and attraction would have become affection, and lust would have then been diverted to . . . chance encounters or the other sex.

Montaigne is sharp about the Greek arrangement of young warrior and pubescent squire, the latter not enjoying–or supposed to enjoy– what the lustful other does with him. Although this relationship might produce excellent soldiers, it was not and could not be, in Montaigne's eyes, true love because man and boy were not equals and the relationship was grounded solely upon the passion of the older and more experienced male for the beauty of the younger. Only in equality can there be love, as Montaigne had uniquely experienced with his friend La Boétie's mind and character if not body. Montaigne thought that if a woman could ever be a man's equal in mind and education, then that relationship might be best of all, but since Montaigne is mildly misogynistic, he gives no examples.

JIMMIE TRIMBLE had applied for the navy V-12 program, where high school graduates of seventeen and eighteen were trained to be naval officers in Stateside universities. As of June 1943, I was in the army's equivalent, the Army Specialized Training Program at the Virginia Military Institute, to be trained as an engineer, for which I had no aptitude. After three months, I flunked out, more or less deliberately, thus saving my life because, with the army's usual brutish haste and ill faith, the program was suddenly dissolved and my inadequately trained classmates were shipped off to Europe as front-line infantrymen. Many were killed in the last German counteroffensive, the so-called Battle of the Bulge. But by then I was first mate of an army freight-supply ship in the Aleutians, more in danger of being killed by my own inadequacies as a navigator in the world's worst sea than from enemy fire. At least, unlike

Jack Kennedy, I didn't get run over by a Japanese destroyer, the trick of the week, I always thought, though the latest biography makes more sense than usual of the harebrained fleet of PT boats to which the ailing Jack had been assigned, a thousand miles to the south of me.

Jimmie, according to a survivor from his unit, failed his physical for V-12, which seems impossible for a professional athlete. Yet, I now learn, he was indeed sickly, prey to a chronic form of pneumonia. But he had no problem in getting accepted, as cannon fodder, by the marines in January of 1944; his basic training was at Camp Lejeune; then, in August 1944, he became a member of a scout and observer group of the Third Marine Division in the South Pacific. He saw action until the end of October, when Guam was secured.

From October to February he seems to have had a quiet time on Guam. For one month he was again a baseball player, helping the division team win the local championship. On February 4, he played his last game for the division. He reports to his mother that he has sprained his ankle; meanwhile, "everything is once again wonderful with Chris and me." He remarks that his mother is a "worse procrastinator than I ever was"–she has not sent him a long-promised picture of herself, so "how about sending one while there is still a tomorrow?" He recalls the Sunday picnics that they used to have in the Virginia mountains. "I'll never forgive myself for refusing to follow your advice to stay in college. After the war we won't receive any credit for having been out here ... Mom, please don't get the blues over what I am going to say, but some insurance should be taken just in case. Mom, you know if anything happens to me you are to have all I possess but I would like to ask one favor. You know the gold ring with the diamonds set halfway around? Well, Mom, if (it won't) anything does happen, would you give it to Chris for me? Kind of a memorial the other way around." Finally, "Well, Mom, I'll write again in a couple of days ... All my love to the swellest Mom in all the world. Your devoted son, Jimmie."

This letter could have been written in the Civil War. The tone is also that of Andy Hardy in an MGM movie, but there were once real boys like that, before the great sullenness spread over the land.

February 25, 1945, Jimmie arrived at Iwo Jima in what turned out to be one of the bloodiest engagements of the war. Twenty thousand Japanese were killed; 6,821 American troops were killed, mostly teenage marines. Jimmie was in the 4th Platoon, a member of what was called the Reconnaissance Company. A survivor of the platoon recalls, "I was with the first observation team that went up there; we stayed three days, then they relieved us; I saw him [Jimmie] when they relieved us, and that was the last time. They relocated their position forward; lost contact with them. In the early morning hours."

There were eight men in Jimmie's squadron as of the night of February 28. They were arranged, as far as I can tell from a news story, two to a foxhole "on a slope overlooking our infantry front line and the enemy's concrete placements beyond. As dawn broke at 4:45, March 1, 1945, all hell broke loose upon them. A Jap raiding party had infiltrated the front lines and attacked their post." Six of the eight were killed: "one . . . was dead in his foxhole. He had been bayoneted in his sleep. Another had been killed by a grenade, and a third by rifle fire. One burned poncho was found in the foxhole shared by the two missing men. . . . Sixty-three Jap bodies sprawled in the observation post's little battleground."

Jimmie was the scout who had been killed by a grenade. Another marine who was there bears witness: "We were all real proud of Jim Trimble, and everybody else was. He was a joy to be around. He had a good personality. He was always joking. I know he wanted to go back and go to school and play professional baseball. He was just a joy to be around. I remember that he went into the ship's store—because it was cold up in Iwo. Everybody thinks of it as the Pacific, but it was their winter up there, and it was only 700 miles from Tokyo. Jim went in and bought a black Navy watch sweater. He was the only guy that kept warm, before this happened. But then, you know, I'll never forget the way the grenade hit him in the back, and that sweater was just all wrapped up inside of him.

"You know, in circumstances like that, you're probably closer to those guys than you are your own brothers. Of course, for me now, we're talking about 50 years. You kind of forget. Like I said, the wars all kind of blend into each other.

"He was tall, blond curly hair. But I'll tell you, he was heavy, carrying back. I though I'd die. At that age, you know, I was 18, and I weighed about 145. He had to weigh 160. He felt like 2,000 pounds by the time I got back to the foxhole."

When the commanding general heard of Jimmie's death, he was, according to a witness, "moist-eyed" for one boy lost in all that carnage.

The Third Division named its baseball field on Guam Trimble Field. That was that. End of Jimmie. Since then, "the wars all kind of blend into each other."

In the summer of 1945, I left Birmingham General Hospital, at Van Nuys, California, on leave to see my father in New York. I had acquired rheumatoid arthritis as a result of a modest freezing (hypothermia) in the Bering Sea; one knee was partly locked and the fingers of my left hand were like thumbs—yes, everything is a bit worse now. When I went before the hospital board, I was told that I could get a disability pension for life, but that would mean two years more of service. If I chose to forgo the pension, I would be let out in less than a year. The European war was over; the Japanese war nearly so. I let the pension go.

En route to New York, I stopped off in Jackson, Michigan, to see my father's sister. We were standing in a sunny garden when we were joined by a boy I had been at school with—which school? Even then Nina's educational enthusiasms had begun to blur: Potomac, Sidwell Friends, Landon, St. Albans, Los Alamos, Exeter. But since the boy spoke of Washington, it must have been one of the local schools—"You know," he said, "Jimmie Trimble's dead." By this time, I had pretty much distanced myself from these stark announcements. I think my first reaction must have been somewhat like that when I heard Jack Kennedy had been shot. I was in a Rome movie house, watching *David and Lisa*. News spread during the interval. I didn't believe it. There had been a mistake. That's not the right plot. But, of course, finally, that was all that Jack was ever to be—a great media monster, now wreathed in garlands of paranoia of a most unpleasant sort. Jimmie was no media monster, but he was already vivid in his own right and, thus, no candidate for death. It took me some months to absorb the fact—or nonfact—of his being *not*-being.

To this day, in another world and almost another century, I have wondered what might have become of our so swiftly completed maleness. Is it only for a season that wholeness endures? On this matter Plato is silent. Experience suggests that desire of any kind is brief. In due course, I wrote a novel in which I described what *might* have happened had we met again years later. The conclusion was too harsh for many readers, but that is the way American society is and I was a realistic writer until, one day, I realized that there is no common reality beyond desire, the pursuit, and, in at least one case, the achievement of the whole. It would be greedy—not to say impractical—to expect a repetition of a lucky accident. I was very much aware of my once perfect luck, and left it at that.

"DID YOU SEND JIMMIE the copy of *Leaves of Grass* he asked for?"

Mrs. Sewell was vague. "If he asked me to, of course I did."

Will I ever know who got him to read Whitman on the island of Guam? No, I am not jealous, only sad I was never to be with him again. Actually, I hope that he did find someone. He was always lucky, except for his death—and maybe there was luck in that, too. Long life, finally, is nightmarish repetition while "Death is beautiful from you." Did he read that in Calamus? Did he read Whitman on "the brotherhood of lovers"? On "How together through life, through dangers, odium, unchanging, long and long, Through youth and through middle and old age, how unfaltering, how affectionate and faithful they were, Then I am pensive—I hastily walk away fill'd with bitterest envy." As who would not?

I have now lived a half century with a man, but sex has played no part in the relationship and so where there is no desire or pursuit, there is no wholeness. But there are satisfying lesser states, fragments.

Dah

BEFORE THE CARDS that one is dealt by life are the cards that fate has dealt. One's family. A cousin has just sent me a 1936 newsreel of my grandfather's last campaign for the Senate. Thomas Pryor Gore looks and sounds weary. He predicts the coming of the Second World War; and he reminds the electorate that he is the last remaining member of the Senate of 1917 and that as he had opposed American intervention in the war then, so he does now. "I will not sacrifice your sons to the dogs of war."

My first memory is of early evening in a room that overlooked the driveway of my grandfather's house in Washington, D.C.'s Rock Creek Park. I am standing up in a playpen—euphemism for cage. I stick my head between the slats of the pen; get stuck; roar. Someone comes and I am freed. If recurrent dreams can be relied on, I also have a memory of being born. I am in a narrow tunnel, wriggling toward the light, but I get stuck before my head is free of the tunnel. I cannot move forward or backward. I wake up in a sweat. Nina's pelvis was narrow and I was delivered clumsily, with forceps, by a doctor not used to deliveries: he was officer of the day in the Cadet Hospital at West Point, on a Saturday, October 3, 1925, at about noon.

Some weeks later, Eugene Luther Vidal, West Point class of 1918, resigned as first lieutenant in the army: He had been the Academy's first instructor in aeronautics, as well as football coach. In 1917, he had been

*My grandfather, Senator Thomas Pryor Gore.
This is pretty much how I recall him,
in his old age. He is being painted by
Azadia Newman, who is soon to marry the
film director Rouben Mamoulian.*

an all-American quarterback as well as a track star who had taken part in the Olympic Games at Antwerp. Gene, Nina, and child moved into her parents' house in Washington, thus richly ensuring the failure of that marriage.

Much of the first ten years of my life was spent on the hill above Broad Branch Road–the branch being Rock Creek itself, a clear, pure stream that rushed shallowly over rocks between wooded hills, a haven for salamanders and all sorts of freshwater life. Senator Gore owned three acres of woods above the creek where, shortly before my birth, he had built a gray stone mansion. Because of T. P. Gore's antiwar and anti–League of Nations positions, the good people of Oklahoma had denied him a fourth term in the U.S. Senate and so, from 1920 to 1930, he practiced law in Washington, D.C., and built his house, now residence to the Malaysian ambassador.

In the crash of 1929, Gore lost most of his money; in 1930 he returned to the Senate. Predictably, he fell foul of the new president, Franklin Delano Roosevelt. By then, Gore was a populist turned conservative. He and the president quarreled over whether or not the dollar should go off the gold standard. "If you do," said Gore, "you will have stolen the money of those who had faith in our currency." Carter Glass, a senator present at the meeting, later told the blind Gore that the president had gone gray in the face. But Roosevelt took the currency off gold. Later, of the half-dozen senators that Roosevelt tried to purge in 1936, T. P. Gore was the only one to lose his seat for good.

I was ten when he was defeated. My stepfather sent him a thousand-dollar bill for his campaign. I had never seen a hundred-dollar bill much less a thousand-dollar one. Even so, he lost the primary to a Roosevelt ally. He came home in the spring. He was melancholy, to say the least, and somewhat bored during the last thirteen years of his life, practicing law in Washington, mostly to get the government to pay the Indian tribes for those lands that it had stolen from them.

For a child–like a cat–the place where it lives is often more important than the people who live there. Rock Creek Park was very much my territory. The house itself was gray-yellow Baltimore stone. On one side, there was a steep lawn that overlooked Broad Branch Road and the winding creek, while, on the other side, there was the front door, approached by a circular drive at whose center was a small fountain. In those days, from the house, one saw only green woods, a rose garden, rows of flags, as we called irises, and a small vineyard of purple grapes. At the edge of the woods was a slave cabin, falling to pieces. In the heart of the woods, there was a spring of cold water that one was warned, even then, not to drink. Magically, water bubbled from soft gray sand, which I used to build elaborate sand cities, usually in the style of those I'd read about in Lane's translation of the *Arabian Nights,* a book I never ceased to read and reread.

The main hall smells of fried bacon, floor wax, irises, books–thousands of dusty books. There is a large dining room on the left, with a fireplace and a niche on either side in which there are two tall gaudy pink-and-gold Sèvres vases. Back of a screen, there is the door to the large white kitchen, where the large, dark Gertrude Jackson presides. I used to watch her cook by the hour, telling her stories that I made up as I went along. She was stout, from Maryland's Eastern Shore; she was also sly. She stole a gold pin from Nina and then, a year or two later, absentmindedly wore it to work. We all thought that the loss of her cooking was rather more serious than that of a gold pin.

To the right of the hall, a living room with a large bay window framed by bookcases. I recall a set of Mark Twain and a set of Voltaire in a red binding; also, the works of Brann "the Iconoclast." A large sofa, covered in pumpkin-yellow and salad-green. Beside the fireplace, the Senator's chair, and a smaller one where I would sit when I read to him, drinking Coca-Cola and trying not to let the ice tinkle. He forbade Coca-Cola in the house because it contained cocaine.

Perversely, the Senator, who had done his best to put his rural origins behind him, insisted on keeping chickens–to impress visiting constituents?–but as there was too much shade, they moped in the woods. I found them a bit dull, but I did my best to keep them amused.

One day at table I was told, "Eat your chicken." A terrible knowledge of Edenic magnitude filled me with horror. This? On the plate? The same? The same. I would not eat chicken for many years, despite my grandmother's cunning ways to trick me into what I took to be a form of cannibalism.

The Senator called his wife Tot, which I rendered as Dot. To her, he was Dad, which I rendered as Dah, an Irish locution, I am told. Her first name was Nina. I never heard her call the Senator by his first name except once, when they were in the small sitting room off their bedroom; he wore a long nightshirt and she was in her usual uniform, a pale pink wrapper over a lace nightdress–since he could not see her, she never bothered with her appearance unless there was company. While reading to him, she noticed that his nightshirt had ridden up to his knees. "Put your dress down, Tom," she said. Otherwise he was Dad or Mr. Gore.

No one that I know of ever called him Tom or Thomas. President Roosevelt, in his squire-of-the-manor way, addressed him once, and once only, as Tom. The Senator ignored him until he was addressed properly. As a boy in Mississippi, he had been called Guv, short for Governor, tribute to an ambition that was noticeable even then. There seems never to have been a time that he was not in demand as an eloquent and witty speaker, particularly at those political picnics which were one of the few communal pleasures during harsh Reconstruction days.

The Gores belonged to the Party of the People; hence, populists. T. P. Gore's father was clerk of Walthall County, an elected post of peculiar power in that state, a sort of regional chancellor. Since there were few blacks in north-central Mississippi, Gores have never been slaveholders, unlike Dot's father's family, the Kays of South Carolina, or her mother's family, the McLaughlins of Meridian, Mississippi. "I still remember how my mother used to just step out of her clothes in her bedroom at night and leave them right there on the floor wherever she happened to be standing and, of course, I'd have to come along and put them away. You see, before the War, there was always a slave girl to take care of her."

Dot and Dah complemented each other. She was dark, with large eyes and high-arched brows; she was also small–hence, Tot. She had a beautiful low speaking voice. When Dah first heard it at a political picnic in Palestine, Texas, where her family had moved after the War, he said, "I'm going to marry you." He was a twenty-five-year-old blind lawyer, practicing law with his father and two brothers. After losing a campaign for election to the Mississippi legislature, he had left the state. The campaign had been unusually dirty. Also, rather more to the point, he was already bound for the United States Senate; this meant that he must leave Mississippi, where one had to wait for an incumbent to die, which could be decades; much too long a time for a man in a hurry. First, he headed west to Texas; then on to the Indian territories, where he helped organize the state of Oklahoma. In 1907, he was sent to Washington as the state's first senator.

I've just come across a clipping from what looks to be *The Washington Post*. It is 1930, and the reporter pays a call on the recently reelected senator, who is baby-sitting me. At five, I am still called Gene.

Stacks of books surround the blind Senator's chair, piles and piles of them, all colors, all kinds. Last week, there was a fire in the house. The bookcases are being repainted.

Baby Gene runs about among the stacks of books. The radio drones on.

"Tell me a story, Dah," begs little Gene, bored with his playthings.

The Senator, eyes tightly closed, says nothing.

"Dah," insists the boy, shaking him. "Oh, Dah! Please tell me a story."

Silence, immobility on Sen. Gore's part.

"Dah, won't you tell me a story?"

Silence.

Baby Gene regards his grandfather with interest, observes naively.

"Why do you keep your eyes closed? You can't see anything anyway."

Sen. Gore, amused, opens his blind eyes, begins sententiously:

"Once upon a time . . ."

Dah was a wonderful storyteller; he also made me pay back in full when I was six by getting me to read to him, which I did by the hour for several years.

Thomas Pryor Gore. He is seated in his heavy wood Mission rocking chair, now in my bedroom at Ravello. He listens as the secretary reads to him; the straight but rather small chin is held high while the head is slightly tilted to one side. The blind eyes are tight shut with concentration. He has a full head of cowlicked white hair, a rosy unlined face, and a large straight Anglo-Irish nose with the curious flaring Gore nostrils that most of us have inherited, including our young cousin who currently lives in vice-presidential obscurity, a sort of family ghost flickering dimly on prime-time television.

Dah is about five foot nine or ten; he stands very straight. He is well proportioned except for an astonishing stomach. A parabola begins at his rib cage and extends half a foot out in front of him before it abruptly rejoins the lower body. The stomach is hard as a rock. Dot would often touch it with wonder. "When you're dead, I'm going to have this opened up. I've *got* to see what's in there. It's like iron, that stomach." Now I am getting the same stomach, but much later in life, and thanks only to alcohol. Dah himself never drank until old age, when doctors prescribed two shots before dinner. Both of his brothers were alcoholic, in the best Confederate tradition. This meant that they functioned as lawyers all day, then, work done, they drank a great deal. So too, I fear, did Dot, to Dah's distress. At dinner, she would begin to ramble in a story or slur her words, ending the meal by sneezing exactly five times and blowing her nose in the Irish linen napkin, to my mother's fury. She lived to be the oldest of my four grandparents, dying in her eighties.

I have a newsreel of Dah from 1931, the year that he came back to the Senate. He is standing in front of the Capitol with another senator, also blind. Clearly, an unpolitical human interest story was on the producer's mind. Gore's voice is measured, precise, more southern than southwestern in accent, with an actor's phrasing. Lyndon Johnson used to imitate him, unsuccessfully. The Gore style influenced at least two generations of regional politicians. Much of his effect depended on a sharp, sudden wit that could surprise a crowd into laughter, very like his friend and fellow Chautauqua speaker Mark Twain. It is said that Will Rogers, in performance, most resembled Gore. But I wouldn't know. Although I often led Dah from his office onto the Senate floor, and even into the holy of holies, the Senate cloakroom, I never heard him make a speech. It was a family complaint that when he was due to make a major speech in the Senate, he would tell none of us in advance. We would only know about it from the newspapers the next day. There was, of course, no television then, and newsreel cameras were not allowed in the chamber. Dah ends the 1931 newsreel with an offhand "Nice to *see* you," straight to camera. Early in his career, he liked to hold notes in his hand that he would pretend to consult in order to disguise the little known, at the time, fact that he was totally blind.

I still cannot get over the wonder of film. I have now seen and heard a man I'd not seen and heard for almost half a century; it is a sort of miracle, and a powerful aid to memory.

.   .   .

WE ARE SEATED ON THE PORCH—a sort of open loggia—at one end of the Rock Creek Park house. It is summer. The irises, in full bloom, have a heavy lemon smell. I am eating grapes that I've just picked in the arbor which separates porch from dilapidated slave cabin. Dah sits in his rocker. A woman journalist rattles away: How did he become blind? We have all told this particular story so many times that we can recite it without thinking. Eight years old. Throwing nails at a cow. Another boy's nail misses. Hits Guv's eye. Still has one good eye; partial, but fading, vision in the damaged eye. Age ten, appointed page to the Mississippi State Senate at Jackson. Boards in a state senator's house. Son of house has a birthday. Guv brings him a gun. When you pull the trigger, a spike comes out. Doesn't work. Guv holds it to his good eye to see what's wrong. "Now I'm blind" were his first words after the spike found its target. The family wanted to put him in a school for the handicapped. No. I'm going to study law. How? Send someone to school with me, to read to me. A relative named Pittman went with him to the Lebanon School of Law in Tennessee. Gore learned to memorize what was read to him, including endless statistics. Learned to recognize people by their voices. Was not surprised when radar was developed in World War Two. "All blind people know about radar. You can feel the sound waves bounce off a wall up ahead of you. Gives you warning."

Woman journalist has a tinkling laugh. Dah winces. "Is there any sound more dreadful than that of a woman's laugh?" he would say. A mild misogynist, he was a true misanthrope, which the public never guessed as they gazed on his serene, kindly face with its crooked thin-lipped smile and the blind gray eyes—one was glass—that had a surprising amount of life to them, particularly when he was about to launch a devastating line.

"You must admit," said the journalist, "that when you lose your sight, your other faculties develop. So there have to be compensations."

"There are *no* compensations," Dah said, grimly; particularly for someone whose greatest pleasure in life was reading. He was read to almost every minute of the day. Once Senate or legal work was out of the way, he turned to history, poetry, economics. He disliked novels. Dot, two secretaries, and, later, I were the principal readers. As our spirits would sometimes start to fail, he would observe, blithely, "Both Milton's daughters went blind reading to him."

He had, surprisingly, a gift for mathematics. At one point he had been offered a job at a university teaching mathematics, but "I couldn't take a job like that. When I think of teaching in a school, I get this lonesome feeling." After one of his political speeches in Texas, a group of Baptist elders approached him and offered him a fine church and house in Houston if he would become their minister. He thanked them and said that the offer was very fine indeed but he couldn't take it as he didn't believe in God. "Come now, Mr. Gore, that's not the proposition we made you, is it?"

Dah had a curious position in the country, not unlike that of Helen Keller, a woman born deaf, mute, and blind. The response of each to calamity was a subject of great interest to the general public, and we children and grandchildren were treated not so much as descendants of just another politician but as the privileged heirs to an Inspirational Personage.

Politically, Gore always thought of himself as a member of the Party of the People even after he had been co-opted by the Democrats, whose more or less populist tribune, William Jennings Bryan, would three times be a losing candidate for president. Although not unalike politically, Gore and Bryan got on uneasily. At Denver in 1908, when Gore seconded the nomination of Bryan for president, he started the longest demonstration in the history of American conventions. Gore made, as they used to say, the eagle scream. I suppose the magic was entirely in his performance, because the text ... Well, as he himself said, a successful speech must reflect the people's mood at the time. He liked alliteration. "I prefer the strenuosity of Roosevelt to the sinuosity of Taft," he would observe in 1912.

After the Denver convention, Gore and Bryan drove away from the hall together. An exuberant Bryan said, "You know, Senator, I ascribe my political success to just three things." Dah would pause dramatically at this point in the telling. Then: "I'm afraid I don't remember a word he said, but I do remember wondering why he thought he was a political success."

I've just been reading a book about the lawyer Clarence Darrow and I'm surprised to note that when Darrow was defending two labor union officials accused of having blown up the *Los Angeles Times* building, who should show up in the courtroom but "Senator Thomas Gore of Oklahoma, the famous blind U.S. Senator, friend of Darrow, who was in town on a lecture tour." Plainly, populist Gore was showing solidarity with the cause of labor. As it turned out, the two labor leaders were guilty and Darrow himself was later put on trial for bribing two jurors. But that is another story.

In 1925, at the Scopes trial, Bryan and Darrow faced one another in a Tennessee village courtroom to argue about whether God created the world in a week or did life take a bit more time to evolve, as Darwin proposed. Bryan spoke for God; and won. Darrow spoke for evolution; and won because the educated minority of the country made a hero of him; and poor Bryan, made to look ridiculous, promptly died. Some thought it was humiliation at being out-argued by a great lawyer. Dot knew better: "Bryan was killed by chicken and rice and gravy. How that man could eat, and in all that heat, too!" Incidentally, a recent poll shows that only 9 percent of the American people believe in evolution. We should be able to do marvelously well in the second millennium.

Although Dot herself did not know how to cook, she knew how to train cooks, a Confederate art lost to the world, along with those black ladies from the Eastern Shore of Maryland who were born with no need to be taught anything about cooking. Dah's standards, when it came to food, were high: "The only true ground for divorce against a wife is if she serves her husband store-bought bread." We never knew there was such a thing. Spoon bread. Corn bread. Buttermilk biscuits. Honey from square waxy combs. "I only live for breakfast," said Dot at the end, bedridden from stroke and Parkinson's disease. "I love my dough." I once asked her what the nineteenth century was like. "Oh, the food! It was so wonderful!"

The Gores were constantly struck by fate. Dot thought that Dah had been born under a maleficent star. After all, the odds are very much against losing an eye in an accident, but to lose two eyes in two separate accidents is positively Lloydsian. But fate had many more freakish misadventures in store for him.

According to family tradition, while practicing law in Corsicana, Texas, Gore boarded in a house where also lived a blind girl. She became pregnant, and the blind boarder was accused of seduction by the blind girl's guardian. A shotgun was produced in the best tradition of

Cavalleria Rusticana. Gore walked away. "Shoot," he said, his back to the guardian, "but I'm not marrying her." Thanks to the scandal, he lost a congressional election but won Dot; and together they moved on to the Indian territories, and glory.

At about the time Gore was visiting Clarence Darrow's courtroom, he was himself about to be tried for rape. Dot thought that this bit of melodrama was far and away fate's masterpiece. Although Gore was often helpful to the oil interests in the state, he was not paid off by them, unlike most of the delegation. Proof? He died a relatively poor man, something that no Oklahoma senator has ever done, particularly one who had, like Gore, written the original legislation for the depreciation of oil resources allowance that made the southwestern oilmen as rich as today's Saudis and quite as unbearable.

Now, here is the family's version of what happened:

An oil company wanted to expropriate Indian land. They appealed to Congress. Gore took the Indian side. The oilmen offered him money to change his vote. Without naming names, he announced to the Senate that he had been offered a bribe. I believe this was the first and perhaps last time that any senator broke one of the most powerful unwritten rules of the club. The resulting storm in the press did not scare off his tempters. Again, they threatened him, not a wise move in dealing with a man of so fierce and righteous a temper. He said that now he would charge them *by name* with bribery. So they played the "badger game" on him.

A woman rang Gore's office to say that she was a constituent and that she would like to propose her son for an appointment to West Point. She was not able to come to the Capitol, but could he stop by her hotel on his way home? He did, in the company of his secretary, Roy Thompson. In the lobby, she proposed that the Senator and she go to the less crowded mezzanine. Unaccompanied by Roy, she led Gore into her hotel room, where she started to scream and tear off her clothes. By prearrangement, a pair of detectives arrived, shouting, "We've got you!"

The threat of exposure was thought to be quite enough to get the Senator to cooperate. But he refused. Charges were brought against him. The newspaper scandal was enormous. Since the defendant may pick the venue of his trial, he, most daringly, chose to be tried in the capital of his state, Oklahoma City. Gore seemed certain to lose until the appearance of a surprise witness, a lady from Boston who had been at the window of a room opposite the one in which the rabid badger had been loosed, and she had seen and heard the woman tear at her own dress, had watched the detectives rush in. Gore was acquitted. But, as Dot said grimly, "All our lives, just as things start going well for us, something awful happens and we have to begin all over again."

PALIMPSEST TIME. Although I have pretty much kept to my system of recording only what a faulty memory recalls (and the written—equally faulty?—memories and biographies of others), I did send away to the University of Oklahoma at Norman for the various accounts of T. P. Gore's alleged "indecent assault" on one Mrs. Minnie E. Bond in the Winston Hotel during March 1913, at Washington City. Minnie wanted $50,000 damages for the agony that she had undergone. Gore said he would not "treat or retreat," and opted to stand trial in Oklahoma City.

On February 19, 1914, the jury took ten minutes to exonerate the Senator. The family's version of events was, more or less, that of the press of the day. Now the story begins to diverge. Minnie had come to Washington to ask Senator Gore to appoint her husband internal revenue collector for the state. On three occasions he said no. She asked to see him yet again; he told her to come to his office, but she said that she would prefer that he come to her hotel. He did, with his secretary-escort, one of Dot's brothers.

As the downstairs parlors were full, Minnie led the Senator upstairs to what proved to be the bedroom of a Mr. Jacobs; she then tore her clothes and gave what the newspapers said was a loud "squawk." Jacobs and two other "witnesses," conveniently stationed nearby, rushed in. Gore had been framed.

But reading the press accounts (I think I shall avoid the actual transcripts of the trial if they exist), I wonder why Dot's brother Harry Kay didn't go upstairs with him. But then I always wondered how on earth Dah managed sex. A blind man can't go into a bar and, with a glance, find a partner. In the course of the trial, the prosecution came up with a number of instances where Dah had allegedly made advances to women, but none of the women ever stepped forward. The fact that he always had a brother-in-law or a man secretary as escort meant that he would have to rely on them for any arrangements which he might have made with women, not to mention guiding him to the men's room in a strange city.

Nevertheless, there are odd discrepancies between the family version and what I have been reading. The famous surprise testimony of "the lady from Boston" who had witnessed the whole thing from her hotel window opposite the one where the "rape" was supposed to have occurred is entirely absent from the story. The jury simply said there was "insufficient evidence" to condemn Gore, and no one took seriously the stories of the three politically interested witnesses. It would seem that the actual reason for the frame-up involved an attorney named J. F. McMurray, who had involved himself in the transfer of some Indian lands and then sued the tribes for $3 million in fees. Gore took the side of the Indians. McMurray did not get his money; hence, revenge in the generous form of Mrs. Minnie E. Bond.

All this was par for the course in the frontier politics of the day. But more disturbing to me was the plaintiff's investigation of the blind girl and Gore in Corsicana, Texas, some twenty years earlier. The family story was that in 1895, the twenty-five-year-old Gore was practicing law with father and brothers in Corsicana. Gore was also the Party of the People's candidate for the House of Representatives. He took music lessons from a young blind girl, the ward of a local couple. The "music lessons" sound truly far-fetched. Gore was tone-deaf. Every time the national anthem was played, he invariably said, "Now, there's a catchy tune."

I cannot tell what is true and what is not true in the deposition of one S. P. Render. But the story is hair-raising. In 1914, Render found the blind girl in Galveston, Texas, where she was giving music lessons and living in genteel poverty. The Gores had, she told Render, thrown her out years earlier. As for the pregnancy, Gore was responsible. "I was engaged to [him] and I loved him as well as a child—for I was at that time, in heart, a child, in mind a child . . . but I did not submit to him of my own free will. He overpowered me and I could do nothing." When she told him she was pregnant, he plied her with medicines, saying that "the fever" must break. When this failed to make her abort, "some little instrument" was used. Mr. Render says that Gore was put on trial—(who was the plaintiff?)—for seduction and abortion, criminal offenses in Texas. Just before the trial, the blind girl told Render that Gore came to her and begged her to answer no questions at the trial on the ground that she would not only destroy his career but also the lives of his "aged" parents, who had never harmed anyone. Finally, she concedes. " 'The little one is gone—you could not shield him and you have done all you can against me' and I said, 'If you promise me you will be a better man . . . I will accede to your wishes, I don't see any good that could come in me doing otherwise;' and then I was almost immediately conducted into the courtroom. I followed out his wishes as far as I could . . ." Render adds that Gore, as a lawyer, knew that no court in Texas would send to prison a blind girl who refused to answer questions of the court.

In the Bond case, the judge ruled that any previous adventures of either plaintiff or defendant could not be admitted as evidence. Was Gore guilty? In the Bond case, most unlikely. It was too obvious a political trap. In the blind girl case, he was indeed guilty, as his brother Ellis said after my 1960 television play *The Indestructible Mr. Gore*, in which I followed the family line, to Dot's dread until she saw the actual program, which delighted her. Ellis sourly noted that not only was Guv guilty as charged but that he got their parents to take the girl as part of a deal made with her. I now understand why he resisted all biographers as well as publishers interested in memoirs. "My life," he said to me, "is a dull one and there is so much that I cannot tell."

I have just learned from a Mississippi relative that two years after the program aired, during the war between Attorney General Bobby Kennedy and me, Bobby sent a request to the county clerk in Eupora, asking for details of the Senator's life. The clerk, loyal to his own, threw the request in the wastebasket. Had he not, there would now be on the bookshelves of the republic *The Thousand Lecherous Days of T. P. Gore*, by Arthur Schlesinger, Jr.

DURING THE INFLUENZA EPIDEMIC OF 1918, Dah nearly died; and never entirely recovered his strength. He was also about to die of diabetes when, like the now legendary lady from Boston, Fate saved him— for more torments? Insulin was invented and so, more or less in the normal course, he died of a stroke from high blood pressure in 1949, age seventy-eight, while joking with Dot at breakfast. The two of them had a merry private language, immediately discarded when others intruded, and he would assume a cool gravitas while she would be gracious lady of the house.

Gore's personal triumph over blindness had become so powerful a myth in his own time that his actual political career was somewhat

occluded, while his intellectual powers and wit, though duly acknowledged, were hardly treasured by the folk he represented, much less by
Americans at large. There is no first-rate biography of him, thanks
largely to Dot's carelessness with papers. In the attic at Rock Creek,
most of his archives were strewn over the floor or stacked in trunks and
broken boxes. Unable to see this mess, he probably didn't realize that
his history was being erased through sloth.

In the absence of primary texts, the Woodrow Wilson biographers
seem not to have got much out of him. A. S. Link regards him as a political manipulator and not much more. But biographers of prophets tend
to be proprietary of their great men, and Gore was always there to say
no to ambitious transgression whether in the name of the Republic, the
common man, or the Almighty.

Bryan's nomination in 1908 had, predictably, ensured a Republican
victory. But as a leading populist-Democrat in the Senate, Gore was
now ready for a winner. He began to engineer an alliance between the
populists of the South and Southwest and the big-city bosses of the East.
The result was the nomination of Woodrow Wilson, a one-term New
Jersey governor who had sworn faithfully to serve the local bosses;
then, more in sorrow than in anger, he double-crossed them. Wilson's
subsequent alliance with Bryan and Gore was a necessity for him and a
convenience for them. The tribunes of South and West, of farm and factory, had their permanent base in Congress; the White House was simply
a pleasant extra.

Gore ran Wilson's campaign out of Chicago. When the Republican
vote was split between Taft and Roosevelt, the truly eloquent, if not
entirely sound of mind, Wilson was elected president. Bryan was made
secretary of state. Later, when it became clear that Wilson was maneu-
vering the United States into the First World War, Bryan honorably
resigned. I've always thought him of far more consequence than historians now do. They remember his ignominious end at the "Monkey Trial"
in Tennessee, not to mention the three defeats for president. But I think
of him–like Gore in the early days–as a literally popular voice raised
against the bold, crude ownership of the nation, and a resolute enemy to
the end, like Gore, of those wars that the ownership never ceases to
wage against what it takes to be enemies of its financial system.

In the Senate, Gore was expected to forward Wilson's ambitious
domestic program, which he did, enthusiastically, even though the two

had personally fallen out after the election, when the Senate was in the process of "organizing" itself—that is, selecting various officers and setting up legislative procedures. The all-important post of secretary to the Senate had not yet been filled. Wilson sent for Gore, on an urgent matter. "I would like," said Wilson, "for the Senate to appoint my brother, Joseph, secretary. He is highly qualified and . . ."

Gore listened, astonished. Finally, he said that he never thought he would have to remind so eminent a historian as the author of *Constitutional Government in the United States* that the legislative and executive branches of the government were forever equal and forever separate and that for the executive to have his own brother, as an executive spy, in the councils of the legislature would make a perfect hash of the separation of powers.

"Wilson never forgave me for that." Dah is in his rocking chair, cracking peanuts, lap covered with their shells; the bushy white hair is in an interesting tangle. "Of course, he was the sort of man who got uneasy if you ever raised your eyes higher than the third button on his waistcoat. As for me"—the crooked smile. "Well, whenever there's a Republican president, I'm a Democrat, and when there's a Democratic one, I'm out of step." He sounded more amused than sad. As a politician, he was a lone wolf. I suppose, at heart, he was more Whig than populist and no conservative at all, at least in the current sense of the word—one who serves unquestioningly the wealthy interests that control American life while parroting official cant of the "better dead than Red" sort. He particularly loathed Franklin Roosevelt's phrase "age of the common man."

"There was never such an age and never will be and it goes beyond the limits of necessary demagoguery to pretend that there could even be such a thing." He also disliked Lincoln's rhetoric. "Was there ever a fraud greater than this government of, by, and for the people?" He threw back his head, the voice rose: "*What* people, *which* people? When he made that speech, almost half the American people had said that the government of the North was not of, by, or for *them*. So then Lincoln, after making a bloody war against the South, has the effrontery to say that this precious principle, which he would not extend to the southern people, was the one for which the war had been fought. Well, he *did* say this at a graveyard for northern soldiers. I suppose that was appropriate." If I got anything from Dah, it was the ability to detect the false notes in those arias that our shepherds lull their sheep with.

I always found him noblest when he put his career at risk for some overriding principle. He thought that no foreign war was worth the life of any American. Neither do I. When the Oklahoma City chamber of commerce ordered him to vote for war in 1917, he wired them, "How many of your members are of draft age?" He was defeated in 1920. But he was reelected in 1930, on the same principles, he liked to say, that had defeated him a decade earlier. The comeback was a dim affair. "I remember asking a political friend, just before I entered the race, what was the mood of the people nowadays, and he said, 'They're a lot harder to tickle now.' "

I used to sit on the floor of the attic, reading newspaper cuttings from every period of his life. I recall a particularly savage attack on him in 1930, mocking his "hoary jokes," along with a photograph of the Rock Creek Park house, supposedly built with the tainted oil money of one Doheney. Out of office, Gore had written a legal brief for the oilman. When Doheney went to prison, for the Teapot Dome oil field scandal, my father took Gore, very nervous indeed, to the prison cell. Why they met, I don't know. But the fact that he had been briefly, while out of office, a lawyer to the master of corruption earned T. P. Gore the sobriquet "Teapot Gore." Such is the nature of reputation: The religious man is known to be an atheist; the generous man is called mean. Some years ago an actress told me that *everyone* knew that Noël Coward liked to eat shit. I was horrified. I knew Coward well. He was as fastidious about sex as everything else. When I saw her recently, she said, "I've never forgotten what you told me about Noël Coward, that he liked to eat shit." Thus I have been transformed into the source of a truly sick invention that will be grist to the satanic mills of Capotes as yet unborn.

Courage was Gore's most notable trait. But then his great-grandfather had been a Methodist preacher of such somber fire and will that he was known as "Rock" Gore. On the demerit side, Dah did not think that government money should go to anybody if *he* could help it. "When I first came to the Senate, there were still *pensioned* widows from the war of 1812. Give someone a pension and you create a Methuselah." Coldly, he refused the request of a delegation of the blind for government aid. He had been able to make his way, he told them, and so could they. This was disingenuous. "When I was young, cheese and crackers was one word to me," he used to say, emphasizing his poverty. Bored with this repetition,

I am said to have responded, at the age of six or so, "Well, ice cream and cake are one word to me."

Actually, the Gores were well-to-do for their time and place. He was born in 1870, among the ruins of Walthall, Mississippi. Yet even then, when the university degree was the principal dividing line between lawyers, teachers, divines and the redneck peasantry, most of the Gore clan was educated.

Not long ago, I visited the house where he was born, set in lush green chigger-ridden countryside. There is a large parlor with a fireplace from whose wooden mantelpiece he had detached a sliver. "I was here," said the old woman who owns the house today, "when the Senator came home. You know he had said when he left Mississippi that he would never come back unless he could came back as a United States senator. Well, he was true to his word. Everyone was very excited. Then he came out here and asked my father if he could have a piece off the old mantel."

Through the middle of the house there is a covered open-ended breezeway, a traditional means in the South of cooling a house, as what air there is sweeps through, providing some relief during the equatorial summers. I stood in the small bedroom where Gore was born; felt nothing. Then I went over to the courthouse, where his father had been chancery clerk, and I sat on the same steps where his father had sat all one day in 1861, trying to decide whether or not to join his brothers and friends in a Mississippi rifle company. The Gores were Unionists, and if they had lived across the nearby border in Tennessee, they would have fought for the Union. As it was, reluctantly they fought for one another rather than for slavery, which they despised, or for the ill-starred Confederacy.

It is a pity that so little is understood today about American isolationism. It is accepted that "hyphenate-Americans," newly arrived from suicidal old Europe, would not want to go back to the continent that they had so recently fled to fight for their new rulers' investments. But less understood is how old Americans clung so tenaciously to the Washingtonian precept that nations have interests, not friends or enemies, and that wars far from home will, in time, erode the state. Finally, rather more mystically, there was the idea of American exceptionalism. We were intended to be like no other country: We were neo–Noble Savages. More to the point, we had territories so vast that without immigration we could never have filled them up with the descendants of the 3 million residents of the Republic of 1789. So much did we want to keep ourselves to ourselves that John Quincy Adams, as secretary of state to James Monroe, invented the Monroe Doctrine, denying any European power a foothold anywhere in our hemisphere while swearing a great oath that we would never meddle in European politics, much less wars. Wilson abrogated that doctrine in 1917.

Of course, from the beginning, we were twice-cursed in our garden of Eden–first, with the peculiar institution of slavery; then, with the systematic dispossession of the original Mongol population, known fancifully as Indians. Ironically, after the Gores had become prosperous in northern Mississippi during the 1840s by taking over what had been Chickasaw land, T. P. Gore went west to the territories to which the Chickasaws had been removed, and in effect, by creating Oklahoma, he helped rob them of their land a second time. Also ironically–guiltily?–he tended to take the side of the Indians in their losing disputes with the government over the stolen lands. From 1936 to 1949, he worked as an attorney for the Apache, Comanche, and Kiowa tribes, and some years after his death, they finally won a judgment against the federal government, Gore's ultimate atonement to the people that we had dispossessed.

The spirit of Harry of the West, as Henry Clay was known, was the spirit of the border people from Clay to Lincoln to Gore. "Internal improvements" were what interested these rustic paladins. When imperialist President Polk gave us the Mexican War, which in turn gave us what is now one third of the United States, including California, Congressman Lincoln denounced him (Lieutenant U. S. Grant did, too) on the ground that we were behaving like a predatory European power. We were supposed to create our unique Arcadia without border raids on other countries. We certainly needed no more land. Wasn't the Monroe Doctrine our holy text?–along with the Declaration of Independence, which proclaimed as a universal human given the right not only to pursue happiness but the implicit right to separate from an onerous foreign master.

Gore came out of the border world. He represented the ruined farmers of the Civil War, who would later be victimized by eastern financiers, playing casino with the price of cotton. "Seven-cent cotton" was one of the first phrases I can remember hearing.

In due course, Bryan and Gore and the other liberals—today called conservatives or nativists or worse—reached out to labor, organized or not. Hence, Gore's mysterious appearance in Darrow's courtroom, where union labor was on trial. The Civil War that had brought ruin to the South had also awakened all sorts of energies that led to new alliances. In effect, the Party of the People took over the Democratic party, and despite the presence of the big-city bosses, who at least represented the working man, unionized or not, the party was for the working people at large in a way that the Republicans could not be, since they tended to agree with Alexander Hamilton that the rich were wiser and better than the poor and so ought to be allowed to rule the country and do business without popular interference. Conflicts between the two sides continue to this day. But for Gore and the other populists, the imperialism of the two Roosevelts and Woodrow Wilson—Polk, too, earlier—was a terrible distraction from our destiny, which was the perfection of our own unusual if not, in the end, particularly "exceptional" society.

I sit with Dah in the living room of his flat in Crescent Place, just across the street from the stately house of Agnes and Eugene Meyer, owners of *The Washington Post,* that official voice of empire. The Rock Creek Park house was sold in the war: impossible to heat. I am still in uniform, a warrant officer back from the Aleutians. Dah rocks in his Mission chair. Discusses my political career and what he calls "the New Mexico option," because "Oklahoma is too volatile." He always winced at the thought of his Bible-loving constituency. "Of course, you were born in New York. Why not take advantage of that? Why not get yourself a district in the city? You pay Tammany Hall your first year's salary and, except for city matters, they leave you alone." I thought this a dead end.

Then we talked of the past. He had got into the habit of answering my long, questioning letters with long ones of his own. I thought that his to me were lost in the war when my mother threw out all my clothes, books, and papers, on the sensible ground that, like Jimmie, I'd not be coming back. But apparently Dah kept not only my letters but carbons of his own to me. Excerpts have been published in *World Literature Today,* by one Marvin J. La Hood, who found the collection at a university library.

It is nice to hear Dah's voice again; disconcerting to hear my own, a sort of schoolboy Machiavelli with, alas, a non-Machiavellian fury to be *in the right,* like my politically martyred grandfather. Apparently, the Senator wrote me an eleven-page disquisition on Roosevelt's character, not quoted in full. But I can guess its gist. Like his fifth cousin Teddy and his former commander in chief Wilson, Franklin Roosevelt had always been eager to play an imperial role on the world scene. To make internal improvements in a country like the United States was as difficult then as it is now.

I always thought Dah somewhat invidious whenever he discussed the ever-more imperial trappings of the presidency and the blaze of world publicity, which, from Wilson's triumph at Versailles to Bush's vomiting in the lap of the Japanese prime minister, was the outward and visible sign of our imperium's military glory and economic primacy. But all that is now quickly fading away and one can see how quaintly prescient we were over fifty years ago.

The correspondence begins on March 9, 1940. I am at the Los Alamos Ranch School, in Otowi, New Mexico. Apparently, I've been reading about the First World War and Gore's ambivalent maneuverings in the Senate.

Gore explains his "resolution [that] warned American citizens not to exercise the right to travel on the armed ships of a belligerent. . . . I introduced that resolution two or three days after the celebrated Sunrise Conference which is now 'historic' . . . I thought then that we were speeding headlong into war—as we were." For someone brought up in the wreckage of the Civil War, any *foreign* war seemed like perfect folly. For someone who detested the country's ruling class, the idea of a war that would be profitable only to the Rockefellers and to the Morgans was insupportable. Certainly, those who actually fought the war would not do well out of it. But then they never do. From one of Jimmie Trimble's last letters to his mother from Iwo Jima: "After the war, we won't receive any credit for having been out here. It's the smart guy who stays in the States earning money. I'm not even getting much self-satisfaction by telling myself that I'm at least doing my part, for peace of mind does no good if anything happens." Three weeks later something happened. When I wrote in a memorial issue of *Newsweek* about the war and Jimmie's death, letters from ex-marines began to arrive. They are still in a rage at what was done to them, not to mention all the dead.

Dah's letters also contain exhortations for me to get better grades. This is a constant refrain throughout my school days. I was thought to be reasonably intelligent by the various schools that I attended; certainly, I was often more widely–if eccentrically–read than many of my teachers, which was not saying much; unfortunately for me–and irritatingly for them–I have never been so bored, before or since, as I was by the courses that I was obliged to take and pass. For an energetic mind, with a passion to know everything, to be confined to translating from the Latin that dismal miniaturist Cornelius Nepos was exquisite torture, particularly when I was being denied, at least in class, Suetonius, Juvenal, Tacitus–and Livy, whom I had read at seven, in English. Worse, what passed for education in those days involved the memorizing of everything from Latin subjunctive verbs to mathematical theorems. Outside reading was not encouraged; neither was thought.

Dah has duly noted my ambition but fears that I will turn out like my mother and her brother, indolent Washington types who believed implicitly in the Law of the Lobbyist: It's not *what* you know, it's *who* you know.

"The power to excel is not the same as the desire to excel," he writes me. "You know, a west Texas jackrabbit has a habit of running on three feet until pressed by the hounds, then he puts down his fourth foot and runs off and leaves them." Dah wants to see my fourth foot in action. I suppose I wanted to see the hounds first.

Dah's socialist impulses eroded with time. He had wanted to nationalize the railroads when he helped write the constitution of the state of Oklahoma, and I believe that this virtuous proposal is still in the text. But despite his expertise on banking and currency in the Senate, he detested Maynard Keynes without quite understanding him. He grasped, reluctantly, tax and spend in bad economic times, but he never took in the other side to Keynesianism: Try to make money in good times and in the classic marketplace.

In the letters, Dah deeply dislikes Roosevelt both personally and politically. "He worships at the shrine of Power and Popularity." There is now, he notes, almost $50 billion of national debt, hardly a "Star Wars" price tag for what was meant to be a New Deal for those millions of people undone by a vast depression. The worst hit, as Dah had prophesied, were the veterans of that war for Wilson's greater personal glory. I had always thought Gore's concentration on one man's vanity too petty a motivation for the American role in the events of 1914–17. But when I came to study Wilson at Versailles, blithely carving up the Austro-

Hungarian empire, I could understand why this ignorant would-be Metternich drove Dr. Freud so mad that he felt obliged to publish a libelous "psychoanalysis" of Wilson, without having met him, of course. Although Freud's analysis is nearly as demented as Wilson's imperial– even messianic–behavior, he does echo Gore's original analysis of a prim American schoolteacher whose ignorant self-esteem never faltered. As I write, Wilson's handiwork is now exploding in what proved to be his dottiest invention, Yugoslavia.

Senator Gore was obliged to observe three American caesars in action. In his youth, there was Theodore Roosevelt's Spanish-American War, followed by the bloody conquest and subjugation of the Philippines. When Gore came to the Senate at thirty-seven, Roosevelt was still president, and an anathema to a tribune of the farmers and workers. Then, twice, Gore helped elect Wilson president. From the start, there had been a vague understanding between them that the egregious Marshall be replaced as vice president in the second term by Gore, but, as of 1916, relationships were so bad between Wilson and Gore that the Senator decided to sit out the election. When it became obvious that Wilson was going to lose, Gore got a desperate call from the White House. The election would be determined by California. Gore was popular in California. Would he stump the state? Gore made one condition: The slogan must be "He kept us out of war" and, presumably, "he" would do the same in the second term. Gore barnstormed California. Then he wired the White House the exact margin by which Wilson would carry the state. That night Wilson's opponent, Charles Evans Hughes, went to bed as president of the United States. But the next morning California was heard from and Gore's predicted plurality reversed the election. Wilson was president; and the war came.

Dah turns on the radio news. He prefers right-wing commentators like Fulton Louis, Jr. He did not live long enough to realize just how conservative a president Roosevelt was at home or how much a radical imperialist he was abroad, breaking up the colonial empires of our allies as well as those of our enemies and, like metal filings to a magnet, attracting their fragments to us. But in the forties, all that Gore can see is the vast amount of debt–so puny compared to what the truly radical Reagan was to give us.

"These debts," Dah writes me, "constitute a first lien, a first mortgage on every dollar's worth of private property. . . . However, all this is not the most fatal defect in the New Deal: it has spoiled the character and the morals, spoiled the souls of millions of our people. I have always thought that self-respect is the sheer anchor of human character. As long as it holds, there is hope. When it breaks there is no hope, there is nothing left." Thus speaks the Protestant conscience, not to mention, alas, Herbert Hoover.

I have always regarded Roosevelt's improvisations in a kindlier light. It was the Depression brought on by the higher capitalism that denied people work, and Roosevelt was there, no matter how opportunistically, to get the people, as well as the capitalists, through bad times. But there is indeed a terrible truth in Gore's observations on the necessity of self-respect—of individual autonomy. In order to exclude the black minority from American society, the white majority decided to pay them off with welfare, thus seeing to it that there would be no "anchor" for many black families for many generations. No wonder so many are now choosing the fire this time as the ultimate "self-respect."

"Those crowds," he begins, turning off Fulton Lewis, Jr. *Amos 'n' Andy* would soon be on, his favorite comedy, swarming with politically incorrect "Negro" stereotypes. "Those crowds that Wilson saw in Europe." He shakes his head; the white hair is now all on end as two cowlicks meet, and Dot will soon have to start unsnarling and combing them straight. "I suppose any man's head would be turned by them. Now Roosevelt has gone to Yalta. At least there won't be any crowds. But he'll be just like Wilson. *He* won the war, and *he'll* make the peace, or so he thinks. But Churchill and Stalin will be too smart for him. Just as Lloyd George and Clemenceau were too smart for Wilson. Then there's the fact he's dying, which doesn't help matters. . . ."

It is curious how everyone knows everything in Washington while the people of the country, at least in those days, know nothing about their rulers. Until television, our capital was always rather like the secret Kremlin in its Stalinist glory days. *We* all knew, but the public did not, that Crown Princess Martha of Norway, the president's last love, had moved into the White House and that Missy Le Hand, *maîtresse en titre* and secretary, moved out and died of a broken heart. When Roosevelt, in front of the newsreel cameras, presented the crown princess with a warship, our *nomenklatura* whispered, "How like him! Most men give their mistress diamonds. But not our czar. He gives her a destroyer."

From Dah's letter to me on my fifteenth birthday: "I compare or contrast your opportunities now with mine when I was your age and I all but envy you. I lived thirty miles from the railroad and attended a school which ran about four or five months a year–in a building 30 by 50 there was no fifth dimension." Nevertheless, by then, he had freed himself of that religion which was–and still is–a terrible blight in his part of the world. At nine or ten, told that if he had faith he could fly, he attached cornstalks to his arms and climbed out onto the roof of a barn and took off, to fly around the world. He broke his collarbone. Later, when his father decided to abandon the family Methodism for the Campbellite variant of fundamentalism, the family was ordered to choose its brand. The mother stayed as she was. Two children became Campbellites, for Father's sake. Gore turned atheist, a daring thing to do then–and now–in Mississippi. On the other hand, he did not let it be generally known that he was a nonbeliever; if he had, he could not have had a political career. A conundrum that he liked. "Can God, the all-powerful, do *anything*?"

"Yea! Yea!"

"No, He can't."

"*What* can't He do?"

"Can't make a year-old heifer in a minute."

"'Course He can. Why, in just a minute, there it is."

"Yes, but no matter how big that heifer is, it's still only a minute old and not a year."

In November 1942, I write him: "I can see now why you aren't in the Senate. It surprises me that people had enough sense to keep you for as long as they did. When I start running I am going to call spades, spades, fools, fools, New Dealers, Jack asses, and I shall be beaten by a comfortable majority." Professor La Hood finds this prophetic but notes that in 1964, had I run again for the House of Representatives, I would have been elected.

From Antigua, I write Dah about my new friend, the president of the Guatemalan Congress: "They respect men of learning here and don't try to reduce them to the lowest possible common denominator."

Dah is amused: "I particularly enjoyed the last paragraph, where you mentioned the fact that in certain localities you have to appear genial and a little half-witted in order to woo the omnipotent public."

*My grandmother, Nina Kay Gore, with her
husband the senator and children,
T. P. Gore, Jr., and Nina, about 1916.
President Harding said that she was the
best-looking lady in Washington.
She rather fancied him.*

Dot

I SEE DOT MOST VIVIDLY on the lawn in Rock Creek Park. Small. Plump. Pink wrapper. Hair uncombed. She has a piece of hardboiled egg in her hand. She whistles. A cardinal—a bright red bird indigenous to the South—drops from a tree onto her wrist and eats the egg. Birds, animals all came to her with no fear.

I came to her in my sixteenth summer. Nina was leaving Auchincloss. She was packing up. I had been on a trip to Canada with my father. He dropped me off at Merrywood. Early evening. I had one suitcase. In a few weeks I would be going back to Exeter for my last year. Nina was drinking; smoking; packing in a haphazard way. I had been given one of Whistler's Venice etchings, which hung in the celebrated small bedroom. She forgot to take it.

Furniture shrouded in white dust covers. Everywhere: open boxes, suitcases, trunks. Nina is alone; her Bavarian maid, Maria, is on holiday. Nina is spoiling for a row. Gene, given to mischief, now gives her a splendid occasion: an insurance policy left over from their married days. As only Gene paid the premiums, he can do with it as he likes. He turns it over to me to use when I'm of age. But she wants that policy. Right now. I say, No, I'll need it later, when I start my career. In New Mexico. She rages, all the while puffing smoke, drinking Queen Anne Scotch, packing linen, silver. A hot, humid August night on the Potomac palisades.

Bloodshot eyes, puffy body. And many, many grievances. The prenuptial agreement ensures that there will be no more money for her other than the agreed-upon thousand dollars a month for life and a certain amount for her two small children, whose custody she somewhat absently demanded and got from Hughdie. A thousand dollars a month, in those days, was like ten thousand now. Enough to get by on. There should have been more, somehow, but there was not, "because, let's face it, I'm always the fall guy. I'm the guy who'll always give you the shirt off his back. That insurance policy was always mine. It's the least he could do for me after I married him and got him into aviation because I knew Burdette Wright. Why, if it hadn't been for me, he'd still be a football coach up at West Point or, worse, Oregon, or someplace just as bad, but lucky for him it was *my* friendship with Amelia and Slim Lindbergh that got him to the Ludingtons and that first airline, which *I* put together out of nothing, *nothing* at all, and even served the first lunch myself, first meal ever, on an airplane from Washington to New York. Consommé in cardboard cups. With those hard-boiled eggs. I mean, let's face it, your father's a failure, or was until he married me and I gave him *entrée. . . .*" This was a favorite lobbyist's word, meaning, I am the daughter of Senator Gore, and if you would like any special legislation passed by his subcommittee, I will be happy to arrange it for you, for a fee.

I don't think Nina ever put her case quite so bluntly, nor was she, curiously, at all greedy for money other than her vague, almost metaphysical, sense that the world's contents were hers by divine right and only the malevolence of others had denied her, to use today's cant word, so many due entitlements. Over the years, she kept adding newer and wilder details to the scenario of her life. As she collected injustice on a grand scale, she reinvented everything. As fellow flyers, Earhart and Lindbergh were my father's friends, not hers, as well as colleagues in several airlines. She contributed nothing other than an imaginary "*entrée*" to the Senate, where none was needed, since my father was a favorite at the other end of Pennsylvania Avenue, the White House, where Senator Gore was by then an enemy marked for destruction.

Years later, after I was on the cover of *Time*, she wrote the editor a long letter denouncing Gene and me. Even *Time* dared not print more than a paragraph, under the title "A Mother's Love."

From her original deposition: "*We* started the Ludington Air Line in 1930 [my italics]. My father, Senator Gore, was going to finance it, but the 1929 crash depleted his resources. After about a year Gene tired of it and retired from the company."

The truth was that between September 1930 and February 1933, the Ludington line flourished; then, as so often happened in those early days, it was merged with another airline and metamorphosed as Eastern Airlines. By then, Gene had left—not at all tired of the company—because President Roosevelt had appointed him director of air commerce, in March 1933; he was thirty-seven, and from what I now read in the press and see in the newsreels of those days, he was not only a highly romantic figure but he was also, as one historian of aviation put it, "the high priest of flight."

Nina's gloss on all this is bold: "Finally, after rough going, my father got the poor man an appointment through Franklin Roosevelt as Director of Aeronautics [*sic*]. Then I felt I'd done my duty, and went to Reno taking Gore with me." Thus, God must have sounded on the seventh day.

Finally, that hot night, with a cry, she threw the inevitable glass at me. Once, in candid mood, she confessed that rage made her orgasmic. I forgot to ask her if sex ever did. But I did enjoy her candor about herself.

In the middle of the night, I left Merrywood forever, carrying a suitcase that got heavier and heavier with each mile I walked.

The house is set back a good distance from what was then a country lane which then connected with the River Road, two or three miles from Chain Bridge. I walked, sweating heavily, as far as the bridge. Found a taxi. Said I had no money but I'd lend the driver my signet ring until my father paid him back. Luckily, Gene was at a hotel in the city. He paid the driver. I slept on a sofa. The next morning I moved back home to Rock Creek Park.

IN THE MORNING Dot was fully dressed for once, and very grim. Nina had rung to say that I am to be thrown out of the house. "She's drinking." Dot was unusually blunt. The matter of drink is almost always euphemized in southern families. But now the line came out hard and clear. Dah was nowhere to be seen.

"I'll go on to East Hampton." Gene's summer place on Long Island.

"You'll stay right here. *And* you'll read to Dah," she added, giving her not entirely altruistic game away. We could hear Nina's car as it came into the driveway.

"Go on upstairs. I'll handle this." Ordinarily, Dot was an affectionate, rather absentminded woman; but she also had very much the gift of command, inherited, no doubt, from her slave-owning mother.

I stationed myself in the room above the front door, with a clear view of the driveway.

Nina stood beside the fountain and delivered her summing up for the prosecution. A formidable brief, replete with detailed instances of betrayals, deceits, and crimes against her goodness to which, she proclaimed, with Jeffersonian splendor, there were finally limits. *She was now going to live for herself at last.* She, who had given too much of herself to me, was damned if she was going to give up that insurance policy that was hers by right, and how could I, with any conscience, take *her* money when she was the guy who had got Hughdie to create a twenty-five-thousand-dollar trust fund for me as part of the prenuptial agreement? As it turned out, Nina pocketed every penny of the small income from that fund until I was twenty-one, when the interest was paid directly to me.

The tirade of self-justification was, as always, of Supreme Court caliber. Ten generations of lawyers, starting back in County Donegal, must seriously affect the DNA code. "Now, you must throw him out . . ."

"He is our grandson." An icy bronze voice that I'd never heard before from Dot. "He stays here."

"*I* am the mother, under law I'm his guardian . . ."

"Under the law, this is my house, not yours. Now, *you* go away."

Nina, stunned, rallied. "I'm coming in . . ."

"Oh no you're not!" With that—I could no longer see Dot from my window, but apparently she had slipped inside the house and slammed the door so hard that the house shook. Nina got back in the car and drove off.

Dot came into the room. I was still at the window. "You heard that." It was statement, not question. "I don't know why it is," she spoke with a kind of wonder, "but whenever my daughter appears upon the scene, it is like an evil spirit."

I said nothing.

Dot smiled. "Remember when this was your room?"

As I have already noted, my first memory is of that room, and of my head stuck between the slats of the playpen. Then Dot told me that it was she who had freed me.

I HAVE ALWAYS BEEN INTRIGUED by the phrase "the long arm of coincidence," invented by a playwright friend of Somerset Maugham. The long arm reached out and touched me yesterday, August 21, which proved to be, after weeks of intense airless heat, the first day of autumn. A cool to cold north wind–the *tramontana*, as they say here–driving rain clouds but as yet no rain. This year's August drought is even longer than last year's. Dah liked to quote a farmer's testimony before his agricultural committee: "Harvests have been below average for the last twenty years."

As I type out memories of Dot and Dah on an old green portable Olivetti whose *m* is half stuck, a letter is placed on my table. It is from T. P. Gore II, my first cousin. I've not heard from him in thirty years. He writes from New Jersey. He has enclosed photographs of the graves of Dot and Dah and Nina in an Oklahoma City cemetery. I don't even know the cemetery's name because I have never been to Oklahoma City or, except for one night in Tulsa during the war, in the state at all. I suppose this is partly due to resentment against the people who defeated Dah when I was ten years old.

Clear color photographs show well-tended grounds. A large altarlike memorial of gray marble bordered by flowers. On one side, an inscription to Dah; on the other, to Dot. Presumably, their remains are in boxes beneath the monument. I read with a magnifying glass: "Thomas Pryor Gore, born Webster County, Mississippi, December 10, 1870, member of the Council Oklahoma Territory, 7th Legislative Assembly District 1903–1905, Elected United States Senate 1907–1921, Re-elected 1931–1937, Died March 16, 1949." On that day, St. Patrick's Day, my father and I took a train together from New York City. At noon we were in the ground-floor flat of an apartment house on Wisconsin Avenue, a block or two from the Gores' first Washington house in Mintwood Place. Full circle.

Dot wept quietly but talked coherently. "He had been laughing at breakfast, joshing me. Then he was in a coma, a stroke. I think he knew what was happening." Next to being blind, this struck me as the worst that could happen to anyone: to be trapped deaf, dumb, blind in a motionless body. Three days later he died. Ancient colleagues came to pay their respects. She greeted each by name. Never got a name wrong. Remembered to repeat Mr. Gore's good opinion of the visitor.

Dah was obsessed with death. But then blindness is a kind of permanent foretaste–prelude? The Greeks thought that death was the absence of light. In old age, he overcame his fear, literally by accident. At the time, I was about twelve years old. One of my St. Albans classmates was the son of the Colombian ambassador to the United States. On a Sunday, I went to have lunch with Alfonso Lopez. I was curious about the gloomy embassy because at the time of the First World War it had been the German legation, and it was from here that righteous Wilson had driven Count Bernstorff from Freedom's land. The house proved to be appropriately spooky. It became even more so when a servant appeared in the dining room door to say that, according to the radio, "Senator and Mrs. Gore have just been killed in an automobile accident."

As it turned out Dot was all right, but Dah had suffered a concussion. When consciousness returned, days later, he observed with wonder, "I could have been dead all this time and I'd never have known a thing. That means there's nothing at all to being dead." Years later, Dot came to the same conclusion when, crossing a room, she suffered a stroke. "And there I was falling slowly, slowly to the floor and I remember thinking, Why, this is death and it's really so pleasant." Unfortunately, she was to survive a number of debilitating strokes.

The automobile accident was to be the last blow from Dah's ironic fate, ironic because he was about to go back to Oklahoma City to be reelected to Congress, this time as a member of the House of Representatives. But his ever-vigilant fate saw to it that Dot's vagueness about left and right had placed them in the wrong lane, and so a truck, not Roosevelt, ended his political career. The Lopezes were understanding; they, too, were a political family. In due course, Alfonso became president of Colombia, but I never saw him again after school. He was the first boy in our class to have pubic hair–*Latin* blood, we little Anglos observed censoriously.

"Unyielding to adversity, conqueror of misfortune, served Oklahoma with indomitable will for two decades. First United States Senator from Oklahoma, he bequeathed us eloquence, wit and learning. Great is the memory of his character."

In Oklahoma there is a fairly large city named Gore, notorious for being one of the most polluted in the United States, thanks to oil refineries and the infamous Union Carbide; there are also numerous lakes, mountains, and streets called Gore, but no proper biography. Although what little remained of his papers did end up in a university, I doubt if there is enough left to reconstruct him. *Character* is the key word when one thinks of him. Martin Luther's "*Ich kann nicht anders*" would have been a good motto for him: I can do no other.

On the obverse side: "His wife, Nina Kay Gore. Born Anderson County, Texas, March 28, 1878. Died May 8, 1963." Dot's father was from South Carolina; fought in the Civil War; then moved west. "See?" She would point to a large daguerreotype of a wild, blue-eyed, bearded man. "He looks just like Robert E. Lee." I've never seen the slightest resemblance.

Once a year the Kay family holds a reunion in South Carolina. I've never gone to one, but a cousin writes to me from time to time. Apparently, that ill-starred president Jimmy Carter had a Kay grandmother, too, and so he and I are, according to the family's vast Alamanach da Gotha of farmers and mechanicals, "fifth cousins twice removed," whatever that means. Once removed, I suppose, by his election to the presidency and permanently removed by his defeat. I've never met him. I did send him a telegram after his failed helicopter strike at Teheran. I said that honor required him to resign. Had I known of our relationship—as close as that of Franklin to Theodore Roosevelt—I would have said "family honor." Earlier, I had been invited to the White House but, rudely, I never acknowledged the invitation. I am told that he proudly mentions T. P. Gore as his cousin. But there is no evidence that he has made a similar claim in regard to me. Anyway, he is a decent man if an inept politician.

A third photograph shows a small slab set in appropriately burnt-out grass: "Loving Daughter, Nina Gore Olds, 1903–1978." "There's room for you, too," Dot would say, enticingly. "We can take four more." I must say they all look so *final* now, their names in gray marble, presumably forever, their terminal dates at last filled in.

Today it is windy; premature autumn. Last night I dreamed of Dah for the first time in many years. We are aboard a ship. There is no stateroom ready for him, and I have no ticket, passport. I can't find Dot. The ship pitches slightly, and I hold on to his arm as I used to do when we negotiated difficult terrain: otherwise, he'd hold my arm. I am worried that he will fall. Then I find a stateroom with an open door and trunks all about. As it is empty of people, I commandeer it. Dah is not well; wants to lie down. I help him into a bunk. I'm afraid that the occupants will come back at any moment. Then I notice that my white cat is missing. More anxiety. I search the ship; cannot find the cat; cannot find my way back to Dah's stateroom. Wake up.

"Do you dream in pictures?" I once asked him.

"Not often," he said. "And when I do it's always from the time that I could see. I've no idea what Tot–or any of you–looks like. I also can't imagine *ladies* with painted faces."

Change in weather alters mood. Energy returns, though not as it once did. I'm beginning not to mind looking into the past, but I certainly wouldn't want to live there. Once was enough. Dah: "The happiest time in anyone's life is when he is working to achieve something that is within his capability. But then, once you get what you want, there is a bit of a letdown..." Miraculously, he had got to the Senate. But, of course, he had wanted to be president; but feared–knew, indeed–that his blindness would disqualify him. In any case, he could only go so far after the quarrel with Wilson; finally, influenza removed him from the great stage.

At forty-eight, he never again was to recover his full strength or momentum. Curiously, at the same age, my father suffered a near-fatal heart attack and he, too, was diminished, never to be the same again. I came as close as I ever have to a nervous "breakdown" in my forty-eighth year, fearful that I, too, would share their fate. But I was spared and allowed what they were denied: twenty-two years more or less at full strength.

"Loving Daughter." Since one can have no idea what really went on in the lives of those now resident in cemeteries, the novel was invented. Back of gravestone pieties there are vivid realities. Theresa Baxter, the black woman who saw the Gores through old age and into the cemetery, said that whenever Nina rang to say that she was in Washington, Dot would say to Dah, "Lulu's back in town." Then they would both roar with laughter. Plainly, some music-hall joke of the nineties.

Nina was very much of the great world. Henry Luce, in my presence– that is, I was in the next room, an unwilling but interested eavesdropper–said that his wife, Clare Boothe Luce, *did not understand him* and would Nina . . . ? Later, I told Nina that it would be a good career move all round if she were to marry the proprietor of *Time* and *Life* magazines. But though she liked the idea of all the money in the world, she was not about to work for any of it, in or out of bed. The most that she had ever done in the way of quo-pro-quid was to allow poor Hughdie to try to exercise his conjugal rights. Incidentally, it was Hughdie who had befriended Luce when both were at Yale. Hughdie paid his way to Europe; later gave him money to start *Time* magazine. The money was repaid without interest. We were obliged to call him Uncle Harry; he had long fingers covered with orange fur, like caterpillars.

There was something very pure in Nina's selfishness, something truly beguiling in her lack of self-consciousness. Lulu really didn't give a damn. She didn't want to have sex with Uncle Harry and so she didn't marry him. She did want sex with an air force general with no money; and she married him, only to bury him a year later, when he died of an obscure blood disease.

MY FAX MACHINE has suddenly become a time machine. My researcher has found a second marine who was with Jimmie at Iwo Jima; they served in the same platoon of scouts.

Jim Trimble came in around the first of January [1945]. *We were all strangers to each other—we were immediately sent out on an ambush. The Japanese were harassing some of the natives in a town on the other side of the island, and this is how we started to get acquainted. I think Jim was on one of those first ambush set-ups . . . Nobody knew too much about him at first, except we knew that on certain days when we were training, if there wasn't too much going on, they'd come and tell Jim, Well, you're pitching today.*

So he'd leave, and it turned out he was our star pitcher. I think he won 21 consecutive games . . .

We left for Iwo Jima on about February 8. Then we were at sea 4 or 5 days . . . we went ashore about the 24th or 25th. The day of the 28th we went up to the front . . .

I remember Jim asking me, in particular, because I had seen combat on Guam and I'd killed my first man over there and everything (I was probably one of the only ones that had already seen combat).

He said, "Now, if anything happens tonight, if you were really up against it and you had no choice, would you surrender?" I said, "Not I, because I saw what happened to guys that did surrender on Guam. They'd be tortured and killed." So we talked it over and pretty well agreed that that's what we'd do, fight till the end, no matter what.

At just about midnight, the Japs came from below this ridge; there must have been hundreds of them. We only killed 68, but there was just droves of them coming. They started by–off to my right, where Jim Trimble was . . . Anyway, all hell broke loose, there were hand grenades, shooting and flares went off. I knew there were some mortar men behind us but I didn't know how far. All this excitement and this yelling and shooting and everything else, well, it was hard for us to make contact.

After things finally settled down about 9 or 10 in the morning, after we had killed all of them we could, I started looking around for our guys. Being that Jim Trimble's foxhole was the closest, why there I found him, and he was dead. And he'd been shot and bayonetted just like the rest of them there. He had, I don't know how many, bayonet holes in him, and was shot. There was nothing we could do with Jim . . . we took some of [his] personal belongings off, like a wallet and ring, and we give them to our officer, who in turn– this was standard procedure–sent them back to their next of kin.

Personal things about Jim Trimble? Well, like I say, I probably knew him only six weeks . . . I remember him telling me, because he was engaged to a girl by the name of Christine White–he said, "Boy, we're going to get married."

As I remember him, he died with his boots on. We had our little talk just a couple of hours before, about what we would do. Instead of getting up and running, which at least one other fellow did, he stayed there and toughed it out like the rest of us. Except he got killed. I'm happy to see that someone is interested enough to find out what happened. Another guy in this platoon had a father who owned a publishing company in New York. Several years after, in the front page of our local newspaper, there was his wedding announcement. But that son of a gun, when it came time to go to Iwo, he disappeared. Got himself transferred or something. You never know who you're bumping shoulders with.

I, too, took much the same route and transferred from what would have been infantry duty—almost always lethal for those eighteen or nineteen—to the relative peace of the Bering Sea. I think I could have given my life for Jimmie, but I was not about to give anything but a reluctant two and a half years to President Roosevelt's imperial longings. I have never thought that entire war was worth Jimmie's life or anyone else's.

Curious, as I've been writing about him, an equinoctal gale has started up in the Gulf of Salerno, and there are whitecaps in the sea below the house where once, it is said, Odysseus, more than usually off course, made landfall at the cave of Polyphemus.

SEVERAL YEARS AGO, the then Malaysian ambassadress showed me through the house in Rock Creek. I stopped on the second-floor landing at the small magic door that I still dream of from time to time, the door to the narrow staircase that leads to the attic, my refuge. Ten—twenty?—thousand books lined the house-length raw-wood room. Originally, the books had been carefully catalogued, but one year when the Gores rented the house, the tenant rearranged all the books according to color. Dah never recovered; and never reordered them. The Malaysians had tidied up the long room and built on an annex, while the books have long since returned to the secondhand bookstores where Dah had found them, one by one, over sixty years.

I walk to the window recess where I used to sit on the floor and read. I have a tactile memory of a chocolate Easter egg, filled with a kind of fondant containing dried fruit and nuts. I had never tasted anything so delicious. Before I settled to read, I would take a single bite out of it. Usually greedy, I made that egg last several weeks.

I am now back there again, in memory, seated on the dusty floor, reading *The Athenian*. I have not thought of that book in years. I have no idea who wrote it, or even if I've got the title right. Somehow, an Athenian boy of the fifth century B.C. ends up with the Spartan army in the Greek war against the invading army of Xerxes, the Great King of Persia. At Thermopylae—the Hot Gates—the Spartans are outnumbered. They will not retreat. This means that they will all die. But before they do, their king, Leonides, sends the Athenian youth back to Sparta with the famous message that they have chosen to die with their boots on and only the foreign boy will survive to tell their story.

As I stand in the window niche, I can still see the book with its maroon binding, smell the dust of the attic, taste the last stale remnant of the chocolate Easter egg.... I also sense Jimmie's presence in this room. As it turned out, he was the Spartan boy; I, the Athenian. I had wanted to re-create him through memory, the ultimate possession as well as the last memorial. But tombs are best left shut. Now it is I who am being possessed by him in fast-fading present time.

Is Christine White still alive?

Briefly,
Schools, War

THE PRINCIPAL ANNOYANCE of living at Merrywood was that I had little opportunity to go home to my grandparents' house in Rock Creek Park. Occasionally, the Gores came to Merrywood– that seems to have been part of the contract between senator-mad Hughdie and Nina–but such occasions usually ended badly, when Nina would quarrel with her mother. One Christmas Day, Nina gave Dot a fur coat, then after Nina had said or done something peculiarly offensive, Dot threw the fur coat at her; and went home.

Meanwhile, every attempt to well-round me failed. I was given a Winchester rifle that I never touched. Paradoxically, I later liked the carbine that the army issued me. I disliked team sports and managed to avoid them almost entirely at St. Albans, to the bemusement of the masters. Then I was sent off to Los Alamos, a "ranch school," where some seventy allegedly disturbed, allegedly rich boys each had a horse. The school's founder, A. J. Connell, was a disciple of Theodore Roosevelt's strenuous life. He was also a pederast who insisted on weekly physical exams for the boys, disturbing, no doubt, even the disturbed, amongst whom, a decade earlier, there had been the disturbed and disturbing William S. Burroughs of the adding machine family.

Fortunately, wherever I was, even Los Alamos, the library was my center. At fourteen, I wanted to know the entire history of the entire world. Although reading was discouraged at Los Alamos in the interest

*I enjoyed debating in the Exeter senate.
I also enjoyed the mock politics, so like the
real world later. I took up public speaking
partly because I intended to be a politician
and partly because I had a stammer,
which I gradually lost.*

of strenuousness, I not only managed to read nearly all of Shakespeare, but I made a solid dent in a vast series devoted to the history of Europe, country by country, beginning with Guizot's *France*. I now understand why my mother, only marginally literate, would find so ravenous an intellectual curiosity distasteful, suspecting, correctly, that it would lead to what every teacher regards as the worst perversion of all, autodidacticism.

At first, teachers used to ask me why I wasn't a football player like my father. Interestingly enough, Gene himself was fascinated by my "erudition," as he called it in a letter to me, and had not the slightest interest in my being an athlete. One reason I didn't like football was the boredom of putting on and taking off all that gear. Even so, at an early school, I made what I thought was an unusually brilliant touchdown against what proved to be, upon closer analysis, my own team. Metaphorically, that said it all. Let coaches bark like dogs, my caravan was moving on, like a juggernaut.

I still recall a baseball game at St. Albans. As I looked at the unfinished tower of the cathedral in the distance, I wondered, close to despair, if I would ever be delivered from this state of perfect boredom. As one means of escape, I had developed a vivid inner life, with a number of fictional narratives going on in my head at any one time. At bad moments, I would simply switch on a story; and be gone. This trick of improvising stories for myself continued until I was out of the army and into the world, where life's narrative took over. Luckily, I never lost the knack of being able to switch on, pretty much at will, a fictional narrative. This proved to be a lifesaver when, broke in my twenties, I was obliged to write five pseudonymous books in less than two years.

Although I am told that I have an eidetic imagination (I can summon up vivid scenes, recalled or invented, in my head), I have no idea how or why I do this. Now, despite my aversion to Freud, I find a most odd explanation of this by Georges Simenon, author of hundreds of novels and copulator of thousands of women:

From the example of Balzac, I wish to show that a novelist's work is not an occupation like another—it implies renunciation, it is a vocation, if not a curse, or a disease ... It is sometimes said that a typical novelist is a man who was deprived of motherly love ... The fact is that the need to create other people, the compulsion to draw

*out of oneself a crowd of different characters, could hardly arise in
a man who is otherwise happy and harmoniously adjusted to his
own little world. Why should he so obstinately attempt to live other
people's lives, if he himself were secure and without revolt?*

LACK OF WELL-ROUNDEDNESS did not affect my relations with the
other boys at St. Albans, who, mysteriously and easily, accepted my
preference for books to their games; in this they were more tolerant of
my eccentricity than some of the masters. The head of the Lower
School, now in his nineties as I write, still remarks with wonder, "The
other boys took it for granted that Gore wasn't going to play games. And
they didn't mind." He did not go so far as to say that I was popular, but
he realized that I had, somehow, decided not to conform and that I had,
somehow, got away with it.

I'd learned, very early, how to transmit, in an interesting way, sufficient knowledge and imagination to charm those that I wanted to
charm. Also, I was physically well developed for my age and managed
to win or neutralize the inevitable fights that stand out like bonfires in
the pages of those memoirists who begin life as shy, misunderstood
youths. I was never shy, and if I was misunderstood, it was because I
was modeling myself on that preteen actor Mickey Rooney, and so
played many parts, including my favorite, that of paramount leader.
Wherever I was, I always formed a gang, and I was boss. At Friends
School, the gang's headquarters was a collapsed frame building in the
center of a large meadow. We had all been warned not to go inside the
ruin, a haphazard pile of lumber with many intricate passageways and
dead ends–a maze of delight where we would hide out, preparing for
wars with other gangs.

AT MERRYWOOD I was cut off pretty much from the Gores and, finally,
from Merrywood itself when I was sent as boarder to St. Albans. A good
thing, as it turned out, because I finally began to make friends.

Once I was in the dormitory, there was Jimmie, and the first human
happiness that I had ever encountered. I do not strike the note of self-
pity because, never having experienced happiness before–as opposed
to my own odd constitutional cheerfulness–I could hardly have pitied

myself for what I'd not experienced. I had always known how to make people laugh and, once free of raging Nina and sad Hughdie, I also laughed a lot; yet, to be fair, in passing, Hughdie was most generous to me; he gave me castles and toy soldiers, and at Merrywood I would deploy them by the hour, inventing stories for them, mostly nonmartial. The life of the imagination became more and more intense as the reality about me became more unendurable. At eleven I started, mysteriously, vomiting in Nina's presence. Words were suddenly failing me.

Of the masters at St. Albans, Stanley Sofield was my favorite. He was a plump young man with thick brown hair, glasses, a tapir's nose and small chin. Musical-comedy mad, he wrote and produced shows of his own making at a summer camp. He drank a good deal, which meant that the class that Jimmie and I had with him, early in the morning, often found us face to face with Stanley in a state of terminal hangover. We could always tell if it was one of *those* days by his gentle grave manner, his slightly pained squint, and the very, very soft voice that he used when he told us to pipe down as we took our seats. Then, like a sleepwalker, he would go through the lesson of the day, often at the blackboard. The tone was always one of gentle expository reason. But we all knew that a storm was now on its way; he was like a benign Nina.

One could never guess what would trigger Stanley: Two boys talking in the back or an unusual display of ignorance could set off the scream. Now, the scream was no ordinary human scream. It was a cry from another species or world. An H. P. Lovecraft ghoul's eldritch howl or the blast Tarzan's Tantor the Elephant made. The entire Lower School would fall silent as that scream slowly rose to a crescendo; while the blood of even the best and the brightest turned to ice. Then books would begin to fly with devastating accuracy across the room, each finding, like a proto–smart bomb, an offending boy. We were ecstatic with terror. This was life. Emotion writ large. Catharsis. Then the voice would return to its normal hangover-level; and class would continue.

Stanley had nicknames for boys he liked. I was still called Gene. (At fourteen I lopped off my Christian name and became Gore.) So, for Stanley, I was "Gene-y with the Light Brown Hair," always sung, while I writhed with embarrassment. Jimmie was also a favorite, though I forget his nickname. If not seated together in class, Jimmie and I would signal each other when a hard-on had arrived unbidden. When the other boys figured out what we were doing, they began signaling, too. At twelve, erections come and go, like T. S. Eliot's ladies, talking, most appropriately, of Michelangelo.

The highlight of my school days was the summer of 1939. The war was almost upon us, but Stanley and another master were hell-bent on getting to Europe for one last look. They cooked up a plan to take a half dozen of the boys to France "to perfect our French" and go sight-seeing. Nina was immediately sold on the plan. I was getting a bit too old to be shipped off, yet again, to Camp William Lawrence in New Hampshire, "to be with the other boys and become well-rounded" and as far from Merrywood and Newport as possible.

For the next to last time, Jimmie and I made love in the woods above the roaring river. I remember his almost-mature body with the squared bony shoulders and rosy skin against bright green. He was already becoming famous in Washington as a baseball player, and I was busy writing, and thinking of a political career. At thirteen we talked about girls less than we did about each other. This was a sign, though I was hardly adept at signs then. Why should anyone happy ever note a sign?

After sex, we swam against the swift, deadly current of the forbidden Potomac River, swam among rocks and driftwood to a special large gray-brown glacial rock, where we lay, side by side. We're going to go on doing this for the rest of our lives, I remember thinking, tempting– no, driving–fate to break us in two. If I had been told that we'd meet only one more time in his short life, I would have . . . done what I have done, no doubt. Happily, neither of us knew the future. I did know that after Europe, Nina intended to ship me off to schools far away while Jimmie would stay on at St. Albans, where I wanted to stay but, alas, the school was far too close to Nina's more and more scandalous field of operations.

Every now and then, in idle moments, I start to hear snatches of the conversation of those two boys on the rock that afternoon. ". . . could play ball, as a pro . . ."; ". . . can't be a politician without a state and I don't come from anywhere, maybe Virginia . . ."; lyrics of some jazz song sung in Jimmie's light tenor; "gotta learn sax . . ."; "writing a novel, trying to . . ."; "I'm going to, maybe, to VPI, but they don't have much of a ball team . . ."; ". . . *hate her* . . ." Who said that? I'm now projecting present feelings upon a cloudless sunny day when Europe was ahead of me and all I cared for beside me.

In later years, whenever I tried out a play at the National Theater in Washington, I'd ask Stanley to come backstage when I gave notes after a performance; then we'd go out on the town and drink. He was thrilled by backstage life, and I was always delighted to be with my one last link to St. Albans, to our European summer, to Jimmie.

"Jimmie." Stanley smiles. "I went on seeing him all along until he left for the marines." Stanley was "closeted," as they say in "gay" circles, but I don't know to what degree he was suppressed. Once grown, I was always candid with him; but he was not with me, as was proper.

A bar in Fourteenth Street. A jukebox plays. The late fifties. I put the question: "Did Jimmie ever talk about me?"

Stanley, now very stout, looks at me slightly glassy-eyed, more from drink than from sadness at all that was lost. "Oh yes. He knew you and I were in touch from time to time," a white lie of great kindness. Suddenly, his eyes focus. "Yes, I do remember one day when you were already in the army and he was about to go off to the marines, and the two of us drove by Merrywood and he said he wanted to stop and look around, and so we did. We didn't go near the house, of course, only to the tennis court where the two of you used to play." Stanley frowns. "I don't know . . ." he begins and stops; then: "He seemed sad."

"Did you know why?"

"I do now, don't I?"

EUROPE. With Stanley and young Hamilton Fish (now old and just retired from Congress) and a number of other boys, as well as a teacher called Barlow and his wife. We set out in June, aboard the *Ile de France,* second- or third-class. Pommes frites. Grenadine. Summer school at Jouey-en-Josas. Classes in a manor house with domed drawing room. (In 1949, I saw the half-ruined Château du Mont Cel by moonlight.) French lessons. Walks into Versailles. Baba au rhum.

Paris, July 14, I stand on the steps of the Grand Palais as the French army parades. Nervous bald man in an open car at the center of all this glory. Premier Daladier, the "Bull of Vaucluse," soon to be a prisoner of the Nazis. In buses, we toured First World War battlefields. Poppies nicely symbolic of blood already shed and of blood to be shed yet again in a year's time. Maginot Line. Cement bunkers. Impregnable. So impregnable that the Germans sensibly went around the line. Bus to Touraine. Magnificent guide whose large nose was streaked with broken veins. He wore a monocle, and tarried over lunch. At Blois, he acted out the murder of the duc de Guise. Played all the parts, rushing from room to room. Chenonceaux. The salamander of François premier. Diane de Poitiers. In the bus I fell in love with an older woman, Hammy Fish's sister, Zeva, perhaps sixteen. Never saw her again, though I've seen him. He succeeded to his isolationist father's seat in the congressional district where I'd been a candidate before him.

At Orléans, an old lady squatted down under a tree near the cathedral and relieved herself. I talked to a soldier. He gave me his name, Louis Gilet, and army address. I wrote him twice from school. Sent him a dollar bill. He thanked me warmly. Nothing more.

Rome. August. Heat. I did not careen and moan from monument to monument like Henry James, but I knew that I was home. Forum full of broken marble. I picked up a head and hid it under my coat. Stanley saw me and made me put it back. Blackshirts everywhere. The crowds–like those of France–smelled of garlic. Ten years later no whiff of garlic in either country. Prosperity. Baths of Caracalla. The opera *Turandot.* We sit outside in a railed-off box, under the hot dark sky. In the next box, Mussolini, wearing a white uniform. At the first interval, he rose and saluted the soprano. Audience cheered. Then he left the box. As he passed me, I smelled heavy cologne. Onstage, he saluted the audience– Fascist arm outstretched. Vanished. Since we were Official Children– Hammy's father was chairman of the House Foreign Affairs Committee–Ambassador Phillips received us in the old embassy. Tall glasses of orange juice, and a large plain girl: daughter of Postmaster General Farley. What a good time the ambassador must have had that day! I wrote of Phillips, years later, in *Hollywood.*

End of August, war about to begin. We take the last train out of Italy before the border with France is shut. A dash across France and the Channel to London. Bloomsbury. Russell Square. Old boardinghouse. Fascinating primitive bathroom.

September 1, we are in Downing Street to watch the prime minister, Neville Chamberlain, leave to go to Westminster to say that war is now at hand. Thin little man. A wing collar, huge Adam's apple, uncommonly small head. No cheers, no jeers. The crowd simply sighs, in unison, on exhalation. Terrible, mournful sound. Chamberlain tries to smile; winces instead. Is driven off.

At Liverpool, we board the *Antonia* for New York. In the Irish Sea we see our sister ship, *Athenia*, torpedoed by a Nazi sub. Longboats carrying passengers to the dull, misty green Irish shore. Consternation aboard our ship. Some wanted to turn back. Captain did not. We zigzagged across the North Atlantic. Canteen ran out of chocolate. No other hardship. I did not know fear because I knew that true history—life and death, too—only existed in books and this wasn't a book that I'd read—just a gray ship in a dark sea.

"Gene-y with the light brown hair," sang Mr. Sofield.

"Shut up . . . sir," said Gene-y.

THE FACT THAT the eight years between my tenth and seventeenth years were spent far from home at boys' schools was, in one sense, a good thing: I did not have to deal with Nina. But it was a bad thing in that those webs of friendships that start at an early age between boys and boys and then between boys and girls were broken beyond repair. Even while I was a boarder at St. Albans, I was still at home in Washington, D.C.; but from the fall of 1939 to the spring of 1943, I was in New Mexico or New Hampshire for most of the year, and brief returns for holidays only reminded me that I was permanently displaced, and those friends that I had started to grow up with were now strangers. By the summer of 1943 I was in the army; after that I only came back to see the Gores.

After St. Albans and Mrs. Shippen's dancing class, I made no friends until I was grown. I did like the fact that, after claustrophobic Los Alamos, Exeter was a large place where you could pursue your own interests. It was also reassuringly brutal, just like the real world, or so they rather smugly assured us. But, in retrospect, the real world, at least for me, turned out to be far pleasanter and easier to handle than dour Exeter. The American hysteria about homosexuality was so extreme in those days that friendships between boys were deliberately discouraged, a cruel and counterproductive thing to do in an all-male environment. Duly intimidated, we became coldly competitive, and expert at the art of the cruel put-down. "I came out like a flower and was cut down," our poet Lew Sibley used to quote as he prepared yet another epitaph for one of us. I fear that I was also good at this sort of thing. The only amicable relations that I had at Exeter were with three teachers, T. Riggs, H. Phillips, and L. Stevens. One could at least talk to them without fear of intellectual ambush.

One of the few boys that I found congenial was Bob Bingham. He was tall and sturdy, with a booming voice. "Flamingo" was a song that he often thundered. We double-dated at the girls' school, Wellesley, and one night slept out on a golf course. He was the editor of the school literary magazine, *The Review.* I was on the board. One would think that with so much in common, the relationship would have been easy; instead, it was edgy. So competitive was the atmosphere that he and I were soon in a struggle over which of us was going to be *The* Writer. He was indolent. I was not. I had begun to write a florid novel; never, happily, finished. But I did turn out dozens of short stories. If Hemingway was correct (he was not) that celibacy increases and improves a writer's output, I was positively Shakespearean, at least in output. There was also no sex for me at the school, or for much of anyone else. On the rare occasions when sex was a possibility, he who made the first move would be forever in the power of the moved upon, no matter what happened. This made for a certain guarded irritability in all relations. Later, I was told that "the boys," as we called the athletes, were somewhat freer with each other. One, a lanky baseball pitcher (baseball yet again) swung his leg against mine in English class. I gave him a startled look. He grinned. I suspected a trap and pulled away.

Although there were four other editors at *The Review,* Bob exercised a power of veto. After I had published one story, he exercised his veto vigorously in my case. He had the head of a huge cherub, with blue eyes that would suddenly fill with tears if he was thwarted or in any way put down. When I denounced him for keeping me out of the magazine and himself altogether too visibly in, tears filled those innocent blue eyes. "How can you say that? I mean . . . well, it's only your *story* I'm rejecting, because it's not as good as you can do."

Since stories were often sent us for submission, I wrote a comic piece to which I signed the name of a boy none of us knew. I presented it to the editors. "I got this yesterday. I think it's pretty funny." Bob read the story aloud and laughed the loudest. The story was unanimously accepted.

It was a lovely victory. Bob never forgave me for what he called my "duplicity." In later life, when *The New York Times* refused, for more than a decade, to review me in its daily paper (and always badly in the Sunday supplement), I recalled Exeter and published three novels as Edgar Box; each was extravagantly praised by the *Times*. Plainly, Exeter, though a bad place for the kinder emotions, proved to be a good training ground for every kind of warfare.

When Bob became editor of *The Reporter,* he got me to be, briefly, drama critic. Then he vanished into *The New Yorker* magazine as an editor, and a very good one I am told. He did write one novel after the war; it was not published. He once told an interviewer that he would rather be a good editor than a bad novelist. This was meant to be the ultimate put-down. But I thought that it was not quite up to our old savage standards. Like several of our contemporaries who had seen heavy combat in the infantry, Bingham came back from the war with—how to describe it? A broken ego? For him, some sense of self was lost for good in France.

I think it was Bingham who had the happy notion to break into the files of the English Department and find out what the various teachers had said about us as we moved from the class of one to that of another. A master complained that I seldom did the required reading but would often be found reading irrelevant books on history or novels not on the syllabus, like Mann's *The Magic Mountain.* Another wrote that as a writer and a speaker I was "a soapbox orator." This was at the height of the struggle between the America Firsters, of which I was one of the student leaders, and the interventionists, which included most of the Anglophile faculty. Of the teachers, only Tom Riggs was on my side. A radical young man, he had, while at Princeton, organized the Veterans of Future Wars. This caused a national stir, particularly when he demanded that we be given our bonuses now, *before* the war and possible death. Riggs and I used to think of ways of discomfiting the interventionists, headed by a boy called Gunnar, whom I dubbed "Give 'em a Gun Gunnar."

One prescient English teacher wrote that I might well be a "credit to the school if we can stand him for another two years." Another teacher, after a class with me, told his colleagues, "I wish that I were a bull." When asked why, he said, "So that I could gore Vidal." Well, I see their point; but I don't think that they ever saw mine. As most of them were dim dispensers of conventional wisdom, I felt, who knows why, an obligation to find out what they really meant, particularly when they got onto politics, and then to contradict them, an unpopular trait that I shared with Mary McCarthy, who once told me, "I was always the one in class to hold up my hand to say no to the teacher. I couldn't stop myself."

Unsuccessful as a child, I was proving to be a perfect failure at pretending to be a conventional adolescent in a New England boys' school. Then, three years after graduation, I published my first novel. I am told that there was rage and despair in the English Department. Only the best teacher that I had, Leonard Stevens, was pleased by what I had done, but in his gentle way, he suggested I try to transcend the national manner—gray literal realistic prose—and read more Henry James. I did; and I did.

In the class behind me was John Knowles, whom I don't remember, but he remembers me, because, I suppose, I was conspicuous at the debating societies as well as in the wars on behalf of America First. We have been friends many years now, and I admire the novel that he based on our school days, *A Separate Peace*. I am the character Brinker, Jack tells me—and soon the world, since he is currently writing a book on the novel and its background. I don't see the slightest resemblance. True, Brinker is the class politician, but in the story he acts as a sort of snooping district attorney, trying to find out whether or not one boy caused another boy to fall from a tree. I've told Jack that since I had almost no interest in any of my classmates, I would be the last person to mix myself in the business of others. My time was spent writing and reading and counting the days to my deliverance not only from the school—and later the army—but from the control of others. Nevertheless, *A Separate Peace* remains an eerily precise reconstruction of how things were in that long-ago world before the Second War.

IN MY SIXTEENTH SUMMER I went to work in Gene's factory in Camden, New Jersey. In the interest of finding a cheap fuselage for his "flivver" aircraft (metal was too expensive), he had developed something called Vidal Weldwood, a laminated plywood that proved to be useful for making, among other things, wingtips for fighter planes, which the Vidal company manufactured.

The war was well under way in the summer of 1942. I lived in a boardinghouse and worked as unskilled labor. I ate my first cheeseburger, a new invention, I think. I also bought a package of Camel cigarettes and tried to learn to smoke, but after a few attempts I gave up. Factory work was as dull as I'd suspected. The only person at home on the floor was a mad Englishman who, in response to the rubber shortage, was busy inventing a molded plywood automobile tire. With each awful failure, his confidence grew.

In the middle of the summer, Gene suffered a coronary thrombosis and was not expected to live long. I saw him in St. Luke's Hospital, New York, eyes a glazed yellow-gray from drugs, the hair on his chest gone as gray as mine is now. Haltingly, he told me to work hard. Neither of us had the right script for this scene. As it was, thanks to his years as an athlete, he had developed powerful ancillary veins to the heart and recovered. But in those days heart-attack survivors were kept immobile for at least a year after the attack, thus truly ruining their health. He was never the same again.

Gene was not interested in business once the initial invention or organization had been completed. Even before the heart attack he had begun to drift away from his companies, to the consternation of his partners, the Pew family of Philadelphia, owners of Sunoil.

Three years later, when I was in the army, Gene wrote me to say that he was playing tennis again. "I am so healthy I don't know what to do with myself now that I am removed from the Vidal companies' activities. My withdrawal resulted in very bad feeling on the part of my associates, the Pews, who now accuse me of not acting in the best interests of the stockholders, etc. Never again will I have associates in business." He does admit, "I was rather a phony president, seldom about and dodging all regular official work."

Later, he would do some experimenting with molded fiberglass; he even put a small factory near my house on the Hudson that I was supposed to manage during the days when I was broke. Luckily, it burned down; unluckily, it was not insured.

Gene was never to be the Henry Ford of aviation, because no one could be. The skies were, even then, too crowded, but he did remark, in a letter toward the end of the war, "I do find that I am also a fair-haired boy now [and] that all aviation people agree that the private plane program I tried to swing ten years ago should not have been stopped up." It should be noted that one of the prototypes that he helped develop, with government money, became the helicopter.

Once upon a time, the highest American distinction that could befall fifty-two men and women in a given year was to have one's face on the cover of *Time* magazine. Even Auden was thrilled when he heard that he was the subject of a cover story, and deeply hurt when it was canceled because the managing editor, nodding beneath his flat rock, had been told that Auden was a fag and no fag could ever be so honored. This changed in time, but too late for Auden.

A lobbyist to her fingertips, Nina believed implicitly in publicity, particularly cover stories. She also believed that had it not been for her life-long selfless service to undeserving husbands, lovers, and children, she herself could have been a very great celebrity indeed, though in what field it was never clear. Once, she had some cards printed, announcing that she was an interior decorator. Certainly, she had talent in that field, but between drink and sloth she never set, as it were, a sofa right. Even so fame, rightfully, should have been hers. The day my father brought *Time* magazine home, she threw the magazine in his face, which was also the one on the cover. Since their relations were relatively good at the time, this was indeed a loud cry from a jealous and competitive heart.

In 1976, some eighteen years after I had got her out of my life for good, I was on the cover of *Time*. A few months before, she had written me, begging for money, and I had sent her seven or eight thousand dollars. Money duly banked, she wrote *Time* the infamous attack on me.

I have a copy of the letter in front of me. Nina notes, apropos Exeter, that they would not take me in after the summer school because I had been caught cheating. "However," she wrote, "with tears and pleading I got them to let him continue." There were no tears or pleading. She never set foot in Exeter, even when I graduated. But there is some truth to the "cheating."

Each class sat at a round table with pull-out leaves. During a written test, the master would wander about the room or look out the window while we answered the test questions that had been put to us. One lad, a heavy breather, often looked over my shoulder to see my answers.

Finally, hot breath on my neck one time too many, I broke. "Here," I muttered, and shoved the paper toward him. At that moment, the master turned around. We were both put on probation. I was not able to explain to the principal my exasperation without getting the heavy breather into even deeper trouble. But, more to the point, I knew that even if I had been able to explain the nature of my gesture–ironic, not collusive–the irony would never have registered in so literal a place.

Since English was my best subject, it was decided that, at worst, I was an accomplice. I was duly warned and allowed to come back in the fall. But honesty now requires me to say that I cheated in almost every mathematics examination; otherwise, I could not have graduated, a matter of some urgency with the war on and a high school education necessary to get into the army's training program. My breach of Exeter's honor system never gave me the slightest pause. After all, it was *their* honor system, not mine, a means of getting us to sneak on one another. None of us had been consulted in the matter, nor had we sworn an oath. We were simply told and that was that, and I have never thought much of rules arbitrarily imposed on me by others for their convenience. For me, in those days, honor was Billy the Kid: Kill my friend and I will kill you. Now honor is to try to tell the truth.

THE TRUTH IS my war was not much. With a hundred other Washington boys of seventeen, I marched into Union Station and onto an ancient train that let us off in or near Lexington, Virginia, where the Virginia Military Institute (VMI) was. The school's cadets continued about their business while we occupied similar but unequal barracks. We were to be trained as engineers–and, of course, soldiers. I was hopeless, as always, at mathematics. But I liked Major Willard, the physics teacher, who told me (July 1943) that the atom had been broken and that somewhere out west we were creating what would be the most powerful bomb in history. So much for the top-secretness of the Manhattan Project.

"Out west," I later learned, along with the rest of the world, was the Los Alamos Ranch School, taken over by the government a year or two after I left. The main house of the original school is now a museum showing how the place looked before the government built its city on the mesa. I am told that there are, in a glass case, the chaps that I left so happily behind, my name pinned to them like a relic.

I wrote a good deal of dark verse at VMI. I also enjoyed the company of a VMI English teacher who was surprisingly literary, but then he was a relative of Ellen Glasgow, an excellent Richmond novelist now forgotten. Since the three-month term was about to end, I realized that the army was getting ready to abandon our training program. I signaled my uncle, the commanding officer of a fighter wing at Peterson Field, Colorado Springs, and so I leaped, as it were, away from the door to the slaughterhouse through which my classmates were now obliged to pass. I already knew too much politics to be willing to die in "Roosevelt's war." Nina, of course, claimed credit for my transfer. "I got Gore," she confided to *Time* magazine, "into the Air Force." But, of course, she did not.

My time Stateside is a blur. At Peterson Field we lived in Quonset huts heated in winter with black iron coal-burning stoves. We alternated as CQs (charge of quarters) to stoke the coals all night long in below-zero weather. I recall a handsome red-haired southern boy who could neither read nor write. When I was CQ, he'd often stay in the hut rather than go into Colorado Springs, and I'd tell him stories, like a child. I even tried Shakespeare on him. Romeo and Juliet. He loved the plot, but then he came from feuding country and, for him, the Hatfields and the McCoys were no different from the Montagues and Capulets. The verse, what I could recall, moved him, and he would idly play with what he called his "fuck-pole," but in no provocative way. As Dr. Kinsey would discover, there was a great deal of same-sex going on. In the States, it was dangerous on post. But in nearby Colorado Springs there were many men eager to know us, and once, after I was blown by an old man of, perhaps, thirty—my absolute cut-off age—he offered me ten dollars, which I took. As a result I, alone in the family, did not condemn Jackie's marriage to Onassis, since I, too, had once been a small player in the commodities' exchange market.

From Peterson Field to Lake Pontchartrain as a deckhand on an army crash boat. I knew more about boats than anything else of use to the air corps, other than being a clerk-non-typist. We were stationed at the so-called Irish Canal; our job was to pick up wet flyboys—pilots in training who had ended up in the large lake. In time, I passed an examination for first mate by memorizing most of a navigation book. My eyes were too bad to get into Officers' Candidate School. So I became a warrant officer (junior grade) and transferred to the Transportation Corps at Fort Lewis, Seattle, Washington.

The night before we went overseas, I was in the Snakepit Bar of the Olympia Hotel in Seattle. Smoky, raw-wood-paneled dive, powerful smell of beer, cheap Ivory soap, fog-damp wool uniforms, and bodies that smelled and looked as different from today's bodies as science-fiction earthlings differ from deodorized androids. We were a lean, sinewy, sweaty race, energized by sex and fear of death, the ultimate aphrodisiac. Bodies *were* different then. No one was fat, unlike most Americans today. These were Depression boys. I recently watched some old "pornographic" films of the period. I had forgotten what the so-called workingman's body was like–thick-thighed, flat-chested, with muscular arms, not as comely as an aerobics-styled body of today, but solider, uncalculated, earthlike.

Certain that I was going to be killed wherever it was that the ships would take us the next day, I thought that I should at least experiment with a potential Jimmie. For the first time, I picked up someone. A merchant mariner. He was delighted. I noted that he wore a wedding ring, but then half the hunters in the bar were fleshing out Dr. Kinsey's as-yet-uncharted graph from 1 to 6 (those exclusively heterosexual were 1; homosexual, 6; 2 through 5 were swingers between 1 and 6). In the Snakepit Bar the golden mean prevailed, as I suspect it does throughout the race.

We tried to get a room in the hotel; all were taken except for a "samples room." We took that. The room was a corridor with a long table where salesmen could line up samples of whatever it was that they were selling. At the far end, in an alcove, there was a bed. I was nineteen, just under six feet, weighing in at one hundred and fifty pounds. He was twenty-five and weighed about one hundred seventy pounds; he was shorter than I, but we seemed a fair fit. Once in bed I realized that I had no plan; this proved to be an error. Suddenly, he was on my back. I tried to push him off. He used an expert half nelson in order to shove partway in. I bucked like a horse from the pain, and threw us both off the bed. We rolled across the floor, slugging at each other. Then, exhausted, we separated. He cursed; dressed; left. That was my first and last experience of being nearly fucked.

By ship we sailed up Prince Rupert's Channel to Anchorage, Alaska. I got drunk for the first time New Year's Eve 1944–45. I was reprimanded. Then out to the islands, the Chain, as the Aleutians were known.

Palimpsest from *Williwaw,* my first novel.

The main street of Dutch Harbor curved parallel with the beach for half a mile. Most of the houses were on this street. Bars and restaurants and one theater, all wooden, also lined the street. The buildings had been painted white originally; they were many weathered shades of gray, now. On a small hill, behind two bars and a former brothel was the old Russian Orthodox church, with two onion-shaped cupolas painted green while the rest of the church was an almost new-white.

On several lanes, running inland from the main street, were the homes of the two hundred odd pre-war residents. Most of the houses had been vacated and the windows were boarded up and the privies leaned crazily in the back yards. Seven trees, which had been imported, were withered now, and their limbs had been made grotesque by the constant wind.

A mile inland from the shore and the village was the army camp. It had been erected early in the war and its many barracks and offices duplicated the military life of the distant United States.

Soldiers from the post and sailors from the Navy ships in the harbor wandered about the crooked lanes and along the main street. They were looking for liquor and women. There was much of one and little of the other in Dutch Harbor. Prices were high for both.

I took over as first mate of freight-supply ship 35, operating between Chernowski Bay on the island of Unimak (according to the atlas–we called it Umnak) to Dutch Harbor. We made a weekly trip carrying cargo and seasick soldiers. The Aleutians were barren volcanic islands, home to huge ravens and small foxes, with beaches strewn with moonstones and jasper.

From *Williwaw:*

Major Barkison contemplated the sea and was pleased by it. Today the water was smooth and only occasionally disturbed by gusts of wind. The Major stood alone on the forward deck. A few miles to his left was the vanishing entrance to Dutch Harbor; before him was the Bering Sea.

The water of the Bering Sea was a deep blue-black [and] the Major . . . watched carefully the ship-made waves: black when with the sea mass, then varying shades of clear blue as they swept up into the large waves, exploding at last in sudden whiteness. When he had the time, Major Barkison appreciated beauty. He had three days now in which to be appreciative.

Several sea lions wallowed fearlessly near the ship. Their black coats glistened in the pale morning light. For a moment they dove and splashed near the ship, and then, quickly, they went away. . . .

Major Barkison had a sure method of foretelling weather, or any-thing else for that matter. He would, for instance, select a certain patch of sky and then count slowly to three; if, during that time, no sea gull crossed the patch of sky, the thing he wanted would come true. This method could be applied to everything and the Major had great faith in it.

He looked at a section of sky above a distant volcano. Slowly he counted. At the count of two a gull flew across his patch of sky. The Major frowned. He had a way, however, of dealing with this sort of thing. He would use the best two counts out of three. Quickly he counted. No gull appeared. The trip would not be bad. In his mind, though, he wondered if it might not be cheating to take the best two out of three. One had to play fair. Not that he was superstitious, of course.

As it proved, the Major was in for a williwaw, a sudden wind out of the mountains that my fictional ship–like my actual one, the F.S. 35– barely survived. I suffered–not then but later–a drenching in below-zero weather. Hypothermia.

A few days later, while docking at Dutch Harbor, I tried to leap from bow to dock, and my knee locked. Something had gone wrong. The hospital at Fort Richardson, Anchorage, X-rayed me: rheumatoid arthritis or rheumatic fever.

Since we could select a hospital near home for recovery, I picked Van Nuys, California, to be near, not Nina, at the Beverly Hills Hotel, but the movies. I would hitchhike into Hollywood and hang around the studios, an endless fascination.

With Anaïs Nin in 1946.
One of her biographers says that I, at twenty,
proposed marriage to the lady, aged
forty-three. She was, the biographer invents,
to be my "front." Needless to say, I never
wanted to marry anyone, certainly not
someone who was to me, in my ageist youth,
a very old woman.

"Today My Nerves
Are Shattered. But
I Am Indomitable!"

IMET THE PLAYWRIGHT John Osborne a year ago, and I told him, with more sincerity than such encounters require, that I had read with delight his two volumes of memoirs. The ongoing portrait of his mother was particularly fine; an unrelenting monster, she is impervious to everything about her and, like all great comic characters, never out of character. "Did you take notes or keep a diary along life's tumultuous way?" I asked in the sepulchral tone we memoirists use when confronting each other in one or another of the many chambers of the charnel house of truth.

"Good God, no!" Osborne is (alas, was–he died a few months after I wrote this) an elegant mustached figure, colorfully tweeded and ascotted–or did he wear the proud tie of some school or regiment yet to be founded or formed? "Actually, I think I make it all up." At last a truthful remembrance of lost time. Plainly, he starts with an emotion, usually vivid in its dislike of, let us say, a less than satisfactory wife; then he taps into the emotion, makes sentences, scenes, a work. This, of course, is the way that most naturalistic fiction is written. Unfortunately, the Osborne method is of no great use to me. I gave up naturalism years ago. I either create–out of air–a parallel Duluthian universe or I re-create, from agreed-upon facts, a figure like Abraham Lincoln. Since a memoir is a memory of those things that one recalls, one can't describe what never happened, as I described my governorship of Alaska in

Screening History. Worse, how am I to reconstruct myself or, rather, my memory of now-shadowy events when, except for thirteen green pages of notes from 1961 and a diary kept for a month or two in 1948, I have made no record of my own days and must rely either on an idle memory or on what others have written about me?

It seems that practically everyone that I have ever met is now the subject of at least one biography–and in the case of my ancient friend Paul Bowles, whose life was mostly spent in the company of people more famous than he, a small library is now devoted to him and to those whom he knew.

I have never known quite what to do about biographers. Usually, I say that I have nothing more to say if I have ever written on the subject. As for my own sacred story, I entrusted it to a journalist who, after hundreds of interviews with the quick and the slow, and now often the dead and the gone, produced not a page in nine years. In one sense, his scam was ideal for me. He kept others at bay.

Now I palimpsest. I erase the next few lines and write: I am rereading this a year later. The journalist gave way to the biographer Fred Kaplan; then the journalist died–nonsequitur–and I started on this series of glimpses of an earlier self.

Meanwhile, almost daily, requests arrive from biographers of–well, who's at hand?–Carson McCullers, Mary McCarthy, Tennessee Williams, William Faulkner–thank God I never met Hemingway–J. F. Kennedy, Truman Capote, Antony Tudor, Anaïs Nin–*Rod Serling*! Apparently, there is no one so obscure that he or she has not at least one biographer. But then that is the order of the day. As fiction ceases to give pleasure, biographies–that is to say *mega*-fiction sometimes posing as gossip–has come into its terrible own. The distress of Jimmie Trimble's mother was due to the sleuthing of a journalist who, in other times, would have waited until I was either safely dead or on the record before making those personal revelations that I am now placing in proper context with, I confess, a certain pleasure at reliving a past which I thought I had either used up in fiction or locked away for others–if so inclined in the future–to discern and decipher.

My last winter in the army (1945–46) was spent at Mitchell Field, on Long Island. As a semi-invalid, I had been reassigned to the air corps, preparatory to mustering out. When off base, I stayed at my father's apartment in Fifth Avenue. It was there that I met a woman who was interviewing Gene for a biography of Amelia Earhart. Through her, I met the managing editor of E. P. Dutton, Nicholas Wreden, a large, amiable Russian émigré. He not only accepted *Williwaw* for publication but offered me a job when I got out of the army.

I DID NOT GO BACK to Washington. I stayed in New York. Rosalind had vanished into marriage, but I saw a good deal of her friend Cornelia Claiborne, a pretty girl with gray-blue hyperthyroid eyes and an interest in literature. She was helping to start a literary paper, *The Hudson Review.* I was roped into escorting her to a mass coming-out party at the Waldorf for those girls, deprived by war, of what used to be called debuts. Among those present, looking strangled in white tie and tails, was James Merrill, still an undergraduate at Amherst. I was condescending older warrior to unpublished ephebe. In later years I delighted in his wit, and read his poetry with pleasure. Now, conforming to this memoir's inexorable law, he has just died. Younger than I.

I also discovered, that magical winter, the Everard Baths, where military men often spent the night, unable to find any other cheap place to stay. This was sex at its rawest and most exciting, and a revelation to me. Newly invented penicillin had removed fears of venereal disease, and we were enjoying perhaps the freest sexuality that Americans would ever know. Most of the boys knew that they would soon be home for good, and married, and that this was a last chance to do what they were designed to do with each other.

The Astor Bar in Times Square was easily the city's most exciting meeting place for soldiers, sailors, and marines on the prowl for one another; few civilians, and no woman, ever dared intrude on these male mysteries. Even the military police and the shore patrol kept their distance. After all, we had—all of us—won the great imperial war, and thanks to us, the whole world was briefly American.

It was my experience, in the war, that just about everyone, either actively or passively, was available under the right circumstances. Certainly, things were pretty open in the Pacific islands, where on one, no doubt mythical, island an entire marine division paired off. Although the traditional hysteria about same-sexuality ran its usual course in the well-policed army camps Stateside (to categorize is to control), bars like the one on the ground floor of the Astor Hotel throve. At any time of day or night, hundreds of men would be packed six-deep around the long oval black bar within whose center bartenders presided.

OVER THE IMAGE of the bar I now see one Alfred C. Kinsey, author of *Sexual Behavior in the Human Male* (human *American* male, Ned Rorem noted, since our habits differ from Moroccans', say, none of whom is "gay" while all indulge, when possible, in same-sexuality).

I got to know Kinsey in 1948–his book came out a month after *The City and the Pillar,* and the shocked *New York Times* would not advertise either. For a time, Dr. Kinsey used the mezzanine of the Astor as a sort of office, where he would interview "human males" about their sex lives. I think that the somewhat phlegmatic Dr. Kinsey was secretly delighted by this warrior display, and I like to think that it was by observing the easy trafficking at the Astor that he figured out what was obvious to most of us, though as yet undreamed of by American society at large: Perfectly "normal" young men, placed outside the usual round of family and work, will run riot with each other. Curiously, there were few effeminate types at the bar. They patronized other watering holes. There was also no consciousness of rank. I recall one tall golden youth, an army pilot who proved to be, on closer inspection, a much decorated brigadier general, in search of likeness.

I can now *see* Dr. Kinsey as he walks me to the steps that connected mezzanine to lobby. He is a gray-faced man who always wears a polka-dot bow tie. He looks uncommonly tired and has not long to live. Yet he is only fifty-four. He never stops conducting his interviews, all questions and answers, in code. Mrs. Kinsey is concerned about his overworking. "Ever since he took up sex," she is quoted as saying, "I never see him."

Dr. Kinsey was intrigued by my lack of sexual guilt. I told him that it was probably a matter of class. As far as I can tell, none of my family ever suffered from that sort of guilt, a middle-class disorder from which power people seem exempt. We did whatever we wanted to do and thought nothing of it. Kinsey told me that I was not "homosexual"–doubtless because I never sucked cock or got fucked. Even so, I was setting world records for encounters with anonymous youths, nicely matching busy Jack Kennedy's girl-a-day routine. I would not have had it otherwise, since, even then, I did not believe in fixed sexual cate-gories; and finally, Kinsey appears not to have believed in them either. But one's primary attraction (for the other half?) is innate and immutable and hardly a "choice," as the ignorant pretend. Of course, secondary attractions are possible; hence the tradition, in patriarchal societies, of a conventional marriage for Jonathan as well as one for David, though their love for each other is the primary fact of their lives. I tried to tell Kinsey about Jimmie. But I had not yet read Plato; I had no theory. Kinsey gave me a copy of *Sexual Behavior in the Human Male,* with an inscription, complimenting me on my "work in the field." Thanks, Doc. But it wasn't *all* work.

When Dr. Kinsey had finished with my history (he liked to question you twice, with an interval between, to catch any inconsistencies), I asked, "If you didn't know who I was—what—*who* would you say I was, according to my sexual history?"

"I'd rate you as a lower-middle-class Jew, with more heterosexual than homosexual interests." Curiously, I have lived most of my life with such a person.

We part. For good. Were we in my *Duluth,* I'd have said, "We won't see each other again, because I'll be going to Europe soon and you'll be dead in 1956, and I'll only get this last look at you in the year 1993 as I type these lines on a portable Olivetti typewriter in Ravello, Italy, long after the Astor Hotel was torn down."

Isherwood and I used to play around with the notion of what it would be like to know the entire future of someone we had just met, rather as if we could skip to the back of a book to see how things turned out, as Montaigne always did, eager to read how the protagonist died even before he knew how he had lived. Then, knowing the ending, one would address the new person accordingly: "Sorry, I have no time to waste on you. Next summer you'll be dead on Route 9W in a car acci-dent, and by the time I'm sixty-five, I will have forgotten your name."

Last glimpse of Dr. Kinsey. He is standing at the top of the broad car-peted steps. He has a clipboard in one hand. He wears a crew cut; so do I. He has just interviewed me for a proposed study of the homo/hetero sexual balance in the arts. Even in 1948 there was a suspicion that far too many creative people were inclined to same-sexuality, which meant, of course, serious mental illness of the sort that makes truly great and universal art impossible. By the 1950s, an all-out war was declared on

the homintern's control of the arts (so like the Comintern's control of the
State Department), a war that still continues into our own enlightened
time, led by Christian fundamentalists and "neo-conservatives" often
dedicated to Zion.

I enter the bar. I am now further back in time—a twenty-year-old warrant officer. It is early winter 1945. The war has just ended. In a few
months I shall be out of the army.

The bar is already crowded at sundown. Suddenly, I see the merchant
mariner from the Olympic Hotel in Seattle. I say hello. He stares at me
for a moment; then frowns and says, "Oh," and turns away.

I am tempted to have a second go with him, reversing roles. I am now
six feet tall, and ten pounds heavier than before. He is as he was. Blue
eyes. Straight thick black hair combed straight back. He wears yellow
socks to show he is not military. Abruptly, sensing my plan for him? he
left—for good now, except in fantasy. I drink beer at the bar. Under my
arm, a Modern Library edition of *Pepys Diary*.

From behind me, someone quotes, "And so to bed": Pepys's usual last
line for a journal entry. I turn. A small, grinning, bespectacled civilian
tells me, all in a rush, that he is Kimon Friar, a Greek-American poet
and critic and professor, and he has a theory of the art of poetry which
he calls the Medusa and he will be happy to tell me all about it in some
secluded place. I take him up to my father's Fifth Avenue apartment,
overlooking Central Park.

Kimon is unduly impressed by the apartment. He tells me that he
comes from a working-class immigrant family, but poetry has given
him wings. I tell him that my first novel has been accepted by Dutton.
He doesn't believe me, but he wants, compulsively, to talk about poetry
(in those days I thought, mistakenly, that I was a poet, too); and so we
talked for a long time. Kimon had already mastered the art of not listening to others with an air of attention. This is a necessity when you
are in the army or psychiatry, but a demerit, I would think, in a
schoolteacher.

Once Kimon saw that sex was out of the question and realized that
Williwaw was actually being published, he became interested in my
case, if not work. Novels did not interest him. Poetry was his passion.
Since I am drawn to obsessive types, I found him agreeable. When not
cruising the Astor Bar, Kimon taught poetry; wrote about poetry; and,
presently, while teaching at Amherst, became mentor to the under-

graduate James Merrill, "whose father," he announced triumphantly, "is a lot richer than yours!" Kimon's vulgarity was–is?–a never-ending, never-failing joy. In due course, at his insistence, I went to hear him lecture at the YMHA.

From Kimon's description, I had expected an auditorium crowded with hundreds of people. Instead, there were a dozen rather damp young men and women in a small classroom. I sat next to an exotic silver-taloned woman with brown-red dyed hair (in those days dyed hair was not as universal as now); she wore a hat like that of Mary Stuart in the famous portrait.

Kimon Friar introduced me to Anaïs Nin (1903–1977), whom I had recently read about in *The New Yorker*. She was the latest of the literary ladies with whom the critic Edmund Wilson would fall in love after first giving them a good review.

I said to her, "You look like Mary Stuart."

She said–soft voice, French accent, "Does that mean you will cut my head off?"

As it turned out, it was she, not I, who was the keeper of the ax, in the form of a diary begun at the age of eleven and still, to this day, being published by her devoted heirs. I suspect that there will never be an end to these publications (the diaries comprise thirty-five thousand handwritten pages); also, she constantly revised the text in order to conform it to her changing view of those whom she had let into her life with such hope only to have hope turn, usually more soon than late, to disappointment or, in my case, to a *chagrin d'amour* that eventually became a *fureur*.

Anaïs was–and remained to the end–the wife of a long-suffering American banker named Hugh Guiler. Under the name Ian Hugo, he did engravings and made surreal films, rather like those of Maya Deren. In 1931 Anaïs began an affair with the down-and-out Henry Miller in Paris. When war came, he retreated to California while she and Hugo returned to New York, and to what she had already decided would be a "legendary" career, based largely on the existence of the diaries which Miller had celebrated in terms that might have turned the head of Aphrodite but not that of Anaïs, who had been named for an Egyptian goddess, usually depicted with helmet, shield, and battle-ax.

Although the ostensible subject of the diaries, as of her life, is Love, the actual theme is Deception. I have the latest installment on my desk:

Incest, from "A Journal of Love": The Unexpurgated Diary of Anaïs Nin, 1932–1934. Hot stuff, plainly. The dust jacket is an ominous mauve and beige. Our heroine is now thirty years old, living near Paris at Louve-ciennes. As always, she is passionately in love; this time with herself. "I am so marvelous to talk to that he [Henry Miller] almost forgets to fuck me. I experience a strange resigned pang–this acceptance that the mind in me eclipses the woman . . ."

She deceives husband Hugh with Henry Miller; then Miller with her psychiatrist; then there is a second psychiatrist whom she beds; as well as several friends of them all. Finally, Joaquin Nin, her pianist-father comes back into her life–he had abandoned her and her mother in New York twenty years earlier and now she seduces him, too. This was the fairly covert theme of *House of Incest*, a book that Wilson admired back in the forties, despite its "vatic" style. I, too, was ensorceled–a favorite Nin verb–by her for a time.

From the beginning, Anaïs wanted to publish the diaries. At one point, she allowed Maxwell Geismar, a critic of the day, to read the lot. Later, when the diaries began to appear, he wrote a piece warning readers that she was drastically rewriting in order to settle, as Mary McCarthy would put it, everyone's hash.

Unable to get her "novels" published in the 1940s, she printed them herself, and thus gained a degree of underground fame. Finally, I bullied Dutton into publishing *This Hunger*, whose first edition is dedicated to me. Over the years, her portraits of me darkened. I have just read, in a breathy account of Anaïs's life by a young Frenchwoman, that I turned against Anaïs because I read in the diaries that she thought me "a talentless gigolo." The inventor of this clinker has outdone her role model, whose lies were far more artful. In any case, I'm only disturbed if the phrase means that I had no talent as a gigolo; I believe that this is actionable in law even if proof is no longer demonstrable by me in life.

"Lying is an accursed vice," wrote Montaigne. "It is only our words which bind us together and make us human. If we realized the horror and weight of lying, we would see that it is more worthy of the stake than other crimes . . . Once let the tongue acquire the habit of lying and it is astonishing how impossible it is to make it give it up."

There are, of course, liars and liars. There are those who must lie constantly for expediency, like the Kennedys and their apologists. Eugene

McCarthy, in his mock bemused way, observed that "Jack used to tell you lies. Bobby told lies about you. And Teddy lies about himself. Now, is there a moral progression here of any kind?" Obviously, sexual bucca-neers who want to succeed in American politics must lie all the time, and I do not think that Montaigne would have objected to this sort of protec-tive lying in a society whose mores one must pretend to honor in order to survive. Even Montaigne's friend Henri IV thought Paris worth a mass.

My own tendency to lie is seldom indulged in except when picking up a stranger. Then, with real delight, I invent a new character for myself, one that I think will appeal to my quarry. Since there will be only one encounter, I don't think these impersonations come under Montaigne's injunction. Of course, I was never more than a part-time politician, and so I can afford to be virtuous and ignore the rules of that particular guild or, as a senator said to me after Jimmy Carter's announcement to the American people that he would never lie to them, "Now Carter wants to deny the very nature of politics."

In Anaïs's defense, I suppose that as a self-liberated woman still liv-ing in a man's world–and brought up a Spanish Catholic–to be a "Doña Joanna" (her phrase) meant numerous disguises. But, by the end, lying had become her first, not second, nature; yet even that would not have mattered so much had she not set herself up as a diarist who told the absolute truth.

From *Incest:* "Lies: to explain to Henry why I could not spend this week with him. Inventions. Color. Drama. To explain to Allendy why I still go out one evening a week. Lies to Fred to attenuate effect of Henry's furious cruelties because Fred steals a kiss now and then.... Lies to conceal from the world my struggles against bad health.... Lies to Hugo to preserve his security. Lies to Emilia. Lies to Joaquin to calm his jealousy.... The only person I do not lie to is my journal." But in the end the journal proved to be the greatest lie of all, as she constantly rearranged the scenarios of her life to suit what the old Stalinists would call new necessities.

By the end, I don't think even Anaïs knew who was who and what was what as opposed to how she was currently reinventing everyone. I do know that she hated satire, wit, intelligence (always "cold," of course). So it was that a very mature Marie Corelli met a very young Jonathan Swift–well, H. L. Mencken. In one sense, bad luck all around. In another, she gave me my most original, or so I thought, creation.

As I read *Incest,* I realized that something which I had always taken to be unique, the voice of Myra Breckinridge, was actually that of Anaïs in all the flowing megalomania of the diaries. Of course, I had not read the diaries then, but even so, if only for that one thundering voice, I am forever in her debt.

I didn't intend to read *Incest,* but the first page made me laugh and so, with true delight, I read straight through to the end. On every page there is something that gives pleasure, and if one knew the diarist, there *is* a strange sort of resonance to the prose, to the humorless obsession with herself and with those to whom she assigns parts in a vast auto-drama through which she canters, on her donkey, always in disguise and always, always the same. "Henry is singing and working, flowing, and I exhaust my newborn strength on him." But there is a terrible flaw in Henry. "He was accustomed to [his wife] June always 'mounting him' . . . this discovery was a great shock to me. All this caused a great revolt in my femininity. I cursed my blindness." Earlier, she had made the mistake of falling for a fag cousin; now the quintessentially macho Henry Miller is turning lavender on her, too. "Defiantly I must abandon him as a lover. I do not want to be the leader. I refuse to be the leader . . . I want a man lying over me, always over me." So that she might lie to the man lying over her?

Here Anaïs parts company with holy Myra, who was definitely in the business of leadership. Eventually, Henry does get on top and that crisis is resolved, but soon she will find other reasons for falling out with him, as she does with everyone. But then what mere man could possibly give her the strength that she gave others? She resembled Nina (no, Freudians–*forget* it) in her conviction that she and she alone could so energize men that they would flow like great rivers into the sea of glory, leaving behind–thrown to one side–the source of their strength, the selfless, the giving, the ultimately used-up and discarded Woman.

"What hurts in caricature is when it approaches truth." Yet for me, the Anaïs of the diary is beyond caricature, thanks to her unique inability to see herself and others not as they are–none of us has that gift–but at least as recognizable human types. "Tonight I'm terrified of my own inexorable goodness. *I do not live for myself . . .*"

I find it impossible to believe that I once listened to all this with perfect seriousness. Anaïs was also an adept in psychoanalysis and astrology, two superstitions that have never attracted me. Once she tried to get me to an analyst to thaw my coldness: She made much of my having been frozen–symbolism!–in the Aleutians, further buttressing the Theme *that I had been abandoned by my mother.* Obsessively, she imposed her own story on others. As her father had abandoned her at eleven, so my mother had abandoned me. *Magari,* as the Italians say: Would that she had! In due course, Anaïs's potted Freudian plant bloomed in *Time* magazine. When hot-tempered Nina saw this shameless hogwash, she wrote her infamous letter: Far from having abandoned me, she had not only written my books, but she had also created my father's airlines, all the while managing to be a pretty swell guy quite used to getting the short end of the stick in life's rodeo.

Nina and Anaïs were well matched. But I don't know how or why, having rid myself of the first, I acquired the second, who was born, as I tactlessly told her, in the same year as Nina, 1903. That day at the YMHA I was twenty, Anaïs forty-two. She called me Chéri, after Colette's eponymous young man. Gigolo?

Here is her final–at least published thus far–version of our first meeting. "Kimon Friar asked me to attend his lecture on love at the YMHA .. ." Surely the subject was not love but his Medusa theory of poetry. She refers to her current state of depression; also to her "small heart-shaped black hat, with a pearl edging, shaped like Mary Stuart's hat . . . Kimon lectured at the head of a long table. At the foot of the table, one chair was empty. I took it. Maya Deren sat a few chairs away. Next to me sat a handsome young lieutenant. During a pause I leaned over to speak with Maya. She said: 'You look dramatic.' I said: 'I feel like Mary Stuart who will soon be beheaded.' "

In the tradition of all great stars, she gave my line to herself. "The lieutenant leaned over and introduced himself: 'I am Warrant Officer Gore Vidal. I am a descendant of Troubadour Vidal.' Later he admitted that he guessed who I was." As I was a warrant officer, I couldn't be a lieutenant, but as she said when she later showed me the text, "You know I never get *those* things right." I also said that I would never have used a military title.

I am reading Edmund Wilson's diaries, *The Sixties.* He, too, is abloom in her conservatory. She shows him what she has written. He notes her "characteristic inaccuracies. She said that I gave her a set of Emily Brontë as if there could be such a thing, actually it was Jane Austen and she had been offended and sent it back–which was not true, she had kept it."

Anyway, it was Kimon who introduced us. But Anaïs had nearly thirty years (from 1946 to 1971) to rearrange the text, not to mention past.

As of 1971 I am still "luminous and manly. Near the earth. He is not nebulous, but clear and bright, a contrast to Leonard." Who was Leonard? Did I ever know him? She always had a court of young men about her, mostly clever queens, though there was usually at least one youthful stud for use. "He is active, alert. Poised. He is tall, slender, cool eyes and sensual mouth. Kimon was lecturing on Plato's symposium of love." I have forgotten that detail, which sounds true, since she had not read Plato's *Symposium*. She also had no ear for dialogue. This is what we really said—*She:* You have a French name. *Me:* Yes. Like Peire Vidal. The troubadour. *Reader:* He's the one who's coming on. *Me:* Maybe.

I came to call. She lived in a fifth-floor walk-up on Thirteenth Street. There was a glass skylight that she had painted different colors. She and Hugo pretended to be poor artists, and when I took them out to dinner several times I would always pay the bill, until she finally confessed that Hugo was really a vice president of a large bank, and he should pay. Despite her lack of ear, it is interesting to read what she *thinks* she hears. It is also curious to watch her turn oneself into herself. "Gore said: 'I do not want to be involved, ever. I live detached from my present life. At home, our relationships are casual. My father married a young model. I like casual relationships. When you are involved you get hurt."

Although this aria is out of my character, it is very much in hers for me and so I sing the tune that she has written for me in the opera of herself. In real life, I was not in the least worried about being "hurt," something that I believe is an occupational hazard for selfless, entirely giving women but hardly for a roaring boy usually in pursuit of the bodies—not souls—of other roaring boys. Then she really turns me into herself: "*My* father's desertion created the opposite reaction in me. I was always seeking new closeness, greater closeness." So, now I am "abandoned" by my mother and "deserted" by my poor father, an amiable man who let me live in the servant's room of his flat until I made enough money to move out, our common dream. On the other hand, I was, as she notes, "no dream-laden adolescent" and certainly no waif; unfortunately, that was the only role that she was able to identify with.

What did she look like then? Tweezed eyebrows in the twenties manner. Beautiful hazel eyes; unbeautiful black upper gum (dead teeth), which she was careful not to show. The body was that of a dancer, very slender, with a long waist; small breasts with pink nipples–like a girl, she said. "Like a Dane," I said. She had had a Danish grandparent, mixed in with Spanish, Cuban, French antecedents.

I give her *Williwaw* to read. "I am startled by the muted tone, the cool detached words. It is writing I do not admire. The once-frozen young man is not as lifeless as the writing. Action, no feeling. Am I wrong to think there is a potential warmth in him? Is this writing a disguise, a mask? Another Hemingway to come?" The first alarm bell sounds. *Williwaw* was a true-minimalist sort of novel and Anaïs was about as maximum as one could be in her be-sequined celebrations of the deep inner core of her own being. In fact, her Paris agent of the thirties, William Bradley, enraged her by saying that her "novels" belong to the 1840s, which was well observed: She *is* like George Sand in her romantic, vague impressionistic scenes, but Sand's own character was monumental in its goodness; and she told no lies.

In short, Anaïs liked pretty writing, while I believed that the plain style was not only harder to write but more apt to be "truthful," the object, I thought in those days, of realistic writing. At about this time Truman Capote was brought to Anaïs's walk-up. When he met me, he whined, "How does it feel to be an onn-font-tarribull?" She thought *his* writing truly magical; he detested hers. La Ronde.

"I think, dear Gore, that you choose to write about ordinary people in an ordinary world to mask the extraordinary you and the out-of-the-ordinary world in which you live, which is mine. I feel in you imagination, poetry, intuition of worlds you do not trust because they are linked with your emotions and sensibilities. And you have to work far removed from that territory of feeling where danger lies." I must say I could listen to this sort of thing for hours; and did, of course. But, privately, she noted: "The direction of Gore's writing distresses me. But at twenty did I know my direction? At twenty I imitated D. H. Lawrence."

Eduardo Sanchez, her Cuban cousin, was an astrologer; she quotes from his horoscope of me: "Neptune, making for high illusions, upsets his Venusian life. He is not satisfied with power. . . . What balances him is the power to rebel against authority. Otherwise, this would be a one-sided horoscope."

Although she notes that I would like to be president of the United States, she lets the subject lie there–stunned–upon the page as something of absolutely no interest to her even as a fantasy. But politics was of interest to me, and in a matter of months I would have to make a choice. Was it to be literature or politics? Truth or—well, if not lies, the harsh consequences of my imaginative writing on my actual life.

Senator Gore had arranged with an old friend and "protégé," Governor Dempsey of New Mexico, to place me on the state ballot in 1948, as a presidential elector. Vidal is a common Hispanic name, which, combined with the Gore clan, would start me off nicely in the state. Incidentally, the hysteria in right-wing circles about my name has always puzzled me. I was christened Eugene Luther Gore Vidal. The first two names were my father's. I lopped them off for political as well as for aesthetic reasons. But this has often been gleefully interpreted as a rejection of my father, whom I liked, in order to become my mother, whom I disliked. How a little Freud can be used to poison almost any well! Sometimes ambition is just a cigar, too.

Between 1946 and 1948 I had planned to move to Santa Fe, not far from Los Alamos; go to work at the local newspaper; and begin a political career. Fortunately—or unfortunately?—by 1946 I was writing *The City and the Pillar*, which I knew would make a political career impossible; also, it made a conventional literary career impossible, a lucky break as that turned out, too, but hard-going then.

During this period, Anaïs finds me edgy. I must have told her of my dilemma, but as this was not the sort of thing that interested her, she does not record my ambivalence. After the success of *Williwaw* in 1946, I published *In a Yellow Wood* the next year; it was every bit as bad a book as she feared it would be, but the theme was poignant to me: A young man must choose between life with a foreign girl outside the conventional world and the boredom of a life inside. Robert Frost's verse, from which I took the title, says it all, "Two roads diverged in a yellow wood, And sorry I could not travel both, And be one traveller . . ." The character in the novel chooses convention, while his author went into rebellion.

"Because it was Gore who presented me to Dutton, because he watched over the writing of *Ladders to Fire*, encouraged me, I said I would dedicate the book to him." This sounds a bit on the grudging side, but then it was probably written long after the fact. "Before the flowers of friendship faded friendship faded," as Gertrude Stein so nicely put it.

Meanwhile, Anaïs is now breaking off with Edmund Wilson, who once sent her flowers, and "a set of Jane Austen. . . . He was hoping I would learn how to write from reading her! But I am not an imitator of past styles." Anaïs told Wilson that she was otherwise engaged with a twenty-year-old Latin poet, me. After Wilson's death, Daniel Aaron found in Wilson's desk a review that I had written of Anaïs's diaries. On the several occasions that Wilson and I met, we never talked of her, though I once brought up the subject to the former Mrs. Wilson, Mary McCarthy, and her face became Gorgonian at the mention of the name.

That winter we acted in a Maya Deren film. "The stars are Maya and a Negro girl, Rita. Gore has a prejudice against Negroes, but he joined us anyway."

As usual, Anaïs missed the point, or at least the humor to the point. Servants aside, I had never known any "Negroes" while growing up and so, when asked to appear in a film with Rita, I said, "If only my grandmother could see me now." The Gores were Reconstruction southerners, and though they got on well with our dusky cousinage in master-servant relationships, they did not believe in equality. In response to my teasing on the subject, Dot said, "If any of my descendants ever mixes our blood with theirs, I'll come back and haunt him." I said, "Well, you've got a lot of haunting to do right now since half the mulattoes in Mississippi are related to us." She changed the subject.

A few months after the filmmaking, I brought James Baldwin into Anaïs's life. He was a vivid creature in 1946, full of energy, with a personality that oscillated between Martin Luther King, Jr.'s (before the fact) and Bette Davis's (after *A Stolen Life*). In the spring I tried to get Dutton to publish Jimmy's *Cry Holy,* later to be known as *Go Tell It on the Mountain.* I can still see the neatly typed manuscript in two torn cardboard boxes on my desk at 200 Fourth Avenue. The book was rejected. The publisher told me, "I'm from Virginia."

Of the film: *Ritual in Transfigured Time,* Anaïs wrote that Maya was "looking for the spontaneous, the accidental. Gore and I decided to act pretty much as we do when we are together, a mixture of playfulness, key words, seriousness, and connections with what we are writing." I have just seen the film for the first time. I look like the second lead in a Paramount musical. Anaïs looks haggard; she is also annoyed at Maya, which comes through in her performance. Maya herself appears in the film–sloe-eyed, almost beautiful, with a tough wit that Anaïs detested. Maya was also capable of great candor, a trait not calculated to ingratiate her with a Romantic Legend. Anaïs was ensorceled by the word *legend,* and though she knew that she was not yet a full-fledged universal legend, she was certainly the only myth living on Thirteenth Street, because if it were Tenth Street, she would have had to compete with the legend of Jane Bowles, whom she once stopped on the sidewalk, as Jane's husband, Paul Bowles, walked on. When Jane rejoined Paul, she told him who the strange-looking woman was. "So why did she stop you?" he asked. As always, Jane was literal and straightforward. "She said that she felt that she had to tell me herself what a bad writer I am."

"People tell me Gore is arrogant and boastful. I have never seen that." I don't think "people" did, either. I had not written anything worth boasting about. On the other hand, to be published at my age caused resentment, and so if I was not arrogant and boastful, I *ought* to have been and therefore, by the inflexible American Law of Reputation, I *was*. Rather worse, I did have political opinions, something unheard of in the circles that I was now frequenting. As it turned out, I never could bear the fashion-magazine world that dominated the arts in New York, a world obsessed with decoration, whether of a stage set or of a prose style. What in the name of God am I doing here? I kept thinking.

At Peggy Guggenheim's, Charles Henri Ford, the bright-eyed poet-novelist-editor and friend of Tchelitchev, approached me and said, "You can't be a good writer because you have such lovely legs!" Years later I came to enjoy Charles Henri, but for a twenty-year-old soldier still thinking about politics in New Mexico, this was too much. I turned to James Agee, a tall, sadly amiable man with bloodshot eyes. He was known then as a poet as well as author of the windy text to Walker Evans's fine photographs of southern sharecroppers. He was also a film critic for *Time,* and duly defensive, since cinema was not yet–quite–an accepted art form. I told Agee that I'd like to break poor Charles's legs. Agee was soothing; then he said, most thoughtfully, "These fairies can be surprisingly tough." I looked up and saw, in the middle distance, pastry-pale, beady-eyed, thin-lipped Parker Tyler himself. Little did he–or I–suspect that twenty years later Myron and Myra Breckinridge would explode onto the world scene as not only saviors of MGM but of the human race as well, their holy text Parker's *Magic and Myth of the Movies.*

APRIL 1946: "Gore buys a house in Guatemala. It was once a monastery. It is beautiful. I must visit it when it is ready." By then, I had made up my mind to write *The City and the Pillar.* Instead of Santa Fe and politics there would be—points south and a truthful novel and a lot of trouble.

I had saved ten thousand dollars while in the army, and my father gave me the bonds that he had set aside to send me to Harvard. I cashed them in, to his horror: In those days one could have lived on a hundred dollars a month, which was the interest from the bonds. But I wanted a house. My head was full of novels. *Williwaw* had done moderately well; *In a Yellow Wood* had not. But I was very much on view with the other young lions of the second postwar generation. Journalists were eager to know if we would be "lost," too.

Life magazine featured several of us. There was a full-page picture of Truman Capote, looking waxy, as if from under a Victorian glass bell; thus he began his career as a celebrity. He had also decided that I was to be the competition. He was twenty-one; I, twenty. But, as he confided to the press, "that Gore Vidal is twenty-five if he's a day." Over the years, this silly line has been carefully reversed and attributed to me, the kind of weird reversal that has been a peculiar constant in my life because, I suppose, what others want you to be you are going to be, despite all evidence to the contrary. Had I read Anaïs's diaries as she was writing them, I might have understood the process better.

During my first civilian winter, I realized that I was never going to get much work done in New York. Also, Anaïs needed stormy scenes of a sort that I did not. I did enjoy my daily meetings with strangers, usually encountered in the streets. We would then go to one of the Dreiserian hotels around Times Square. Most were poor youths my own age, and often capable of an odd lovingness, odd considering the fact that I did so little to give any of them physical pleasure. But then, even at twenty, I often paid for sex on the ground that it was only fair. Once Truman said to me, "I hear you're just the lay lousé."

"At last, Truman, you've got it right."

The ruined church of El Carmen in Antigua, Guatemala. Next to it is the convent I bought for $2,000 in 1946 and sold some years later.

Guatemala

I N T H E S U M M E R of 1946, I quit my job as associate editor at E. P.
Dutton in New York. As Europe was still closed to tourists, I headed
south of the border. I wanted to get out of New York and what had
been for me, thus far, a life term in prison–twelve years of school,
almost three years of army, half a year in a publisher's office. Fifteen
years of doing what I did not want to do was most of my life. When I
arrived in Guatemala City, I was twenty years old.

I stayed in a pension; worked at *The City and the Pillar;* met people.
Guatemala was starting to flourish. The old dictator, Ubico, an American client, had been driven out. A philosophy professor named Arévalo
had been elected president in a free election. He was a democrat socialist or social democrat, or whatever. He had brought young people into
government; tamed the army; behaved tactfully with the largest
employer in the country, the American company United Fruit. I visited
the *fincas,* or estates, of wealthy coffee growers who lived much as they
had lived for two centuries, feudal lords on amiable if less than generous terms with the Mayan majority.

In due course I moved on to Antigua, a volcano-circled sixteenth-
century town in the highlands. For two thousand dollars I bought the
earthquake-damaged convent of El Carmen; there were several livable
rooms and a large chapel that I left empty. Life was cheap. The foreigners who lived in Antigua were either remittance men or ladies of a cer-

tain age, like Nina, for whom the perfect martini was the Holy Grail. I did not fit in awfully well with the foreign colony, but visitors came to stay with me.

Easily the most interesting person in–and out–of the town was Mario Monteforte Toledo. Less than thirty, he was a thin, energetic intellectual who wrote poetry. He had a wife in the capital and an Indian girlfriend in Antigua, and when he came to visit her, he and I would meet and talk, and talk. President of the Guatemalan Congress, Mario was regarded by everyone as a future president of the republic. In politics he was vaguely socialist, as was the style for the young in those days. I, of course, reflecting my family's politics, was fiercely Tory. We had splendid rows.

Scene: patio of my house. Overhanging it, the high wall of the adjacent church of El Carmen. Under a pepper tree, near an ugly square fountain like a horse trough, we would sit and drink beer. He told me the gossip. The president's car had run off the road recently; he was being driven by an American girl from a news magazine. Then Mario twitted me about my grand friends, the Vasquez Bruni family, great landowners whose house in Guatemala City filled a city block. The family patriarch was Colombian in origin, and he held what seemed to be the lifetime hereditary rank of minister from Colombia to Guatemala. There were three sons–one a true wit named Ricardo–and a beautiful daughter named Olga. They comprised an enchanted world. I often thought that I was luckier than the protagonist of my then-favorite book, *Le Grand Meaulnes*–I was able to find my way back to the big house and its marvelous occupants, all presided over by the ancient minister in his throne, two equally ancient mastiffs at his feet.

After a ritual denunciation of the rich and the indifferent, Mario started to talk politics. "We may not last much longer."

"We . . . who?"

"Our government. At some point we're going to have to raise revenue. The only place where there is money to be raised is *el pulpo.*" *El pulpo* meant the Octopus, also known as the United Fruit Company, whose annual revenues were twice that of the Guatemalan state. Recently, their workers had gone on strike; selfishly, they had wanted to be paid $1.50 a day for their interesting work.

"What's going to stop you from taxing them?" I was naive. This was long ago and the United States had just become the Leader of the Free World.

"Your government. Who else? They kept Ubico in power all those years. Now they're getting ready to replace us."

I was astonished. I had known vaguely about our numerous past interventions in Central America. But that was past. Why should we bother now? We controlled most of the world. "Why should we care what happens in a small country like this?"

Mario gave me a compassionate look—compassion for my stupidity. "Businessmen. Like the owners of United Fruit. They care. They used to pay for our politicians. They still pay for yours. Why, one of your big senators is on the board of *el pulpo.*"

I knew something about senators. Which one? Mario was vague. "He has three names, like us. He's from Boston, I think . . ."

"Henry Cabot Lodge? I don't believe it." Lodge was a family friend; as a boy I had discussed poetry with him; in fact, he was a poet's son. Years later, as Kennedy's ambassador to Vietnam, Lodge would preside over the murder of the Diem brothers.

As we drank beer and the light faded, Mario described the trap that a small country like Guatemala was in. I can't say that I took him very seriously. With all the world—except the satanic Soviet—under our control, it was hardly in our national interest to overthrow a democratic neighbor no matter how much its government irritated the board of directors of United Fruit. But in those days I was not aware to what extent big business controlled the government of our own rapidly expiring republic. Now, of course, everyone knows how the subsequent empire, with its militarized economy, controls business. The end result is much the same for the rest of the world, only the killing fields are more vast than before and we make mischief not just with weak neighbors but in every continent.

At the time I didn't realize that Mario was giving me the idea for a novel: A dictator (like Ubico) returns from an American exile as the Octopus's candidate to regain power. I would tell the story through the eyes of a young American war veteran (like myself) who joins the general out of friendship for his son. The more I brooded on the story, the more complexities were revealed. I called it *Dark Green, Bright Red.* The Greens, father and son, were the company, and dark figures indeed, haunting green jungles. Bright Red was not only blood but the possibility of a Communist, Red, taking power. Primary colors keep shifting. Nothing is as it seems in this story.

"No novel about–or from–Latin America has ever been a success in the English language." As of 1950, my publisher was right.

Four years after the book was published, Senator Henry Cabot Lodge denounced Arévalo's popularly elected successor, Arbenz, as a Communist because Arbenz had expropriated some of the company's unused land, which he gave to one hundred thousand Guatemalan families. Arbenz paid the company what he thought was a fair, if humorous, price: their own evaluation of the land for tax purposes.

The American empire (or National Security State) went into action. The CIA put together an army and bombed Guatemala City. American ambassador Peurifoy behaved rather like Mr. Green in the novel. Arbenz resigned. Peurifoy made the Guatemalan army's chief of staff president, and gave him a list of "Communists" to be shot. The chief of staff declined: "It would be better," he said, "if *you* sat in the presidential chair and that the Stars and Stripes fly over the palace."

Peurifoy picked another military man to represent the interests of company and empire. Since then, Guatemala has been a slaughter ground, very bright red indeed against the darkest imperial green. Later, it was discovered that Arbenz had no Communist connections, but the "disinformation" had been so thorough that few Americans realized to what extent they had been lied to by their government, which had now put itself above law and, rather worse, beyond reason. Five years later, in Cuba, Castro drove out our Greens and established himself as a bright–if now faded–Red presence.

The book is still read in Spanish and Portuguese editions, and I'm told that many readers are unaware that it was written almost a decade before Castro, as well as four years before my friend Monteforte Toledo went into exile. He settled in Mexico City. Wrote a book called *The Fish,* which he sent me. Then I lost track of him, and of all that sunny ambiguous bright-colored world which, for me, nowhere survives except in the pages of an old novel.

IN DUE COURSE Anaïs came to Guatemala. She has not published any of that section of her diary. I was suffering, I thought, from a chronic complaint, spastic colon, but this proved to be acute hepatitis–I used to eat in the marketplace out of caldrons where chicken was boiled in bitter chocolate. I soon lost twenty pounds. Like a hidden treasure at low tide, the outline of my swollen liver could be seen beneath the rib cage, while the whites of my eyes turned dark gold and my urine, black; it was not a joyous time.

Before the worst stage had developed, a college student I had met in East Hampton arrived on the scene with a friend. I should note that even before Anaïs met me, she was a relentless chicken hawk, as fags used to describe those men who preferred boys–chicken–to men. Of course, most people do; after all, young males are better-looking than old ones, and they have more stamina. I never blamed Anaïs for sharing in a universal taste. But with characteristic secrecy, Anaïs made a date to meet the student's friend in Acapulco. She should have known by then that sexual jealousy was–and is–an emotion denied me. I calculated, at twenty-five, that I had had more than a thousand sexual encounters, not a world record (my near contemporaries Jack Kennedy, Marlon Brando, and Tennessee Williams were all keeping up), but not bad, considering that I never got a venereal disease like Jack and Marlon or suffered from jealousy like Tennessee. But Anaïs could not resist intrigue; in fact, I now think that deception was more important to her than sex. Only last year did I learn of all this from the *ci-devant* lad himself, the journalist Dominick Dunne, who told me that after a week in Acapulco, "Anaïs dumped me for a Mexican beach boy." Romance!

I arrived at the Miramar Hotel in Acapulco, and went to bed. Jaundice. A Swiss doctor fed me charcoal and corn flakes. Anaïs, between visits to the beach, nursed me, and I give her credit for taking time from her busy schedule to look in on my last days, a somewhat casual Severn to my nonterminal Keats. Since this was the only time in my life, thus far, that I had been seriously ill, the whole thing is still a nightmare, including my attempt to read William Blake, whose work I still associate with heat and longed-for death and a Hieronymous Bosch–like memory of the last thing that I ate before being felled, oily chicken served in half a coconut full of nauseous yellow cream.

I have just checked the published diaries, 1947–55. Happily, I have been replaced by the young man she was soon to marry while still remaining married to Hugo! "I am a bigamist," she would whisper to every interviewer; then she would beg him or her to keep the terrible secret. Of course, by the 1950s, we had been through many ruptures. I had once said in an interview that the best American *woman* novelist (such divisions were made in those oh so vile, sexist days) was Carson McCullers. This brought on a tantrum; and we did not speak for a long time.

The worst scene occurred after she had read the manuscript of *The City and the Pillar.* I expected sympathy, if only feigned; after all, my life was about to change, and not for the better. An editor at Dutton had told me that if the book were published, I was in for twenty years of bad reviews, and my literary reputation would be finished for good. My answer was a sort of whistle at midnight. "If any book of mine is still remembered in the year 1968–then that's fame, isn't it?"

As I write–I am now in icy Ravello, first week in March 1993, planting roses–the forty-fifth anniversary of the publication of *The City and the Pillar* is being celebrated with a symposium at the University of New York in Albany come April. A number of academics, many not born when the book was published, will present papers on what effect this "crossover" book had and still has. These pieces will be published in book form. Will I read it? Probably not.

But the old editor was right, in a sense. For twenty years–and more–I was regularly attacked for insufficiently worshiping at the altar of the Family. One Orville Prescott, the daily reviewer for *The New York Times,* told my editor that he would never read much less review another book by me. *Time* and *Newsweek* followed suit. Seven novels went unnoticed in their pages. I was also carefully erased from the glittering history of American Literature, where once I had had long, dull chapters devoted to my work. Twenty years ago, there was an academic study of the five hundred–or was it five thousand?–truly great American novelists since the Second War. I was not of their company. I had slid down the page to a footnote, where I am described as a sort of Lucifer who had turned his back on "modernism," a movement that had ended, I always thought, in the year of my birth. During the fifties, a university student told me that when he had wanted to write a dissertation on me, he had been warned that he would be thought a fairy and that no university would ever hire him.

In order to make a living, I was forced into television, movies, theater, and the essay. During this bad time (actually, a very good time as long as I wrote no books under my own name) was Anaïs at my side, encouraging me as I had encouraged her, even to the extent of forcing

Dutton to publish her? No. Anaïs was involved in a thousand exciting scenarios, starring herself, not me, and so I got exactly what I deserved for my uncharacteristic lapse into self-pity. Nothing.

AT ANAÏS'S INSISTENCE, I met her at the bar of the Ritz Hotel in Madison Avenue. She had prepared a position paper on *The City and the Pillar,* which she proceeded, grimly, to read to me. I must have a copy somewhere. The gist was how could she–the exquisitely wise character in the book, known as Marie Verlaine (I, of course, was Rimbaud)–have been attracted to such a colorless clod of a boy as Jim, so unlike those plumed, serpentine Mexican beach boys that she had fancied. Incidentally, by an odd coincidence, Henry Miller called the Anaïs figure "Ida Verlaine" in *Sexus,* a book not published until the sixties.

Finally, rather densely, I realized that Anaïs was concentrating entirely on a minor character, the French enchantress with whom Jim goes to Mexico but not to bed. "And then–*worse*–you say that she–that she–that she has *lines* about her eyes!" In the Ritz bar, Anaïs's fierce lines were unlike anything that I have ever seen except the first time that I opened my fax machine and quickly shut it not because of the resemblance of all those wires to the wrath of Anaïs but because I don't like machinery.

"No woman wants to read that," she actually hissed, "about herself." Politely, I pointed out that she was not exactly a household name, and though the book was, as it turned out, read in several languages, I don't think any reader ever connected her with it. But she was in full flow, and I remember an interesting verb that she used: "When a woman gets older, there is always the fear that she may never *win* again." The word *win* has stayed with me. Love was contest as well as deception. Love meant defeat for one, victory for the other. I thought this ugly.

Anaïs then denounced the promiscuity of same-sexualists. I was polite about her own powerful–and eclectic–appetites, but I did suggest that there was both a beauty and fulfillment in sex with strangers that one seldom enjoys with people one knows. Even at twenty, I had pretty much decided that the most interesting sex would be *de passage* and not with friends or acquaintances. I am now reading about Jack Kennedy's "reckless youth"; and I recall, suddenly, how hated he was by the legions of girls of his generation that he had got into bed, because they were attracted either to him or to his fame and then discarded.

But Anaïs belonged to the heavy-breathing school of lady's fiction; she also had a touching belief in psychiatry. "There was a side of Gore which I saw, which existed in my presence, a Gore which might have flowered if a deeper love had been possible." Yet that "deeper" love was all in *The City and the Pillar* and she had missed it; apparently, those tiny lines about the eyes blinded her to all else. But then the idea of male completeness with male went against her Spanish Catholicism, shored up as it was by patriarchal Freud and made literally celestial by astrology.

"I went to dinner with him. Same place. But not any longer the same relationship. We had dealt each other deathblows. I could not be his mother, with no other life of my own." Here she was truly undone by Freud. I already had one mother too many. Also, in our relationship, I was the man–the father–who had got her published and then introduced her to a world that she had longed to figure in–my new post–*City and the Pillar* friends, Tennessee Williams, Christopher Isherwood, and all the rest.

Years later, in Hollywood, when Paul Newman and Joanne Woodward and my friend Howard Austen and I shared a house at Malibu, we asked her to lunch. Later, she deplored to others my life with "starlets." Yet she joined us one evening at the Mocambo nightclub, where Edith Piaf sang only to us; there were no other customers. I'd like to read Anaïs's account of that evening. For the record, she and I were on fairly amiable terms for a number of years. When I started to write about books, she was eager for me to celebrate her at length, but I never did because, after my early ensorcelment, I did not like her writing but, compassionately, never said so.

We saw one another occasionally in the sixties. She was working hard on her legend, which was, ironically, taken seriously by the sixties feminists, whom she derisively labeled the "Kotex brigade." She still wanted me to write about her, but although I can perjure myself in a short blurb for a book, I cannot sustain deceit over any great critical length.

One odd detail came back to me as I read *Incest.* "I imagine what a beautiful piece of cruelty it would be to give Henry the four or five volumes which concern him and our love just before parting from him for good . . . to read that night, alone, with the knowledge that I have vanished."

Anaïs gave me a green journal. "I've copied out everything that I've written about you in the journals. I want you to have it, to read it." She was radiant with what I now realize was malice. But her stratagem was undone by my lifelong reluctance to read anything about myself. Over the next few weeks, she would ring me to ask what I thought, felt. Finally, I had to admit that I had no intention of reading her "portrait." She was angry: "Then I want it back!"

"Can't I keep it—as a souvenir?"

"No." So I gave it back to her. After her death, her Hollywood husband mislaid it.

Sudden vivid memory: East Hampton. Summer 1946. I stay at my father's house. Anaïs stays at a hotel. It was her idea, not mine, for her to come. We go together to the public beach by back roads. I am terrified I'll be seen with her—an older woman, who was less than radiant in the full sunlight. I cringe now at my snobbism.

One day on the beach she told me that she had not been able to sleep the night before. Anxiety. Unhappiness. She had walked up and down the deserted main street of the village. The night watchman, an old Irishman, stopped her. He gave her coffee. Sympathy, too. She was grateful. I was moved. But now, as I write these lines on a warm day in May of 1993, I realize that Anaïs had invented the encounter with the old Irishman, a surly soul not given to kindnesses of this sort, and so, once again, she was able to net me in her ongoing fiction of herself, her world.

*John Kriza in one of my favorite ballets of the
forties, Eugene Loring's* Billy the Kid.
*I got interested in Billy the Kid when I was
at school in New Mexico, Billy's turf.*

Dancers:
An Interval

I<small>N A FIT</small> of uncharacteristic generosity, the American government
had agreed to pay for the higher education of its former indentured
servants, the armed forces. I waived a college education. But when,
as physical therapy, I began to attend a ballet class given by George
Chafee, I let the government pay. At first, I was only interested in the
barre exercises, for my arthritic knee. Then I got interested in how ballet worked technically and so, for a season or two, I took class, talked to
dancers, went to the ballet, and learned the language of ballet.

In the late forties, balletomania hit New York City. For years there had
been the Ballets Russes de Monte Carlo, a spin-off of the prewar
Diaghilev company with a small but loyal audience. The principal
dancers were Alexandra Danilova and Frederic Franklin, as well as
Leon Danielian, a character dancer best known in such Massine ballets
as *Gaîté Parisienne*. Leon and I became friends; he was exuberantly
funny about his fellow dancers; himself, too. Whenever he played the
prince's friend in *Swan Lake*, a very showy part indeed, he would bring
down the house with his turns, "which consist of," he would grin,
"three turns to the left and, with luck, two to the right. They applaud
because of how I hold my head, and shake it triumphantly when I finish. Also, I've got almost no elevation, so I make my leap on the down–
not on the up–beat. No one knows the difference and I seem to
soar–just an inch or two off the ground."

I was backstage once when Anton–known as Pat–Dolin was guest-partnering Alicia Markova in *Swan Lake*. Pat was an amusing, vain Englishman, now a bit long in the tooth. Backstage, during the overture, he was doing barre exercises in the wings. Leon whispered as he passed him, "Too late, Pat, too late."

From the wings, I watched Pat and Markova. The two quarreled constantly during the pas de deux, and I was amazed that the audience didn't hear them over the music. "Put me down! It's the third beat," muttered Markova. "Since when could you count?" he snarled as she struggled free from him, landing on beat, on perfect point, and then to fifth position. Thus was one of my pseudonymous novels born, *Death in the Fifth Position*.

But the real art of the dance was not to be found at the Ballets Russes in those days; rather, it was Ballet Theatre that excited a public that would never have gone much–if at all–to the ballet. The master whose work I became addicted to was Antony Tudor. Tudor had lived many years with a handsome dancer called Hugh Laing, who in turn had taken up with Diana Adams, a rising ballerina. The *ménage à trois* looked to be comfortable. I met Tudor in 1948 or 1949 in the entr'acte of a ballet at the Paris Opera House. Bald and lean, with a sly crooked smile and a deadly sense of humor, he said, "I've always wanted to see Serge Lifar. Now I have. And it's all true . . ."

"What is true?"

"He is every bit as bad–no, dreadful–as I've always heard." Even I could tell that the flabby-buttocked man onstage was, if not bad, oddly repellent as he struck his poses. Years later, Nureyev said that when he was in charge of the Paris Opera Ballet, his most difficult task was to exorcise the malign ghost of Lifar. "Is everywhere. In rehearsal halls. Backstage. We name rooms after this one, after that one. *They* make me name Lifar Room. Always evil in that room." Rudi would shudder. "Bad ghost."

Between Tudor ballets and Tennessee Williams's new plays, something visceral was happening to those of us lucky to be in New York at the time, and able to go from play to ballet. Now, for the time being (which may be the only time–being or not–we may ever have in either dramatic form), there is not much excitement, or if there is, then that passionate, hungry, postwar audience no longer exists.

As an artist, Tudor tends to vanish in one decade to be revived in the next, but revival is never the same thing as *now* in the sense that what one is experiencing is truly novel or new. Tudor made a place for himself between classical ballet and modern dance, between Diaghilev and Martha Graham; his ballets were known as "psychological"; that is, they had real–as opposed to fairy-tale–plots. But they were classically balletic in movement. With *Pillar of Fire,* Tudor managed to define an entire generation that was finding a transient religion in psychoanalysis. Nora Kaye was his principal interpreter. She was a droll woman with a good business sense. At fourteen or so, she had been married to James T. Farrell, a marriage that was annulled. I told her once that I knew about Farrell.

"No one's supposed to know about that," she said, more resignedly than annoyed. "How do you?" I said that Farrell had told me. We had met at Milton Klein's, our common dentist, in Fifty-fourth Street. At seventeen I had got Farrell to autograph my copy of *Studs Lonigan.* Over the years, I came to like him rather more than the books–naturalistic stories of proletarian life in Chicago–that I had devoured at Exeter.

Other Nora marriages were equally haphazard: One was to a descendant of Martin Van Buren, whom I would write so much about in *Burr.* Then there was the violinist Isaac Stern. I went to their wedding reception on New York's West Side. Neither looked as if he had met the other, but all the town was on hand. A hot summer day, I remember, with white curtains billowing at open windows. That marriage was soon over. "I couldn't stand it," said Nora. "That squeak, squeak, squeak all day when he practiced."

Onstage, Nora was like no one else. As a classical dancer, she was barely in the second rank. As a dancer-actress, there has never been, and perhaps never will be, another like her. Nora's scream at the end of Agnes de Mille's *Fall River Legend* still resounds in my head forever as an actual scream, although it was soundless as she stood, writhing, at center stage, white dress splashed with parents' blood. In Jerome Robbins's *The Cage,* Nora played a sort of preying mantis–"queen of the bugs," we called her: She was terrifying.

A few years ago, Nureyev and I got to know each other when he moved to an island off Positano, and I would come down from Ravello to visit him; then, with seigneurial courtesy, he would come to me by sea and let his AIDS-wasted body collapse beside the pool.

Nureyev's knowledge of American ballet before his defection was spotty. One day, he asked me to tell him everything that I could remem-

ber about the Tudor ballets that were no longer in the repertoire. After
I had described several pieces, no doubt inaccurately, he said, "Is different now." He knew, of course, the Tudor ballets that are still done
occasionally, like *Lilac Garden,* but works like *Undertow* have slipped
away forever. I'm told that one of the last ballets, *La Gloire,* was recently
revived. Antony was uncommonly slow, which meant expensive, as he
endlessly pondered moves, particularly in the case of *La Gloire,* based
upon the life of Bernhardt and set to the music of Beethoven's "Egmont
Overture," an unlikely piece for dancers to dance to. "But then," as the
sharp-tongued composer Samuel Barber observed, "Tudor only uses
music that he happens to already have in his notoriously small record
collection."

On Nureyev's last visit to us in Ravello, the August before he died, he
lay, exhausted, on a sofa, drinking white wine, not speaking, until we
got on to the latest ballet gossip. "Peter Martins—he kill wife, no? No.
Sad. Saw him when sixteen. In class. Big cock hangs there. I make
move. Erik Bruhn say, 'No. Too young. Go to jail.' " Rudi smiles; face
ravaged but beautiful, still very much Tatar king. The upper body has
begun to waste away, but the lower is still unaffected, legs powerful, and
the feet—for a dancer—not too misshapen, no hammertoes.

"Two kinds of dancer," he said, suddenly. "Perfect steps. Perfect tech-
nique. Then there is *music* dancer. Not so perfect. Make mistakes. But
music go right through body and onto audience." He did not say which
he was, but then he had always been both in youth. Now, with age and
illness, he was saying that he relied on the music to use up what was
left of him.

One of my favorite ballets of the period was Loring's *Billy the Kid.* It
was exciting to see my early role model incarnated by John Kriza, a
manly youth from Berwyn, Illinois. Copland's music certainly flowed
through that strong body, particularly the percussion. Loring's Billy
killed sadly, with revulsion. In life, many men and women loved
Johnny, who responded wholeheartedly in an absentminded way. He
had a large car that he called Florestan, and together we drove down the
east coast of Florida, receiving the homage of the balletomanes in their
beachside houses. Eventually, he married another dancer; drank too
much; went swimming one day in the Gulf of Mexico and drowned.

Harold Lang was a short, stocky, blue-eyed dancer, best known for
Jerome Robbins's ballet *Fancy Free*: three Second War sailors "on the

town," as the musical based upon it would be called; the other two sailors were played by Kriza and Robbins himself. For a time Bernstein's music from *On the Town* was a sort of marching song for all of us set free from war and, as the lyric went, "Lucky to be me." By the time I met Harold, he had moved on to musical comedy; and he was about to be starred in *Look, Ma, I'm Dancing.* Harold was a chameleon-lover who could become, instinctively, whatever the other person wanted. Since I thought (for only an instant) that this was Jimmie come back again, I did not in the least mind that Harold was, simultaneously, having affairs with the author of the musical and its star, Nancy Walker, not to mention as much of the British navy as he could take aboard when we were in Bermuda for a week. This hardly bothered me, since I was almost as promiscuous as Harold. But during our short time together I was obliged to face the fact that I was never going to make the journey from homoerotic to homosexual and so I was never going to be able to have anything other than one-sided passing sex. Thanks to Harold, this belated revelation was to prove a great time-saver over the years.

When Lenny Bernstein, in his sixty-ninth summer, came to stay with us in Ravello, I mentioned Harold. "Oh, God! Not *that* conversation! Practically everyone I know—or used to know—liked to tell me how one thing we have in common is the cast of *Fancy Free.*"

"Well, I did go to bed with two thirds of your cast."

"And I," said Lenny, competitive to the bitter end, "went to bed with all three. But I will say Harold's ass was one of the seven—or whatever number it is—wonders of our time."

In 1982, I was a candidate for Senate in California and I came to speak at the university in Chico. There was Harold in the audience. He taught ballet; and had his own undergraduate company. He was unchanged except for a rosy blotch or two about the nose. He drank more than any athlete that I've ever known, but then, like the other hard-drinking dancers of that day, he sweated it all out the next day in class.

After I had made my speech, Harold and I went off to a bar. He bought a cellophane bag of pretzels. "Dinner," he said. He still looked as he did in *Pal Joey* on Broadway. He seemed content. He had come originally from Daly City, close to San Francisco. As an adolescent, he had been a Western Union boy, delivering telegrams on a bicycle; then someone—upon receipt of a telegram?—proposed he become a dancer. He did. He was prodigious; with an astonishing elevation. In *Fancy Free,* he would leap, without perceptible preparation, from floor to tabletop, as the audience gasped; then, without a break, do his *tour en l'air* on the beat.

He was dead a year after I last saw him. Cirrhosis, I heard. But I wonder if he might not have been an early AIDS victim. Because of his methodical heart breaking, he was known as the Beast of the Ballet. In the bar at Chico, I asked him why he felt so great a need to enchant then desert others.

"It all started with the nose." Like everyone else in those days, Harold had done a grand jeté or two through psychoanalysis. "I had this big nose, and no one would go with me. Then, after I started dancing, I cut the nose off and everybody who'd ignored me before now said they were in love with me, and so I . . ." He munched on a pretzel, analysis finished. Plainly, those who did not like his real nose deserved what punishment they later got when they were attracted to the new one, and its bright protean attachment, Harold himself.

My days as a balletomane—and lover of dancers—ended when Balanchine appeared on the scene and swept *American* ballet off the stage. Balanchine's ballets have mathematical charm, but I wanted Nora Kaye to illuminate our generation, to the music of Copland or Bernstein.

My knee was helped by barre exercises. Finally, I learned from Harold that an affair with a man was neither possible nor desirable for me, and so, with relief, I gave up any further attempts along those lines. Women were sometimes tempting, but my early exposure to the Marriages of My Family proved to be a reliable, unbreakable prophylactic. I might have negotiated Tolstoy's last station with style, but it was the first station that looked ominous, to say the least. Thus, I was able, at twenty-five, to settle down with Howard Austen, age twenty-one. We had met anonymously at the Everard Baths.

"How," we are often asked, "have you stayed together for forty-four years?" The answer is, "No sex." This satisfies no one, of course, but there, as Henry James would say, it is.

"Gene Collins"

THE YEAR 1948 was the year that I became, overnight, as Michael Foot put it in an English review, like Byron, "famous." *The City and the Pillar* came out in January. As a best-seller that year it was somewhat ahead of Capote's *Other Voices, Other Rooms,* somewhat behind Mailer's *The Naked and the Dead.* Only Mailer and I have survived that year's best-seller list, headed by George Orwell's *1984.* In those days works of literature were often popular, something no longer possible. But then, for someone young today, 1948 is as remote as the year 1903 was for us—the year that Henry James published *The Ambassadors* and Jack London, *The Call of the Wild.*

Although my book had generally very bad reviews—*sterile* was a favorite adjective, code word for faggot—the book was being read not only by the crushed and closeted inhabitants of Sodom but by a great many other people as well, including Dr. Kinsey, as I have noted. In the same season he and I made, jointly, a nice assault on the Leviticus Committee Report, and the United States was never to be the same again, on that subject at least.

I have often been asked what family and friends thought of *The City and the Pillar.* The Gores did not finish the book; and the Senator never mentioned it to me. But our relations were unchanged. After he died in 1949, my grandmother used to come and stay in my house on the Hudson; we would also go to Key West together in the winter. The most she

*My father, Gene Vidal (1895–1969), when
he was a football and track star at the
University of South Dakota. The local
congressman was so excited by his playing
that he appointed him to West Point.
Had he not been a great athlete he might
never have got out of South Dakota, and so
I would not have existed–in present guise.*

ever said was, "You mustn't stir up more snakes than you can kill." When I asked her if this was an old South Carolina saying, she said, "No, I think I just made it up."

Nina was thrilled by my subsequent failures–five books unreviewed by the daily *New York Times, Time,* and *Newsweek.* "You see," she would confide to anyone who would listen, "he isn't really a novelist, he's only a journalist, with just the one book in him, and now of course he's finished." Heaven knows who gave her this line, but she reveled in it. Then everything changed rapidly when I became a "hit" playwright on Broadway. Carlos Fuentes tells me that once he came to her house in Cuernavaca and, not finding her in the sitting room, he went to the next room, which proved to be her bedroom. She was lying on the bed, paperback editions of my books all around her–this was years after I had sent her away for good. Odd.

My father–I now realize–was being deliberately cryptic when he'd say, "I think it's a very interesting book." Thus closing the subject. Actually, it must have been of more interest to him than I ever suspected. At the time I had heard of–but never read–Robert McAlmon. He was from my father's hometown of Madison, South Dakota. Like most of the bright and restless young of the heartland villages, he got out. He was a writer. He settled in Europe and was friend and editor to Pound and Hemingway. I have an impression that, at some point, he wrote me a letter that I never answered.

I cannot remember when or how I first heard that McAlmon had been romantically involved with Gene. I know that I always kept forgetting to ask Gene about him–because McAlmon had the reputation of being Capote-like in his inventions?

Although McAlmon was neither a good writer nor "a good person," he was a good editor; he also wrote an interesting autobiography called *Being Geniuses Together*, which Kay Boyle later reissued, adding her life story to McAlmon's text. No, I never talked to Kay Boyle about him, either.

Finally, I read McAlmon's novel *Village: As It Happened Through a Fifteen Year Period.* There, on the first page, is my father at fifteen, consulting a Ouija board in order to discover whether he will be appointed to West Point or to Annapolis or to neither. The narrator is McAlmon, aged fourteen; he is in love with Gene, whom he calls Eugene Collins. At first I took this to be a reference to war pilot Paul Collins, my father's airline partner in the twenties and thirties; but the dates didn't work out. Then, in the spring of 1994 at the University of South Dakota, I saw a fraternity photograph of Gene sitting near the strikingly handsome head of the fraternity, a youth named Collins.

What is McAlmon up to?

The book covers fifteen years in the life of a village, based on Madison. Gene grows up. Goes to West Point. Becomes an all-American football player. Marries Nina. McAlmon himself comes and goes, recording the rather sad life of a village where the bright boys and girls all move away, as he himself does, too.

If I had had the sense to get to know McAlmon, I might have learned a great deal about Gene, not to mention Hemingway, whom McAlmon had fingered as a fellow fag, to Hemingway's fury. Whatever McAlmon may have said about others later in life, right or wrong, he is plainly working from the facts in *Village*. My aunt, Margaret, who is about to be born at the beginning of the book, testifies to the accuracy of his description of life in that box of a house in South Dakota where winters were arctic and summers hot, and Peter Reynalds (McAlmon) would visit Gene Collins, and they'd discuss the facts of life and Gene, after some stammering, says,

"Well, you know what happens to fellows our age—I wonder if it's happened to you yet."

Peter answered quickly: "I guess so; I thought Chemo had talked to you. I told him about the scare I had one night after I got to bed, and I thought something had burst in me. He said he'd been afraid when that happened to him, and went to see Dr. Douglas who only laughed and said: 'That's all right Chemo, my boy. You just take a girl and you'll be all right,' and Chemo thought he had to or he'd be sick. But you don't have to at all because your dreams take care of you."

Peter wondered to himself if he really liked Gene as a friend as he liked Lloyd Scott. The unspoken understanding that had existed between him and Lloyd was not here with Gene. He almost resented his affection for Gene; he wondered if he'd have liked him at all if many other boys of his own age were about. It was simply that all of the other boys in their classes at high school were such dumbheads. Gene had an attraction for him, however, that Lloyd had

never had. He wondered, was that simply now, and because both of
them were adolescent? But if that was so, why did it exist more
between him and Gene than between him and other boys in that
period? He saw that Gene felt about him as he did about Gene;
attracted, and antagonistic too. That was rivalry, and jealousy,
because the two of them led their class easily.

This is right out of *The City and the Pillar*, including the clumsy gray
all-American prose. Gene never mentioned McAlmon to me. Had he
forgotten him, as Bob had pretty much forgotten Jim?

The years pass and the passion cools on McAlmon's side:

Gene Collins, after two years at the State University, was appointed
to West Point, and his first year there made a great name for him-
self as a football player. By this time any friendship that had existed
between him and Peter Reynalds had evaporated. Six years had
passed. Peter . . . found that they were completely antipathetic to
each other. Gene's attitude about money, a tightfisted one, was the
first symptom; and his intentness on making a good marriage was
a second.

This is, plainly, a bit of a projection. It was McAlmon who was
obliged to marry the wealthy English lesbian novelist Bryher, in order
to survive. In any case, Nina had no money.

Later, in a memoir, McAlmon writes of Eugene Vidal, the director of
Air Commerce, whom he had once known, and remarks that boys like
Gene and himself were a lot more articulate than Hemingway was
currently rendering them in his mannered stories of dumb-ox Midwest lads.

After Aunt Margaret, at my suggestion, read *Village*, she said, "Well,
it's pretty clear he liked Gene too much," exactly the same words that
Jimmie's mother used about Jimmie's stepfather. Recently, when I visited Madison, I asked about McAlmon. A few people had heard of *Village*, but every time a copy arrived at the library, the librarian locked
it up.

Although I was once held in the arms of my grandparents Vidal in a
Chicago hotel room, I have no memory of them. But at Madison I did go
to the cemetery to see their graves, two small yellow lichen-covered

stone markers: F. L. Vidal and Margaret Vidal. They died less than a year apart: in 1934. My uncle–the youngest child–said that for days on end they would not speak to each other. Then, after their sundown supper, they would go to bed and make love; hence, his "scandalous" birth when she was in her forties.

McAlmon:

Mrs. Collins, Gene's mother, came into the room to say goodnight. She was retiring early, exhausted, as she might well be, carrying her great flabby person about all day.

"I'm not one to brag," she said, "or to want my children to be snobs, but I just tell them about their forebears so they will know they can hold their heads up anywhere they go. Of course the debt will never be paid, but if the French government ever would pay back all it owes to our family from away back since the Revolution, we'd be one of the wealthiest families in the world. I don't remember very clearly, but some ancestors of ours lent some king or other all kinds of money years and years back. We aren't one of those families which can't trace back more than a generation; though I'm very democratic myself, and not one to boast."

Fifteen-year-old Gene looked sheepish, and mumbled: "Peter doesn't give a darn about all that rot, mother," but Mrs. Collins pattered on for a few minutes. Her mind and her conversation never stayed fixed on any one point for long, so that before finally saying goodnight, she was rambling on about the marriage that her father, the gay, rakish old Mr. Dubois, had made. "He wrote me the woman was wealthy but I've heard nothing from him since, and from other reports that are drifting back, I'm thinking both he and that Atlantic City widow played a joke on each other, each pretending to have money they don't have."

Old Mr. Dubois was my grandmother's father, Luther Lazarus Rewalt, a Pennsylvanian Dutchman from Morristown. He was known as Foxy Grandpa, after a natty cartoon character of the day. He had served, he said, as a doctor in a Pennsylvania regiment in the Civil War. I looked up his army record. Apparently, he was a civilian doctor employed by a Washington hospital to look after the wounded. He was fired for drinking and playing cards with enlisted men while on duty. In his last years, he did very well with something called Rewalt's Elixir, a patent medicine containing sugar and gin by which many a Midwest temperance lady swore. Always on the lookout for a rich widow, he thought that he had found one in California. They met. Unfortunately, she was on the lookout for a rich widower. Each fooled the other only briefly. That winter he came back to Madison. After a night in a tavern, he passed out in a snowdrift. The temperature was below zero. The next morning, what everyone took to be the frozen body of Dr. Rewalt rose briskly from a snowdrift, brushed the ice from his overcoat, and said, "You see? The virtues of my elixir." The alcohol in his veins had kept him from freezing solid.

McAlmon's Gene is hard and calculating. I never saw that side to him, and perhaps McAlmon's view is colored by the Jim-Bob syndrome that results from rejection.

The University of South Dakota yearbook hails Gene as their greatest athlete but notes that he "lacks aggressiveness." A Senate committee came to the same conclusion about his administration of the Bureau of Air Commerce. I suspect that what he "lacked" was the single-minded ambition that most people are accustomed to. He was restless, curious, inventive. In general, people bored him, and since he had no wish to exert power over them, he was not "aggressive"—or much of anything else—in his relations with them. When a journalist once remarked to him on my "courage," his response was to the point: "What's courageous if you don't care what people think of you?"

One detail that establishes the authenticity of McAlmon's report on "Gene Collins" is the mother's long ramble about the loan to some long-dead "French" king. One of the first things that I ever knew about the family was the loan which, if ever repaid, would make us all incredibly rich.

My great-great-grandfather, Jost Josef de Traxler, of Stans, Switzerland, had been a member of the Swiss guard of Louis XVI at Versailles. During the revolution, he survived the general slaughter of the guard and escaped to Madrid, where he was employed by Louis' cousin Charles IV, king of Spain. This was 1803. When Napoleon invaded in 1808, Traxler and his son-in-law Ludwig von Hartmann of Lucerne raised a regiment with their own money to fight for the Spanish king against Napoleon, who wanted to include Spain as well as Portugal in what Napoleon tidily referred to as his "continental system." Charles IV, to whom my great-great- and great-grandfather had sworn loyalty, abdicated in his son Ferdinand's favor, only to be replaced by Napoleon's brother Joseph. Meanwhile, the Spanish people resisted Napoleon, and our family's regiment played a considerable part in the resistance. Once Napoleon was gone and the royal family restored, the *cortes,* or parliament, of Spain was presented with the family's bill for services rendered and the government acknowledged the legitimacy of the claim as well as the sad emptiness of the treasury. Finally, in the 1930s, just before the republic fell, the debt to the family was honored and my father received his share of the many millions that the family in Madison, South Dakota, had dreamed would enrich them—some three hundred dollars, I seem to remember.

I saw a photograph of my great-grandmother's grave in Wisconsin. She was born Carolina de Traxler, and her place of birth is given as "Carthage." It took me some time to realize that Carthage was the Wisconsin translation of Cartagena in Spain, where she had been born. Professional Swiss soldiers seldom lived in Switzerland: Her father, Jost Joseph, had been born in Naples, where his father had been commander of the guard of the king of the two Sicilys. By my grandmother's time all this was a glamorous blur, involving royal rich birth for us all.

Robert McAlmon: It is curious—to say the least—to encounter one's father as a boy of fifteen as seen through the eyes of a boy of fourteen who is in love with him. I was as intrigued by the possibilities of all this as I was by Jimmie's sudden interest in Walt Whitman.

I replay in my head Gene's comment that he had found *The City and the Pillar* "very interesting." Had I, without knowing it, told *his* story? With Gene as Bob Ford, who forgets about a youthful idyll, and Robert McAlmon as Jim Willard, a writer who is still writing about what may or may not have happened in their common boyhood. If nothing else, the very ordinariness of the story makes it a good deal more universal than I realized when I wrote it at the age of twenty—I turned twenty-one as I wrote the ending in Guatemala City. Certainly, McAlmon must have been intrigued that the son of "Eugene Collins" had written a variation on *Village* without ever having heard of the book or its author.

Rome and the
Glorious Bird

O N JANUARY 10, 1948, *The City and the Pillar* was published. When it reached number five on *The New York Times* best-seller list, I rented out the Antigua house and headed for Europe on a Greek ship, bound for Naples. I checked into the Excelsior Hotel, much damaged by the war. My bathroom was half paved with marble, the rest raw cement.

I moved on to Rome, not visited since 1939. The streets were empty of cars. The bar of the Excelsior on Via Veneto was the center for the foreigners who were beginning to flock to the city, where prices were cheap; sex, too. I stayed at the nearby Eden Hotel. Frederic Prokosch, whom I had met at East Hampton two years earlier, was also on the scene. We would breakfast together at Doney's while observing, with pleasure, my future lunch companion, Orson Welles; he was usually seated alone, reading a book called *Decadence;* he was in town trying to make a film about Cagliostro. Prokosch was mildly annoyed at my success, and chided me for wanting to know where I stood on the weekly best-seller lists.

That year, in my youthful eagerness, I wanted to meet every writer that I admired. I met several; as a result, I never again wanted to meet, much less know, a writer whose work I admired. But the apprentice stage is a useful one, if only as a means of placing oneself. Otherwise there is nothing to be *done* about those already in place, except take their place in time. Golden Bough, or Golden Age?

February 1948. The Glorious Bird and I
on Rome's Pincio with the jeep that he
had just bought. We drove south through
war-damaged towns to Amalfi, where on
an excursion one day we visited Ravello.

RAVELLO, APRIL 17, 1993, I have a number of things going through my mind. Some seem more urgent than others, but none wants to line itself up in an orderly narrative. First, the white cat: She is a stray that has lived with us for seven years; she is sitting on my hand, bumping her forehead against my chin, and I am disturbed that her ears are not only covered with bloody scabs but a spikelike tumor decorates the tip of the right ear. Cancer? She knows that we are going away because the baggage is in the hall.

Baggage. The mind shifts from the cat's ear to the Naples/Frankfurt/Washington, D.C., airports. Despite half a beta-blocker this morning, I can feel my blood pressure rise. In Washington, I will visit the Kennedy Center, where they are showing, all during April, the thirty or so movies that I refer to in *Screening History*, the films that I grew up with. I will introduce *That Hamilton Woman*. What to say? Then a chat at the Shakespeare Folger Library—improvise? Then Chicago, where I perform in a Warner Bros. movie, starring Joe Pesci. I play a Harvard Law professor who mixes in high policy: a scoundrel like Henry Kissinger. The story is more charming fable than real life in the American academic-governmental jungle, where evil (my character) must struggle for the soul of a Harvard student with a Whitmanesque bum who lives in the stacks of the Widener Library, a nice touch. At ten I wanted to be a movie star like Mickey Rooney. At sixty-seven I am one, and not unlike the current Mickey Rooney, in appearance if not in talent.

I have just come from the *cisterna* above the house, set in a jungle that a team of gardeners is clearing away, revealing old walls, paths, rare trees—a whole new property with rich earth. The air intoxicates. We are in a planting mood.

The furniture from the Rome flat, given up after thirty years, is slowly fitting in down here. Much confusion over the placement of this and that. I have a powerful urge to burn everything, past included. I think it is at fifty that the good Buddhist takes to the road with no possessions, only a begging bowl. I am overdue.

I have just been studying a poll that pretends to investigate the sex lives of Americans. It is wonderfully preposterous (average woman has two sexual partners—in her life), but it will be useful when the dictatorship is in place and the aberrant woman who chooses a third partner can be punished. Apparently, only 2 percent of the male population has ever had a homosexual experience. Forty-five years ago, it was 37 percent: Are Dr. Kinsey's figures really off by 35 percent? Are there now entirely different "preferences" (to use a loaded political word)? Due to the fear of AIDS or to the general unattractiveness of the American male?–now the fattest on earth. Or did the Pentagon fix the poll in order to keep that now-insignificant minority "gays"–the weirdly inappropriate word used to describe a nonexistent category–from serving in the military without harassment or concealment or disgrace?

Interestingly, all the questioners of the men were women; as a result, over 30 percent of those approached refused to participate, while the rest were obliged to lie. After all, to tell a strange woman that you had no intention of ever fucking anyone of her sex could be construed as a harassment on a titanic scale, not to mention posing a grave threat to the baby supply, punishable by death in a free society.

Last year, in a book called *The Day America Told the Truth,* a megapoll discovered that 91 percent of our population admits to lying regularly. Of course if 91 percent were lying to the mega-pollsters about their propensity for lying, one is back to the oldest of recorded jokes. "All Cretans are liars," said a Cretan. True or false?

NOW IT IS JUNE 7; equatorial heat. I am home from the trip to the United States. I arrived at the Kennedy Center in a storm. Ugly movie theater. Intelligent audience. Even so, the usual bewildered question: Why, asked a young woman, does this story of Lord Nelson glorify war? I explained that that was why the film was made, to glorify resistance to a predator-tyrant, like Hitler. British propaganda in the thirties and forties was most effectively deployed in Hollywood films so that the American people would be emotionally ready to fight, yet again, with England against Germany. But the questioner was mystified. She just *knew* that all war was bad somehow, and though, from firsthand experience, I incline to her view, I did suggest that it was not such a good thing for her–or for anyone–to be so unaware of history. Once we had been attacked by Japan, we had no choice except to fight back. Naturally, she identified war entirely with men; once women are in power, war will be politically incorrect, as Mrs. Thatcher demonstrated.

The Elizabethan gallery at the Folger Library is reminiscent of Chastleton, the last inhabited "pure" Tudor house, where once, on an icy February morning, I performed two Shakespeare sonnets for British television. One was my favorite, the thirty-fifth, which begins: "No more be grieved at that which thou hast done."

I was introduced by a St. Albans classmate, Barrett Prettyman, now a constitutional lawyer nobly opposed to the death penalty. In the audience a dozen people from my past, including Oatsie Leiter and Evangeline Bruce as well as Roger Stevens, who produced my play *The Best Man* only to end up as a White House courtier as well as creator of the Kennedy Center, a real estate metaphor for the arts in America. As a member of the Advisory Council on the Arts (my advice had been, Don't build the center), I was at the groundbreaking. The Kennedys were all on display; Hughdie and Janet, too. President Johnson wore a white camel's hair coat and a suit of rich green never before seen on a first magistrate, or perhaps anywhere else on earth. He shoveled the dirt with casual contempt, more Kennedy gravedigger than keeper of the flame.

Two weeks in Chicago was a pleasant distraction. To be an actor in a movie is to be out of time and space. The part keeps driving everything else out of my head. During the long waits in my trailer, I find it hard to read even *The Chicago Tribune* as the unconscious mind deals with the part to be played. Happily, I have no anxiety about learning lines: My dialogue is written on cards scattered around the set. All I need to concentrate on is energy. Joe Pesci munches hard candies; suggests I do the same thing–quick energy. The days are long–seven in the morning until seven in the evening; then I go watch the rushes of the previous day.

The director is twenty-eight. Last year he did a documentary about the omnisexual-singer Madonna, who rings or faxes him every day. "I am the most hated woman in the world," she wrote, with what I assume–hope–is pleasure.

Three boys and one girl in the cast. The boy that I work with is so soft-spoken in our scenes that I can barely hear him. Then, rather late, I realize that with the latest sound technology, actors have taken to whispering into the mike, which adds considerably to their character range, while I continue to speak as in life. Happily, Joe Pesci is satisfyingly loud in our big scene before several hundred students. I have always hated making eye contact on camera, because my concentration, not much to begin with, dissipates when I look at someone else. I'm told that when Ronald Reagan was a film actor, he never made eye contact, either—lack of concentration?

But when my character is in a rage at being outdone in his own lecture hall by Pesci, I finally look him in the eye. An electrical switch is turned on and I start to get *his* energy, which is formidable. Later, Paul Newman rang. When I told him what I'd done, he said, "Well, that's the whole fun of acting, finding out all these things with other people. I've never understood how you loners do it."

I arrive back in Ravello. Three new offers to act, but the agent is firm: "The parts are too small." Now I begin to fret about a visit to seven German cities, as well as Oslo and Salzburg in July, for the USIA and my German publisher. For years I was a nonperson in Germany, as was any critic of the American empire, whose east-most province was Germany. But the legions are now in retreat, and critics of the imperial American system are suddenly of interest to the Teutonic tribes. I don't look forward to the rushing about, a different city a day. I also have no speech ready, and no clear idea what line to take. The migration of tribes will, I suppose, be the theme—a subject full of danger, which is attractive. We are in for a century or two of race wars unless, of course, nuclear weapons are employed early on, in which case we join the dinosaurs, our irradiated remains shining in the museums of our heirs, the sage cockroaches.

The house is full of workmen. The electrician—rather sulky—has come and gone with the telephone, so I cannot ring out. The carpenter repairs furniture, carefully replacing eighteenth-century patina with a bright and shiny chocolate veneer whose formula will die with him. The cook has gone to the village to do the shopping. In this heat, tuna-fish salad. A characteristic of Italy is that no job is ever properly finished, thus maintaining an eternal and often highly irritable relationship between contractor and artisan. For the artisan, a finished job is like a finished tomb was for Pharaoh: a signal that he is now ready to die.

My own mood is irritable this morning. A kaleidoscope of impressions keeps thought at bay. My collected essays have just been published. The reviews are arriving. I look at them; Howard reads them. As the book represents forty years of essay writing, the reception is benign.

I am plainly at the end of the road. So, I suspect, is literature, a serious matter that I cannot say I take very seriously. Each culture plays the games it needs to play. The novel has given way to the audio-visual just as interactive computers now replace conversation and sex for Americans, if that recent poll is to be believed.

Not to want, was the Buddha's recipe for the blessed absence of pain. As it has turned out, I have got so much more than I ever wanted–or needed–that I am close to serenity. Even so, when I wake up, I take my blood pressure–normal this morning; blood sugar, too. Were I to follow the Buddha's fivefold way, I should not bother about such things. But I am a child of the sick West and cannot be other.

I look about the room where I have been at work for almost a quarter century. Proofs of unread novels accumulate on the coffee table. I sit at a large table that was in the house when we bought it. Everything since *Burr* has been written at this table. Lately, we have acquired a television set to watch the news on CNN and old movies. Videocassettes are beginning to crowd out the books. To the left of the fireplace, a chiaroscuro Neapolitan painting by Viola. "Typical of early eighteenth-century South German painting," boomed the journalist Joe Alsop. As Joe was an expert on everything, he was generally wrong on almost everything, particularly his subject, politics. For thirty years we were losing to Communism, according to Joe; he was a romantic goose, but endearing.

To the right, a Eugene Berman painting, a ruin whose perspective is slightly off; next to Eugene, a Tuscan landscape by his brother, Leonid. Eugene lived in Rome, surrounded by a vast illegally acquired Etruscan collection that the director John Huston tried, illegally, to buy. Where is it now? Eugene was a friend of Carmen Angleton, sister of James Jesus Angleton, the madman of the CIA, and an associate of my sister's friend Cord Meyer, whose wife, a mistress of Jack Kennedy, was mysteriously murdered and her diary vanished, supposedly taken by Angleton. . . . Everything has so many chains of association in our unexpectedly Jacobean republic that nothing any longer surprises.

Ordinarily, I don't think much about the past. A friend was surprised to hear me say that there was not one moment of my past that I would like to relive. Apparently, I am unlike others in this. In fact, everyone I've put that question to has a list of times and places and people to be revisited. I am only at home in the present, and view with dislike the numerous letters from biographers. On my desk there are now two new requests for recollection–of Alec Guinness and Terry Southern. Who next? I like both, but what on earth has one got to say about either that will be interesting? Little anecdotes are not my style. Of course, I could review their life work, but I charge for writing reviews.

When I last saw Alec, he was about to move into the Connaught Hotel in London, where I was staying. "Good," he said. "We shall see each other. I shall be filming for a month in town. A TV thing." I said that, alas, I was leaving the next day for Pittsburgh. "Why Pittsburgh?"

"I, too, am filming, a movie. As an actor this time." Alec's pale brows knit. "A *television* film?" he asked. "No. A theatrical film." The eyes became, as Daphne du Maurier would say, *mere slits.* "How *long* will you be in Pittsburgh?" When I answered two days, he sighed with quiet pleasure, "Ah, a *small* part."

While filming *With Honors* in Chicago, I was told that since the star, Joe Pesci, had a degree of control over the cast, the producer proposed five names to him for the part of the villainous Harvard professor. Four English actors and me. Alec's name headed the list. Pesci is supposed to have said, "Why do we always have to go get an English asshole for this sort of part when we have one of our own?" Thus, I was hired.

The above is a demonstration of how memory works–or doesn't work. One thing recalls another, and then the mind starts to shape the material. As I am supposed to be remembering myself, I am central to these memories; I am, however, happier to be at the edge, as one is in an essay, studying someone else or what someone else has made art of, like Alec's splendid caricature of Kenneth Tynan in *The Lavender Hill Mob,* eerily precise even down to the way that Ken, who was to die of emphysema, stagily held a cigarette between ring and little fingers. Ken also, despite–no, I am sure, because of–his lifelong stammer, was the Player King in Alec's *Hamlet.* What was Ken's performance like? Alec sighed. "He elected to play the part as a Chinese, a curious choice. But then I was bad, too. The only original thing about the production was that I insisted that there be no staircases on the set. I have found in life– if not onstage–that I have *never* had an intelligent conversation with anyone–much less a monologue–on the stairs of my house."

I have always preferred the company of actors to writers. But given the choice, who does not? Of the two professions, actors are the most modest and the least secure; they also tell better stories. Writers tend to self-pity and crude envy. I suppose my own self-pity is adequate to the task of being, for half a century, a writer, but as I have never experienced sexual jealousy of anyone, I have also never been envious of another writer. If a reviewer prefers X to me, I will dislike the reviewer, not X. Also, the reverse of envy, I am drawn to those writers who do what I cannot do. In reading someone wonderful–full of wonders–like Calvino, empathy takes over and I start to feel that what he wrote I wrote. This can be exhilarating. Whenever Tennessee had a successful play, it was like my own. When I wrote a successful play, Tennessee would be distraught. The Glorious Bird, as I called him, would make hissing sounds through that sharp beak, feathers aflutter, beady eyes wide with alarm, nest invaded.

Now, after much circling, I am ready to take the plunge into the heart of 1948.

"I particularly like New York on hot summer nights when all the . . . uh, superfluous people are off the streets." Those were the first words Tennessee addressed to me; then the foggy blue eyes blinked, and a nervous chuckle filled the moment's silence before I said whatever I said.

As I later wrote: "Curtain rising. The place: an apartment at the American Academy in Rome. Occasion: a party for some newly arrived Americans, among them Frederic Prokosch, Samuel Barber. The month: February 1948. The day: glittering. What else could any day be in the golden age?"

I am pleased that I can remember so clearly my first meeting with the Glorious Bird. Usually, I forget first meetings, excepting always those solemn audiences granted by the old and famous when I was young and green.

I thought Tennessee ancient. After all, I was twenty-two. He was thirty-seven. *A Streetcar Named Desire* had been running in New York for more than a year when we met that evening in a flat on the Janiculum hill with a view of what was, in those days, a quiet city where hardly anyone was superfluous unless it was us, the first group of American writers and artists to arrive in Rome after the war.

In 1946 and 1947 Europe was still out-of-bounds for foreigners; hence, my Guatemalan phase. But by 1948 the Italians had begun to pull themselves together, demonstrating once more their astonishing ability to cope with disaster, so neatly balanced by their inability to deal with success.

Rome was strange to all of us. For one thing, Italy had been sealed off not only by war but by Fascism. Since the early thirties, few English or American artists knew Italy well. Those who did included mad Ezra Pound, gentle Max Beerbohm, spurious Bernard Berenson, and, of course, the wealthy Anglo-American historian Harold Acton, in stately residence at Florence. By 1948 Acton had written about both the Bourbons of Naples and the later Medici of Florence; he was also prone to the writing of memoirs. And so, wanting no doubt to flesh out yet another chapter in the ongoing story of a long and marvelously uninteresting life, Acton came down to Rome to look at the new invaders. What he believed he saw and heard, he subsequently published in a little volume called *More Memoirs of an Aesthete,* a work to be cherished for its remarkable number of unaesthetic misprints and misspellings.

"After the First World War American writers and artists had emigrated to Paris; now they pitched upon Rome." So Acton begins. "According to Stendhal, the climate was enough to gladden anybody, but this was not the reason; one of them explained to me that it was the facility of finding taxis, and very little of Rome can be seen from a taxi. Classical and Romantic Rome was no more to them than a picturesque background. Tennessee Williams, Victor [he means Frederic] Prokosch and Gore Vidal created a bohemian annexe to the American Embassy . . ." To like Rome for its available taxis is splendid stuff and I wish I had said it. (Did I?) Certainly whoever did was putting Acton on, since the charm of Rome, for us, if not the Italians, was the lack of automobiles of any kind. But Acton is only just easing into his formidable stride. More to come.

Toward the end of March, Tennessee gave a party to inaugurate his new flat on the Via Aurora (in the golden age even the street names were apt). Somehow or other, Acton got himself invited. I remember him floating like some large pale fish through the crowded room; from time to time, he would make a sudden lunge at this or that promising bit of bait while Tennessee, he tells us, "wandered as a lost soul among the guests he [had] assembled in an apartment which might have been in New York. . . . Neither he nor any of the group I met with him spoke Italian, yet he had a typically Neapolitan protégé who could speak no English."

At this time Tennessee and I had been in Rome for only a few weeks and French, not Italian, was the second language of the reasonably well educated American of that era. On the other hand, Prokosch knew Italian, German, and French; he also bore with becoming grace the heavy weight of a Yale doctorate in Middle English. But to Acton the author of *The Asiatics,* the translator of Hölderlin and Louise Labé was just another barbarian whose works "fell short of his perfervid imagination, [he] had the dark good looks of an advertiser of razor blades . . ." Happily, "Gore Vidal, the youngest in age, aggressively handsome in a clean-limbed sophomore style, had success written all over him. . . . His candour was engaging but he was slightly on the defensive, as if he anticipated an attack on his writings or his virtue." Well, the young GV wasn't so dumb: Seeing the old one-two plainly in the middle distance, he kept sensibly out of reach.

"A pudgy, taciturn, moustached little man without any obvious distinction." Thus Acton describes Tennessee. He then zeroes in on the "protégé" from Naples, a young man whom Acton calls "Pierino." Acton tells us that Pierino had many complaints about Tennessee and his friends, mostly due to the language barrier. The boy was also eager to go to America. Pierino was enthralled, Acton tells us, by Acton. "You are the first *galantuomo* who has spoken to me this evening." After making a date to see the *galantuomo* later on that evening, Pierino split. Acton then told Tennessee, "as tactfully as I could, that his young protégé felt neglected. [Tennessee] rubbed his chin thoughtfully and said nothing, a little perplexed. There was something innocently childish about his expression." It does not occur to the memoirist that Tennessee might have been alarmed at his strange guest's bad manners. "Evidently he was not aware that Pierino wanted to be taken to America and I have wondered since whether he took him there, for that was my last meeting with Tennessee Williams." It must be said that Acton managed to extract quite a lot of copy out of a single meeting. To put his mind at rest, Tennessee did take Pierino to America, and Pierino is now a married man and doing, as they say, well.

"This trifling episode illustrated the casual yet condescending attitude of certain foreigners towards the young Italians they cultivated on account of their Latin charm, without any interest in their character, aspirations or desires." This sentiment or sentimentality could be put just as well the other way around—and with far more accuracy. Italian "trade" has never had much interest in the character, aspirations, or desires of those to whom they rent their ass. When Acton meditates upon the Italian Boy, a sweet and sickly hypocrisy clouds his usually sharp prose and we are in E. M. Forsterland, where the lower orders (male) are worshiped and entirely misunderstood. But magnum of sour grapes to one side, Acton is by no means inaccurate. Certainly he got right Tennessee's indifference to place, art, history. The Bird seldom read a book, and the only history he knew was his own; he depended, finally, on a romantic genius to get him through life. Above all, he was a survivor.

From the Bird's memoirs: "Life that winter in Rome: a golden dream, and I don't just mean Raffaello [Acton's "Pierino"] and the mimosa and total freedom of life. Stop there: what I do mean is the total freedom of life and Raffaello and the mimosa . . ." That season we were, all of us, symbolically, out of jail. Free of poverty and hack work, Tennessee had metamorphosed into the Glorious Bird while I had left behind me, as I've already noted, a lifetime of servitude. So it was, at the beginning of that golden dream, we met.

Tennessee's version: "[Gore] had just published a best-seller, called *The City and the Pillar,* which was one of the first homosexual novels of consequence. I had not read it but I knew that it had made the best-seller lists and that it dealt with a 'forbidden subject.' " Later, Tennessee actually read the book—the only novel of mine that he was ever able to get through. Tennessee was so taken in by the style that he thought that I was writing, most artlessly, the story of my own life.

"My parents were just like yours," he said, "particularly my father." At first, I didn't know what he was talking about. Then I recalled my description of Jim Willard's lower-middle-class family in Virginia, which I had simply made up out of my head with some help, perhaps, from James T. Farrell's *Studs Lonigan.* I told him that everything in the book was made up except the passion of Jim Willard for Bob Ford.

Tennessee didn't care for the ending, "I don't think you realized what a good book you had written." He found the fight at the end melodramatic—that from Tennessee, whose heroes, when not castrated, are eaten alive by small boys in Amalfi, just below where I live. I should note that whenever *Suddenly, Last Summer* appears on Italian television, the local boys find it irresistibly funny.

My paternal great-great grandparents.
Born in Lucerne, Caroline de Traxler von
Hartmann was the daughter of the Traxler who,
with his son-in-law, raised a Swiss regiment
to fight for the Spanish king against Bonaparte.
Ludwig von Hartmann, a professional soldier, married
Caroline in Spain. Their daughter, Emma, married Eugen Fidel
Vidal of Feldkirch, Austria; they emigrated to Wisconsin in 1848.
Their son, my grandfather Felix, was a 33-degree Mason; his
son, my father, disliked him for reasons I could never discover.

Carrie Wingo Gore, mother of my
maternal grandfather, Senator
Gore. A woman of great character,
she took in the girl that her son is
said to have seduced and betrayed. At left, Carrie's husband,
Thomas N. Gore, corporal with a Mississippi rifle company
in the Civil War. Although Unionist, he joined up to be with
his kin. He was wounded and taken captive at Shiloh. For
many years he was clerk of Webster County. "I was," he
used to say in later years, "the *only* corporal in the
Confederate army."

My maternal grandmother's mother,
Marcella McLaughlin, was from a
landowning, slave-owning Mississippi
family. She had Creole blood, via New Orleans. At right, John
Kay from South Carolina. He fought in the Civil War, then
moved to Texas, married Marcella, and, in due course,
prospered modestly. My grandmother, Dot, always said
he looked just like General Lee.

In 1913, my grandfather, the blind Senator T. P. Gore, was offered a bribe to help some oilmen rob Indians of their land. He rejected the bribe. The oilmen, duly incensed, played the "badger game" on him. A constituent rang to say that she wanted to talk to him at a Washington hotel. He arrived; she led the blind man not to the mezzanine but to a hotel suite where she suddenly "squawked" and hired witnesses rushed in. He was accused of attempted rape, stood trial in Oklahoma City, was found not guilty. At left, below, my grandfather in 1908, the year after he was elected the first senator from Oklahoma, at thirty-eight. At right is my grandmother, Nina Kay Gore, making the transition from gracious Washington hostess to politician. In the senator's last campaign (1936), when asked at a meeting how long they would be in the state that he represented, Mrs. Gore was horrified to hear herself say, "Oh, we just drove over from New York for the day." The Senator lost.

A BALD-FACED FRAME-UP DECLARES SENATOR GOR DENYING BOND CHARG

Led to Room He Thought P lor; Proved to Be Bedroc Infested By Political Enemi Bent His Ruin; Banker Te of Offer to Drop Suit F Money.

ENTERS REALM OF NATIONAL POLIT

MRS. THOMAS P. GORE
The brilliant wife of the blind senator from Oklahoma who is one of mittee of the leading society women of the east who are forming an org tion to further the interests of the democratic nominee for president. the next three months they will bend every energy toward securing th tion of Governor Woodrow Wilson

Rock Creek Park, Washington, D.C.
My true home. T. P. Gore built the house in
the early twenties. After his defeat in an
election for the Senate in 1920, he was able,
as a lawyer, for the first time in his life to
make money, which he lost in 1929. Luckily
he was re-elected to the Senate in 1930. The
house is now the residence of the Malaysian
ambassador. At left, a studio portrait of the
Senator and me when I was about ten.

My father, Gene, at West Point, where he won three sabers—football, track, basketball. He was also at the top of his class scholastically, and, in 1917, he became one of the army's first fliers.

My mother, Nina Gore, beautiful in youth.

The recently elected president, Franklin D. Roosevelt (*at left*), summoned Gene to Warm Springs, Georgia, to offer him the directorship of the Department of Air Commerce. Seated is Henry A. Wallace, just chosen Secretary of Agriculture. Below, Gene with Amelia Earhart. eight or nine, I proposed to them that they get married. (I wanted another mother.) Amelia w delighted; Gene blushed. Together they were involved in the founding of TWA, Eastern, and Northeast airlines.

he *Time* cover that Nina hurled in Gene's face because it was his face, not hers, on display. But then he was the famous director of Air Commerce; she was not.

Here I am in Eden, the Gores' house in Rock Creek Park, more or less my home until I was ten and moved to Merrywood with my mother and her new husband, Hugh D. Auchincloss.

The Merrys of Merrywood, around 1940. Hugh D. Auchincloss, my amiable, long-suffering stepfather; his son, Yusha; my grandmother, Dot; my grandfather, Senator Gore; and Nina and me. Nina's defiantly phallic hat betrays her inner need.

The only picture of Jimmie Trimble and me at St. Albans.
We are about thirteen. He is squinting in the sun, thinking about baseball.
I'm thinking about him.

At left, me at Merrywood. At right, graduating from Exeter in 1943, when I was seventeen. Below, the Los Alamos Ranch School in 1940. I couldn't wait to get out of there.

Jimmie Trimble in the Marines. This was taken in 1944, a few months before his death.

The winter of 1944–45, at Fort Richardson on mainland Alaska. Home until I was assigned my ship. Below, I am at the wheel of the F.S. 35, preparing for yet another perilous landing in the always bad weather of the Aleutians.

Anaïs Nin in a Maya Deren film of 1946. She had a major part. I was an extra. She fell out with Maya afterward because Maya had *deliberately* made her look old. Below, left, *Williwaw*, my first novel, which was published in the spring of 1946. I was twenty years old and everyone said that we were all too close to the war for a war novel, but the book was well reviewed and sold respectably. At right, Antigua, Guatemala, in the forties. In 1946 I bought a house there in which I finished *The City and the Pillar* and *The Season of Comfort*. High above sea level, Antigua had a perfect climate, as well as earthquakes.

WILLIWAW
a novel
gore vidal

In a piece on young writers in 1947, *Life* magazine posed me in front of a ship considerably larger than the one that I had been first mate of.

Paris, the summer of 1948.
I am still wearing my soldier's crew cut.

Dancers: above left, Harold Lang, "the beast of the ballet," as he was known; we are together in Bermuda (1947). Above right, I am with John Kriza–Billy the Kid–on a Florida beach in 1948. We spent a lot of time on beaches in the golden age. Now, homely skin cancers sprout. At left, a long-time friend, Leon Danielian: at his best in the ballets of Massine and Fokine.

To Jane
from Leon

Above, a party given by Tennessee, October 6, 1948, for the opening of *Summer and Smoke*. I am chatting with Marlon Brando's girlfriend, Celia Webb, as Marlon glumly picks his nose. I am twenty-three; he is twenty-four. We were usually the youngest people at such parties and always eyed each other warily. Below, same party. As far as I know, this is the only photograph of me with Capote and Tennessee. I am seriously staring out of frame.

Paul Bowles ready to go someplace, anyplace not in the United
States. We met in 1946 or '47; we are still corresponding friends after
a half century. He hates Italy. I hate Tangiers. So we write letters.

The most reproduced photograph from the forties. A number of writers at the Gotham Book
Mart welcome Edith and Osbert Sitwell to town. In the back, Tennessee and me. On the
ladder, Auden. At left, Stephen Spender. On the right, Marianne Moore, Randall Jarrell,
and Delmore Schwartz, going mad.

This picture, taken by Karl Bissinger for the first issue of a new magazine called *Flair*, best sums up the forties as I experienced them. Here is the ballet dancer Tanaquil LeClercq, soon to be Mrs. Balanchine; Donald Windham, a writer; Buffie Johnson, a painter; the Glorious Bird; and me.

I told Tennessee about Jimmie Trimble, and how I had no idea what would have happened had we ever met again and so, aware of the American panic on the subject, I had visualized the worst possible ending, rather, I added slyly, as Shakespeare had done for *Romeo and Juliet* and as Tennessee himself would do over and over again. Love is Death is Romance.

"Gore was a handsome kid, about twenty-four, and I was quite taken by his wit as well as his appearance." Incidentally, I am mesmerized by the tributes to my beauty that keep cropping up in the memoirs of the period. At the time, nobody reliable thought to tell me. In fact, it was my impression that I was not making out as well as most people because, with characteristic malice, Nature had allowed the actor Guy Madison to look like Guy Madison and not me.

"We found that we had interests in common and we spent a lot of time together. Please don't imagine that I'm suggesting that there was a romance." I don't remember whether or not I ever told Tennessee that I had actually seen but not met him the previous year. He was following me up Fifth Avenue while I, in turn, was stalking yet another quarry. I recognized him: He wore a blue bow tie with white polka dots. In no mood for literary encounters, I gave him a scowl and he abandoned the chase just north of Rockefeller Center. I don't recall how my own pursuit ended. We walked—cruised—a lot in the golden age.

"I believe we also went to Florence that season and were entertained by that marvelous old aesthete Berenson." No, that was someone else. "And then one afternoon Gore took me to the Convent of the Blue Nuns to meet the great philosopher and essayist, by then an octogenarian and semi-invalid, Santayana." I had to drag Tennessee to meet Santayana. Neither had heard of the other.

In 1985, after the Bird's death, I wrote:

Thirty-seven years ago, in March 1948, Tennessee Williams and I celebrated his thirty-seventh birthday in Rome, except that he said that it was his thirty-fourth birthday. Years later, when confronted with the fact that he had been born in 1911 not 1914, he said, serenely, "I do not choose to count as part of my life the three years that I spent working for a shoe company." Actually, he had spent ten months, not three years, in the shoe company, and the reason that he had

changed his birthdate was to qualify for a play contest open to those
twenty-five or under. No matter. I thought him very old in 1948.

I must say I was somewhat awed by Tennessee's success. In his *Mem-oirs*—and life—he went on and on about the years of poverty, yet, starting with *The Glass Menagerie* (1944), he had an astonishingly productive and successful fifteen years. But even at that high moment in Rome, the Bird's eye was coldly realistic. "Baby, the playwright's working career is a short one. There's always somebody new to take your place."

TENNESSEE WORKED every morning on whatever was at hand. If there was no play to be finished or new dialogue to be sent round to the theater, he would open a drawer and take out the draft of a story already written and begin to rewrite it. I once found him revising a short story that had just been published. "Why," I asked, "rewrite what's already in print?" He looked at me, vaguely; then he said, "Well, obviously it's not finished." And went back to his typing.

In Paris, he gave me the story "Rubio y Morena" to read. I didn't like it. So fix it, he said. He knew, of course, that there is no fixing someone else's story (or life), but he was curious to see what I would do. So I reversed backward-running sentences, removed repetitions, elimi-nated half those adjectives and adverbs that he always insisted do their work in pairs. I was proud of the result. He was deeply irritated. "What you have done is remove my *style*, which is all that I have."

Tennessee could not possess his own life until he had written about it. This is common. To start with, there would be, let us say, a sexual desire for someone. Consummated or not, the desire ("something that is made to occupy a larger space than that which is afforded by the indi-vidual being") would produce reveries. In turn, the reveries would be written down as a story. But should the desire still remain unfulfilled, he would make a play of the story and then—and this is why he was so compulsive a working playwright—he would have the play produced so that he could, at relative leisure, like God, rearrange his original expe-rience into something that was no longer God's and unpossessable but *his.* The Bird's frantic lifelong pursuit of—and involvement in—play pro-ductions was not just ambition or a need to be busy; it was the only way that he ever had of being entirely alive. The sandy encounters with his first real love, a dancer, on the beach at Provincetown and the dancer's later death ("an awful flower grew in his brain"), instead of being forever lost, were forever his once they had been translated to the stage, where living men and women could act out his text and with their immediate flesh close at last the circle of desire. "For love I make characters in plays," he wrote; and did.

I had long since forgotten why I called him the Glorious Bird until I came to reread his stories for a preface that I would write. The image of the bird is everywhere in his work. The bird is flight, poetry, life. The bird is time, death: "Have you ever seen the skeleton of a bird? If you have you will know how completely they are still flying." In his last story, written at seventy-one, "The Negative," he wrote of a poet who can no longer assemble a poem. "Am I a wingless bird?" he writes; and soars no longer.

ONE OF THE BIRD'S academic biographers wanted to know if he had ever said anything witty or wise. I suppose too much had been made of his later years, when he was often on pills or drunk and not always coherent. But, at his best, he was corrosively funny. After listening to a boorish youth in a bar repeat for the hundredth time, "Live and let live is my motto," the Bird finally said, with grave courtesy, "Surely, in your situation, there is no alternative philosophy."

The fiercely busy and tragical director Kazan was Stanislavsky to the Bird's Chekhov. Where Tennessee or Chekhov intended a comic effect, the two directors insisted on fierce passion and tears. Invariably, at the end of *A Streetcar Named Desire,* when the audience was barking like seals as the broken Blanche DuBois is led away, with the poignant cry, "I have always depended upon the kindness of strangers," the Bird's whoop of laughter would echo in the snuffling theater, and he would say, loudly, "Now she's off to the bughouse."

In London I acted as interpreter between the Bird and Claire Bloom when she was about to take on the role of Blanche. The Bird didn't think she was right for the part, but he had agreed to the production. Claire was jittery. He offered her a cigarette. "I don't smoke," she said, grabbing the cigarette and inhaling deeply as he lit it. "Except one, just before dinner, always in the evening," she babbled. The Bird looked at her suspiciously; then he said, "Do you have any questions about the play?"

"Yes." Claire pulled herself together. "What happens *after* the final curtain?"

The Bird sat back in his chair, narrowed his eyes. "No actress has ever asked me that question." He shut his eyes; thought. "She will enjoy her time in the bin. She will seduce one or two of the more comely young doctors. Then she will be let free to open an attractive boutique in the French Quarter . . ."

"She wins?"

"Oh, yes," said the Bird. "Blanche wins." The result was splendid. Claire gained greater and greater strength as the play proceeded and, at the end, she leaves for the bin as for a coronation. Audiences cheered, not knowing how one psychological adjustment, made in the smoke of one cigarette at dusk, had changed the nature of a famous play.

AT ELEVEN-THIRTY every morning, a tourist boat passes below the house, and from four hundred meters below, I hear a woman's voice describing, first in Italian, then in English, the villa of Gore Vidal. I hear my name clearly but cannot make out exactly what she is saying. Last year Nureyev said that she also discussed him as he lay in bed on his island off Positano. "She come to me first. *Nine* o'clock." He rather enjoyed her. I don't. I feel as if I were being forced to listen in on an extension telephone where I am being discussed. Doubtless, I am reacting against my mother who was a compulsive eavesdropper, as well as interceptor of the mail of others.

Nina's spying backfired during a September-July romance that she was having with an actor in Southampton. On an extension telephone, she heard him speak lovingly to a man in New York whom he was to see the following day. Furiously, Nina confronted him. Not only was he two-timing her, he was, as she had always feared—let's face it—a sexual degenerate. He admitted the first; denied the second because "That was not a man," he said. "That was the actress Edith Atwater. She has a very deep voice, and we are being married tomorrow." Later, Edith was in a road company of my play *The Best Man*. Once we made eye contact at a rehearsal and, without a word, both laughed at Nina.

The Guest of
the Blue Nuns

YEARS AFTER 1948, Frederic Prokosch was to write a book called *Voices* in which he described every famous person he had ever met. He had kept careful notes, he assured the reader. I gave him a wary review, and praised him for literary virtues that had been unfairly overlooked for more than a generation. But I was uneasy with his "voices" of the great, since it was plain to me that he had simply made up most of them. The few that he did catch from real life, like Auden, are sharp and one does hear a real voice; but with George Santayana, say, whom I took him to meet in Rome, he simply invents, rather lazily, what he thinks Santayana *ought* to have said as opposed to what he did say.

Santayana is largely forgotten now, but he was once a commanding philosopher known for his silver style and elusive persona. In 1935, he published his only novel, *The Last Puritan,* an attractive story that I read as a boy, half guessing at the emotional currents that he sets in motion when he describes how a New England Puritan youth, Oliver Alden (alpha omega, beginning and end) tries to find himself. Even I, a pubescent, could identify with his search. But then it is a book for the young. Later I read *The Idea of Christ in the Gospels.* I also made a number of partially successful attempts to grasp Santayana's formal philosophy. This was the background to our meeting, which took place simply enough.

*George Santayana (1863–1952). I saw him
a number of times in the spring of 1948. He
was, to me, in every way admirable. It is
ironic that he is now pretty much forgotten
except for a single aphorism: "Those who
cannot remember the past are condemned
to repeat it."*

I presented myself at the convent of the Blue Nuns on the Celian hill. A sister—the nuns are Irish—met me in the hall. What was my business? I would like to see Professor Santayana (Professor has more resonance in Italy than it has for us). I am a young American student, I added, as bait. Well, I was American and twenty-two.

The nun left me at the entrance to a long hallway with doors to left and right. She opened one of them, on the right. A small figure glided toward me, the light behind him. Santayana's routine with callers was simple. If he was interested, he would invite them back to his cell; if not, he would say a few polite words and withdraw.

We shook hands, he looked up at me with bright round black eyes that reminded me of someone I knew well. He wore a dressing gown, a Byronic shirt open at the neck, and a faded mauve-gray waistcoat from the 1890s. The voice—although I have an aural memory and can usually mimic almost anyone, I cannot recall his voice other than that it was agreeable, very much Harvard of the last century, where he had taught alongside William James . . . well, *counter* to William James. Santayana's father had been Spanish, as was his mother, who later married a Sturges of Boston. He looked Spanish but sounded Sturges; he had made himself the first—and perhaps last—Epicurean Puritan.

"Come in," he said after a few words of exchange. As the bright eyes stared at me, I realized that they were the eyes, and indeed the face, of my beloved grandmother Gore, gone mysteriously bald.

The cell had an iron bed, with a screen partly around it, a small book-case with fewer than a dozen books; a writing table with chair; a second chair for visitors. He had lived at the Bristol Hotel during the war, but when the Nazis came, it had seemed politic to vanish into the convent-hospital. He was eighty-five when I met him.

"I shall talk and you shall listen," he said, with a smile. "You can ask questions, of course. But remember I am *very* deaf." I felt like Phaedo with Socrates. He held up a section of a book whose binding he had removed. As he finished reading each section, he would drop it into a wastebasket, "I am reading someone called Toynbee. Do you know him? No? I gather he is some sort of preacher who involves himself with history. The footnotes are not entirely worthless. Perhaps you know my *new* young friend, Robert Lowell?" I said that I had met him. "He writes to me regularly. He is gifted as a poet, isn't he? I no longer write poetry." This seemed to mean, Nor read it either. But he had read

Lowell's *Lord Weary's Castle*. "What a difficult time he is going to have, though I don't dare tell him so. He is a Lowell. From Boston. He is also a poet and now . . . now . . . he is a Roman Catholic convert. Isn't that all perhaps too much for one young man?"

I did not know Lowell well enough in 1948 to be able to remark that Lowell was also, periodically, mad as a hatter and a great torment to the three talented women he married. I always liked to compete with the sane Lowell in conversation–and competition was what he most enjoyed. Once at my house on the Hudson, we talked of Caesar. I remarked on Cicero's report to Atticus on Caesar's visit to his house, and how delighted Cicero was when Caesar–the true politician–praised his consulship.

Lowell moved smoothly in to take the trick. "And remember," he said, "Cicero's remark on how unnerving it was to have Caesar for a house-guest?"

What is the point to any knowledge unless one can share it? Did we learn these things in school? No, we read them on our own in order to meet the personages of the past with whom Lowell was as eager to compete as with his contemporaries. He was forever making up lists of the best, second best, third best this or that (usually poets). I told Mary McCarthy that he was currently making more and more far-fetched comparisons, like, Is Mary McCarthy a better critic than Saint-Beuve? Mary's eyes become adamantine. I recovered quickly: "Well, that's too reasonable as you're both critics. It's as if he . . ." Mary finished for me: "As if he had said, Is Mary McCarthy a better general than Joan of Arc?"

"Tell me, do you know a Mr. Edmund Wilson? He came to see me. He led me to believe that he was a very famous man of letters, which no doubt he is. He said that I had sent him a book. I said that he was mistaken. He said that, no, I had signed it to Edmund Wilson. At first I was firm, but then I remembered that when the American army came–and, oh! how glad we were to see them in Rome!" The black eyes glittered with a fine obsidian malice. "And an army major came here with several of my books for me to sign and as I was so grateful, so *very* grateful for this liberation, I threw caution to the winds and signed copies to this one and to that one. Edmund Wilson was apparently that one."

Wilson had paid his call on Santayana three years before me, in April 1945. He wrote it up immediately, and so his detailed account is apt to be more precise than mine forty-five years later: "He received me with simplicity and courtesy and excused himself for reclining on a little chaise longue with a blanket over his legs." I don't remember a chaise longue. The comedy of the autographed copy of his memoirs, *Persons and Places,* was duly played. Santayana told me that although he sometimes signed books for people, he never wrote the person's name unless he knew him. Wilson had taken it for granted that Santayana had sent him a book as an *hommage* to the powerful critic of *The New Yorker* magazine. "Santayana seemed to want to slip away from the subject, but I was nonplused and embarrassed at coming to see him when he did not know who I was." Fame. "With a freedom that surprised me, however, he at once began talking about his recent books: *Persons and Places* and *The Middle Span.*"

I didn't talk to him about these two memoirs because I'd not yet read them. I did ask about *The Idea of Christ in the Gospels,* written in the convent. I had had a long argument with a friend about Santayana's chapter on Christ's miracles. As Santayana gravely—even reverently—describes each miracle, the analyzed miracle becomes ever more absurd as, all the while, he maintains the usual priestly line that since all life is a miracle, then what we may not understand could be . . . and so on. I was blunt: Does *he* actually believe in them? The answer was quick. "Oh, no." He smiled what Wilson called his "mischievous smile" and paused: "On the ground, of course, that there is not enough evidence." Wilson remarks that someone said that Santayana was a Catholic in everything but faith. Santayana himself is supposed to have said, "There is no God and Mary is his mother."

I asked about Henry James. He gave a sort of imitation of Henry's paraphrastic style; then sighed. "Oh, the James brothers!" He sounded as if he were invoking the outlaws. Perhaps he was; Santayana was about twenty years old when Jesse James hit the dust. "One was a novelist who thought he was a philosopher," the old man said—for the hundredth time?—"and the other was a philosopher who thought he was a novelist." I cannot remember much else, though I did take notes in a diary that winter and spring in Rome. I must look them up.

I brought the composer Samuel Barber, Prokosch, and Tennessee to meet him. He was amused, I think, by the first two and mystified by the Bird. Although the Bird had never heard of him, the Bird's bright eye watched him carefully and the Bird's perfect ear picked up Santayana's reading of the line "That was in the days when I had young secretaries." Later, the Bird repeated the line with relish and rolled his eyes heavenward.

I saw Santayana two or three times alone. He never asked me a question about myself, and I never volunteered information. He had given Wilson the same treatment: "One of the wonderful things about him was the readiness and grace with which he played a classical role: that of the sage who has made it his business to reflect on all kinds of men and who will talk about the purpose and practice of life with anyone who likes to discuss them—as with me, whom he didn't know from Adam . . ."

I recall two arias. One that began on the subject of the mystics, in which he tended to include the egotists, as he called them, of German philosophy. This ended on the pure Santayanan note, a plainspoken, even wide-eyed statement, swiftly canceled by an unexpected comment: "I am not a mystic." Full stop. Then the eyes—yes, widened, and the mischievous smile switched on: "But I can *imagine* what it must be like." This reopens the door to reveal . . . what? Another door, I should think. What is mysticism but imagination?

Finally, on the transience of reputation and of history itself. "In America literary reputations come and go so swiftly," I complained, fatuously. The answer was swift. "It would be insufferable if they did *not*."

I commented on how bloody the century that we had lived in was. He looked surprised. "Why, I have lived most of my life in one of the longest periods of peace ever known. I was born at the end of the American Civil War while those two German wars together lasted—how long? Nine years? Out of the eighty-five years that I've been alive, nine years of war is nothing." Plainly, he was suggesting that I must cultivate the long view. We spoke of the coming election in Italy. American propaganda daily told us that Italy was in danger of going Communist, and if that happened, Western civilization would be extinguished.

I have just shut my eyes. I used to be able to summon up scenes at will, but now aging memory is so busy weeding its own garden that, promiscuously, it pulls up roses as well as crabgrass. In any case, the room is too full of light for me to see clearly what is—much less what was. I ask him why he never wrote another novel.

A great smile: "How could I? You see, I've never really knocked about that much." I liked the "knocked about."

I open my eyes in present time but continue to hear, if not see, Santayana talking about a possible Communist takeover of Italy. He is disconcertingly blithe. "Why not? After all, they have tried everything else. This will be something new for them, something perhaps even useful, because who knows what life will be like in a . . . in a wolf pack? Who knows what sort of new energies, relationships, loyalties will emerge?" The irony shone along with the morning sun on the pale bald head.

Then he opened a picture book and showed me colored sketches of Guards officers in some nineteenth-century regiment. "The illustrations are nice."

I rose to go. This was my last visit. Alarmed by our imperial propaganda machine, I feared that Italy was about to undergo the standard "bloodbath" that our press is always eager to draw for other people. I said goodbye.

"I shall give you a book," he said. From the bookcase, he took a copy of the second volume of his memoirs, *The Middle Span.* "What is your name?" I told him. "You see," he said, as he carefully wrote at his table, "I shall write 'for' you. I rarely do this, except of course when liberated by the American army." I have the book on my desk: "For Gore Vidal, George Santayana, April 1, 1948."

"It is your April Fool's present." He led me to the door to the corridor. "How old are you?"

"Twenty-two."

"You have written a book?"

"Three, in fact."

"You look young for your age, but then your head is small in proportion to your body." In those days I wore a crew cut. "When I was your age I wanted to be an architect at Harvard. But there was an opening in philosophy . . ." He walked me slowly down the corridor to the entrance hall. "I've often wondered what life would have been like as an architect. I'm not sure that I could have handled the mathematical part very well, but I believe that I would have been good at decoration."

He gave me his cold old hand. I shook it. "I think you will have a happy life." He smiled and the black eyes glittered. "Because you lack superstition. If you come back to Rome, pay me a call, assuming that I'm still here." I did, but did not see him. He was to live four more years.

Prokosch's Santayana is entirely made up: "His head sags a little. His eyes begin to water. His voice rose imperceptibly, as though for a final effort. 'We are sailing ever deeper into the dark, uncharted waters. The lights in the lighthouses are beginning to go out. Is there anything to guide us? Is there anyone worth listening to? I wake up in the middle of the night and I'm cold with terror.' " I fear this is a libel, and I grow irritated with my dead friend Fritz.

Wilson gets the tone right: "This little husk of a man, at once so ascetic and so cheerful, sustaining at eighty-one so steady an intellectual energy, inhabiting a convent cell, among the layers of historical debris that composed the substance of Rome, intact and unmoved by the tides of invasions and revolution that have been brawling back and forth around him; and when he talked about these outside occurrences it was as if he attached them to history: the war was an event like any other which would presently belong to the past." A past that Santayana belongs to—as well as Wilson and Prokosch and nearly everyone else that I knew in 1948, all past and gone.

Years later I became a friend of Philip Rahv, a literary critic as well as editor of *Partisan Review*. The only row that I ever had with Philip was when he remarked, in passing, that Santayana had sent him an essay from Rome (probably a chapter of *Dominations and Powers*), which Philip had sent back, unread, because, "What's *he* got to say to us now?" I said, "Everything," and more.

There is a strain of flippant anti-Semitism in Santayana's letters and *obiter dicta* that makes uncomfortable reading, but it is all a part of a general dislike of both nationalism and tribalism. As he wrote to his Jewish assistant at Harvard: "[Nationalism] is at once interior and exterior, or political; how can Italian, Balkan, Irish or Zionist Americans combine in an entity between the two? . . . It is the difficulty of realizing either of these ideals that seems to me to make nationality a problem rather than a solution." The idea of any people as "chosen" he finds romantic in the worst sense; finally, it is not the Jews that disturb him but the Germans. As early as the First War, he found that in their tribes there was "something sinister at work, something at once hollow and aggressive." *Egotism in German Philosophy* describes how, after Napoleon's invasion, Fichte and Hegel cobbled together a worldview that Providence intended for the German people "to occupy the supreme place in the history of the universe." Of this "revealed philosophy" Santayana notes, "It is the heir of Judaism," and he finds it to be not so much religious as a mad idealism in service to the state: "In this philosophy imagination that is sustained is called knowledge, illusion that is coherent is called truth, and will that is systematic is called virtue." This was written in 1916.

The most famous of Santayana's aphorisms is: "Those who cannot remember the past are condemned to repeat it." A generation later the forgetful Germans made a second bid for supremacy, and again failed. Santayana despised fanaticism; after all, the title of his five-volume "philosophy" is *The Life of Reason.* He was a materialist of the Epicurean school of Democritus and Lucretius; and he suspected that despite all his notions of the tribe and self and will and God and *"Skepticism and Animal Faith,"* "Chaos is perhaps at the bottom of everything."

THE PRESENT INTRUDES. Yesterday was the longest day of the year, June 21, 1993, and always to be celebrated if only with full attention. Hot, dry, luminous; a cool wind starts up as the sun passes the limestone cliff to our west. I sat at the pool, idly reading Hazlitt's political journalism, deploring his exclamation marks, while noting, rather grimly, how this sort of journalism tends, in future time, to die upon the page.

Swifts dive-bomb the pool. Dragonflies skim the dark blue water. The pool's navy-blue interior produces a pale star-sapphire effect when the noon sun strikes it.

The past is now working overtime for me. In the mail, a set of photographs of the fiftieth reunion of my class at St. Albans. I recognize only two or three of the stout, gray old men. There's an accompanying letter from a master, first appointed in the year that the class graduated. He, too, found it hard to recognize the golden youths of a half century ago. He reported how one of them, an athlete named Carter, had gone to see Ted Smith, now in a "mental home."

Ted was a droll, gangling dark-haired boy whom Jimmie had bedded before me. Ted's life has not been happy—alcoholism, divorces, and now he is institutionalized. When Carter first heard that Jimmie had been killed, he had had a nervous breakdown. Now, long since recovered, he sat with Ted, who babbled of "green fields." When Carter mentioned

Jimmie, Ted was galvanized. Sat up straight, and said, "Why, he was just here. He just now left. If you hurry, you can find him in the hall."

Was there ever so furious and restless a ghost? Or is it that we, the survivors, are so traumatized to this day by his abrupt absence from our lives that we are still trying to summon his ghost? For years, whenever I was in a numinous place like Delphi or Delos, I would address the night: Jimmie, are you anywhere? and almost always the wind would rise. But I am neither a believer in an afterlife nor a mystic, and unlike Santayana, I cannot begin to imagine what it must be like. Yet I still want Jimmie to *be*, somewhere, if only on this page.

A new biography of Anaïs has just arrived. It is a joy. According to the biographer, I wanted people to believe that Anaïs was my mistress. I, who skulked along country lanes for fear that I be seen with her. Then, after the biographer reveals that Anaïs was a compulsive liar, she blithely writes that at twenty I had wanted to marry Anaïs, as a cover for my sex life! No source is given for any of this nonsense. She also proclaims that we had no "affair." This is true. I have never had an affair with anyone. Sex, yes. Friendships, yes. The two combined? No. Jimmie, of course, was something else–me.

Paris,
Proust's Whorehouse,
Gide, Bowles,
and Isherwood

I WENT FROM ROME TO CAIRO where I finished *A Search for the King* in the old Shepheard's Hotel. Cairo was like a French provincial city, relatively uncrowded and presided over by a fat young king, Farouk. I watched him one evening at the Auberge des Pyramides, a nightclub near the Sphinx. Like a mafia don, with dark glasses, he was surrounded by plainclothesmen, also in dark glasses. Farouk was on the prowl for large blond women. Later, when he was in exile in Rome, I used to see him at the Café de Paris on the Via Veneto, always at the same table, always with a different large blonde. One night a thief grabbed the blonde's purse and fled with it into the *dolce vita* night. She screamed; Farouk laughed with delight.

In Cairo I was taken up by some wonderfully shady characters. One was the sad, plump, middle-aged son of the last sultan of the Ottoman Empire; he had married a sister of King Zog of Albania. He wooed me sadly and hopelessly beside the pool at Mena House. He looked like a sensitive dentist. He was also the only person I ever met who sighed the way that characters are supposed to sigh in novels, which is where, of course, he ended up–in *The Judgment of Paris*, the first book where I abandoned the somewhat affected, plain-plywood style of what I long ago christened "the national manner" and spoke, as it were, in my own voice. It was a bit like being let out of the army. With that book, I felt that I could try–if not do–anything.

Paris, spring 1948. Clifford Coffin, an American photographer who worked for Vogue, *was commissioned to photograph me. Coffin preferred natural light, and so we spent a morning on the left bank of the Seine, waiting for the right light to come off the river.*

Under the influence of Karnak and the Valley of the Kings, I wrote a powerful play. I forget the subject, but I thought the result sublime. After Tennessee read it, he said, rather thoughtfully, "You must not have been well in Cairo. The water's bad, I am told. I think this is the worst play I have ever read."

In Cairo I was also beginning to invent some of the characters that I would use in *Messiah*. At Luxor, I started to hear the voice of the narrator of what was to be my first novel in the first person.

I moved on to Paris, where I stayed at the Pont Royal Hotel. Sartre and de Beauvoir held court in the downstairs bar: Tourists had driven them from the Café Flore. Now, at century's end, I find it hard to believe that I once lived in a time when writers were world figures because of what they wrote, and that their ideas were known even to the vast perennial majority that never reads.

The world paid close attention to Sartre and Camus, and people took sides in their duels. Gide and Mauriac and, my favorite, de Montherlant, were like oracles to be consulted. It was as if literature, in its last act, decided to have one final great Paris season and we Americans–British, Italians, too–came dutifully to Paris to see the gods in what proved to be their twilight, though none of us suspected that we had come at the end of the day and that the horses of the night were, contrary to Faust's prayer, running very fast indeed. In our youthful innocence, we mistook early evening for morning. In Paris, there were Bellow and Mailer and Capote and Baldwin and Bowles, while Tennessee and I shared a floor of the small Hôtel de l'Université. As the century unfolded, we would all be duly admired and known while becoming, simultaneously, mere coda to a more and more irrelevant Western literature.

This summer at a Salzburg seminar, I described what it had been like to live at a time when writing was still central to the culture if not *the* culture. One of the schoolteachers was indignant. "What a romantic view! As if Sartre and Camus were of any literary consequence." For her, they had been surpassed and replaced by Derrida, Foucault, and a lady who teaches currently at the Sorbonne. But Derrida is faded now, while Foucault's fateful, fatal adventures in the San Francisco bathhouses made him, briefly, a secular saint in the time of AIDS. I suppose that that is some distinction: But a half million people attended

Sartre's funeral, and of that number, perhaps half had once read him, with passion.

Tennessee decided to celebrate his arrival in Paris with a party at the hotel. The translator, Duhamel, was told to invite the gods. He did. The gods did not come. Sartre sat nearby, alone, in the bar of the Pont Royal, conspicuously *not* attending the Bird's *vernissage*. A few actresses showed up: interested in the part of Blanche DuBois, which they had read about in the press.

The angry Bird sent Duhamel to Sartre. Duhamel returned to say that Sartre was on his way. In general, the French gods kept their distance from all of us. But then they were some twenty years behind in their reading of American literature. Dos Passos's *Manhattan Transfer* was the popular American novel that season. They also liked Horace McCoy and James M. Cain. They were barely up to Hemingway, while Fitzgerald was unknown. I made a reference to him in a novel that was translated into French a few years later; the publisher provided the reader with a footnote explaining, helpfully, that F. Scott Fitzgerald had been the English translator of the *Rubáiyát of Omar Khayyám.*

John Lehmann, my English publisher, appeared. Tall, with ice-blue eyes, he had been an editor at Virginia Woolf's Hogarth Press. During the war, he had published Penguin's *New Writing,* a monthly anthology; then he started his own publishing house. He got me through Isherwood, while I got him the Bird and Paul Bowles. He also published Bellow and Delmore Schwartz, a prescient American list for the late forties.

I AM READING Rousseau's *Confessions* as I write what now seems to be a sort of travelogue in past time. I am curious to know how others manage their memoirs. Tennessee made a mess of his–too much sex and not enough about the work or even the people that he met. But then, as he told me, he had simply dictated a lot of material and left it to an editor to shape. "I have never actually read the book in question." I believe him.

Now I break in on myself. Where is this narrative going? I suddenly appreciate the value of *conscious* fiction, where the protagonist, at least in his creator's mind, moves toward some goal or calculated terminus.

But in this text I am not moving toward anything that I am aware of, and the flora and fauna that I observe along the way are getting to look a bit random and incoherent and too much like life, of which we all have the same chaotic impressions.

Rousseau himself barely holds my interest. He is now describing his early life; he runs away from home; falls in love with an older woman, who keeps him for a time; then he converts to Catholicism in order to get a place to live during the period of conversion. I've always liked the idea of Rousseau if only because conservatives so hate him. Burke makes him responsible for the French Revolution. And once, in my presence, a Tory publicist declared that he was evil incarnate. I find him, so far, a humorless bore, while Santayana found Rousseau, along with Martin Luther, both "intensely unintelligent . . . yet the world followed them, not to turn back."

"I desire to set before my fellows the likeness of a man in all the truth of nature, and that man myself." My immediate response is *why?* For one thing, you cannot do it. You can confess to all sorts of crimes that most people hide, but at the end, what has one got? A list. At least Augustine was working for his church when he decided to confess to having stolen some pears as a boy, an episode which the bemused Oliver Wendell Holmes described to Harold Laski as "a bit rum." One should do better than that when it comes to crime. Perhaps at the end of his confession, I will be in a mood to absolve him but thus far, his monotonous self-love is Nin-like in its intensity.

Ominously, he writes, "Nothing that concerns myself shall remain obscure or hidden; that I shall keep myself continually before [my] eyes . . ." Yet there are few strong scenes and not much remembered dialogue. What one does get is a querulous tone of voice. One feels that he is obliged to write in this way because he has spent a lifetime solemnly regarding himself and rehashing the various injustices that he has collected along his sacred way. One doesn't feel that one knows him as one knows Flaubert or Byron from their letters and notebooks. Worse, one doesn't really want to know him at all.

I do begin to understand why Rousseau liked to assert that the arts and sciences have conferred no real benefits on mankind. He thought that only by a return to nature could man—the noble savage—find his true identity. Since "man is naturally good, and only by institutions is he made bad." Paradoxically, he thought the only merit to be found for man was in war; at the time that he was writing, 1750, civilized Europeans were mopping up the noble savages of the two Americas. Certainly he is true ancestor to Marx when he writes, "The first man who, having enclosed a piece of land, bethought himself of saying 'this is mine,' and found people simple enough to believe him was the real founder of civil society." As well as the real founder of those wars that, paradoxically, appeal to Rousseau; were it not for the notion of private property–real estate or women–there would be no wars and so, for Rousseau, no merit in life. Thus, contradictions define as they undo us.

When Rousseau sent Voltaire his "Discourse on Inequality," the great man was amused: "I have received your new book against the human race, and thank you for it. Never was such a cleverness used in the design of making us all stupid. One longs, in reading your book, to walk on all fours. But as I have lost that habit for more than sixty years, I feel unhappily the impossibility of resuming it. Nor can I embark in search of the savages of Canada, because the maladies to which I am condemned render a European surgeon necessary to me; because war is going on in these regions and because the example of our actions has made the savages nearly as bad as ourselves."

A few years later, in "The Social Contract" Rousseau questioned the divine right of kings and spoke up for democracy. One is not surprised to learn that he was befriended by two kings, Frederick the Great of Prussia and, surprisingly, George III of England. Burke found Rousseau vain. Hume noted, "He has only *felt* during the whole course of his life..." Certainly he does not seem to have thought much. In fact, he, more than any other philosopher, puts feeling ahead of reason, and so made romanticism inevitable for those who were moved by such rhetoric as: "Man is born free, and everywhere he is in chains. One man thinks himself the master of others, but remains more of a slave than they are." This reverberates still. Yet "what does it mean?" as I was taught at Exeter to ask myself when faced with any statement. Man is born a baby; and what baby was ever free?

YESTERDAY, JULY 15, turned out a perfect day in what today's newspaper assures us will be a brief, very brief interregnum before a hot phase followed by the arrival, I suppose, of glaciers, now overdue by several millennia. A slice of glacial ice has revealed the weather of the last 250,000 years. Apparently, dramatic shifts from hot to cold are the rule, not the exception. The last ten thousand years has been so comfortable for our breed that we have bred like a mutant strain of bacteria. But the hot and the cold will come again and it is possible that we may not have time to adjust from the present moderate temperatures to a sudden heating up and melting of the polar ice caps, the flooding of coastal cities, and then new glaciers. We are apt to become extinct, a consoling thought on one of the most beautiful days that I remember here on the coast or anywhere else for that matter. The light is an intense gold that irradiates the rooms that overlook the—yes, cobalt sea four hundred meters below the cliff onto which the house is built.

I walked in the chestnut woods that grow on a fairly steep incline—the property is some seven acres of terraces, each with its own character; vines on one, a lemon orchard on another, as well as olive trees and rose gardens; each terrace has its own view of the sea below and beyond. Only in the woods can one see nothing but green. The reflection of the intense gold light through the green leaves is dazzling. I ponder the eventual scorching of these woods, to be followed by the creeping flow of sterile ice. World disaster is always comforting to contemplate if not to undergo. My imagination is often triggered by the "what if" that leads to the end of things.

The perfect day continued until moonless night. I swam in the pool and saved a small lizard from drowning. I recalled the grubby pool at the Royal Lodge at Windsor, where Princess Margaret and I, in mid-pool, saved a number of bees from drowning, she exhorting them in a powerful Hanoverian voice to "go forth and make honey!"

Mention of her here reminds me that I read too many of those magazines that seem to have taken the place of books for those still able to read. Yet, without much pleasure, I am reading Hazlitt's political writings. I had the same experience with Orwell once he got off literature and popular culture and onto the politics of his day. How quickly our day's urgencies turn tedious.

Popular revue sketch in London circa 1930: An earnest woman, in fustian evening gown with a necklace of wooden beads, crosses to lectern at center stage and says, in a loud voice, "India." The curtain falls to ecstatic applause.

When Orwell writes, "Spain," or Hazlitt, "Napoleon," one's eyelids droop. Surely this does not happen when *I* write "Ron and Nancy" . . . At least my characters are inherently comic, or so I find them. Today, I wonder why I am so content, inhabiting as I do a body so keen to disassemble. Then I realize why, perfect day to one side: I do not want anything. I am past all serious desire for anything–at the moment, anyway. The Buddha was right: To want is to suffer.

TWO WEEKS IN Germany, Norway, and Austria. Good to get away from paradise. The point to paradise is to get away from it in order to want to get back. Spoke at the America Houses in Leipzig, Berlin, Hamburg, Cologne, Frankfurt. Stuttgart and Munich. A weekend in Norway, where I spoke at a festival in the north, at Molde. I also experienced the Arctic white night, which never ends in that season. It is no wonder that the natives take to drink. Sat on a boat in a fjord, eating freshly caught shrimp. Herons decorated the green woods, and perched on gray rocks. The horizon at Molde is a circle of more than a hundred mountain peaks, each capped with snow year-round.

I am followed about by a journalist from the principal Oslo newspaper. He keeps asking, How is it possible for so famous an American writer not to be translated? Only my worst novel, *In a Yellow Wood*, 1947, has been published in Norwegian. I keep saying that he must ask a Norwegian publisher, not me. The usual answer is that *everyone* reads English in Scandinavia, which is not true, though a number do, as I discovered when asked to sign ancient paperbacks in English.

Finally, a novelist explained to the journalist that I had been critical of the American empire, to which Norway was humbly attached. "We were always cringing toward the English, as our protector. Then, since the war, we have had the same relationship with the United States. So any American writer that our American master doesn't approve of we ignore."

Though I am published in Germany, I am usually invisible, and a German editor in Berlin said, "As a conquered province for forty-five years, we would never do anything that might displease the Americans. Germans are very disciplined, you know; that's why there is no need for censorship. Everyone censors himself automatically. Even our left has hardly any idea that people like you and Chomsky exist in America.

They think the U.S. is a capitalistic monolith where everyone writes like John Updike, supporting the consumer society . . ."

"And empire," I added helpfully. Then, to be fair to Updike, I add to my addition, "He is very radical on the subject of adultery . . ."

"A great theme," the editor agrees. "Perhaps the only theme."

"Certainly more important than politics or . . . or radicalism." I say the terrible word: taboo in Germany as well as America. "What else is literature," I intone, "but marriage by other means?"

I have just noted that *The City and the Pillar* has never been published anywhere in Scandinavia, while it was only published in Germany a few years ago, by a gay ghetto publishing house. On the other hand, Eastern Europeans, freed of *their* imperial puritan master, are publishing it in a half-dozen translations. The Czechs have also just brought out *Duluth*. At least I have arrived in eastern Mitteleuropa. Curious that a career like mine should be almost as conditioned by the political weather as that of any writer in the old Soviet Union.

Philip Roth told me how, years ago, he used to meet with a Czech writer who was popular only in the underground samizdat. The writer naturally longed for aboveground publication. Philip said that it wasn't all that wonderful; in fact, he envied the Czech's dedicated audience. What the Czech wrote mattered a great deal to those who read him, while nothing that is written matters much to anyone in the United States. The Czech was not convinced. Philip gave him the American reviews of his latest book. The Czech read them: "I see what you mean," he said. "You must carry about with you a great deal of stupidity."

I have made a tentative peace with *The New York Times*. The editor of the editorial page just rang up; he's in Positano; he will come to lunch on Monday. Meanwhile, a magazine in London offers me what I am told is "a fortune" to interview the prime minister. I pointed out that if they really wanted to make a splash, John Major should interview me. After all, he too reads Trollope. We could talk about the Master. I say no to all book chat now. No book reviewing after forty, said the critic F. W. Dupee. I am well past the cutoff. Actually, to do a piece well takes a long time, and time is not a thing that I am eager to fling idly through life's transom window.

I find ruminating upon the past interesting when I focus on someone else; less so when confronted with my youthful self, an elusive–even blank–figure whom I don't remember much about. Meanwhile, as the day's blue, gold, and green rush by, one wonders just how much more time one has before extinction. If I live as long as my father, five years; as long as my mother, seven years; as long as the Senator, ten years; as long as my grandmother, fifteen years, the last few shaking to pieces in her bed with Parkinson's disease and crying out for Demerol, which Dr. Huffman, the morphine-giver to my mother, refused to give a woman in her eighties for fear that she might become an addict.

I admire Fred Dupee's departure; he had lunch in his house at Carmel with friends and wife. He remarked upon the beauty of the day; was in excellent form even though he was soon to go into the hospital for an operation, cancer of the bladder. Later, alone in the house, he wrote a farewell note–a distinguished literary critic, Fred had an allergy to writing anything at all by this time and so the composition of a last letter must have annoyed him; then he took pills, a most elegant stoic departure. I believe he is the only writer ever to begin a book with the word *although*.

SOMETHING ABOUT DESCRIBING John Lehmann wrenched me away from the time machine. I return. He had a tiger's grin, liked to call people Ducky. Sexually, it was his pleasure to beat working-class boys; otherwise, he lived a life of perfect domestic virtue with a ballet dancer called Alexis Racine, an uncommonly plain, uncommonly effeminate man.

I had not taken into account that when I wrote *The City and the Pillar* I would become a figure of great interest to the fag world, about which I knew rather less than the book suggests. I sensed, correctly, that the grand queens would dislike the book not only for its lack of chic, but because the "hetero" boy gets fucked by the protagonist, an act very much against their nature.

Meanwhile, a pack of queens were on the move that summer in Europe. Some lived by their wits, others on remittances from home. In 1948 they converged on Rome and Paris and Tangier. In the next decade, it would be Athens and Istanbul; later Tokyo, where life was cheap in the seventies and Americans honored. Then Tokyo extruded them and the survivors fled the setting sun for San Francisco. Of the peripatetic group that centered on Tennessee, Capote, the Bowleses–

not me, I was fugitive—all but one is dead. In America I had steered clear of them, though I would sometimes visit the Blue Parrot on Lexington Avenue, a faggot bar above which General Dwight D. Eisenhower had his office. Did he know? I once took my stepsister-in-law, the actress Ella Raines, to the bar. My stepbrother was regular army, West Point. "Why," Ella said, "it's just like the officers' club."

I went to the Blue Parrot not for sex but wits, like Sam Lurie, a rotund publicist for Ballet Theatre. Sam had the profile of Louis XVI and a wit as sharp as Wilde's. Once, at a party, someone referred to trade (boys who sold their sex) as "angels in disguise," a phrase from the Bible. But from which book? Someone suggested the Book of Hebrews. The host duly checked a Bible. "I can't find the book of Hebrews," he said. "That's because," said Sam, "You have the Racquet Club edition."

Tennessee writes to Donald Windham in the summer of '48 that "Gore gets on even less well with people than I do." Certainly, I never got on with the remittance queens for whom Tennessee was a magnet, which meant that if one saw him, one saw them.

Tennessee and I occupied the second floor of the Hôtel de l'Université, on the Left Bank. The second floor was two rooms and a bath for him on the street side and one room and a bath for me in the back, with the stairwell between. Not long ago, a would-be biographer of the Bird, an American academic, wrote me to ask if we had had an affair. I told her that although it was not my habit to comment on private matters, it had been my experience in real life that it was unusual for colleagues to go to bed with each other. Of course, I added tolerantly, to show that nothing human could be alien to me, I did understand that it was well known for tenured lady professors to go to bed with each other, and I was certainly not about to cast a cold eye upon their sapphic revels.

The Bird and I did like the same type, and we would pass boys back and forth. Once, after an unsuccessful evening's prowl of Saint-Germain, we returned to the hotel, and the Bird said, "Well, that just leaves us," to which he says I said, "Don't be macabre." I don't recall any of this, but he enjoyed telling the story, so I suppose it happened. When he made a similar suggestion to Donald Windham, a fellow hunter, Windham's response was sharp: "I deplore," he said, "your taste."

I would lock myself in the back of the second floor and work while Tennessee watered the queens, who then repaid his hospitality with exuberant mockery of his plays, his appearance, his generosity.

Summer afternoons, I would prowl the streets, empty of traffic in those days. Sometimes I would go to the male brothel that Proust had set up for his own voyeuristic purposes. It was now called Hôtel Saumon and lugubriously furnished with Mother Proust's furniture, of which Oscar Wilde had observed, on his one visit to the Proust family apartment, "How ugly your furniture is!" But the beds were comfortable, as I discovered in the summer of 1948, the terrible year in which a woman senator in France and a woman senator in Italy each got her country's brothels shut, increasing the spread of venereal disease. Although Hôtel Saumon was forced to shut down in 1949, regular customers could still use the rooms, presided over by an old bald Algerian named Said.

The hotel was in an arcade just off the Place de l'Humanité. To the right of the entrance, a small office; to the left, stairs. Said himself looked like an evil djinn in the *Arabian Nights*. But looks belied an amiable and gentle nature. He would loll at one end of a dirty divan and I'd sit at the other and ask him questions about Monsieur Marcel. "He would sit there, where you sit, always in a great fur coat. Even on a hot day like this, he was always cold." What did Proust *do*? I could not resist asking. Paul Bowles had told me that Proust had once become ecstatic when he watched a rat bite a youth's hand—or was it the other way round? "Oh, he would just look. That's all. There were holes—you know, in the walls." Said was vague: after all, I was a customer and might not want to be spied on. Said had somehow been involved with the first manager of the hotel, and in due course, he had inherited the business.

On the first floor there was a sitting room. One could look through a crack in the door at the room's contents, a half-dozen working-class boys, smoking, reading newspapers, drinking wine. Choice made, Said would send the one chosen to the room. To exoticize the Victorian solidity of Mme. Proust's furniture, Said had hung, wherever he could, beaded curtains while in dark dusty corners tarnished bronze pots and pipes gleamed.

The boys were polite and rather shy; and they urgently needed money. Whatever their primary sexual interests, they took easily to their own sex, and I often wondered how Kinsey would have rated them. The ghettoization of "gay" and "straight" had not yet begun. I suspect that all of them would marry and have children and then, in due course, with age, they would pay for women and perhaps boys, too, since that taste had been awakened, if nowhere else, amongst Said's Algerian beads.

I particularly liked one blond rangy youth, as tall as I, rare in France in those austere days. He was a student, he said, and this was the quickest way to raise money to put himself through university. Was he telling the truth?

A week later, as I was crossing the Pont Neuf, a couple passed me, pushing a baby carriage. She was pretty and pregnant. Despite thick glasses, I recognized the blond student. He gave me a smile, and walked on.

John Lehmann introduced me to Denham Fouts, *un homme fatal* from Jacksonville, Florida. Denham was in his late thirties, very pale, with dark lank Indian hair and blank dark eyes, usually half shut: He smoked opium, and the light hurt his eyes. He was being kept by Peter Watson, usually identified as the "oleomargarine king of England"; a tall nervous man, Peter had financed Cyril Connolly's *Horizon* magazine, at that time the most interesting literary paper in the English-speaking world. Watson established Denham in a flat on the rue du Bac, then more or less abandoned him. Denham spent his days in a great bed beneath a Tchelitchev painting, the paraphernalia for his opium pipe close by. In the salon there were four Venetian shell chairs and nothing else. A large white frizzle-haired dog occupied the far side of the bed.

Lehmann and I sat on the edge of the bed while Denham, eyes shut, free-associated. "Cyril was just here. His first trip to Paris since the war. Peter and I took him to a restaurant down the street where he ordered a huge lunch—he's very fat and greedy, you know—and he ate it all up very fast and then he ordered a second lunch and ate that, too. Then he fainted. The waiters carried him back here and put him over there on the floor. Isherwood is on his way, he writes me. He's with someone new, he says. I took up Vedanta when I was in California because of Chris and he did because of Gerald Heard, who is a real fraud. I want to meet Truman Capote. I have his picture here." There, under the opium pipe, was Truman's picture, as posed for *Life* magazine.

I said that they were bound to get along. Denham was very much a denizen of a world that Capote was intent on breaking into. "Café society" was the phrase then used. "Jet set" was later coined to describe people with money who liked publicity, and the collection of marginal types like Denham and Truman—for their beauty or news value or simply gossip. Denham's legendary beauty was not visible to me. He looked like the ghost he would soon be, dead of a malformed heart. He was slender and boyish, with a markedly asymmetrical face. He was at his best with pubescent boys; but then he was one himself, I should think, a southern Penrod who still spoke with a North Florida accent.

Denham prepared the opium pipe, an elaborate process that involved melting a pellet of opium in a metal dish set over a flame; then the pellet was placed in a metal cup atop a long wooden pipe. Denham inhaled deeply and exhaled slowly blue medicinal-smelling smoke. "Here." He handed me the pipe. I said that I didn't even know how to inhale cigarette smoke. But I tried and had a coughing fit. Lehmann abstained. The large dog eagerly sniffed the air. Contact high?

"I've just had a telegram from Prince Paul—only he's King Paul now. We lived together—well, traveled a lot together before the war, but then he had to get married to Frederika and so we stopped seeing each other because I was living in Santa Monica by then anyway and working in that bookshop and seeing Chris and Gerald . . ." The names kept flowing evenly, without any particular emphasis, and I assumed that most of them were inspired by opium. As if he sensed my skepticism, he produced a crumpled telegram from the floor beside his bed. I read: "My dear Denham so thrilled to hear from you I am much better than papers report hope you can come to Athens love Paul," and the venue duly noted "Royal Palace." This story, at least, was true. Isherwood, Capote, and I each dealt with Denham in short stories. It is a pity that he himself never wrote a memoir.

On the other hand, Lehmann wrote several volumes of memoirs, and Isherwood and I used to marvel at how so deeply malicious and interesting a gossip could be so boring when he came to review his own life and times. John describes his failure, as a publisher, to sign up Truman; so he "decided to take a chance on Gore Vidal, whose homosexual novel *The City and the Pillar* had just caused a considerable stir." Then he gets wrong the story about Truman's "twenty-five if he's a day." John also believes that our "rivalry" was as intense on my side as on his. I recall no rivalry—as opposed to anger at what Truman said about me. Besides, how could two writers so unlike be in competition? "Thank God *we're* not intellectuals!" Truman once said to me, to which my dusty answer was, "Speak for yourself."

Of 1948, Lehmann reports: "It was already perfectly clear to me, in those early meetings, that Gore had limitless ambition and confidence in himself. . . . I grew fond of him, but in spite of my estimate of his abilities and energy, I could not then have envisaged his blossoming out, a decade later, as one of the most successful American writers of plays for television and stage, author of extremely clever and successful film-scripts, and even a controversial figure in Democratic politics of the Kennedy era."

As I type this out, I am delighted by the exquisitely malicious choice of adjectives, each an alarm bell for an English ear but music to an American one. For the English, *clever* is almost the worst thing that a writer can be. *Successful* is something to be avoided if possible—if not possible, as in the case of E. M. Forster, say, the writer of true worth and human modesty is expected to let slip the feather and withdraw into silence, surrounded by loving friends whom he has refused to surpass. To be a writer of any kind in England is to be very humble indeed, although for the Bloomsburyites, among whose relics and heirs I had fallen, the moral superiority of the writer was contingent on his shy lack of worldly ambition and his capacity for making precise, even terminal, moral judgments on the behavior of his fellows. Maynard Keynes had been, finally, detested by the other Bloomsburyites because he had gone into the world as an economist and money manager: then he had triumphed as an adviser to nations; and, worse, after a string of intense unsafe-sex partners, he married a *woman,* a ballet dancer whom the others disliked and, finally, hell's last circle, he became uxorious. Forster was the Madame Lafarge of this set, as I was soon to discover.

I am reading Edmund Wilson's diaries kept during the sixties. I note, with amusement, that Auden harangues him as he did me on the subject of class. Auden "told me that one reason for his coming to America was that . . . he had discovered that there were no . . . social distinctions. He said that he had regretted not having been sent to Eton."

The English disease affects them all, and the apparently shy, modest literary folk are still, in their hearts, proud of their schools and professional or civil-service families while deeply envious of other people's schools and families and accents, and though they will cringe in the presence of someone of a higher class, they are quick to shoot down anyone lower than they who dares move above *his* station, starched serviette held on high. As a result, most English humor is based on someone being caught out in his pretensions and firmly put down.

They speak with irony of their betters, but if royalty's shadow should fall across their path, they come, as Tom Driberg would say, all over queer. Wilson tried to set Auden straight but I suspect got nowhere.

Americans have the same social distinctions as the English, but we play the game so subtly that anyone who does not choose to play can do so as long as he does not wonder why it is that certain worlds are closed to him and their glittering prizes beyond reach. Also, we have a tradition of the self-invented millionaire from nowhere, like Gatsby, as well as our Truman Capotes and Lillian Hellmans, who keep right on inventing themselves before our eyes. The English could never allow—much less be taken in by—their kind of deception: The island is far too small, while the islander's ear is far too sharp for so much as a single diphthong to fall, swallowlike, undetected.

"One day, I persuaded André Gide to let me bring young Gore Vidal to be introduced to him. This was an event that Gore had dreamed of for years, and he was in a high state of excitement as we rang the door bell in the rue Vaneau." I like that word *persuaded*. Noble John? It is true that I wanted to meet the literary great that season, but having me "dream" of meeting Gide, or of any other writer, is far-fetched. After all, I had been brought up with far more famous people than the old writers to whom I was now paying homage, as the young Gide had once done to Oscar Wilde. But John knew nothing of my background, nor was I about to tell him. In those days, I liked to give the impression that I was a professional tennis player turned hustler. John Bowen, then editor of Oxford's *Isis Magazine*, titled his review of *The City and the Pillar*, "Kiss me again hot lips, I'm asbestos." We have been friends ever since.

"The master was in his most cordial mood, and questioned Gore closely about sex in American writing. At the end Gore rather nervously mentioned that he had sent Gide a copy of his *The City and the Pillar*, though he had received no acknowledgement. Gide replied that he remembered perfectly well; and then immediately switched the conversation onto the stranger perversions that were prevalent, he was told, amongst rich spinsters and widows in New York. Afterwards, Gore sighed and said he supposed that just meant that Gide had not read his book. I was not so sure." Actually, I had not sent Gide a copy of the book. Joseph Breitbach, a French novelist of the day and friend of Gide, told me that Gide had said, with some amusement, that he had received several copies of the book from those who thought that he should keep up with the latest work "in the field," as Dr. Kinsey would say. Breitbach said that Gide would be pleased to receive its author. Then Breitbach left town and so it was generous John who was able to fulfill my lifelong dream to shake the hand that had shaken the hand of Oscar Wilde.

Actually, my memory of the meeting is pleasant indeed. The flat was sunny. Gide's plain wood desk looked onto rue Vaneau, not far from Mrs. Wharton's Paris flat on the rue de Varenne. Gide was seventy-nine, short-legged, deep-chested, with a large egglike bald head on which was perched a *vie de bohème* velvet beret; he also wore a dark green velvet jacket. The voice was deep and rather stagy, like the Comédie Française actor that I had seen in de Montherlant's *Le Maître de Santiago.*

I congratulated the master on having just won the Nobel Prize—a great sea change in Scandinavian academe, because Gide was the first acknowledged admirer of same-sexuality to have got the prize. He beamed; then intoned, "*Premier le Kinsey Report, et après ça le Prix Nobel.*" John missed all this.

I told Gide about my meeting with Dr. Kinsey. The master was fascinated with Kinsey and his report, which he felt had indeed made him, if not respectable, plausible and prizable. He knew that *The City and the Pillar* had been coupled with the Report. Yes, he had discussed the book with Breitbach. Yes, I would have liked an endorsement from him, but none came, at least not directly to me. I thought our encounter significant because Gide himself had spent much of his life under the sort of cloud that had now materialized over me. Luckily for him, France had a degree of civilization, and he was able to prevail in the literary world; unfortunately for me, the United States has never had a civilization and so survival is not easy if one goes against the grain of so fiercely superstitious a land. But as Gide had survived in his world, I intended to do so in mine. It was a pity that I met him with the supercilious John instead of our common friend Breitbach, who could have guided the conversation along more interesting lines than my Phillips Exeter French and John's *cher maître*-ing could lay down.

"I get so many books," Gide said. "Such interesting ones." The dark eyes glittered with amusement. "Here." He gave me a thick illustrated manuscript with red handwritten capital letters. "From a vicar, living in the English countryside." The drawings were beautifully rendered tableaux of naked schoolboys indulging in every sort of sexual act. I studied the drawings with pleasure; then I asked, "How is the text?"

"Un petit peu trop littéraire." The telephone rang. Gide picked it up. "Ah, *cher maître."* A high nasal voice spluttered out of the receiver. Gide held the phone away from his ear so that we could listen. "Henry de Montherlant," he whispered. Later, I came to admire de Montherlant's books rather more than Gide's. A few years ago, I was much moved to find on the cover of a Dutch translation of *Julian* an endorsement from de Montherlant, saying that this was a book which he liked to read and reread, because of my "beautiful" rendering of the last glimmer of paganism.

THAT SEASON I was keeping track of Capote's lies. As I was the only one who found them offensive, why should I have cared? I don't know why, other than a constitutional dislike of liars, not to mention Truman himself. Jack Knowles, in later years Truman's neighbor on Long Island, tells me that Truman had told him that he'd been in love with me and that I had rejected him. "Easily," I said to Jack, "one of his finest spur-of-the-moment inventions."

I caught Truman out in a dozen or so lies that everyone else preferred to believe. I can't think what labor of Hercules I thought I had undertaken, and certainly to no useful end, because the instant lie was Truman's art form, small but, paradoxically, authentic. One could watch the process. A famous name would be mentioned. The round pale fetus face would suddenly register a sort of tic, as if a switch had been thrown. "Eleanor Roosevelt. Oh, I know her *intimately*! I was with her when Franklin died, she hated him you know, and of course she was in love with Marlene. In fact, she and Marlene and I were together in Marlene's suite at the Pierre when, suddenly, Eleanor came rushing in–oh, she was so big–stark naked too–from the bedroom, to say that the president was dead, so Marlene . . ." To watch Capote's face as he added detail after detail was to observe the raw creative process in all its primal fury.

During the summer of 1948, Truman and I met Camus at a party given by the publisher Gallimard. Camus was much involved with actresses in those days. But before summer was over, Truman was telling everyone that Camus was so madly in love with him that he would come to his hotel, importunately, in the middle of the night, wanting yet again to hold that dwarfish body in his loving arms. When I told Truman's biographer that there was no way that someone as dedicated to the other sex as Camus would have been interested in Capote, the biographer, unscrupulous in his bio-porn, did modify the story to say that it had happened only once. Truman had also shown me a gold ring with an amethyst set in it. "André Gide gave me this. He never stops calling." Before my eyes, Truman turned himself into a gemlike flame with the aged Gide as suicidal moth. Now I was able to ask Gide, "How do you find Truman Capote?"

"Who?"

I repeated the name. Lehmann was mysteriously disturbed, as if I were somehow cheating. Did he feel that Capote's lie should not be questioned? Gide finally understood whom I was talking about. "No," he said, "I haven't met him, but several people have sent me this." From his desk he held up the photograph of Truman from *Life*. He grinned. "Is he in Paris?"

We talked of Oscar Wilde. I cannot remember a word that he said. He also wondered what it was that Anglo-Saxons found to admire in Henry James.

When it was time to go, he asked me if I would like a book. I said, "Yes, *Corydon*." He looked surprised. This was his first work "in the field," a rather fin de siècle dialogue on a Virgilian shepherd's loves. "I never give that book," he said, leading me out of the room. "Mind the step," he said in English, his only words to me in that language. But he did say that he was particularly proud of the fact that he had translated Conrad from English into French.

Gide's library was on two levels, with a gallery separating lower floor from upper floor. He gave me a copy of *Corydon* and wrote *avec la sympathie*. Thus, old and new world met on a title page.

SUMMER DAY. Long blue shadows on the cobblestones. Paul Bowles, slender, blond, exquisitely turned out, and I walk down an empty street off Saint-Germain. Suddenly, a radio is turned on behind a shuttered window and the street is filled with the music of Bizet. Paul complains that composers now think of him as a writer and writers as a composer and that, as a result, he is nowhere. He is writing a novel, *The Sheltering Sky*. It will be published the next year, and Tennessee will review it in *The New York Times*, with a somewhat gratuitous swipe at Capote and me: At last a *mature* artist has come on the scene, so unlike . . .

"Why did the Bird feel he had to attack us?" I later asked Donald Windham.

"Because he's jealous of anyone younger who writes." The Bird was a late starter, which he blamed on all those years—actually, months—spent in a shoe factory.

When the *Times* delayed publication of the review, the Bird was positive that I had used my "influence" there to kill the review, or so he wrote in a letter now published, long after the fact. He knew, of course, that I had no influence at the *Times,* rather the reverse.

As we walked toward the Seine, Bowles said that he had just met Saul Bellow. "Numerous inside jokes about the Torah," he reported. I said that I had liked *Dangling Man.* Paul had not read it. He had just bought a Pleiade edition of de Sade, whom I'd not read. He talked at length about him. When I wrote a preface to Paul's collected short stories, I mentioned de Sade as an "influence." Paul wrote a friend to say that I was wrong and that he had never been able to read, much less be influenced by, de Sade; plainly, the parsimonious author of the Sadeian "The Delicate Prey" had wasted his money on the complete works.

One day, walking alone—what a time for walking that season was—I passed the Café des Deux Magots, where sat Christopher Isherwood with his friend Bill Caskey. I had sent Isherwood the manuscript of *The City and the Pillar.* He had responded with praise. I was grateful. I needed all the support that I could get.

I introduced myself to Isherwood. Thus began a friendship that was to last for the rest of his life. The common denominator in the rare friendships that I have had with other writers is laughter. With Christopher and the Bird, I laughed a great deal. The Bird's humor ran to the grotesque, Christopher's to shades of meaning, often involving colliding class systems, which he could play upon like a comic virtuoso at the xylophone. We would make extravagant statements; and then develop them.

"I am American literature," I announced one day.

"I feared as much," he said; although the voice was controlled, I saw the mounting terror in his eyes as we deconstructed American literature not only past but yet to come, making, as we did, spacious room for ourselves among the ruins. We did parodies. I would improvise in the manner of the later James, setting up clause upon clause like fences in a steeplechase, while Christopher would respond with Edgar Wallace.

He often saw himself as a detective or doctor in a mystery movie. He is discovered on camera. *Al fresco.* He is kneeling beside a crumpled body. He wears a trench coat. He looks keenly up, into the camera, and says, tonelessly, "He's . . . dead."

The three of us went out to Versailles. Christopher and I talked. Caskey glowered; he was an ex–merchant mariner, from Kentucky. I suppose he was jealous. He need not have been. Even *he* was too old for my taste.

Summer 1948. In London, my English publisher, John Lehmann, took this picture of Christopher Isherwood and me and a ballet dancer friend of John's (at left). This was the beginning of a lifelong friendship with Christopher.

London, E. M. Forster, as well as Friends-to-Be

I STAYED WITH John Lehmann at 31 Egerton Crescent in London. Eagerly, John collected the ration book that I had been given on entry into that hungry island. My reward was a mess of fish with one egg clotted over it at breakfast. I ate the rationed egg and left the fish.

John tells us that "there were several passages in *The City and the Pillar*, a sad, almost tragic book and a remarkable achievement in a difficult territory for so young a man, that seemed to my travellers and the printers to go too far in frankness. I had a friendly battle with Gore to tone down and cut these passages. Irony of time and taste: they wouldn't cause an eyebrow to be lifted in the climate of the early sixties." I suppose that *they* would not, but in 1968 a publisher's lawyer insisted on several hundred changes in the English edition of *Myra Breckinridge.*

The principal change John wanted was the ending. When protagonist again finds the beloved after a long search, he is rebuffed. Instead of making love, they fight; and the story ends somewhat ambiguously. Did Jim actually kill Bob or simply–as I intended–kill off the obsession? Since homoerotic fixation was my theme, I thought that this was the logical conclusion for my character, Jim Willard, who had forfeited an emotional life for love of a boy, now a man, who had forgotten him. *The New Yorker* dismissed the original story as more suitable for a "police blotter" than a novel. A critic recently wrote that all in all, most police blotters were a lot more interesting than most novels. To placate not so much John as those who felt that I was making a case that same-sexualists were homicidal psychopaths, I made it clear that Jim does not literally kill Bob, only the idea of him.

Lehmann gave a party for me, to which he added Tennessee as co-guest of honor. Christopher and Caskey were there. It was Christopher's first visit since he and Auden had moved to America before the war. For this transfer, they had been duly pilloried by, among others, that self-invented Catholic gentleman Evelyn Waugh, proud esquire of a smidgen of English dirt.

Graham Greene arrived, gray-green as his name. Forty years later, we got to know each other, through a shared admiration of William Dean Howells and Mikhail Gorbachev. V. S. Pritchett was amiable. The novel? Yes. Yes! The novel. "Ought to have a lot of sex in it," I proclaimed. "Oh, quite. Yes, yes a lot!" One laughed a good deal in those days in those circles. The war was over, of course, but to an American eye, English life was of a terrible rationed drabness.

The entrance of E. M. Forster caused a mild stir. He was all gray, tweed-gray. Face and paws–hands, I mean–like those of Rat in *The Wind in the Willows.* Christopher was nervous. He had sent Forster his latest novel, *Prater Violet,* and had heard nothing. I then observed a ritual English social blooding, not unlike the American one toward the end of *The Age of Innocence.*

A dozen people at one end of the room. Much chatter. Then Christopher asked, "Morgan, did you get the copy of *Prater Violet* I sent you?" Even my transatlantic heart sank: This could only be trouble.

Forster went on chatting to William Plomer and seemed not to have heard. Christopher swallowed more gin. "Morgan!" The voice had gone up half an octave. The room was quiet. Forster's eyes twinkled in Christopher's direction. "Did you get the copy of *Prater Violet* I sent you? I know there's a lot of difficulty mailing things across the . . ."

"Yes, Christopher." Morgan's twinkle never ceased. "I got it." Then he turned back and continued his conversation with Plomer, leaving Christopher garroted in plain view. That was the night when the very drunk Christopher beat up Caskey and then blamed it on me the next morning. "Gore beat you up."

I took an instant dislike to Forster, which did not improve when he came over to Tennessee and me. With Tennessee, he was excited fan.

Would we come to King's? For lunch? We'd never seen Cambridge? Oh, this was the perfect time of year. He would meet us at the college entrance, seated on a stone lion. We would have lunch.

Morning found Tennessee and me at the railroad station. We had missed the first train to Cambridge. The next was not for half an hour. Tennessee was getting claustrophobic. "I must have a drink. The pubs aren't open, are they? Well, I'll go back to the Savoy . . ."

"You can't. Your fan is a very old man, sitting on a stone lion and waiting for you, not me, to come to lunch."

The Bird became lofty. "I do not choose to lunch with old gentlemen with urine-stained flies."

That pleasure was to be mine. Forster's look of disappointment was disheartening. But, dutifully, he took me on a tour. We crossed the river to the chapel, which I coldly termed "pretty," thus disheartening *him*. Lionel Trilling had just published a study of Forster's novels. After the book came out, Capote told Trilling that Forster, subject of his book, was queer. For once, Capote was not inventive. Trilling had been astounded; had never suspected; had not, plainly, a clue to what the books that he had praised were about.

We had a bad boiled lunch. "You must have the steamed lemon curd roll," Forster said. But as there was only one portion left, which he so clearly wanted, I opted for rhubarb. "Now," he said, contentedly tucking in, "you will never know what steamed lemon curd roll is."

I went back to his rooms. He was interesting on music. On Britten. On librettos. He showed me the manuscript of *Maurice*. "I couldn't publish it while my mother was still alive. But now there are other people . . ." I knew all about his married lover, a policeman. There were no secrets in London's literary world.

Forster had developed to the highest degree not only Bloomsbury's love of gossip, the more intricate the better, but, rather worse in my view, an unremitting censoriousness. He was always in court, seated on the high bench, passing judgments, a black cloth on his head. Christopher was hanged not so much for *Prater Violet* but for having left England before the war. This constant weighing of others in one's own scales is, I should think, somewhat perilous; after all, you yourself might find that what looks to be a pleasant literary tea in Egerton Crescent has suddenly become a gaudy kangaroo court. I think that that was the moment I decided no more great men of letters for me. I really disliked Forster; worse, I really liked his books. This is a ridiculous situation to put oneself in–him, too. But Forster's example is contagious. Now *I'm* the censorious one and all because he had not amiably lied and said, right off, "Yes, Christopher, I got the book. We'll talk later." Lying is the worst of sins, but there are times when it forestalls what the Bird regarded as the *very* worst of sins, gratuitous cruelty.

In London, Tennessee's first play, *The Glass Menagerie,* was about to go into rehearsal. Except for the adaptation of *The Heiress,* no American play was to have a London success for thirty years after the war. In those days, Tennessee's London reviews were always bad and his audiences meager. The director was John Gielgud, hardly an ideal choice for so American a play; the star was Helen Hayes, whom I liked but the Bird could not bear. At one point in the rehearsal, Hayes picks up the typewriter from her son's table and marches about with it as she declaims one of the Bird's major arias. Suddenly, she stops and turns to Gielgud, "What do I do with the typewriter?" As usual, Gielgud had no idea, and so Hayes answered her own question: "I think that this loon would put it right back where she picked it up."

Beside me in the darkened theater, the Bird said in my ear, "Did you hear that? She called Amanda a loon." Amanda, of course, was the Bird's mother, Edwina, a woman of joyless pomp and circumstance with a number of patented arias. I called her the good gray goose. In her last days she was positive that the blacks of St. Louis were signaling each other during the dark summer nights by banging the lids of trashcans, preparatory to rebellion, rape, and rapine. One of Tennessee's earliest memories was listening to her denounce his father with the words "You are the reason that I was obliged to have my womb removed." Yes, she talked like that; and talked and talked.

In Edmund Wilson's journals, I find that he too, at my age, had bad dreams, the result of heavy drinking. Like mine, his dreams have to do with frustration. There is also a recurring dream that I thought unique to me. In one's familiar house, there is an unsuspected door that opens into suite after suite of splendid rooms. I also dream that I have gone into an unfamiliar brownstone house in New York City only to realize that I own the building but can never recall its address.

Wilson liked to ask friends if they ever dream of flying. Most of them have. He wanted to know how high they fly, and are people watching, and do they fly easily or with effort? Answers vary. Some fly smoothly above an astonished crowd; some are too embarrassed to want others to know that they can fly; some beat the air with their arms in order to attain altitude (I do) while others tread air as if it were water. Wilson himself glides over the countryside with the greatest of ease.

At exactly my age, he has angina, arthritis, gout. Thus far, I have controllable high blood pressure, a tendency to diabetes that is no problem if one eats carefully. On the other hand, my half to two thirds of a bottle of whiskey in the evening might give me cirrhosis one day, but then, after so many healthy days, why fret over the famous "one day" that arrives sooner or later–in my case, already later–for everyone? In the current great August heat, I can take no exercise other than a couple of laps in the pool. At times, I miss my once vigorous body.

Wilson was intensely social to the end. He needed people to talk at, and he liked to perform magic tricks. (I am reviewing his last journals.) Unlike Wilson, I am not social; I also like giving up things, letting go. The British embassy in Rome has just rung. Will I come to dinner for Princess Margaret in September, two months away? I say no. I don't want, ever again, to sit at a formal table with a strange lady on either side of me and make conversation. As I say no to dinner, I wonder if I am a bad friend. The princess and I have known each other for exactly thirty years. She has been here; I have stayed with her at Windsor. But in the last few years neither has made an effort to see the other; for some reason I am relieved not to see most people, even those I like–or once liked. I understand now why the old enjoy the obituaries of contemporaries. I used to put this down to play-acting in the face of *memento mori;* now I think it is a sense of relief in letting go for good of people whose presence one no longer needs. I recall something Santayana said as he led me into his cell at the convent. "As you see, I live as if I were already dead."

Princess Margaret was operated on last year; a close call. She was told, again, to give up cigarettes and whiskey. Kathleen Tynan has just arrived with a message from M: "Kick him in the shins for me. He never rings up. Then give him a big kiss." Just how detached is one supposed to be in what the Bird used to refer to as the "crocodile years"? I suddenly recall Princess Margaret's grim admonition, "You must meet young people, or else. The others are going or gone." But "or else" is not so bad.

Some days I don't walk beyond the property. The several acres that we have here are now quite enough of a world for me, and far more beautiful than most other worlds. I've not set foot in Rome since April, when we gave up the apartment, after thirty years. Old age is turning out to be like youth; there is a tendency to daydream, but never about the past. I am so much in the present that I don't seem to need recollected time at all. What I am doing now is an act of will that, occasionally, becomes exciting when I detect a puzzle, a mystery, something unexamined. Now, thanks to Kathleen, Princess Margaret's voice is beginning to sound, unbidden, in my head.

"I detested Queen Mary." The blue eyes sometimes look as if they are illuminated from within. "She was rude to all of us except Lilibet, who was going to be queen. Of course, she had an inferiority complex. We were royal, and she was not." I took the princess and her two children to the monastery above Naples. In the refectory, there is a row of carved wooden seats for the abbot and the other high-ranking members of the order. "Here's my seat," said the boy, David, taking his place several places to the right of the abbot, "and here's yours," he said to his sister, who took her seat. Each knew his exact place in succession to the crown.

"Stop *that*," thundered their mother, in her best Lady Bracknell voice. She is far too bright for her station in life, which she takes altogether too solemnly. A bit of Scandinavian modesty might have seen the family through. But Shakespeare has enchanted them quite as much as he has their subjects, enchanted and created not only their family but their nation, too, through his fanciful re-creation and celebration of their predecessors. He was a Tudor flack of genius. M. looks, at times, exactly like Charles I, whose bloodstained shirt she borrowed from the museum at Kensington Palace and wore at a fancy dress party.

LONDON DAYS, sometime in the sixties, a stranger came up to me at a party and said, "*You are in Chips.*" Chips? Had I won a lottery? or–fried potatoes? The stranger stared at me as at someone demonstrably historic. Then he explained: The diaries of Sir Henry Channon had just been published, some ten years after his death. He had been known to me, and everyone else, as Chips. He came from Chicago; drove an ambulance in the First War; married a Guinness, by whom he had a son; became British and a Conservative member of Parliament. In the process, he shed the wife but kept her fortune. He lived splendidly in Belgrave Square and also at a country house near Plymouth. Sexually, he preferred men to women and royalty to either. He was good company, and everyone, as they used to say, came to his parties. At my first London party at the house of Oliver Messell, Chips fell upon me, round rosy face flushed with drink, rather like an antique depraved schoolboy. He had just read *The City and the Pillar*. I must come stay in the country the next weekend. I was moderately alarmed. I tried to put him off. "I'm here with Tennessee." I pointed to the Bird, who stood nearby in a crumpled brown suit and mismatched shoes.

Chips did not know who Tennessee was, but he was game. We would both go. He would send a car for us. He introduced me to his companion, Peter Coates, a classic English queen who had been aide to Field Marshal Wavell when he was viceroy of India.

Chips writes: "27 June, Kelveden. Gore Vidal, the American novelist, and Tennessee Williams the playwright, and I drive to Kelveden. Vidal wears his hair like a Nazi, *en brosse:* he is dark." To look like a Nazi was, I fear, to rank high in Chips's rating for masculine appeal, for he had been part of the prewar pro-German Cliveden set and had been fetched by Hitler's envoy Ribbentrop. Actually, I wore a standard American crew cut, as most ex-soldiers still did three years after the war. I was not dark but fair. At least he does not mention my blue eyes, a staple of interviewers over the years. Actually, my eyes are the color of very weak tea, a variation on my father's near golden eyes, an Alpine racial characteristic that I noted when I was in Friuli and saw my father's eyes eerily staring at me on every side. "He has written four [*sic*] novels, and the most startling is *The City and the Pillar*, a book which has practically knocked America out. However, he is pleasant to talk to and not at all spoilt. Tennessee is thirty-four . . ." The ellipsis is interesting. Chips's son, Paul, had the book edited so that any potential embarrassment to him in *his* political career might be minimized. Hence, numerous ellipses. What, I wonder, was cut out?

I came to know Chips pretty well over the next ten years (he died in 1958), and he always said that he was writing the sort of diary that not even Saint-Simon had dared write. Chips would tell everything about the sex lives of the people who comprised his world. Since, obviously, he himself didn't know everything, he could, at least, report what was said at the time, thus providing that context of gossip in which everyone

moves, an aura that death entirely eliminates, leaving only a few anecdotes and a bare chronology. I can't imagine Chips not confiding to his
diary *why* my book had had such an effect.

He talked to us of his own sex life. Apparently, he was hopelessly in
love with Terrence Rattigan, "the most beautiful man in England and
the greatest playwright." In the journal, he says of Tennessee: ". . . a terrific Rodinesque character of force and vitality and a great writer of
poetic prose." He had done his homework since the beginning of the
week. "Both were immensely impressed by Kelveden, as they have
never seen an English country house before." I let Chips think this; let
everyone think that *The City and the Pillar* was my autobiography.
Actually, Merrywood was about the same size as Kelveden.

"We were joined at luncheon by Field Marshal Sir Claude Auchinlech
and Violet Wyndham . . ." (Another ellipsis? I wonder what was cut out
there.) "An odd mixture but it went well. Tennessee retired to his room,
and began another play." That afternoon Auchinlech and I took a walk
amongst the foxgloves, to the delight of Chips and Peter Coates, who
kept suggesting romance between June and November. The sad-faced
Auchinlech was indeed a sad man. He had been removed from the
North African command by Churchill, "an unconscionable bully, with
no knowledge of military matters." Auchinlech had returned to the
Indian army. "I don't really know this country." He gazed glumly upon
the blue-gray countryside. "I spent my life in India, you know. That's all
I really care about." He later retired to Morocco.

Dinner was pleasant. Chips had written a number of books, including
a fairly good one about Ludwig of Bavaria. He talked of Paris after the
war, when he was setting out on his social career; he had some family
money but not enough for the grandeur that he craved. He toyed with
the idea of literature; told me how Proust used to write him long letters,
which he never kept. "How was I to know he was a genius?"

Chips had been drawn to Proust, whose ostensible subject was the
world that Chips meant to play a part in. There could never be enough
glamour for Chips, who had found Gide "a dreadful, unkempt, poet-
looking person."

I reported to him on Gide; and on Cocteau, whom he did admire, for
his glamour rather than for his work. I described the lunch at the Grand
Vefour that Tennessee and I had had with Cocteau and his lover, the
actor Jean Marais. I had been the translator. It was like an exam at

Exeter. Neither the Bird nor Cocteau had any very clear idea of who the other was. But Cocteau knew that *A Streetcar Named Desire* was the most successful play of the postwar era and he wanted to mount it as a vehicle for Marais, who was threatening to leave him. As it proved, Marais did leave and Cocteau's *Streetcar*, with Arletty cast as Blanche, was a glorious mess of incomprehension full of writhing befeathered and sequined black bodies.

Everyone mocked Chips, but he more than sang for his supper; in fact, he himself provided the supper in his great silver and crystal din-ing room copied from one of Ludwig's castles. He always said that *every-thing* would appear one day in the diaries, but his son told me that what was published was pretty much all there was. I doubt this. Though Chips certainly lacked the obsessiveness of a Saint-Simon in pursuit of the Lorraines, I did think of him as a potential Boswell, describing randy times in what for him was the most splendid world there was. But the result was more a catalogue of dinner parties and Westminster gossip as observed from a back bench. After an hour's disquisition on various royalties, the Bird, squirming with boredom, said, "But what do they talk about?"

"Each other," said Chips, shutting that book smartly. He wanted us to stay for lunch the next day, but the Bird wanted to get back to London and a swimming pool that he had discovered. As Chips was showing us to the waiting car, a second land yacht glided into view. He rushed over to help out a small aged lady, whom he led into the house. Then he came back to us. "That," said Chips, "is the queen of Spain." And shut the door on us.

When Grace Kelly married Prince Rainier of Monaco, Chips gave a party with a long seedy red carpet that unfurled from his door halfway across Belgrave Square. Peter Coates stood, nervously, at the door, say-ing to each woman as she arrived, "A small one will do." Exasperated, I asked Chips, "A small what?"

"Curtsy." The Chicago Saint-Simon was now Arbiter in Belgrave Square.

THE KITCHEN of a flat near Victoria Station. Full of sunlight. Summer of 1948–or 1949, which was to be pretty much a rerun of the previous year. Again, I started in Rome, then on to Paris and London. The son of

the woman who owns the flat is Auberon Herbert, a tall amiable eccentric, with royal longings. But unlike Chips, he does not want to be a
courtier; he wants to be a king. During the First War, Auberon's father
had been at the Foreign Office, a specialist in the Middle East. After the
war, at Versailles, he invented Albania. For this dubious bit of work, the
Albanians wanted to elect him king. As he–and they–had no money, he
proposed to the British government that he be paid an allowance as
Britain's king in the area. The British government refused. "They are so
envious, you know." Auberon poured me bad coffee in the kitchen. "I
mean no one wanted any of *them* for king of anything."

That proffered crown denied had so entered the son's soul that he
now wanted one of his very own. He would become king of Poland, a
country that often elected outsiders. During the Second War he worked
with the Polish government in exile. He served with "his" Poles in the
field. He learned Polish. He had an enviable gift for languages. "It's easy,
really. Each morning you put a card with some new verbs on your mirror. By the time you've shaved, you're that much ahead with the language." But Stalin prevented Auberon from taking up the Polish crown.
In revenge, Auberon now had his eye on the Ukrainian crown. "Really
more interesting when you analyze it. I mean, the true crown of Holy
Russia is at Kiev and as the Soviet is bound to break up one day, I shall
be ready. In fact, I've already made the arrangements." The large pink
face had a faraway expression. As it turned out, he ended his days in a
country house surrounded entirely by Malcolm Muggeridge, a bright
fool, who reported to me, after a "debate" between us on BBC television,
that "Auberon has lost all sense of smell and taste, and so he eats and
eats but tastes nothing. Now he's absolutely enormous, as are his dogs.
But unlike Auberon, they are very bad-tempered and they have taken
over the house. Each has his special chair, and if you try to sit down,
they lunge at you, breaking wind all the time."

Into the kitchen comes a large, plain young woman. It is Judy Montagu. Her mother was Venetia Stanley, who married Edwin Montagu of
Asquith's cabinet. Asquith was chastely in love with Venetia and wrote
her brilliant letters during cabinet meetings when he should have been
conducting the First World War. Over the years, when Judy and I both
lived in Rome, I would advise her about the letters that were eventually
published after her early death. Now she enters my life.

"Auberon, how is poor Laura?" Poor Laura was always pronounced as one word. Poor Laura–Auberon's sister–was so named because she had the malign fate to be married to Evelyn Waugh, a drunken social climber who wrote small funny novels of no great appeal until television realized that the books–particularly *Brideshead Revisited*–contained soap opera elements, which, properly exploited, could fill with vicarious joy the dismal lives of consumers everywhere. Thus Evelyn, belatedly, became popular in the English-speaking world and he is now to English literature what Winston Churchill is to politics, and written about at endless length as if he were a great writer, like James Joyce or Rupert Everett.

"I can't remember. I don't think he struck her, actually. He shoved her from what I can tell. He grows worse, of course." Judy, perversely, liked the monster. She was staying with him and poor Laura on that Easter weekend when he died after Mass, straining at stool. "The teeth were like black pearls by then. He was suffering from the attentions of a dentist."

"Good," I said. My last meeting with Evelyn was at Annie Fleming's house in Victoria Square. Evelyn was placed beside me, a small man with a red round face. He pretended, as always, not to know me and so I affected not to know him, either. But he had the advantage of deafness, so he could affect not to hear my polite inquiries about his business, something in the line of estate planning, I had decided. On this occasion he had what looked to be a mandolin but was actually a Victorian hearing aid. The long end of the mandolin had a cup, which he placed over his ear as he swung the bowl beneath one's chin. "And how long have you been in London?" he cooed.

I leaned over the bowl to begin my inquiries into estate planning when he swung the mandolin away from me, and I was left speaking down to the table. I was not to be caught a second time. Eventually, the mandolin was swung my way again. But before the question as to my travel plans was completed, I seized the bowl of the mandolin with one hand and with the other gave the bowl a smart crack; this must have sounded like the last trump to Evelyn, who gave a wounded cry and let drop the mandolin.

After dinner, we were joined by Tom Driberg, chairman of the Labour party. A sort of stout Dracula, Tom was forever being caught in lavatories with rough youths, many of them not his constituents from proletarian Barking. Tom had been at school with Evelyn. From time to time during that evening, Evelyn would announce, "Tom is not as nice as he looks." At about two in the morning everyone fled into the night, as none dared go first from a room that contained, in addition to our sharp-tongued hostess, Waugh, Nancy Mitford, Debo Devonshire, Osbert Lancaster, Eddie Sackville-West, and Ann's lover Hugh Gaitskell, due to be the next prime minister had he not, abruptly, died. He was quick-witted and literary in a way no American politician has ever been—or could ever be. He was also candid about everything. I saw him several times that season.

At one point, Tom asked me to ask Gaitskell if he had any plans to include Tom in a Labour cabinet. At first, Gaitskell laughed. "How can we? He's bound to be arrested in some loo." Then he said, "Well, maybe, if the old thing could stay out of mischief, he could have the Ministry of Works. I think he'd like mucking about with stuff for embassy windows."

Recalling how, at Annie's dinner, Gaitskell and I had each done his best to outrage Waugh's mandolin by our fervent protestations of atheism, I proposed that as Tom was such a dedicated Christian, the new prime minister should make him Archbishop of Canterbury. Tom would be soaringly happy, and England would be a pagan country in a year. Gaitskell thought this a splendid, statesmanlike solution.

I always enjoyed the English connection. I was also grateful for it during the years of my American blackout. My books were reviewed as books, not as pretexts for sermons on what are now called "family values."

But I have left Judy in the kitchen near Victoria Station.

"I am going to marry Joe Alsop," she said.

"Why?" I had known Joe since I was ten and he was in his early twenties, a young journalist in Washington. Joe used to come out to Merrywood, and once, he watched Jimmie and me play tennis. In later years he would say, "I knew the cast of *The City and the Pillar*."

"I want children. A home . . . Washington suits me; it's political and I like that. So does Princess Margaret." Judy was the princess's best friend. "Joe's in on everything and I like his cousin Alice Longworth. So unless there's someone else . . ."

I'm afraid that I told her that the only romantic attachment that Joe had ever had that I knew of was to Frank Merlo, a Brooklyn sailor of

Sicilian extraction, who was soon to move in with Tennessee, more or less permanently. In later years, I would never have volunteered such information, but at the time, I thought that I was doing everyone a favor. All in all, I believe that I did. At least Judy finally married a man who gave her a daughter, and her friendship with Joe continued happily until she died at forty-nine.

*In the gardens of the Villa Fortino, Capri,
in the fifties: me, with a new mustache,
Mona Williams Bismarck, and the English
entertainer Gracie Fields, who lived on Capri.*

"I Was the Last King-Emperor, You Know"

A T SOME POINT in the summer of 1948 I met Eddie Bismarck. He was the youngest son of the youngest son of the chancellor, and he must have been about forty-five. Although his brother Otto more or less served Hitler, Eddie took after his mother, who detested the Germans; Eddie ended up interned by Italian Fascists on Capri. He told me that as a child, during the First War, "One morning I was sitting on Mother's bed in the house in Berlin when her maid came rushing in to say that the empress was downstairs and was asking for her, and Mother said, 'Tell her to go away. And then count the spoons.' "

Eddie looked exactly like the chancellor's pictures, but he had been born too late to have known his grandfather. Eddie was a talented decorator as well as an expert on the eighteenth century, and he was often called in by antiquarians to identify this or that object. Penniless, he had been taken up by the beautiful Mrs. Harrison Williams, who had, before the war, bought a place on Capri. Now that the war was over, she intended to settle there, despite a house on New York's Central Park, a place in New Jersey, and a Paris flat in the Hôtel Lambert. Harrison Williams had been, for a moment at the start of the Depression, the richest man in the United States. He had wanted to be the first billionaire in history and so he held on a bit too long to his portfolio as the economy came apart. In any case, he was worth about a tenth of a billion dollars, quite enough to keep the beautiful Mona and her decorator-companion in comfort. The three of them were the envy of the grand world, although I'm not so sure how happy Eddie was at being a sort of superior servant; but when, in due course, Harrison died, Mona became Countess Bismarck and all was as it should have been.

Mona proved as good a friend to me as Eddie, and when I came to live in Ravello, down the coast from Capri, I used to visit them from time to time. She had remarkable blue eyes and hair–supposedly, the first woman to handle gray hair by dying it blue. The result should have been like Halloween but was not. Dali painted her, blue hair and all, standing barefoot on a sheaf of newspapers. She was often referred to in the press as "the best-dressed woman in the world." Then she set out, with Eddie's help, to make her houses and her life into works of art in every detail. I cannot say that this was perhaps the most useful sort of life, but for the rest of us it was a fine spectacle to see her seated beneath a Goya in the Paris house or working by the hour in the acres of garden that she had created on Capri, with water shipped in from the mainland.

Eddie's Austrian-Bohemian cousin Cecilia Sternberg came to stay in the New York house in 1948, shortly after the Russians had taken away the Sternberg lands in Czechoslovakia, land recovered from the Nazis only three years earlier. Now they were again in exile, with their young daughter, Diana, who was to make her way in New York and London as a decorator. To everyone's amazement, after Havel's "velvet revolution," Diana got back several castles (but no money) and so she has vanished into her native Bohemia–the country, not the state of mind–and I only hear reports of her, armed with staple gun, attaching fabric to castle walls.

That summer in New York at the Harrison Williamses' house, Diana sat on the marble stairs one night, watching the grown-ups arrive for dinner. Mona, in a sudden bohemian mood, placed Tennessee on her right and me on her left. On the Bird's right was Cecilia. After dinner, Eddie asked Cecilia just how she'd managed to ruffle the Bird's plumage. In her memoir *The Journey*, Cecilia quotes Eddie:

> "He asked me who that unpleasant foreign woman was who'd made fun of him. When I told him you were my cousin he nearly fainted. What on earth did you say to offend him?"
>
> "I can't imagine, but he was most unfriendly. I asked him what business he was in and he said he wrote–does he?"

"Do you mean to say you've never heard of Tennessee Williams?"

"No, should I have?"

"But, darling, he's only the most famous young American play-wright we have–and his A Streetcar Named Desire *is the greatest hit ever. It's playing in every theater all over the world by now,"* Mona said.

"Though obviously not known in Czechoslovakia. It doesn't matter," Eddie added kindly. *"I explained to him how shut away you've been for years from everything of importance and made him understand that it was just ignorance, not malice. He's very sensitive, and plagued by self-doubts like all artists, in spite of his success.*

"You'll like Gore Vidal much better. He's well on his way to fame too. I must give you his novels to read and I'll bring him to talk to you later. He's brilliant, but in a way more like us. Suffered as much from family tradition as we did in our youth. These things still exist in this country in isolated patches and since things grow bigger here, if not better, than anywhere else, so does family pride, and eccentricity, but he's certainly risen above it."

"Is he by any chance the boy who looks like an archaic Apollo?"

"Why, so he does, rather," Eddie laughed, *"though his wits are far from archaic."*

. . . Eddie came to introduce Gore Vidal to me. His face was indeed curiously of the antique world, like a Greek mask, but by no means a tragic one. The wide eyes were alive with humour and so was a smiling mouth. We talked for a while and I thought him as charming and amusing as Eddie had told me I would.

I have always liked Apollo and so, of course, I liked Cecilia. I last saw her at Diana's London house. Cecilia had taken to her bed out of boredom. On one side of the bed was a parrot. On the other, a spaniel. Nearby, a bottle of some fiery liquid. Fully clothed, I got into bed with her and we passed bottle back and forth, and spoke blithely of the dead.

I used to spend Easters with Eddie and Mona on Capri, a cold season in those parts. I spent two successive Christmas Eves with the Bismarcks and their edgy friends the Windsors in Paris. I liked Wallis. She had a flapper's wisecracking charm. As for the duke–well, Hughdie had made me permanently susceptible to the charms of the born bore, to which time had added to this peculiar lust of mine an equal passion for the deeply stupid. David, as Wallis called him, always had something of such riveting stupidity to say on any subject that I clung to his words like the most avid courtier of the ancien régime. The duke described coronations—not that he had ever seen one, either: He had missed his own. I remarked that much of Westminster Abbey's ritual was Byzantine in origin. The word *Byzantine* was not seared in his memory. I quickly moved on to the *sic transit gloria mundi* moment, when two masons appear and ask the newly crowned king for instructions as to his tomb. "Masons? Masons! Yes. You one? I'm one. But I've forgotten all the odds and ends. Dull, really."

As a French accordion player did his best to play "Stille Nacht"—(the duke only knew the German lyrics for Christmas hymns), he suddenly said, "British Empire. First trip to India. Glorious. Never would have believed that it would all be gone in my lifetime. Not possible, I'd've thought. I am the last king-emperor, you know. My brother was, for a time, but had to give it up. I didn't."

Mona said, "Did you see Gore's play *The Best Man* when you were in New York?"

"Of course not," said the duke, genially. "Don't like plays, only shows." He meant musical comedies.

I got the duchess in a reminiscent mood. "I never wanted to get married. This was all *his* idea. They act as if I were some sort of idiot, not knowing the rules about who can be queen and who can't. But he insisted." She took a long drink of vodka. She had square ugly hands covered with large jewels.

"I remember like yesterday the morning after we were married and I woke up and there was David standing beside the bed with this innocent smile, saying, 'And now what do we do?' My heart sank. Here was someone whose every day had been arranged for him all his life and now I was the one who was going to take the place of the entire British government, trying to think up things for him to do. My life's not important. But I think his was. Such a waste, really, for everyone. Of course, it's all a woman's show over there now...." Then the denunciation of the royal ladies would begin, and very entertaining it was. Actually, Wallis would have made a very successful consort, but he was clearly no one's idea of even a figurehead monarch.

I used occasionally to go to their house in the Bois de Bologne, filled with loot from the royal family, or so the family claimed. Like Mona, Wallis lived a "perfect" life. Everything was exactly right. The two ladies liked each other to a point, though I did catch the Windsors standing in a corner of the Bismarcks' drawing room; the duchess had just turned over a plate to see what its marking was; then a loud whisper: "They *must* be living on capital, too."

I've just finished reading Caroline Blackwood's book about Wallis's last days, the prisoner of a French lady lawyer. Caroline describes the duchess as non compos mentis, the result of age. Actually, it was the result of a fourth or fifth face-lift. After a certain age, few people can take much anesthetic. Wallis was warned that she might die during the operation, but she went ahead: The result was splendid, but of course, she died on the operating table for several minutes, quite long enough to scramble her oxygen-denied brain.

My last dinner with her was in New York after the operation. We were four at a French restaurant. Most of the time she was her old self. But then she would lose her train of thought. Suddenly, she announced, "I did learn one sentence of Chinese after all those years out there." She clapped her hands. The waiter came over. "Champagne, *chop chop!*" she said. When he looked at her blankly, she frowned. "They do that deliberately, you know. Pretend they don't understand *perfect* Chinese." I tried to point out to her that as the waiter was Puerto Rican, he could not understand her elegant Mandarin. But she was already on another subject; and in another world.

The only thing of a "historic" nature that I learned from the duke was apropos Mona's current reading about the czar and his family. "I was there," said the duke, somewhat portentously. "In Russia?" I asked. After all, the prince regent had convinced himself that he had fought side by side with Wellington at Waterloo. "No. No." The duke was irritable. "I was there at *breakfast.*" "Ah," we all said, and Eddie, I think, reprised the key word *breakfast.*

"Yes. With the king . . . and the queen. Just the three of us. Suddenly an equerry comes in. I meant this was *breakfast,* for heaven's sake!" We looked, I hope, suitably horrified at this breach. "Not done, you know, ever. The king was furious, but the man went straight up to him with this note, which the king read and gave my mother, and she read it and gave it back and said, 'No.' The king gave it to the equerry and said, 'No.' Later that day I asked my mother what that was all about and she said the government was willing to send a ship to rescue the czar and his family but she did not think it would be good for us to have them in England and so the Bolsheviks shot the lot of them."

One suspects that the present princess of Wales, in a recently published private telephone conversation, may have got the mot juste when she referred to the family into which she has so unhappily married as "this fucking family." They are certainly tough as nails when it comes to survival. On the other hand, I suspect that Princess Margaret would think Queen Mary's decision typical of someone resentful of real royalty, like the czar. When she was reading *Nicholas and Alexandra,* the princess said, with a shudder, "They're so perfectly ordinary. I mean, it could be *us.*"

The last time that I saw the Windsors together was at a screening of a documentary about their lives, shown at a theater in the Champs-Elysées. I sat across from them and watched them as they watched their lives unfold. He had certainly been a beautiful youth. In fact, the audience, chilly, grand Parisians, gasped when they saw him at the front in the First World War, hair gleaming gold.

When the picture ended and the lights came up, the two small people rose in their seats and responded to an ovation for . . . what? Survival, I suppose. To my surprise, he was weeping and she was dry-eyed and hard-looking.

As I passed them, I heard him say, "I'd like to do it all over again." I am convinced that she said, "Well, I wouldn't." But I was by then too far away to hear what she said. Caroline Blackwood reports that in Wallis's last days she turned black.

Eddie told me that Wallis's sexual hold over the duke was that only she knew how to control his premature ejaculation.

"How is it done?"

"I don't have a clue."

"She should open a school . . ."

"I do know," said Eddie, somewhat precise and Prussian in these matters, "that before they were married, he could never keep a valet. Afterward, he had a very good one."

IN THE COURSE of one year, from January 10, 1948, when my third book was published, to year's end, I had met most of my life's cast of characters. There were to be later additions, but the principals are now all in place.

*Jack Kerouac at the time of our fateful union
in the Chelsea Hotel.*

"Now
You Owe Me
a Dollar"

ODAY ALLEN GINSBERG is thin and wan and beardless and
his right eyelid droops.

"I have diabetes," he says, "high blood pressure, a heart that's
irregular. I can eat only macrobiotic food. The doctors say that if I live at
half speed, I'll last a while." He is a year younger than I. But despite his
new fragility, he is almost as busy as he was when I last saw him at the
Democratic convention of 1968 in Chicago, when we were together on
television with a local district attorney, in place to defend and celebrate
what the courts later termed a "police riot" against not only godless hip-
pies and anarchists and all the other enemies of the Vietnam War but
against the nation's rulers as well, the delegates to the convention. The
police were unselective in their porcine fury, and so, for once, they got
a moderately bad press. Allen used the occasion to scream at the police
champion, who smiled tolerantly and made fag gestures to show that
he knew a thing or two about enemies of the human race. I thought
Allen misplayed it. But to each his style.

Now, twenty-six years later, we meet again on a cold January night at
something called Rockefeller University. I'd never heard of this establishment before, but Jean Stein's gentleman friend is its president, and
she has been allowed to give a party there to celebrate my receiving a literary prize, an event as uncommon in my native land as Halley's comet.

I have known Jean since she was a child. Now she has daughters older than she was when I first met her, the child of my mother's Hollywood friend Doris, wife to Jules Stein, an agent who had invented something called MCA that later absorbed Universal Studios only to be bought by a Japanese concern where, until recently, confused Asians struggled hopelessly with the inscrutable accounting practices of the film business, so different from the Shinto simplicities of their faraway islands.

I talk to Allen about Kerouac, Buddhism, and Paul Bowles, whom he has just seen in Tangier. Allen is en route to see William Seward Burroughs, now in his eighties and living in Kansas, where he paints pictures and shoots guns. We are all fading, at different speeds, to black.

I am writing this recollection in our house in the Hollywood Hills two weeks after the New York party and three weeks after the worst earthquake ever reported in our region: January 17, 1994. At 4:31 A.M. I was awakened by what sounded like aerial bombardment. For almost a minute the house shook. All power, lights, and telephone were cut off. I hurried down swaying stairs to the patio. Outside, in the dark, Howard and I sat for a time, responding not unpleasantly to several dozen aftershocks. Then I went back to bed.

At ten o'clock, the car that we had ordered to take us to the airport arrived and we were driven through a strange yellow haze, past traffic lights that had ceased to work. As the principal freeway had fallen in, we drove out La Brea Avenue, where Hispanic and black families were gathered on sidewalks in front of cabinlike houses, their belongings arranged all about them. Their mood was more festive than apprehensive. Also, what I had suspected to be true was indeed true: Had the evil Soviet empire launched even a small aerial attack on our great, evergood republic they would have shut the whole country down. Henceforth, we must have no enemy larger than Panama, and certainly no enemy with an air force, much less nuclear weapons.

Allen thought the first and last time that we had met was at a party for Kerouac's *Dharma Bums,* but that was in 1960. He had forgotten our 1968 meeting at the Democratic convention, where he had kissed my hand as Jean Genet looked on and Mayor Daley shouted "Sheeny!" at Senator Ribicoff. We were both surprised that we had met only three times in the past. I told him that in my haphazard pursuit of lost time, I have been reading a dozen or so books about the Beats. "In fact, I'm now reading a biography of you."

"There are two." Allen grinned. "I haven't read either of them." Up to a point, I believed him. There does come a time when one stops reading about oneself. But I find that I do enjoy reading about people that I have known, despite the prose of their biographers, a sort of frantic–in the case of the Beats–mindless journalese.

"The fifties are making a comeback." Allen was mildly complacent. "At least those of us who used to be knocked for smoking dope are still around and all the drinkers–including Jack–are dead."

We are in a room with large plate-glass windows overlooking the East River; on every side there are fellow survivors of the forties–now I fall into the journalistic habit of breaking up eras into meaningless decades. Most of the original cast is more or less recognizable, particularly Saul Steinberg, who must be ninety. But Terry Southern is now large and unlike the lean, sharp youth I first knew, while Norman Mailer is now as wide as he is tall, but, despite deafness, he is still seriously in motion with his seriously handsome wife at his side. Ken Galbraith, tall and ghostly white, joins us for a moment: We recall, with mock importance, that we last met at Gorbachev's plenum in the Kremlin, where the second Russian revolution had been announced, and Mailer, who had sat next to me in the great hall, disbelieved Gorbachev, but I believed him because he had used the sacred word *revolution* for what he was doing, sacred because it had always meant 1917, when the world was supposed to have been reborn once and for all; to use the word again really did mean a new revolution, and so it is coming to pass. Shortly before Chou En-lai died, he was asked whether or not, all in all, the French Revolution had been a good thing. "Surely," he said, "it is far too soon to tell."

Allen is coming soon to California, where we shall meet and sort out the past. I am amazed that in his somewhat fragile condition he's still on the go, giving readings, teaching, attending Buddhist groups. Years ago, I had said that I thought, once he had got over his bohemian phase, he would settle down to a successful career in advertising. But he stayed the course as a poet and a champion "of my two masters, Kerouac and Burroughs." There is something curiously selfless about his promotion of his two friends. Since I did not particularly admire the work of either, I tended to ignore the whole lot except for Paul Bowles, whose only connection with them was geography–Tangier in the fifties. Paul was almost twenty years older than we were, and two decades younger than the so-called Lost Generation. Yet in this morning's *Los Angeles Times,* I read that Paul is "the last and the best of the Lost Generation," who lived in "the fabulous pre-war Paris of Cocteau and Bowles." This is rather like New England's fabled Indian summer of Hawthorne, Melville, and Vidal. I must say these confusions give me vast joy; in fact, without a constant diet of them, my city of Duluth might never have flourished on the Mexican border.

Actually, Bowles had a small reputation as a composer in the early forties. Otherwise, he was unknown until 1949, when he published *The Sheltering Sky.* Subsequent books did less well, and he was entirely out of print in 1979, when I wrote an introduction to his collected short stories. He was duly, if briefly, grateful, and in a year or two all the books were back in print.

As I read my way through the various biographies of the Beats, I realize how much in the true American grain they had been. Restless, gabby, artless, on the road–the *yellow brick* road–to something transcendental, which turned out to be drugs for a time and then, for the survivors, there were transcendental fixes like California Buddhism, Scientology (briefly, in the case of Burroughs), higher meditation, anything to transcend the everyday. As I write this, I can't help noting that they were, perhaps without knowing it, heirs to the likes of Henry Miller and Anaïs and all the other naturals–I don't think primitives is quite the word–that go back, in the United States at least, to Whitman. I also begin to understand that in a nation dedicated not only to uplift but to transcendental experience, whether it be the Blood of the Lamb or automatic writing or the Ouija board, it was necessary for Henry James and Edith Wharton and T. S. Eliot to get out for good, while echt-American writers as Hawthorne and Cooper and Mark Twain spent a good deal of their time outside their native land; even that master of sly American incoherence Gertrude Stein settled in Paris, where the seventeen-year-old Bowles got to know her.

Stein read Paul's poems. "You are not a poet," she said. So he turned to music. Years later he started, guiltily, to write short stories. Guiltily, because he was the musician and Jane Bowles, his wife, the writer. But she had difficulty writing; and he had none. As he became successful, she became more and more odd until, after a stroke at forty, she was mad. But he persevered. Now, in old age, he is finally made much of for himself and not because of his connections with Stein or the Beats or

Tennessee Williams (for whose plays he wrote incidental music) or his music master, Aaron Copland.

"I just saw Paul in Tangier." Allen keeps track of everyone. "He's pretty much bedridden with sciatica and there's a blood clot in his leg, which he won't allow the local doctors to touch."

"Very wise," I said. After a certain age—eighty? (free of the cruel and insane master, sex)—one is soon going to be free of the greatest tyrant of all, life itself, and so any time given over to surgeons is apt to be time abandoned when not altogether stopped. A few years ago, Paul went to Switzerland for an operation and nearly died of a subsequent infection. "Swiss germs are particularly lethal," he observed to me on my last visit to Tangier; he was then in his seventy-fifth year and happy to be once more at home in familiar Tangerine filth. He lives in one room in a cement-block apartment house with a broken lift, uncertain electricity, and evil djinns all about.

As Paul has no telephone, I simply knocked on the door. "I can't believe you're here," he said. He was as dry and elegantly turned out as ever; some of his Paris suits are sixty years old. The hair is blond-white and the pale blue eyes are somewhat milky with age. Later, when I saw him in the film of *The Sheltering Sky,* his face looked like a sand dune just swept by wind; but then so did everything else in the film. "Down Among the Sheltering Palms," Capote used to sing whenever Paul's name was mentioned.

In the first years of our long friendship, he used sadly to say of my youthful success, "Too much too soon." When I saw him last, surrounded by tape recorders and eager camera crews, I reprised, with mock sadness, "Too much too late."

At the end of 1949, I made a date to join Paul in Ceylon, where he had bought an island off the south coast. From photographs the place—with house—was idyllic; it was also so isolated that it might as well have been on the moon. I booked passage on a ship, spent my last evening in New York with John Latouche and the actor Burgess Meredith, who was hilarious on the subject of his recent divorce from Paulette Goddard. "She even wants my donkey, which she hates." The next morning I went down to the docks only to find that the ship had sailed the day before. I had, for the first and last time in my life, got a date wrong.

Paul's letters were furious: I could at least have written that I was not coming. But I had written, and in due course he got my letter; on the other hand, he still does not believe that I made a mistake. In one of his letters to someone else, he said that he had been told I was in love. But that was not the case. At a loose end, I spent the winter in New Orleans, in a shabby flat on Dauphine Street.

I did not realize until recently, when I read the letters of Jane Bowles, that I had become, for a time, one of her numerous obsessions. In a letter dated November 1948, from Tangier, there is a mysterious allusion to a "cabin," presumably a ship's cabin. "In your letter you said you were sharing a cabin with Gore? Perhaps you thought I wouldn't know who Gore was (I know only too well) and would therefore understand better if you mentioned Tennessee. Kif-kif." (Moghrebi for "six of one, half dozen of the other.") "In other words, you might have been trying to show that you were involved with someone in a cabin and could therefore not wait over in New York." I have no idea what any of this is about. We never shared a cabin or a room, and I never go to bed with friends, much less with anyone older than I. But this does help date my first meeting with Paul: autumn 1948, in New York. Tennessee introduced us. I now see why my relations with Jane were so uncomfortable from the beginning.

The next month, Jane writes, "You mentioned Tennessee and Gore driving through Spain before coming here. Did you want to go with them? Or did you want us both to . . . ?" Jealousy? At being left out? Yet each had his own life with his own sex. Jane had Cherifa, the market woman, as well as a lady named Helvetia in New York. She could be droll about herself: "Word has come to me that Taormina is full of lesbians. Since they all come by ship through the Straits of Gibraltar, they pass right under my window here in Tangier, so you'd think that perhaps a few—well, even one—might just stop off and pay me a courtesy call."

On February 13, 1950, Jane wrote Paul in Ceylon: "Now that Gore is with you I suppose you are less lonely and you may even put off your return." But I was not there. I had missed the boat, the previous month, in every sense. Had I gone to Ceylon, I might have ended my days a permanent resident outside the United States. Instead, by the midsummer of that year, I had bought a house on the Hudson River, and settled into an American life. I cannot imagine what my life and world would have been like had I stayed all this time in Europe—neither Morocco nor Ceylon appealed to me.

Allen spoke of Kerouac. I think he is still in love with the idea of him; at least as he was in early days. Later, as Jack became more and more alcoholic, he would denounce Jews and faggots. "And sound just like his mother," said Allen, "a true horror who never let loose of him. . . ."

"Or he of her," I added.

Allen nodded. "You know around 1968, when we were all protesting the Vietnam War, Jack wrote me that the war was just an excuse for 'you Jews to be spiteful again.' I sometimes think maybe he was right."

"No, right-*wing*," I contributed. Drunken Jack had made a fool of himself on Buckley, Jr.'s television program; and then never ceased to admire that profound political thinker. I have only just learned that Buckley figures benignly in a current documentary film of Allen's life. Political kinship? Or simply a naive love of celebrity in any form? I can't tell. Anyway, Allen's gift for public relations has always been masterful.

I said that I had read Allen's version of what happened between Jack and me in the Chelsea Hotel. "Well, he did say that he had blown you." Allen on sex is rather like a doctor describing, neutrally, the symptoms of a case. "He was sort of proud of that." Jack gave out many different versions of what happened that night, including a chapter in his novel *The Subterraneans* and a poem dedicated to me in *Mexico City Blues.*

Allen was surprised that I had known Jack since 1949. "I suppose back then he would have come on to you like a dumb football jock."

"Quite the opposite. Anyway, that was *my* come-on, only with me it was tennis, not football. No, we met at the Metropolitan Opera House, in the club circle, in evening dress." I've always found this first encounter satisfyingly incongruous. Jack was with a publisher, and I was with a friend of the publisher, a brilliant alcoholic writer with a fortune that he was systematically losing. The writer had paid both Jack and Jack's beloved Nemesis, Neal Cassady, for sex.

Allen asked for the names of our two johns. I gave them. "I'm starting to remember," he said at last.

"Jack came on to me as one writer on the make to another. Only, his first book, *The Town and the City,* wouldn't be published until the next year, and I'd already done *The City and the Pillar.*"

"We all read that," said Allen, who seems to have stopped reading me at that high point in my career. "Because of the sex. Nobody had gone that far then."

I can still see Jack vividly. We are standing at the back of the opera box, which is so crowded that our faces are only a few inches apart. I feel the heat from his body. The eyes are bright and clear and blue; the body muscular, not yet bloated; a drop of water slides alongside his left ear and down his pale cheek, not sweat, but water that he must have just used to comb his thick black Indian-like hair. We were also coming on to each other like two pieces of trade—yes, I was attracted.

"I used to blow him every now and then." Allen stared at Kenneth Galbraith as he loped like a benign camel across the room. "Jack liked company in bed, but he wasn't all that keen on the sex part—with men. He blew me once to see what it was like. He didn't like it."

Allen spoke of Jack's sad last days, when he and his mother retired to Florida, where he drank himself to a death which finally came when, after he ate a tin of tuna fish, his liver exploded and he bled to death, like William Burroughs's son, who, in his twenties, thanks to drink and drugs, underwent a successful liver transplant, then promptly used up the new liver and died.

We discussed the unpleasant things that Jack had said about us in his last years, every word excitedly recorded by passing journalists. "He was a mean drunk," said Allen. "Like his father. What did you and Jack do?"

"Well, I fucked him."

"I don't think," said Allen thoughtfully, "that he would have liked that."

"Maybe that was the point." I changed the subject; I said that I was preparing a new edition of *The City and the Pillar*.

"Put more sex in!" Allen was cheerful.

"But everybody does that now. Maybe I'll take it all out." As I revise these pages, Allen is coming to call this afternoon. He is in Los Angeles, giving readings; meeting Buddhist groups; promoting the film about himself. He is a born executive. Why then did he take up literature when he seems happiest with religion of the somewhat dopey American kind? Maybe I'll ask him about that. Maybe not. I suddenly remember that I introduced him to Mailer. Paul Bowles was staying in a friend's Manhattan house. Ginsberg and Peter Orlovsky were already there. Time for the Beats to meet the War writers. I arrive with Mailer. Mailer makes a speech. Then lies down on the floor and goes to sleep. Allen puts his bare feet comfortably on Mailer's paunch. "Of course, he's crazy," he observes. (When I told Allen this, he grinned. "How could I have been so disrespectful?") Paul had switched on a tape recorder to memorialize our conversation: "But all I could hear later on the tape was the parrot shrieking." Or was it Allen's friend Orlovsky?

At Jean Stein's dinner party, Galbraith describes our adventures at the 1968 convention in Chicago and proposes a toast. Then Mailer speaks at length of our "small but famous quarrels." I respond.

Jean goes to Howard's table with a birthday cake and a speech that she is too shy to give. Saul Steinberg recalls in precise detail our last meeting forty years ago. This is, plainly, the last round-up.

A BBC PROGRAM CALLED *Omnibus* is doing a two-hour documentary of my life and times. So we now move on to Washington, D.C. As always, I am mildly depressed when I am in the city, not that it any longer resembles the southern town of my youth. With a camera crew, we go to the house that T. P. Gore built in Rock Creek Park. I am received graciously by the new Malaysian ambassadress, who turns out to be Spanish. She has prepared us a grand tea.

"I love this house. I wish I could turn it back to the way it was when you lived here, which was . . . ?"

"I arrived from West Point in November 1925. As there was no bed for a baby, I slept in a bureau drawer." Does this explain my claustrophobia?

Outside the house, there are sheets of ice and thick snowdrifts. I note sadly that from every side but that of the creek below, unattractive new houses are visible: Dah's original three acres have dwindled to less than one. But then all the woods that I knew both here and across the river in Virginia have given way to houses and what are known as developments.

"This certainly looks a lot better than when my grandmother was here." I praised her honestly. The living room is beige and ivory, with Malaysian artworks in glass cases. There is the inevitable photograph of the ambassadorial couple with President Clinton, as well as a large portrait of the king of Malaysia, whose father once gave me lunch in Johore, where he was sultan.

I go up to the attic. The long room that once ran the length of the house has been broken up into small rooms. I sit in a chair near the window where I once ate the Easter egg and read *The Athenian* and I hear myself say to the camera that this attic, with all its books, was my only real education. Did I know I was going to be a writer then? I said yes, which is not quite true: I just wanted to read all the books in the attic.

We cross the river to Merrywood. Again, new houses everywhere. The original forty acres have dwindled to five or six. The new owner–a real estate developer–has completely redone what was a rather chaste house in the Georgian style. Two wings have been added, and a turret sprouts mysteriously on the roof. The developer and his wife are not there, but an amiable housekeeper shows us through the downstairs. The interior is like a Las Vegas casino. Artworks of great singularity clutter expensive rooms. A ceramic near-life-size giraffe dominates a new end room. Also on view: dozens of heavy silver-framed portraits of Reagan and Bush and other Republicans to whom the owner has contributed some of the money their regime made it possible for him to make.

I walk from room to room like Wilde's Canterville Ghost. I go to the stairs and sit in the same spot where my mother sat after her disastrous wedding night. I talk to the camera. Then I go up to the landing and the door to the small room where Jimmie and I had made love. I put this demurely, ignoring Ginsberg's ukase about sex. I had told the producer that this had been my room for six years and then it was Jackie's room until she married Jack. With some apprehension–rather like opening one's own tomb on camera–I open the door to reveal not the now-legendary room but a linen closet. We have all been erased, the object, I suspect, of the exercise, since it would have been far cheaper for the owner to build himself a Las Vegas casino rather than to wreck so deliberately and elaborately what was, in the words of Virginia's senator, "a historic house." An embroidered pillow says, "Better *nouveau* rich than not rich."

Only the old pool house, described at the beginning of *Washington, D.C.,* is still as it was; the pool has been filled in. Bright sky. Cold air. Brown trees. Suddenly, I hear the roar of the Potomac River, now clearly visible through leafless woods.

For a moment, things are magically as they were. I sit in a chair–and listen to the river. I think about Jimmie. Curiously, the ghosts of Nina and Hughdie and all the others that I knew then have faded away. But then these woods and this river had been specifically his and mine. I try to imagine him now, a sixty-eight-year-old former baseball star, with grown children and the obligatory second young wife. Would he still seem to me my other half? No. But my "unfinished business" with him would have been long since finished had he lived. I am now trying to solve a mystery: Would he have continued to recall what was for me a completing of the self but might have been for him nothing at all? Before I had ever heard of Blake, I had stumbled–blindly?–on his great truth. "Never seek to tell thy love . . ." Until, of course, it is too late. Meanwhile, ". . . the gentle wind does move silently, invisibly," whenever I think of him.

There is now a swimming pool near the house. Beside the pool, the gilded necks and heads of two giant plaster horses emerge from the earth like Pluto's chariot, surging upward from Hades in pursuit of Persephone and the spring of the year–to put a classical gloss on all this horror. In front of the house, a half-dozen life-size plaster sheep, painted brown and white, await a plaster shepherd. If the 1 percent that own the country spend their money in this way . . .

We drive to the Capitol. The place is aswarm with police and Secret Service as this evening the president will deliver his State of the Union address. Even so, it is my impression that the Capitol is now rather more like the Kremlin during Stalin's feisty reign than a place where the citizens used to wander about and feel at home. Metal detectors everywhere; stern black guards who, very slowly, examine the BBC's television equipment; we have made so many enemies all around the world that, in the name of terrorism, a quite effective police state has ever so gradually replaced the old republic. Also, to bring a television crew in, one needs the invitation of a senator. "What about Kennedy?" asked the naive producer. I explained that as we got deeper into my life story, he would discover that there is little traffic between me and the doomed family. I suggest John Warner, senator from Virginia. Over the years, we meet occasionally. He is now white-haired, but still lean and handsome; he is also ranking Republican on the Armed Services Committee, the principal engine of our financial distress; but he and I never discuss politics seriously, only gossip.

John walks toward me. We are wired for sound. "Button your jacket," he advises. Together we walk toward the camera at the far end of the north corridor, with its painted walls, the work of an Italian who had been overexposed to the Vatican's decor.

I note many more blacks on duty, or passing through, than in the old days, when the guards were not only redneck to the core but often poor relations of members of Congress. As we walk, I report on my visit that morning to Merrywood. John sighs; he has been to the house for political fund-raisers. He likes the new owners, but he also liked the house the way it was before. "We thought about buying it, but then my wife got worried about security. I mean, there you are, off in the woods, no police nearby."

I said that Merrywood is now ringed with houses, many of them resembling bunkers. As one of them had belonged to a head of the CIA, he must have been well guarded. Although our cameraman had once filmed him there, he has forgotten his name. That is Washington at its imperial best: Out of office, everyone is forgotten. Only the offices continue, brief sources of honor before long-term future profit, trading off them. Theoretically, the cliff dwellers, as the permanent inhabitants are called, should remember more than they do, but luckily, in these United States of blessed Amnesia, who can recall how many secretaries of agriculture have come and gone? Each famous for at least a week on a magazine cover; then gone. Even the presidents blur for those of us of a certain age. Recently, a novelist thought to make a joke by putting President Ford's name in the title of a novel; thus, he sank his own book dead. Henry Ford, yes; Glenn Ford, too; but never the long-lost Gerald, who now neither is nor was.

John Warner describes for the camera the table in front of the door to the Committee on Foreign Affairs. A treaty is sent by messenger from White House to Senate and placed upon this table; then it is reverently (or roughly) taken inside for senatorial "advice and consent"; dissent is rare as, over the years of empire, the executive has usurped Congress's only two great powers, the purse and war.

John then leads us into the Rotunda, where there is a copy of Magna Carta that he personally got from England. The cupola has just been painted, while set against the walls, like a cordon sanitaire, the statues of our great men are unnaturally white, like soap carvings. Tourists take pictures. Several ask me for my autograph. John and I part, aptly, beneath a statue of Lincoln. He has been a good friend to my sister. He has also, that day, come out against a fellow Republican who is running for the Senate in Virginia. "I expect to get into some trouble for this." He frowned. "But we just can't have people like Oliver North in the Senate." He is genuinely outraged. I say genuinely because in a state where there are so many staunch Jesus-Christers, it is not wise to challenge

their idols. But John is a romantic who still thinks that the Senate ought
to be a place for gentlemen.

I walk down the steps of the Capitol and into the winter-bleak park
that separates Capitol from Supreme Court. A number of trees have been
planted in memory of distinguished senators. There is a tree to my
grandfather, but I have never been able to find it. This time we got a map
and located a tall forty-five-year-old chestnut oak with THOMAS PRYOR
GORE OF OKLAHOMA on a tag. The tree must have been planted not long
after his death, in 1949. So, except for one tall tree, hardly the most eternal of monuments, he too has been erased. My mood is now as grim as
the day. I don't like the imperial bustle of the Capitol. The guards. Guns.
No, it is not Stalin's Kremlin; rather, a camorra stronghold in Naples or
one of the courtrooms of the currently beleaguered Italian government,
as Italy's First Republic draws to a confused close. When the people dislike the state as much as the state dislikes them, what happens next?

Just beyond the handsome snow-white Supreme Court building are
streets that look to have been bombed out in some long-ago-lost war.
Here live the black majority of the city. Yet the occupants of the Capitol
speak mindlessly of democracy and justice and human rights and the
free world. Well, happy nation to have no collective memory. But then,
as one looks at the paintings and statues that decorate the public buildings and parks, one realizes that everyone has either been swallowed
up by time or else remodeled to serve current necessities, like Lincoln,
whose icon is currently being peddled by schoolteachers as that of a
born-again abolitionist.

The current senator from Oklahoma sits at Gore's desk. "Harry Truman also used it," he told me, "right after your grandfather left the
Senate. But now, of course, your cousin Albert's vice president." The
senator laughed. "When Albert was running for president in 1988, he
came to Oklahoma, and to hear him tell it, old T. P. Gore was *his* grandfather." So the web of kin goes on if the individual strands do not.

At least Gore's house in Rock Creek Park still has much of its charm,
thanks to the present occupants. One of the Malaysian servants, who
had been in the house for several years, wanted to know what the original place was like. I told him that there had been a slave cabin on the
lower terrace. He was delighted: "I dug up the foundations. I wondered
what it was. I've planted a vegetable garden down there." The ambas-

sadress liked the wildlife. "I feed the birds and all these squirrels and raccoons. They are quite tame." I said that Dot had trained several generations of them to come to her; so there is at least some continuity on that dwindling acre above the narrow creek that rushes over rocks between banks of laurel and, of course, poison ivy, which meant for me, one week each summer, white chalky calamine lotion to cover oozing blisters.

I like Dah's tree. It even reminds me a bit of the way that he always stood, very straight, in an almost military brace, chin high, blind eyes upon some bleak horizon. He was stoic: "In old age time passes like a snowflake upon the river. Then, just as you start to make some sense of life, you're gone." Well, most of the cast of my life is now gone. I assume that the tree will outlast me, though the ozone level in the city is doing the trees no good while making my eyes burn and water.

That night I dine with my sister in the old Jockey Club, a restaurant in what used to be our cousin Grady Gore's hotel, the Fairfax, now called something else. The senators Albert Gore, senior and junior, used to live there, free of charge one always heard. Young Albert went to St. Albans, as I had done years before. A master who knew us both said that Junior's ambition was so obvious at an early age that his canny schoolmates—most of them also children of Congress or of high officialdom—called him "Ozymandias, king of kings: look on my works, ye Mighty, and despair."

"On the other hand," said the master, "the boy painted the most beautiful miniatures."

I suspect that I shall never again set foot in the Capitol or Merrywood or Rock Creek. But I might visit the chestnut oak again, the family's last Washington monument—Ozymandias indeed. Gladly, I returned to Los Angeles, to yet another earthquake. But this time I stayed in bed and slept through it.

YESTERDAY, Allen Ginsberg came to our house in the Hollywood Hills; accompanied by a psychiatrist cousin, who proved to be enthusiastically "literary," unlike Allen, who, more and more, resembles a Reform rabbi of the "nurturing" school—to use an adjective much loved by the New Agers here in Southern California, where I am sitting in the sun on trembling earth.

We wondered—*he* wondered yet again—why it was that, as we had known pretty much the same people for forty years, we had so seldom met.

"Of course, I was this poor little poet in Greenwich Village and you were this famous rich best-seller," he said, failing to look undistinguished. He has humor, but as he has spent most of his life talking to the young and ignorant, one must help him break through a pedagogical style that sometimes inspires him to tell you things that he must suspect you know. When I said that, yes, I had actually read Blake and, no, I was not much of one for the transcendental (and quoted Pope), he was surprised.

"When do you read all those books?" I said that that is what I do. He, on the other hand, is surrounded by students, would-be writers, disciples, while I see hardly anyone who reads, much less writes. My appearances at universities are political.

The night before, we had had dinner at Don Bachardy's house, and Allen had said—I forget the context—that he was "insular." I noted politely that as I live in Italy, I have the obvious advantage of being "peninsular." As we drank tea and his cousin discussed Céline, Allen wanted to know why I had agreed with him that he was "insular."

I didn't answer directly—the word had been his—but I did say that I had been alarmed at the sudden appearance of the Beats in the fifties. "Just as I was beginning to get a grip on what writing could be and how best to examine one's life, you come along, preaching a fuzzy sort of Star-of-the-East mysticism. I wanted people to think. You wanted them to *be*. Well, they *are*, anyway. But to encourage the worst educated and the most resolutely propagandized public in the first world *not* to think about why things are as they are is cruel." My *On the Road* was *The Judgment of Paris,* the first of the books I wrote when I moved to the Hudson Valley. I tried to touch many bases in that book. Our differences were polar.

Allen thought that they had made a positive contribution by introducing Eastern thought into American culture. "Jack wrote a wonderful book on the Buddha." I confessed that I had read none of his "Eastern" books but that, long before Jack, Hinduism crops up not only in Emerson but in the author of *The Wizard of Oz.* Allen started to tell me about the Buddha's fivefold way. I said I knew all that. This surprised him. But then except for *The City and the Pillar,* he has no idea of anything that I have written. But then, to be fair, I don't read him, either. I suggested, if he wanted to understand the historical background to the Buddha, Confucius, as well as their contemporaries Socrates and (possibly) Zoroaster, that he read *Creation*. "Chomsky liked it," I said, rather too quickly, giving the book a good review at second hand. "Particularly my 'discovery' that the entire human race appears to be as programmed as the human child is programmed to speak, replicate, die." He asked for a copy; I gave him one.

Allen still does too much rushing about. He looks worn-out and worried. "Today my sugar count's in the four hundreds. I've just taken more insulin." I worry when I'm at 127—seven points above normal. Howard promised to find a teacake for diabetics. But the cake turned out to be sugary, and I brought out cheese and crackers. Again, Allen noted that the Beats who smoked pot had all survived while those writers who drank died early. I said some of us alcoholics survive, too. Allen's cousin, a medical man as well as psychiatrist, discoursed on the liver. Kerouac's had simply exploded at age forty-seven. We tried to figure just how much he drank in a day. I suspect, like Capote, it was all day long every day.

I said that I was dealing with the fifties in this chapter. Could Allen recall the order of our three meetings? "I thought the first had been with Paul Bowles at Libby Holman's house in New York, early fifties."

"No. I didn't meet Paul until Tangier in 1956. You and I met at that party for Kerouac around 1959." I recalled the evening.

Louis Auchincloss had married a lady younger than himself. In the tradition of wellborn young wives, Adele had carefully separated Louis from his old and sometimes raffish friends, of whom I was not only one but "*Hollywood*," too, as she remarked, eyeing with cold distaste my unfamiliar Savile Row suit. Nevertheless, in due course, she asked me for dinner at their flat. Dinner done, a lively woman who worked for Louis's publisher rang to say, "There's a party downtown for Jack Kerouac." *The Dharma Bums* had just been published. "You've *got* to come."

Louis repeated this message to the amused diners. Politely, Adele ignored the invitation. But I did not. "I think I'll go," I said. Louis's great black Byzantine eyes were suddenly those of a suffering Christ Pantocrator set in Adelian gold. Thus, I fell, like the son of morning, from Adele's dinner table to Greenwich Village, never to rise again, and so it was there, in all that chaos and old night, that Allen thinks we first met.

Peter Orlovsky, Allen's friend, declaimed, "I have a clean asshole." When I reminded Allen of this, he said, yes, he would have said that because in India they had given up toilet paper and now washed in the Indian manner.

Jack was thick and sullen, and about to lose his beauty for good. I told him that I had read *The Subterraneans*, in which I figure as Arial Lavalina. Meticulously, Jack describes an evening that he had arranged for Burroughs to meet me.

Burroughs had written Jack from Mexico, November 2, 1949, "I was certainly gratified to hear of your success as a novelist, and meeting all them celebrities.... What is this Vidal character like?" I would like to read what Jack wrote him.

Then, April 1952, Burroughs wrote: "Have you read Gore Vidal's latest?—*The Judgment of Paris*? Funny in places. The man is primarily a satirist and should avoid philosophizing and tragedy." There is, of course, no tragedy of any kind in the book, but the "philosophizing" is of the classical sort, inspired by Rome, Cairo, Paris—my journeys in 1948 and 1949. But at least Burroughs got the satire, even if the classical world in which I had perhaps oversteeped myself was to be permanently alien to the reputed heir to the Burroughs Adding Machine fortune, whose own satiric style was, at its worst, like that of Sinclair Lewis; at its best, I am told, when he would drift into what he called his comic "routines" or monologues.

"Why will people insist on attempting what they are not fitted to do?" He continues in his letter to Jack about my tragic longings. "A man who writes beautiful prose will insist to produce excruciatingly bad poetry and so forth. Is Gore Vidal queer or not? Judging from the picture of him that adorns his latest opus I would be interested to make his acquaintance. Always glad to meet a literary gent in any case, and if the man of letters is young and pretty and possibly available my interest understandably increases. By the way what ever became of Al's normality program?" Earlier, when Allen asked me if I'd ever gone to an analyst, I said no. Had he? I'd quite forgotten Bill's note that Allen had gone to one to become "normal."

Vague answer: "Oh, I went for someone to talk to, I suppose."

"But isn't that what writing's for?" Then I recall just how young Allen was compared to Jack, much less to Burroughs, already a Harvard graduate, a married man, a father, a junkie, and "killer on the run." From the letters, Bill is infatuated with Allen, who is in love with Jack, who is in love with Cassady as well as various women.

Allen ended his sexual relationship with Burroughs because "Bill was trying to get into my mind." He frowned. "It was too much."

August 23, 1953, Jack brought Burroughs and me together at the San Remo bar, on the edge of Greenwich Village. Hot night. Jack was manic. Sea captain's hat. T-shirt. Like Marlon Brando in *Streetcar*. Drinking beer. Burroughs looked like a traveling salesman who had traveled far too far in a wrinkled gray suit. He had published a good novel, *Junkie*, under the name William Lee. He was just up from Mexico. I think Jack had told me all about Bill's problems with the police after he shot his wife dead in a game of William Tell. I also knew he was a junkie. Since I knew nothing about drugs then, if Bill or Jack had been on anything that night, I would not have known. Bill was quiet. Jack was loud. I supposed he was drunk.

I have no idea what we talked about. I now learn, from Burroughs's letters, that Bill had asked me about Europe. He was on his way to Rome. He had liked my description in *Judgment* of a Turkish bath in the Via Poli where boys were available. Unfortunately, the bath was closed when he got there in the freezing winter. He denounces me in a letter to Jack as a "lying bastard" for having given the town such a good review. Then he moved on to Tangier and made, as it were, his name, not to mention literary self, with a good deal of help from Brion Gysin, a brilliant creature, who was to suggest to Bill that what he wrote might be magically enhanced by cutting it up and then piecing together the fragments, presumably at random. Gysin also made a painter of Burroughs, and that is what he mostly does now. Why, I wonder, to paraphrase Burroughs on me, does a natural painter, say, want to be a writer? Or a natural composer, like Bowles, want to be a writer, too? The true answer to this question lies in the question itself; why "why"? Why not.

After I read Burroughs's letters, I reread *Naked Lunch*. The novel is taken from the letters, which are generally sharper and better written than the now very mild book. Burroughs seems to be one of those writers who must go into character to tell a story. When he does, he can be very funny, but too much of the time he is just muttering to himself like old Uncle Ezra—the traditional Yankee as well as the Ezra Pound, whose epistolary attempts at being a funny yokel are so unfunny.

I also, suddenly, recall with shame the only time I was a judge for a literary prize (with Elizabeth Hardwick and Professor Harry Levin of Harvard). Lizzie and I wanted the prize to go to *Morte d'Urban* by J. F. Powers. Levin argued powerfully for Nabokov's *Pale Fire. Lolita*, yes, I said, but to this latest overelaborate bit of academic funning, no. Levin then said that he would accede to our bad taste if we would drop from the list of finalists a book so terrible that it might destroy literature. Cravenly, we erased *Naked Lunch.* Yet even then, I suspected that Levin's hatred of the book was proof of its merit. I was never again a judge.

I am struck, as always, by the desperate need of the Beats for some sort of transcendental experience or faith. Burroughs is drawn to L. Ron Hubbard's *Dianetics.* Jack and Allen, to Edgar Cayce's Zen Buddhism. Curious that three essentially realistic writers should so crave mystical experience or, perhaps, the first part of this sentence answers the question I was going to pose. Without much imagination of one's own and yet eager to achieve some higher estate, it is natural to turn to those who claim to have achieved it and appropriate their "vision." Drugs also enhance reality as my great-grandfather Luther Lazarus Rewalt discovered when he peddled gin and sugar as "Rewalt's Elixir."

The night of August 23, 1953. This is how Jack described it in *The Subterraneans.* He has changed the San Remo in New York City to the Mask in San Francisco. Carmody is Burroughs. I am Arial Lavalina. In a letter to his agent, October 7, 1956, Jack writes, "Perhaps the only libelous point is 'Ariel' [*sic*] Lavalina, a perhaps recognizable portrait of Gore Vidal."

> *The night Arial Lavalina the famous young writer suddenly was standing in the Mask and I was sitting with Carmody also now famous writer in a way who'd just arrived from North Africa. . . . I saw Lavalina and called his name and he came over. When Mardou came to get me to go home I wouldn't go, I kept insisting it was an important literary moment, the meeting of those two (Carmody having plotted with me a year earlier in dark Mexico when we'd lived poor and beat and he's a junkey, "Write a letter to Ralph Lowry find out how I can get to meet this here good-looking Arial Lavalina, man, look at that picture on the back of* Recognition of

Rome, *ain't that something?" My sympathies with him in the matter being personal and again like Bernard also queer he was connected with the legend of the bigbrain of myself which was my WORK, that all consuming work, so wrote the letter and all that) but now suddenly (after of course no reply from the Ischia and otherwise grapevines and certainly just as well for me at least) he was standing there and I recognized him from the night I'd met him at the Met ballet when in New York in a tux I'd cut out with tuxed editor to see glitter nightworld New York of letters and wit, and Leon Danillian [sic], so I yelled "Arial Lavalina! Come here!" which he did.—When Mardou came I said whispering gleefully "This is Arial Lavalina ain't that mad!"—"Yeh man but I want to go home.". . . Finally (she laughing) depositing her in a cab, to get home, wait for me—going back to Lavalina and Carmody whom gleefully and now alone back in my big world night adolescent literary vision of the world, with nose pressed to window glass, "Will you look at that, Carmody and Lavalina, the great Arial Lavalina tho not a great great writer like me nevertheless so famous and glamorous etc. together in the Mask and I arranged it and everything ties together, the myth of the rainy night, Master Mad, Raw Road, going back to 1949 and 1950 and all things grand great the Mask of old history crusts"—(this my feeling and I go in) and sit with them and drink further—repairing the three of us to 13 Pater a lesbian joint down Columbus, Carmody, high, leaving us to go enjoy it, and we sitting in there, further beers, the horror the unspeakable horror of myself suddenly finding in myself a kind of perhaps William Blake or Crazy Jane or really Christopher Smart alcoholic humility grabbing and kissing Arial's hand and exclaiming "Oh Arial you dear—you are going to be—you are so famous—you wrote so well—I remember you—what—" whatever and now rememberable and drunkenness, and there he is a well-known and perfectly obvious homosexual of the first water, my roaring brain—we go to his suite in some hotel—I wake up in the morning on the couch, filled with the first horrible recognition, "I didn't go back to Mardou's at all" so in the cab he gives me—I ask for fifty cents but he gives me a dollar saying "You owe me a dollar" and I rush out and walk fast in the hot sun. . . . "I'll write a letter at once to Lavalina," enclosing*

a dollar and apologizing for getting so drunk and acting in such a
way as to mislead him.

I challenged Jack. "Why did you, the tell-it-all-like-it-is writer, tell everything about that evening with Burroughs and me and then go leave out what happened when we went to bed?"

"I forgot," he said. The once startlingly clear blue eyes were now bloodshot.

"You remembered what I said to you the next morning." We had woken up in a low double bed. As I didn't drink much in those days, I was reasonably brisk. Jack was hungover. After we had dressed, he said he would have to take the subway to wherever it was that he was living with a black girl. "Only I don't have any money." I gave him a dollar and said, "Now you owe me a dollar," which he reports in *The Subterraneans*. In fact, everything is verbatim from our meeting at the San Remo and our visit to Tony Pastor's, a dyke hangout, and then, outside, on a streetcorner, as Jack, with one arm, swung his body round and round a lamppost, a Tarzan routine that caused Burroughs to leave us in disgust.

I said I was heading uptown. I was staying at my father's apartment. But Jack had other ideas. "Let's get a room around here." The first law of sex is never go to bed with someone drunk. Corollary to this universal maxim was my own fetish—never to have sex with anyone older. I was twenty-eight. Jack was thirty-one. Five years earlier, when we first met, I would have overruled the difference, but I had also arbitrarily convinced myself that Conrad's "shadow line" extended to sex: So from the age of thirty on, a man or woman was, for my purposes, already a corpse—not that I ever had much on my mind when it came to sex with men. In my anonymous encounters, I was what used to be called trade. I did nothing—deliberately, at least—to please the other. When I became too old for these attentions from the young, I paid, gladly, thus relieving myself of having to please anyone in any way. But now here I was stuck with Jack, who had certainly once attracted me at the Metropolitan when that drop of clear water slid down his cheek. Now there was real sweat. I stared at him. We were the same height and general build. With some misgiving, I crossed the shadow line.

At the nearby Chelsea Hotel, each signed his real name. Grandly, I told the bemused clerk that this register would become famous. I've often wondered what did happen to it. Has anyone torn out our page? Or is it still hidden away in the dusty Chelsea files? Lust to one side, we both thought, even then (this was before *On the Road*), that we owed it to literary history to couple.

I remember that the bathroom was near the entrance to a large double room. There was no window shade, so a red neon light flickering on and off gave a rosy glow to the room and its contents. Jack was now in a manic mood: We must take a shower together. To my surprise, he was circumcised. Under the shower, for a moment, he rewound himself to the age of about fourteen and, for an instant, I saw not the dark slackly muscled Jack but blond Jimmie, only Jimmie was altogether more serious and grown-up at fourteen than Jack . . .

I have just recalled Tennessee's aversion to sex with other writers or, indeed, with intellectuals of any kind. "It is most disturbing to think that the head beside you on the pillow might be thinking, too," said the Bird, who had a gift for selecting fine bodies attached to heads usually filled with the bright confetti of lunacy.

Where Anaïs and I were incompatible–chicken hawk meets chicken hawk–Jack and I were an even more unlikely pairing–classic trade meets classic trade, and who will *do* what?

"Jack was rather proud of the fact that he blew you." Allen sounded a bit sad as we assembled our common memories over tea in the Hollywood Hills. I said that I had heard that Jack had announced this momentous feat to the entire clientele of the San Remo bar, to the consternation of one of the customers, an advertising man for Westinghouse, the firm that paid for the program *Studio One,* where I had only just begun to make a living as a television playwright. "I don't think," said the nervous advertiser, "that this is such a good advertisement for you, not to mention Westinghouse." As *On the Road* would not be published until 1957, he had no idea who Jack was.

Thanks to Allen's certainty of what Jack had told him, I finally recall the blow job–a pro forma affair, which I put a quick stop to. At what might be nicely called loose ends, we rubbed bellies for a while; later he would publish a poem dedicated to me: "Didn't know I was a great come-onner, did you? (come-on-er)." I was not particularly touched by this belated Valentine, considering that I finally flipped him over on his stomach, not an easy job as he was as much heavier than I as was the merchant mariner in Seattle, whom he—only now does it strike me—physically resembled. Was I getting my own back on Jack's back?

Jack raised his head from the pillow to look at me over his left shoulder; off to our left the rosy neon from the window gave the room a mildly infernal glow. He stared at me a moment—I see this part very clearly now, forehead half covered with sweaty dark curls—then he sighed as his head dropped back onto the pillow. There are other published versions of this encounter: In one, Jack says that he spent the night in the bathroom. On the floor? There was a shower but no tub. In another, he was impotent. But the potency of other males is, for me, a turnoff. What I have reported is all there was to it, except that I liked the way he smelled.

Morning. Hangover. Gray light. Dull blue eyes. Clothes pulled on in silence. Now you owe me a dollar. We meet only one more time, with Allen, when *The Dharma Bums* is published. Why didn't you say what really happened . . . ?

Allen now answers that question for me. "He didn't dare write anything like that because he was afraid of his mother. She was a monster. She hated me because I was a fag. Worse, I was a Jew, too." Allen laughed. "But I did go see her after Jack was dead, in Florida. I'd shaved off my beard, and then it all came out. She was terrified of bearded men. As a child, she had been molested by one. So, beardless, I was all right now." Quick thinking, Memere.

I cannot say that I ever took much joy in Jack's writing, but a few years ago when I reread *On the Road*, I found the experience somewhat—well, romantic. There is so much energy and youth in his wild ramblings, and if the result is more like Looney Tunes than Cervantes, then so much the worse for high literature. What was irresistible in Jack at his sanest was the sweetness of his character; what, I am told and read, was the saddest part of the alcoholic decline was his anti-Semitic, anti-fag ravings, and, of course, the loss of that animal charm.

Thirty years after the head on the pillow, I am at the Paris airport, Orly. Next to me, a French youth; he is wearing a T-shirt with Jack's face on it. I ask if he has read Jack. Yes, he has read one book—had I read him? I said that I had; in fact, I'd known him. The boy was stunned, as if I had said that I'd known Rimbaud. Did he really look like this? He patted his thin chest. I was tactful. Yes, he did for a time, and that's all that's necessary, to look like that–to be like that–for a time, as time is an eminence most famous for running out on all of us.

"I am in love with him," said the boy, simply.

"So was I," I said, to my own surprise. "For a few minutes, anyway." I added this last in English. Of course he never paid me back the dollar.

At Home
on the Hudson
in the Cold War

IN THE SPRING OF 1950 I left New Orleans for New York City. I was twenty-four. I had just published *The Season of Comfort*, written earlier in Guatemala. Although I have never reissued the book, it was as close to an autobiographical novel as I was to write until *Washington, D.C.* Dot told me that Nina had gone on a bender when she read it. I suggested that the bender was an excuse *not* to read what she could not have got through anyway. Where Dah, like some ancient vampire, had turned me into an undead voracious reader like himself, Nina and her brother, in rebellion against him, were resolute illiterates.

I was ready to settle down, somewhere near but not in New York City as the Russians were coming and the Bomb would soon fall in the night. The American people were now being systematically terrified by the country's ownership. Schoolchildren were told how to "save" themselves when the Bombs fell. If in school, they were to hide under their desks. At home, parents were exhorted to build shelters in backyards or basements. The great perpetual American war machine was now humming smoothly, and though it was still officially peacetime (soon we would have a proper war in Korea), Truman had reinstituted the draft, something unknown in the United States except in wartime. Income taxes were as high as 90 percent in order to pay the defense cartel to keep the arsenal of democracy full of weapons so that we could help all the peace-loving little countries everywhere on earth whether they

*On the lawn at Edgewater. I still dream of
this house, which I owned from 1950 to about
1968. This picture was taken in 1960, shortly
after I was nominated by the Democrats
for Congress.*

wanted to be helped or not. When we learned, apropos the 1954 Geneva accords, that the people of North and South Vietnam would, in a free election, vote for Ho Chi Minh and godless Communism, Kissinger wailed, "Don't we have the right to save a people from themselves?"

Later, when Kennedy was preparing for an all-out war, somewhere, anywhere, he got *Life* magazine to assure the American people that in an atomic war, "Ninety-seven out of one hundred people can be saved," if they would only get out those shovels, and take Civil Defense seriously. Jack knew, of course, that this was nonsense, but the White House film critic and historian Arthur M. Schlesinger, Jr., assured his master that, if nothing else, this was one way "of making foreign policy less abstract or remote." Arthur thought that the idea of being blown up would strengthen the fiber of the American people; he did fret that an appeal only to those with backyards might be too narrow an electoral base, since most of those who traditionally voted Democratic could not afford houses, much less backyards.

This was the nonsense that first began to be seriously spouted in 1950 by Harry Truman and Dean Acheson and the lords of the defense industry, who did not want to lose their vast revenues from the War Department, now humorously renamed the Defense Department. Did I see through all of this at the time with these sharp eyes that have always been fixed intently upon a future that never works? No. I believed the whole nonsense. I did have informants at the heart of the empire–Gene would be made chairman of a Pentagon committee on secret weapons, mediating between army and newly autonomous air force, while my uncle was an air force general and ex-Senator Gore was not without his contacts with what he had been the first to refer to as that "first-rate, second-rate little man Harry Truman." But, as far as I can tell now, only a small group at the heart of the National Security State knew just how weak the Soviet economy was and how far behind us they were in modern weaponry.

Meanwhile, charges of Communism at home were beginning to ruin the careers not only of those few who had actually been Communists, but of many others who held unpopular views on politics or sex or race or religion. Truman introduced the loyalty oath for federal employees; this, in turn, made it possible for the likes of Senator Joseph McCarthy– our Titus Oates–to flourish. Who was loyal? Who was disloyal? American or un-American? Fascism was taking off, never to come to earth again, though it is, occasionally, put briefly on hold.

Allen Ginsberg thinks of those years as a liberating time. I don't. I remember only conformity and fear and silence. The Beats thought that they had made a great gesture by opting out and going on the road to Morocco, not to mention to pot, but they were never in anything to begin with. They were marginal people who would have gone unnoticed had it not been for Allen's genius as a publicist. But then, once they had finally made it to a degree of television fame, they let themselves be patronized by *lumpen*-imperialists of the far right like Buckley, Jr.

At that time no writer of my generation was truly political except Norman Mailer, who had nobly spoken out for Henry Wallace, the sole politician in the 1948 election to draw attention to that great con game the National Security State. Wallace was duly demonized as a Communist and flushed from the system.

Two years later I met Mailer at the novelist Vance Bourjaily's house. Vance and his wife had organized a sort of New York literary salon, which tended to net writer-writers rather than teacher-writers. Fags were shunned (if not well closeted), while the Jewish writers tended to center around *Partisan Review*. Except for Tennessee and Bowles and Louis Auchincloss, I never really got to know many of my contemporaries. I had the impression, no doubt an unjust one, that most of them were only playing at being writers, each modeling himself on one of the three prototypes of the previous generation–Faulkner, Hemingway, Fitzgerald.

Mailer tells me that I was curious about his age, and that of his parents. He says that I then calculated that I would "win" as I was bound, actuarially, to outlive him. I do think that this ancient saw has a limited truth. Between outliving one's contemporaries and the ignorance of journalists, there is something–not very much–to be said for living a long time.

Years later, Norman told me, "I thought you were the devil." I found him interesting if long-winded. I never finished *The Naked and the Dead*, but I liked the next novel, *Barbary Shore*. He was trained at Harvard as an engineer, and I have a theory that the mind of an engineer, though well suited for many things, is ill suited for either literature or politics. For the engineer everything must connect; while the natural writer or politician knows, instinctively, that nothing ever really connects except in what we imagine science to be. Literature, like the politics of a Franklin Roosevelt, requires a divergent mind. Engineering (Mailer and Solzhenitsyn) requires a convergent mind. Compare Roosevelt's inspired patternless arabesques as a politician, artfully dodging this way and that, to the painstaking engineer Jimmy Carter, doggedly trying to make it all add up, and failing.

As of 1950, if I had been thinking seriously of politics instead of the mechanics of election, I would have been as one with Mailer. But I had missed all the wars of ideology that for twenty years had convulsed New York intellectuals. Debates at school and around the family dinner table concerned "real," not theoretic, politics: Do we go to war or not? That was a poignant question indeed for someone my age and a matter of profound philosophic implications to a populist like Gore.

In any case, I was now interested only in reading and writing and anonymous sex. Although I have had several lifelong friends who were writers, I have never much enjoyed the company of writers. I also did not realize, nor did the others at Vance Bourjaily's gatherings, that we had arrived on the scene to witness the end of the novel. Today the word *novelist* still enjoys considerable prestige, so much so that both Mailer and Capote chose to call works of journalism novels. But that was thirty years ago. Today an ambitious writer would be well advised to label any work of his imagination nonfiction, or, perhaps, a memoir.

One day, in the spring of 1950, I was invited to lunch by a very ambitious, very young southern novelist who wanted to shine in those social circles that are, for the most part, closed to very young ambitious southern writers. Like Capote, he wanted to be accepted by what was known then as café society, and like Capote, he had mistaken it for the great, and largely invisible to outsiders, world that Proust had so obsessively retrieved from lost time. In later years, I liked to pretend that Capote had actually picked the right ladder and I would observe, most unctuously, "Truman Capote has tried, with some success, to get into a world that I have tried, with some success, to get out of." Truman was surprisingly innocent. He mistook the rich who liked publicity for the ruling class, and he made himself far too much at home among them, only to find that he was to them no more than an amusing pet who could be dispensed with, as he was when he published lurid gossip about them. Although of little interest or value in themselves, these self-invented figures are nothing if not tough, and quite as heartless as the real thing, as the dying Swann discovered when he found that his life meant less to his esteemed duchess than her pair of red shoes.

"Can you come to lunch with Alice Astor Bouverie?" The maiden name was trumpeted in my ear. When I paused, not knowing who she was, he said, "*Truman* will be there." Plainly, he believed that Truman's presence, as arbiter, would convince me that the extended ladder was secure. But I had already observed various Astors at Newport, Rhode Island. The Auchinclosses tended to disdain the Astors as flashy even though the Auchinclosses were far newer on the scene and, despite Hughdie's healthy infusion of Standard Oil money through his mother, nowhere near as rich as John Jacob Astor, who had gone down with the *Titanic*, leaving three children, Vincent, Alice and, by a later wife, the posthumously born John Jacob IV, whose stepbrothers had been in school with me.

I forget where the lunch was held or who else was there. I now note that Alice was a year older than my mother, while Anaïs was exactly Nina's age. Since I so little liked Nina, why was I drawn to women her age? More understandably, I was also drawn to women my grand-mother's age, like Eleanor Roosevelt and our mutual neighbor on the Hudson, Alice Dows. In those days, girls one's own age meant mar-riage. This made any sort of friendship with them uneasy if not impos-sible. Later, when I turned dramatist, I got to know actresses, and as we were all in the same business, relations entirely changed. Most of them didn't want marriage, either. I relaxed, for the first time, and enjoyed myself.

Alice was slender, dark, pale-skinned; from some angles she was beautiful. Out of boredom, her mother, Ava, had divorced Astor in order to marry the rakish Lord Ribblesdale—nicely sketched by Sargent; they settled in England, where Alice was brought up while her brother Vin-cent remained at Rhinecliff on the Hudson in a huge McKinley Gothic wooden mansion. Once, when a guest was leaving, he thanked Ava for a splendid weekend and wondered what on earth he could do to repay her hospitality. "On the way out," she said in her deep Edwardian voice, "drop a match."

Ribblesdale's first wife had been a sister of Herbert Asquith, that most civilized of prime ministers, and I used to ask old Ava questions about him and his sharp-tongued wife, the sometime novelist Margot. "I remember," said Ava, eating a chocolate soufflé as Alice looked humbly

·

on, "when she wrote a novel–she always needed money–and the publisher said that she must put some sex into it. She was mystified, of course. She only cared about politics. Then she was inspired. 'I did just as he asked,' she said to me in triumph. 'I wrote the most marvellous scene of a woman giving birth.' "

By four husbands, Alice had four children. In order to accommodate the latter, she had built herself a gray stone manor house at Ferncliff, the Astor estate high above the Hudson. The house was set far back from the river road, which winds through the wooded estates of Delanos, Vanderbilts, Aldriches, Roosevelts, not to mention Edith Wharton's House of Mirth, built by Ogden Mills. But by 1950 there was not a good deal of mirth in any of the houses. Families had died out or broken up while the postwar economy had eliminated that principal support of any hereditary aristocracy, the servant class.

Alice inherited $5 million from her father; when she died, in 1956, she left exactly $5 million, despite the extravagance of her husbands as well as generous gifts to all sorts of mysterious adventurers aprowl in the psychic world. Alice had once been Queen Tiy in Pharaonic Egypt. She had also come into possession of the queen's necklace, which looked cursed to anyone like me, who had been brought up on the film *The Mummy.* I make her sound silly. But she was not. She liked the arts and artists. She liked the night best of all. With a few friends she would talk, play Chinese checkers, speculate on mysteries, and watch the sun rise as gray lawns turned green. She always seemed to me to be somewhat misplaced in America. She disliked her brother Vincent, a drunken slow-witted creature, but, to give him due credit, he had an ingeniously malevolent sense of humor. For one of his houseguests, a lady notorious for her gallantry, he prepared a special edition of a Hearst Sunday newspaper. The details of her love life were on page three, provoking a most satisfying set of hysterics. As owner of the magazine *Newsweek,* he could indulge his passion for mock newspapers.

Alice had intended to spend her life in England, where she had grown up. Nobly, she stayed in London through the worst of the blitz; then, at war's end, she came back to the United States, for the sake, I suppose, of her children; ironically, two of them moved to England as soon as they could. At Rhinecliff she lived as if she were still English. Frederick Ashton, the Sitwells, various Churchills came to stay. I used to visit on weekends.

Alice also undertook considerable research to establish, to her own satisfaction if not that of brother Vincent, that the Astors had once been kosher butchers in Waldorf, Germany. She thought this a nice antidote to the snobbism of her grandmother Caroline, "the Mrs. Astor" whose delicious task it was, through her court chamberlain, Ward McAllister, to exclude from society all but the four hundred old-guard New Yorkers whom she could insert into her ballroom. Alice preferred more raffish– not to mention more interesting–company.

Paradoxically, like so many of her class and generation, Alice had legitimate doubts as to her paternity. She was fairly certain that she was not John Jacob Astor's child, and so the hot kosher blood of the butcher of Waldorf did not run through veins that contained the blue-tinted blood of one Sid Hatch, an elegant figure about New York at the turn of the century.

I never met Mr. Hatch, but a friend described a lunch that Alice gave for him at a restaurant in New York. As usual, Alice arrived late; and her half-dozen guests were already seated. "Too sorry. The wind, too terrible. The trees. The telephone . . ." She had a series of murmured cryptic remarks to serve as excuses for habitual lateness. Meanwhile, as she took her place, she was still screwing on a pair of earrings. Then she noticed an empty place at table. "Where is Sid?" she asked.

"Here is Sid," said a tall, thin, dark-haired man, hurrying to the table. He looked not only exactly like Alice, but he was even later than she, while, the telling detail, as he took his place, my informer noted, he was hurriedly screwing on his cuff links.

ALICE WAS IN LOVE with the choreographer Frederick Ashton, who was not in love with her but accepted, sometimes with ill grace, her numerous gifts; he often stayed with her at Rhinecliff, where I got to know him. He affected to be in love with me. I said no; but enjoyed his company. He was pouter-breasted, with a permanently crooked finger that was ideal for a wicked witch in pantomime but not so good in other roles. I watched, with him, the first Ashton ballet that I ever saw in New York, *Les Patineurs*. I thought it very pretty but not Tudor, Robbins, or de Mille.

Freddie was a great mimic–mime, too–and one of his best numbers was that of Ida Rubinstein, a rich woman who commissioned ballets for herself to dance, with decor by the likes of Picasso, music by Stravinsky, and so on. Somehow, the young Freddie ended up with her company. As a prima ballerina, Ida had but a single flaw: She could not, properly speaking, dance.

As "Madame," Freddie would take the floor in Alice's drawing room. Slowly, awkwardly, he would get on point. Arms in a spaghettilike adage. Then a stricken look as he realizes he is about to fall off point. Teeters toward sofa. Clutches sofa. Radiant smile as he gets behind the sofa and comes off point with a crash, accepting the cheers of a great audience.

One winter day Alice drove several of us north along the river road to a deserted house called Edgewater, so named as the lawn ended at river's edge; three acres of locust trees, willows, and copper beech provided a miniature park. The house was Greek Revival; six tall columns fronted a cinnamon-colored stucco facade. The house was built in 1820 for a branch of the Livingston family, to whom a Stuart king had granted close to a third of what would become New York State. At one end of the house an octagonal library had been added, the work of A. J. Davis. In time, Alice's relatives, the Chanlers, acquired the place. A Chanler lady married John Jay Chapman, easily the most original of American essayists, and he lived at Edgewater while he built a house for himself nearby. "Coldest winter I've ever spent," he said of his brief stay. He also wrote, "The thing that stirs us in any man's writing is the man himself–a thing quite outside the page, and for which the man is not responsible."

We approached the house from the unimpressive back, where the original driveway had been replaced by the New York Central railroad, thus making the house unlivable for two generations. By 1950 the trains were cleaner and fewer, though no less noisy. A speculator now owned the more or less abandoned place.

Through tall grass where once a lawn had been, we came around the house and there I first saw the row of columns and the wide view of river with the blue Catskill Mountains beyond. "It's like the Austrian lakes," said Alice. She had acquired a romantic lakeside villa during her marriage to Raimond von Hofmannsthal, son of Hugo and himself a man of considerable charm, as well as expensive tastes. When Alice finally noticed that they had spent a million dollars of her money on castles and other toys, she divorced Raimond and married a poor

Englishman of modest tastes. Raimond married again, most grandly. He worked for *Time* magazine in London and gave pleasure to all, including the British army, in which he served during the war. Once, in the barracks, while Raimond was reading in his bunk, the charge of quarters announced, "Attention! Side arms inspection." Everyone scurried to get pistols in order as the officer proceeded down the center of the barracks, examining side arms. Raimond, as vague as Alice, had heard not "side arms" but "short arms," which meant an inspection for venereal disease. So, as the officer came abreast of him, Raimond presented his short arm. I last saw him pursuing a girl in the street in front of London's Connaught Hotel. He stopped when he saw me. He grinned and mopped his sweating face. "I am too old for this sort of thing, of course . . ." We chatted amiably. A few days later I read that he was dead.

Although I was short of money that year, I managed to buy Edgewater for six thousand dollars and a ten-thousand-dollar mortgage, which, had I not discovered television four years later, I would have had a hard time paying off. Alice lent me some of the furniture that she was obsessively acquiring for the return to London that would never take place.

In July 1950, I moved in. I was not yet twenty-five and oblivious of what I had taken on.

I set about putting the place in order. With a borrowed scythe, I painfully restored the lawn. A small island went with the property and on hot summer days I'd swim out to it. In winter I'd walk to it over glacier-thick ice that creaked and groaned as the river's current broke the shifting ice floes. Summers were too hot; winters too cold. Spring was best. Lilies of the valley grew wild. A huge weeping willow at lawn's edge. A collapsed boathouse with copper roof. White red-bordered peonies in a row beneath the colonnade. Locust trees with white, densely rose-fragrant blossoms. Idyllic season. John Latouche wrote the lyrics to a song called "Lazy Afternoon" at Edgewater.

The first novel that I wrote in the house was *The Judgment of Paris*. When a writer moves into the house that he most wants or needs, the result is often a sudden release of new energy. Henry James's move to Lamb House produced *The Wings of the Dove*, Somerset Maugham's move to Villa Mauresque resulted in his only satisfactory novel, *Cakes and Ale*. In my case, there was a burst of energy and imagination of a sort not accessible to me before. Overnight–the result of the octagonal library?–I jettisoned what I called "the national manner," the gray, slow realism of most American writing, not to mention the strict absence of wit and color, and I made a sort of bildungsroman about a young man loose in Europe after the war, preparing to make his own judgment of Paris. Would he give the golden apple, his life, to wisdom, power, or love? Mysteriously, Burroughs misread my high comedy for an attempt at "tragedy," but then no one else was writing like that in those days, and what would a literal American reader make of a text full of classical allusions? At Edgewater, when I first read Petronius and Apuleius, an electrical current was switched on. Simultaneously, late at night, I read straight through Meredith and Peacock; and felt at home in their company. I even read most of Scott's novels, and longed to write my own *Count Robert of Paris*. Meanwhile, my contemporaries–the ambitious literary ones–were trying to find sustenance in the likes of thin Hawthorne or wafer-thin Hemingway, then in high fashion.

I have just read a bad review of *The City and the Pillar* in *The Harvard Advocate*, spring of 1948. The writer duly notes that I am about the same age as the editors of the paper but that I have obviously done myself in by not having gone to college. In a sense, for a conventional writer, the reviewer was right. It is probably a good thing that the dwindling company of twentieth-century readers and the hugely expanding company of writers share the same syllabus. Although the voluntary reader will have read many books that schoolteachers will never have heard of, he may not know all of their required reading. *Required reading!* I have noticed over the years that those who go on to become teachers or critics–or even novelists or poets of a hyphenate kind–tend, as time passes, to dislike, even resent, all literature. But then the secret worm in their brazen apple is careerism, which kills off the amateur or the dilettante, the very best sort of reader, if not writer.

During my first four years at Edgewater, I could not stop reading. I got through James (the New York edition, for which I paid $125, all that I had in the bank). I read through Smollett, too. Then–secondhand books were cheap in those days–I discovered George Saintsbury, unaware that he was out of fashion. Saintsbury led me into French literature. He also led me to the essay; and, best of all, to Montaigne. Although I had written occasional book reviews in the papers of the day, I never wrote a proper essay until 1954, when I read a new translation of Suetonius' *Twelve Caesars*. Suddenly, I had so many new thoughts on the subject of sex and power that I was obliged to write an essay on the subject, not for publication but just to clear my own mind. Eventually, it was published (though a dozen papers turned it down as much too radical), and that is how I became an essayist. I wrote first for myself; then for those few readers who might be interested in the resulting *essai,* French word for "attempt."

Meanwhile, I was going broke. Labor Day, 1950, I met Howard Austen. He worked for an advertising agency in New York; on weekends he came up to Edgewater. Alice and her group liked him; that is, the new group that I had helped her assemble, based on John Latouche, whose wit delighted her almost as much as their shared passion for the night.

John Latouche was one of "the little friends" that I had got to know when I was first in New York. Others were the set designer Oliver Smith, his cousin Paul Bowles, the composer Virgil Thomson, and a half-dozen other originals or near originals. Touche had written "Ballad for Americans" in his youth, a becoming patriotic ballad, much loved by A. J. Connell of the Los Alamos Ranch School. He also wrote lyrics for *Ballet Ballads* and *Cabin in the Sky.* He was a wit of the hard-drinking Irish school; he was always broke; he pretended to be a Communist, and was much blacklisted in the fifties. Alice was enchanted with him.

In the city, the two of them would go from one smoky club to another, all through many a night. Whenever Touche appeared, musicians would play his song "Takin' a Chance on Love." For a time, Alice fell in love with him, and he was charmed by her. She helped him out financially, and he helped her through one splendid night after another. In one very dark club, as she sat in a booth, long white fingers entangled in the enamel necklace of Queen Tiy, Latouche returned from the lavatory and presented her with the chain to the toilet. She often wore this chain, usually wound around a ruby-and-emerald necklace. I don't think she ever dared offend her earlier self, Queen Tiy, with so flippant an ornament.

AT THE HEIGHT of my literary blackout—late forties, early fifties—I used regularly to lunch with Victor Weybright, the inventor of New American Library, whose paperback series, Signet and Mentor, sold millions of copies at fifty cents apiece. Victor was a jolly bon vivant from Maryland whose accent shifted from Eastern Shore to West London as occasion required. He had distributed Penguin books in the United States. Then, in 1945, he set up shop for himself as the first "quality paperback" book publisher in the United States. Before Victor, paperbacks were mostly mystery stories.

"Then, one day, while I was home, reading Faulkner, I thought to myself, if this book were to be marketed like Dashiell Hammett or Thorne Smith, we might be able to sell quite a few copies, considering all Faulkner's sex and violence–the fine writing, of course, doesn't help–but in the end, presentation is all. A sensual cover can do wonders even for a good book."

We are at lunch at the Brussels Restaurant. Victor has started on his second martini. I settle back in my chair: I always enjoy this story. "So I rang up Bennett Cerf, Faulkner's hardcover publisher, and I said I'd like the paperback rights to, oh, maybe a half-dozen Faulkners." A low Maryland chuckle as Victor started in on his first oyster. "Bennett was confounded. 'We've never been able to sell more than two or three thousand of any of his novels and you want to put him in the *mass* market! You're crazy. Anyway, he's out of print.' I told Bennett that, as a good southerner, I not only read but collected Faulkner, so we would set type from my personal copies. Well, that was the beginning. Faulkner was– is–one of our biggest best-sellers." This was also the beginning of paperback editions of literary writers. As of that lunch in the early fifties, all of my contemporaries were in paperback except me. Victor was only mildly apologetic. He blamed my absence from the list on his partner, Kurt Enoch, who not only hated *The City and the Pillar* but feared that it might be banned. Several years later, when I had several plays on Broadway, Victor published all my novels, and *The City and the Pillar* was the first to sell a million copies, a large number in those days.

But, in the end, the blackout affected even my relations with Victor. I had decided that what was needed was a good eclectic nonacademic literary paper, like the recently expired English paper *Horizon.* More or less simultaneously, Victor had decided that he'd like to publish some sort of periodic anthology in which he could try out writers whose later novels he might want to publish, or attract writers that he very much wanted but who were not available to him. We joined forces. I would edit the first collection with the understanding that, if it was successful, I would continue to edit. I borrowed John Lehmann's *New Writing* for the title, inserted the word *World* before *Writing* to show that we would be as broadly based as possible. The first issue was mostly my doing. Friends like Tennessee, Isherwood, Louis Auchincloss, and Philip Johnson rallied around.

Victor gave a triumphant vernissage for the first issue. He spoke gracefully of his passion for the best in literature as exemplified by those not only present in the room but by those published in the first issue of *New World Writing*. (I was one of them, under a cautious pseudonym.) During this, Victor stood beneath a portrait of himself as master of some Maryland hunt, occasioning the odd snigger. At one point, as he paused for breath, the gobbling voice of Auden was heard: "How much are you going to pay us?"

Victor serenely evaded this coarse question and proceeded to thank those who had helped with the first issue. He mentioned one of the editors who had been assigned to the project; she had done little or nothing, but she was an amiable woman and she was useful with the printers. Then, gracefully, as always, he did not mention me.

At the Brussels, another lunch: "Gore, I simply couldn't allow any writer–particularly a controversial one–to appear to be in charge of what I've announced as new writing from all around the world." Victor died confident that he had thought of the title of what was to prove to be a successful series of collections. Admittedly, in a prefatory note, several people were thanked for their help and I was one. "So, you were mentioned, of course. You seem to have forgotten that over the years." Then Victor did me a curious favor. "I'm quite aware that whatever you publish these days will be ignored or attacked. But I have a hunch that if you were to write something–well, *popular*, under another name, we could sell it." Victor puffed comfortably on his cigar. "You know, I've had great success with this Mickey Spillane–fantastic success . . ."

"For God's sake, Victor, I can't even read him much less write like him."

"Of course not. What I was thinking . . . you will recall S. S. Van Dine?" I did; he was a popular mystery writer of the twenties and thirties. "Elegant stuff, you know. Of its sort. Well, we have Spillane, the lowbrow mystery writer. What we need now is an elegant one, to balance Spillane." Later, at a party, Victor introduced me to an English couple who made movies; their name was Box. "How's that for a name?" I asked. I was already writing a mystery called *Death in the Fifth Position* (it took me eight days to write, seven chapters of ten thousand words each, and on the eighth day I pulled it all together). "Excellent. Easily remembered. Now, what about a first name?"

"Edgar," I said.

Victor's rosy face was beatific. "For Edgar Wallace. Good."

"For Edgar Allan Poe," I said grimly. If I was going to whore, I might just as well follow in a master's footsteps. For several years I lived on the proceeds of the three novels I wrote as Edgar Box. *The New York Times* lavished praise on Box; then, years later, when I published all three in a single volume, confessing to their authorship, the *Times* retracted its three good reviews to give me a bad one.

I last saw Victor in the lobby of the Beverly Hills Hotel. He looked ill and haggard. But he was as cheerful as ever. I introduced him to a famous film producer. I knew that Victor had been forced out of New American Library by his partner and he was now at something of a loose end. I praised Victor to the producer as the man who had made William Faulkner a best-seller. As the producer had not heard of Faulkner, I don't think he was greatly impressed; then the producer moved on.

"You know, Gore," Victor was suddenly confiding, "it's true what you said. I *did* make him a best-seller and all that. As I made you one, too, and a lot of others, but the damnedest thing is something that we didn't discover for the longest time, and I've always kept it a secret." He lowered his voice. "The *contents* of a paperback book mean absolutely nothing. It is the cover that sells the book. I first got suspicious when *Absalom, Absalom* outsold *Sanctuary*. How can this be? *Absalom* is almost unreadable. So I changed the covers. Put a sexy one on *Sanctuary* and a distinguished one on *Absalom. Sanctuary* took off. It really was *all* in the presentation. I'd appreciate it if you *didn't* discuss this with too many publishers."

As I write this forty years later, a handsome new—tenth?—edition of *Death in the Fifth Position* has arrived from France. It is in hard cover and, perversely, the dust jacket could as easily be used for a new edition of *La Princesse de Clèves*. I can hear Victor murmur, "How publishing has changed."

ALICE BROUGHT the Sitwells into my life. On their first visit to the United States, the literary world turned out for them, a tribute, I suppose, to that great white elephant Publicity, which they rode so triumphantly throughout their lives. When the famous 1949 picture of them in the Gotham Book Mart was taken by *Life* magazine, almost all our major poets, from Auden to Marianne Moore, were on hand as spear carriers, while Tennessee and I, part-time or would-be poets, were added to the picture, from which James Merrill, the best poet in the shop, was excluded, along with William Saroyan and James T. Farrell. I cannot think of a photograph more often reproduced as almost everyone present in the picture is the subject of multitudinous ongoing biographies.

When Truman saw the picture at Tennessee's flat on Fifty-eighth Street, he was furious. "Of course," he said, inventing rapidly, "*Life's* devoting a whole issue to a day in my life." Tennessee and I were quick to say that an entire issue was, if anything, too small to record even a half day in a life of such busy importance. But Truman was now beginning to lose control. "Edith, Osbert! *Intimate* friends! I can't think why . . ." He turned on me. "*You're* not a poet." I said neither was he, but at least I was still publishing verse, such as it was. He compared our novels, to my–yes, yes!–detriment.

"At least *I* have a style!" he concluded.

"Of course you do." I was soothing. "You stole it from Carson McCullers, along with a bit of Eudora Welty and of . . ."

"Better than stealing from the *Daily News*." During this highly satisfying exchange, the Bird was flapping nervously about the room. "I have never heard such conversation!" The Bird's eyes rolled to heaven. "Please! You are making your mother ill."

Edith and Osbert stayed with Alice in the country. They were not royalty in exile so much as true monarchs who had come from over the seas to claim their rightful kingdom. Osbert was publishing volume after volume of rococo memoirs, while Edith's *Canticle of the Rose* was on the coffee table of everyone in the world who knew–and knows no longer–what was fashionable in poetry or prose. Today they would have not a book but a videocassette of the latest Peter Greenaway movie.

Paul Bowles wanted to meet the Sitwells ("a lifelong dream," John Lehmann would have written) and so Osbert, Paul, and I had lunch at the Madison Hotel. Osbert was rosy-cheeked, with small sharp eyes alongside an important nose. He mumbled, due to Parkinson's disease, which had also affected his walking. Even so, lunch was a success. Paul was always good with difficult cases–not that Osbert was anything but charming, as befitted a newly crowned king. There was no problem of any kind until we were in the street on our way back to the St. Regis Hotel, where Alice had arranged for the Sitwells to stay, gratis, as the hotel belonged to her brother Vincent.

On Fifth Avenue, Osbert's shuffling gait began, uncontrollably, to quicken; faster and faster he went, taking longer and longer steps. As he was a tall, long-legged man, this was very fast indeed. I motioned to Paul to take one arm while I took the other in order to act as anchors. But Osbert was now too far gone to be slowed down. I raced beside him, trying to hold him back—and down to earth like a balloon—while Paul, who is short and slight, had now left the pavement and was flying through the air, clinging to Osbert's arm for support. We hurtled toward the hotel, where we let go of Osbert, who cannoned into the chasseur's arms.

"Too kind," Osbert mumbled, falling into the lobby.

But it was Edith that I most enjoyed, and whenever I was in London, I'd go and lunch with her at the Sesame Club in Grosvenor Street.

Among the colonials, Edith was capable of saying such astonishing things as, "Ah, Lady Macbeth! An ancestress of mine," while Osbert merely looked shyly Plantagenet. But in London, surrounded by military-looking ladies at her club for gentlewomen, Edith was a cozy figure despite her six-foot frame, flowing robes, huge rings on long alabaster fingers, pendant slabs of jade hung from ears, while golden snakes entwined to form a crown in thin tea-colored hair.

I would arrive to find Edith already enthroned in the lounge as the military ladies, one by one, marched up to pay her tribute: To each she gave a winning girlish smile while whispering to me, "This one we call the field marshal." A bobbed-haired figure, in sensible shoes, with swagger stick—if there was not a swagger stick there should have been one—bowed low over Edith's hand. "Dame Edith," the gruff voice saluted her.

Edith responded with gay girlish giggles. Then the field marshal went off to war, and Edith said, "Now, I *know* that you Americans always want a drink of something before lunch—something light for me, of course. Now, what was that lovely drink that Osbert and I became so fond of in New York? Something amusing and—I think—Italian . . ."

A waitress appeared with a small goldfish bowl: "Here's your martini, Dame Edith."

Edith's last years were alcoholic but not too oppressive until she began to fall and break those Gothic bones. But in the fifties she was still a splendid companion. "We shall have a *red* lunch. I have no money, you know. It all goes for lunch here." She would not let me pay. The red lunch was always lobster and strawberries and a bottle apiece of red burgundy.

Toward the end of one splendid lunch we discussed the *Lady Chatterley* case. Lawrence's novel was being prosecuted for obscenity and most of literary London was in court, defending the novel and condemning censorship. "*We* never forgave Lawrence, of course. He based a character in that book on poor Osbert, and we had been so kind to him."

"Actually," I said, the wine working its way into my brain, "Lawrence did *not* write *Lady Chatterley's Lover*. It was entirely Truman Capote's work. You can tell from the style, and, of course, the dates," I added, in a burst of creative scholarship, "conform."

"Really!" Edith mulled this over. Then, slowly, she nodded. "Yes. How stupid of me not to have seen it all along. There are so many clues, aren't there?"

"Far more than *Finnegans Wake*."

"Far, far more, but now this means that we must strike quickly before the case is decided." She summoned a waitress. "Paper, pen, quickly." Tiny red-rimmed eyes gazed into mine. "These girls think that I am about to write a poem. Little do they suspect."

Pen and paper were placed in front of her. "Shall I write directly to the judge?"

"No." I was firm. "Write the editor of *The Times*."

"Whole hog, then?" Edith began to talk as she wrote, "Dear sir, I am a little girl of seventy-four and I have it, on the best authority, that the actual author of *Lady Chatterley's Lover*..." I remember her best like that, in a pool of light in a corner of the Sesame Club dining room.

My last glimpse of the third Sitwell, Sacheverell, and wife, Georgina, was at the Roman flat of the James Dunnes in Palazzo Caetani. Recently, an English book-chat writer sneered at the Sitwells in general and Georgie in particular. He adopted a curious–because so unlikely–stance of superiority to his subjects and then, when he had told us that these glittering figures had not been as Good and True and Aristocratic as the reviewer, he savaged them, getting the facts all wrong, for which he was no doubt modestly paid.

Georgie had a deep cigarette-whiskey voice; she also had a sense of humor. Sachie had just finished telling us the recent horrors of trying to pay a Roman hotel bill with a personal check instead of a credit card, which he did not possess.

"I could hear him all through the lobby of the Hilton." Georgie shuddered. "Sachie's voice got louder and louder. He had no cash, the lobby learned. He had no credit card, and never would, he confided to the mezzanine. The management was sorry but . . . At that moment I knew what was coming next and I raced toward the door. But not fast enough. I heard *it,* tolling like some great bell, that terrible phrase, 'Don't you know who I am?' I nearly swooned."

IT IS THE DAY BEFORE EASTER. Daffodil, forsythia; spring flowers are bright yellow as autumn ones are dark red. Cold wind. The Mediterranean has gone from a deep uncharacteristic blue to slate-gray. Wisteria in bloom on the loggia, as it used to bloom on the colonnade at Edgewater. Purple and white. I inspect the rosebushes. All survived the winter. As homage to Edith Wharton, I put in several General Jacqueminot rosebushes. She must have had some special liking for the general himself, whoever he was, because his roses are candy-red, odorless, and grow in fussy clusters. Yet when she is in a good mood in a chapter, she tacks those roses, like a special charm, to her page.

I am still recovering from three months of the Hollywood Hills. Earthquakes, fire, mud slides, race riots to one side, life is comfortable there. Though the cast, for me, is smaller than ever. Isherwood is gone, but Don Bachardy carries on in their house, which now has an ominous split down the middle. Christopher's diaries are taking forever to edit. "They are just like him," said Don. "His voice, just the way he sounded, written all in a hurry, the way he talked, not labored over like the writing."

The movie magnates are now all younger than I. Curiously, I have known many of them since they were very young men indeed. As always, paranoia reigns in movieland. To make a film is to make a choice which, should it be the wrong one, means the loss of a career. One evening I introduced the editor of *The New Yorker* to several hundred of the essential players, as stars and magnates of the largest magnitude are currently known. I quoted myself: "To be truly commercial is to do well that which should not be done at all." Silence like the tomb engulfed these words. But the commercialites have their own weird integrity, and their productions are often rather better than those of solemn *auteurs,* as "serious" directors are inappropriately known in these parts.

I was offered three films to write and one part to act. Since my price had been lowered for screenwriting (I had forgotten that I had done nothing for the *American* screen in years), I said no to what was on offer and no, as an actor, to the director of *My Own Private Idaho,* a movie that I liked. Unfortunately, the part that he had in mind for me is bound to be edited out. I am beginning to think like an actor. I wonder if I will seem like one when *With Honors* opens at the end of this month. Odd to be trying something new at my age. I feel like an imposter when I see the old man from my mirror up there on the screen.

I LOOK BACK OVER what I've been writing about the fifties. Alice Bouverie, and John Latouche; both died, a month apart, in 1956. In each case, murder was hinted at. Latouche died of a heart attack in a Vermont cabin with a boyfriend. Pains in the night. Always the autodidact, he immediately got out a medical encyclopedia and diagnosed himself. The friend wanted to go to the nearest house with a telephone and ring for a doctor, but Latouche thought the spell was passing. He was also enthralled by the medical description of what he was going through. The friend went to sleep. When he woke up the next morning, Latouche was still seated on the bed, encyclopedia open on his lap, dead. A small amount of blood on the floor gave rise to his mother's accusation of foul play. I am sure there was none. Everyone was most impressed that the page he was reading was exactly the right one for someone suffering from an arterial embolism nourished by too much brandy and too many cigarettes. He was not yet forty.

The last telephone call that Touche had made to me was a week earlier, to discuss Alice's sudden death in her New York house; she had fainted in the bathroom, and was found dead in the morning. What grim mornings! "We must hold a memorial service for her. That's the least we can do." But with him gone, too, the least proved to be too much for the survivors. For the first time, I was diagnosed with high blood pressure. I was given pills guaranteed to produce suicidal depression. I stopped the pills; and normal pressure resumed.

Why have I jumped to the end of their lives? I suppose those years up on the Hudson were too filled with incident for me to concentrate on them or, perhaps, much of anyone, including myself. I envy Bowles's diaries, or whatever he used when he wrote his memoir *Without Stopping* (called by Burroughs *Without Telling*). He is full of incident, if not always accurate. He describes how he joined the Communist party with Jane: "Touche was already in but for some reason would not admit it." The reason was that he had tried to join the party but the Communists would not take him: He was too *un*serious for them.

I have just been reading parts of *Without Stopping* and note that Paul never tells us who anyone is, and he fires a great many names at us. Does he think that the reader will know who Libby Holman is? Does he care, and does it matter if there is sufficient anecdote? It is an odd performance both in the telling and in the selection of what is told. He defends his method by saying the text is "covered." But how to lift the cover? Shall *I* explain Libby? No. She's not a part of this story.

I am also feeling slightly out of time; the telephone rings only for business. Howard misses the company of Los Angeles or New York. I don't. Yet I read less than I did in youth; and watch too many movies and documentaries. Last night we saw a series on the Depression in which I am a talking head, recalling the Bonus Army's march on Washington and how I was well and truly traumatized by the fragility of our social arrangements, today more fragile than ever as the poor grow desperate, the rich arrogant, while the ubiquitous television set keeps showing consumers without cash how well the few live, not a wise thing to do.

After the crash of 1929, our ruling class vanished from the public scene—no more tiaras at the opening of the opera. Celebrities now fill in for them, and the shadowy Mellons will be chuckling softly as Capote's jet-setters, filling in for the last time, are driven off in tumbrils, especially constructed for the revolution by the Ford Foundation.

I HAVE RECURRING DREAMS about Edgewater, and sometimes I wonder if I should have given it up. The dream always starts in the same way. I have just bought the house back from the man I sold it to. Before I cross the railroad tracks to the house, I stop to say hello to Mr. Navins. He is postmaster and storekeeper in a one-room cabin opposite the small Barrytown railroad station house. Mr. Navins has never left home except for one daring trip to New York City in his youth. When he walked out into Forty-second Street, he was so horrified by what he saw that he went back into Grand Central Station and took the next train home to Barrytown. Though long dead, he is very much alive in my dream. "Always thought you'd come back," he says.

Edgewater is in almost as great disrepair as it was when I first moved in. Worse, as I look out the window of my bedroom on the second floor, I see that the river has eaten away most of the lawn. In fact, the water is alarmingly close to the house, while some sort of factory has been built on my nearby island.

Then, as I wander through the house, I come to a door that I'd never noticed before. I open it. Yes, a long vista of splendid rooms, with painted ceilings, like a Roman palace. The same dream.

A LITERARY BIOGRAPHER said recently that the one period in American literature in which he would have liked most to live was the fifties at Barrytown and its surrounding countryside, which includes Bard College. Saul Bellow and Ralph Ellison shared a house nearby. Mary McCarthy taught for a time at Bard, where she assembled that nosegay of deadly nightshade, the novel *The Groves of Academe,* later to be countered by Randall Jarrell's equally witty *Pictures from an Institution,* in which Mary is satirized satirizing Bard. The political journalist Richard Rovere also lived nearby, in Rhinebeck. Best of all, for me, there was F. W. Dupee, with his wife and two children, in a handsome old house called Wildercliff.

Perhaps the only time that an American university could be said to be a legitimate center of culture was Columbia in the years just after the Second War. Richard Chase, F. W. Dupee, Lionel Trilling, Andrew Chiappes, Mark Van Doren, Jacques Barzun, and even Gilbert Highet made the place interesting not only for undergraduates like Kerouac and Ginsberg but for those who wished to participate in what Barzun, too neatly perhaps, called "the long conversation," as good a definition of civilization (intellectual division) as one is apt to get. I suppose that Harvard at the time of William James, Peirce, and Santayana might have been as interesting.

So it was, quite by accident–the accident being my friendship with Alice–that I found myself at the geographic center of as lively a group as our culture had to offer.

My own position was anomalous. I was associated with the likes of Tennessee, Capote, and Bowles–that is, everything those steeped in the political and cultural wars of the thirties and forties deplored. Most of them wrote for *Partisan Review,* where William Barrett used to fret about the rising tide of fagdom that threatened to engulf heterosexuality, that bright but unexpectedly brittle perfect mean. When Barrett moaned that "all *they* can think about and write about is sex!" Philip Rahv responded, in his thick Russian-cabdriver-from-the-Bronx accent, "You mean just like us?" He and I were to become good friends. But at the time I was even further suspect, because I associated with the Hudson River valley families; then, in 1954, I took the plunge into live television– where I wrote some thirty plays and saved myself financially but, in the process, between the blackout on the one hand (due to the rising tide, and so on) and a conspicuous commercial success on the other, I became doubly devilish in the eyes of those who taught as well as wrote.

As I recall, Fred Dupee came into my life the year that Alice died. He was the most charming of men, with a wit that generally slipped unnoticed past most of the Hudsonites, including the teacher-writers. He was of middle height, with Kerouac-blue eyes, thick gray hair, parted in the middle, and the most elegant manners of anyone who had made the quantum leap from Joliet, Illinois (home of the penitentiary), to the Yale of Rudy Vallee to the Communist party to the heights of Columbia. At one point, Fred had gone to Mexico with the scatterbrained director-to-be Nicholas Ray. As a teacher, he was handicapped by no wife and no children and, most significantly, no Ph.D. Eventually, he married a student, whose charm, though hardly equal to his, was reinforced by a truly passionate and radical political nature that sometimes made him nervous. Despite Fred's time as a Communist, he was apolitical; yet, ironically, the last piece that he was to write before he gave up writing for good was a description of the 1968 riots at Columbia. Fred no longer took seriously the politics of the day; he also had little interest in the politics of old days–that is, history. He was fascinated by aesthetics. He could discourse on the correct attire for the Yale undergraduate of 1930 just as easily as he could on a close reading of Milton, whose bust brooded over the Wildercliff drawing room. Fred at work on a text was a joy to anyone who thinks criticism can be a high literary art and not simply a mechanistic process for the production of theory.

It is a usual condition of the American writer to have no one to talk to about literature, assuming that the subject has ever attracted his own interest. I asked Bellow, years later, why he still went on teaching in Chicago. "Because," he said, "I don't have anyone to talk to. I only know people here, which is fine, except every now and then I get the urge to talk about books and so I call my class together."

Until I was seventeen, I had my grandfather to talk to. But we were limited to American politics, history, and melodious verse. "I like the sound of poetry. I don't much care for the meaning." He was without affectation. Luckily, he got me onto Poe, who, as Allen Ginsberg and I were to agree, is the primal fount of American literature, as the French discovered long before we did. Later, at Exeter, there was one teacher, Leonard Stevens, who was knowing and enthusiastic; he himself had been a favored student of F. O. Matthiessen's at Harvard. Need of money for a large family obliged him to leave Harvard for a prep school that gave him a large house. At first, he didn't know what to do with us, a special class of seniors with literary longings. Then he said, half to himself, "I think they should read Plato's *Republic.*" No one had ever used that as an English Department text. He also got us onto Milton's prose; and laid the foundation for my last great experience as a reader when, at forty-five, I finally read, over a period of a month, *Paradise Lost,* sounding every word.

My most intensive period as a reader coincided with meeting Fred, himself self-taught in the sense that he had never truly joined the English Department trade union, which tended, doggedly, to narrow, if not to deepen, the mind through specialization. I never heard him lecture, but I am told he filled the hall. He could range easily from Shakespeare to James, for whom he had a deep affinity, somewhat exacerbated by the presence nearby–but, for him, so far away–of the River Road families who figure in James as well as in Wharton. Fred did get to know the ancient Margaret Aldrich, who had known the Master. She lived at Rokeby, a crumbling old house just south of Edgewater. Fred's obsession with these characters was more than balanced by Saul Bellow's loathing for them, particularly of Saul's landlord, Chanler Chapman, son of John Jay Chapman. Chanler was a large booming creature with an eerie and entirely unjustified self-assurance. He had once married a James. He published his own dotty newspaper, and flirted with libel. He was a hereditary Democrat.

Chanler was very much lord of the manor to the writer-teachers who surrounded him. With Saul, he was very lordly indeed as Saul lived in one of the tenant cottages on the Chapman estate. The rows between thick-skinned master and mutinous serf gave us all joy; later, they gave those able to read equal joy when Saul turned Chanler into his finest invention, *Henderson the Rain King*. Saul also made wine from berries.

I could never tell Saul's wives apart. He seemed always to be married to–or accompanied by–a new variation on some, for him, Platonic-model woman, with a tendency to nag: "Of course you forgot to pick up the yogurt after I *especially* asked you to . . ."

One day Saul showed me his family's passport, signed by the Russian foreign minister Adelberg, whose son, I noted, was staying with Alice Bouverie a few miles away. Saul wrote close to life in a way that ought to have limited his work, but somehow, he could transcend a great deal of forgotten yogurt–yet never forgot that the yogurt is essential to a story, one of those *"human fringes"* as Edith Wharton remarked to James, that "we necessarily trail after us through life," and which she had found sadly missing in *The Golden Bowl*. Stricken, James maintained that they were *there*, or so he thought, when he was writing. They are certainly all present in Saul's *Herzog*, which we read with astonishment at how fully he seized reality–nothing of significance is made up–and made it art, not the easiest task, particularly for someone writing in the American realistic manner. The original of Valentine, the adulterer, was Saul's most devoted admirer, Eckermann to Saul's Goethe. He was some sort of writer-teacher, long since forgotten. I can still remember the afternoon when the president of Bard introduced him to me because, "you are both writers," and Valentine said, in his thick impenetrable English–he was German, I think–"At least *I* write English." As it proved, he was optimistic. But in *Herzog* he has a permanent life on the page.

By and large, except for, perhaps, an inordinate concern with reputation, the conversation of an American writer is no different from that of a realtor–money and the storms of domestic life. What little reading most writers do tends to be of a competitive nature. Who has written what, and why it has failed or, worse, succeeded. A contemporary book is seldom praised by contemporaries, while books older than *The Great Gatsby* are simply a blur. The writer-teacher, of course, must know the syllabus, which he often comes to hate, as who would not, reading, year after year in class, one's old notes on *Middlemarch*? Thirty years ago, the shattering of the canon was supposed to free the teacher-writer so that he might explore the terra incognita outside the sacred maze where once resided that devouring Minotaur tenure. Now Harold Bloom tries to . . . But this is not the place for literary theory or bookish musings. Memoir. The people and places that I remember.

Memory: Dupee and his wife bring Lionel and Diana Trilling to Edgewater. Lionel is pale, with dark-rimmed eyes like a shy nocturnal raccoon; Diana is proud, opinionated. Bellow and a few others are at the end of what we call the Green Room (painted dark green, that is—a nontheatrical term), on the south side of the house. I am polite, as a host must be. Lionel seems truly pleased that I admire his political novel *The Middle of the Journey*. On the other hand, anyone who could write a book about E. M. Forster and not be aware of his intense, almost religious, faggotry is not much in the way of a critic.

Diana's book chat for *The Nation* has plainly gone to her head, as one discovered in her recent memoir. Apparently, people, the *right* people, took her very seriously indeed, she tells us, and she very much enjoyed, she confesses . . . well, *fame:* Publishers took her to lunch. Later, she would distinguish herself with an inadvertently hilarious piece called "One Night at Columbia" when, after a fine introduction by Fred, Allen Ginsberg gave a reading, obliging Diana to meditate on the difference between the Beat barbarians and those high-culture figures who had really made it, like Lionel and herself. For many years, whenever I would ring Fred, I'd say, in a thundering bass voice, "Fred! This is *Diana*. Diana *Trilling*." And Fred would respond in his most gravely courteous manner, "Why, Diana, how good of you to call. I was just reading again your review of *The Man in the Gray Flannel Suit*. It holds up so well. No, really. I mean it. It is like Matthew Arnold."

The Trillings follow me into the Green Room. Merrily, Saul greets Lionel. "Still peddling the same old horseshit, Lionel?" In due course, Saul broke with New York and retreated to Chicago. Although Chicago is a better city to live in, I've never understood his disaffection for the New York literary scene, whose prince he was. The Jewish literary establishment wanted a great writer. They picked him; and he left town. But then he has always had universalist tendencies.

Another couple in another year are in the Green Room. Norman and Midge Podhoretz. Norman is a chatterbox who never listens. Midge does listen, sternly. "Look at that rug, Midge!" Norman turned over one edge of the rug and gave its weave a professional stare. "Persian . . ." I almost sold it to him on the spot.

I was writing *Julian* then, so this must have been in the early sixties. Midge had a scholarly bent, totally undone by the family's occupation as polemicists for Israel. I told her that Julian was an odd sort of Zionist; he had wanted to rebuild the Temple at Jerusalem in order to disprove Christian prophecy. But then, in one of his letters, the emperor describes a disappointing meeting in Jerusalem with the rabbis. Why the disappointment? Midge was brisk: "Because they weren't serious." Since she was not a fourth-century scholar, I thought that she had just made a quick guess. But if she had, it was a lucky one. Research proved her as right as one can be in these matters.

Poddy was always trying to get me to write for *Commentary* (in those days a liberal literary paper, financed by the American Israel lobby). Years later, I criticized him and the lobby, and he denounced me as an anti-Semite who had been totally undone by the triumph of Israeli arms in 1967. As always, in his zeal, he got everything wrong. Since 1948, I had been a somewhat offhand Zionist; but in 1982, when Israel criminally invaded Lebanon, I publicly attacked Israel and its American lobby. In any case, before these interesting exchanges, I finally wrote a piece for *Commentary* called "Literary Gangsters." I named four book reviewers. Poddy wanted me to add all those critics who had given him bad reviews for his autobiography *Making It,* a wonderfully silly book. I declined. Since my piece appeared in *Commentary* in 1970, three years after the famous victory in the desert, this meant that I had been as guileful as a serpent in keeping my anti-Semitism to myself while consorting almost entirely with Jews, penetrating, one by one, their innermost secrets in order to betray their arcane blintzes.

During what was called Vidalgate, one of my Jewish defenders said, "How could he be an anti-Semite when he wrote two pictures for Sam Spiegel?"

"*Two* pictures? For *Spiegel*?" was the shocked response. "Then of course he is."

I had just put on a play at the nearby Hyde Park Playhouse. It was set in the Civil War. Poddy was mystified. "Why, the Civil War is as remote and irrelevant to me as the War of the Roses." I was later to elaborate on this.

The Podhoretzes, in due course, started a curious racket called the Committee for the Free World. One by one, they accused the country's major writers of being "anti-American." (Code for insufficient enthusiasm for those military budgets whose beneficiary was—what else?— Israel.) Saul Bellow let them have it:

"They gave all these editorial opinions about books, and my name was on their masthead. It looked as though I had a part in their opinions. So I wrote to Midge Decter and told her I was through with it . . . If I want to make enemies, I'll do it on my own. I mean, who are they to drag me into abuse of other people—Gore Vidal, for instance?"

Third couple in the room. Norman and Adele Mailer. Norman had stabbed Adele; been sent to Bellevue Hospital; now he was out. I asked them both up to Edgewater. This caused some stir among the writer-teachers. At last, a Moral Problem. Should they meet someone who had done such a thing? Controversy raged over many a glass of gin—we were heavy drinkers in the Valley. As it turned out, most came to the house to greet the Mailers. Adele was surprisingly cool; Norman much subdued. Bellevue had been an alarming experience.

"I was really in danger of being put away as insane, because the doctors there were all Jewish, and I'm a Jewish writer, and Jews just don't do this sort of thing unless they are really crazy." But he was let out.

For some reason Mailer and I drove back together to the city on that, or another, occasion. We were talking about Kerouac's *The Subterraneans,* and I said that I did not appreciate Jack's invasion of our common privacy. Norman wanted to know what had really happened. I told him. Norman almost drove us off the Taconic Parkway. Later, he worked up a mystical case that I had deliberately removed the steel from Jack's sphincter and that is why he took to drink and self-destruction. When Norman arranged a confrontation between us on a television program (I'd criticized his stand against women's liberation, as it was then known), he tried to tell, as proof of my evil, the Kerouac story, but as I was more experienced at television than he, I spoke through him within the same decibel range, thus erasing what each was saying.

Another couple: Eleanor Roosevelt and Alice Dows, a contemporary and neighbor of Franklin Roosevelt, who had once, it is said, fancied her. But Alice married the dim Mr. Dows; she was also, for years, the queenly mistress of Nicholas Longworth, Speaker of the House and husband to president Theodore's daughter Alice, who was complaisant as she was having an affair with Senator Borah, who fathered her daughter. Both Alices attended Nick's funeral. "We went in a private train, like *two* widows," said Alice Dows, with quiet satisfaction at a quartet–she, like Nick, was musical–that performed every bit as well in death as in life.

"Franklin always loved this house." Eleanor went out on the porch. "It was usually empty, you know. And he'd drive up from Hyde Park and sit on the porch and look at the river."

Alice stood with me in the doorway as Eleanor crossed the porch to the lawn. "Such a pity," said Alice of her eighty-year-old rival, "the way Eleanor has let her figure go."

It was well known that Eleanor was careful to serve the most inedible meals on the river and, later, in the White House.

"Franklin came to me, every chance he could get, to be fed properly."

To the mystification of the Valley, Alice Dows and I were a sort of romantic couple until her death; I suppose it was assumed that I was some sort of gerontophile. When she died, she left me the red Chippendale secretary in which she kept her letters from Nick Longworth and the Irish writer Shane Leslie. She was buried with my letters. Plainly, I lack all compass when it comes to the geography of love.

WALKING INTO THE PAST, I see Gore as he was back then, some thirty years ago, relaxing in the autumn sunlight on the lawn of Edgewater, his stately Hudson Valley house built in the Greek revival style. In an ecstasy of unconditional love, he is slobbering over his two spaniels, Billy and Blanche, and receiving their licking-wet kisses in return while he prattles away to them in some arcane version of baby talk. He is handsome, yes, I had long ago conceded this point; there was no denying his crisp good looks and his dimpled smile.

From Elaine Dundy's memoir of those years. We had met in London. She had just written a splendid comic novel, *The Dud Avocado;* and she was still involved in a not-so-splendid, not-so-comic marriage to the London theater critic Kenneth Tynan.

Gore, who made an amusing, if provocative, if provoking guest, came into his own as a host. It is one thing to throw good parties as Ken and I did and have your guests (figuratively) swinging from the chandeliers for three or four hours. But it is quite another to have them (literally) underfoot for a weekend and keep them as Gore did, in a fairly blissed-out state of satori.

In memory those weekends I spent at Edgewater in '58, '59 and '60 are luminous. Just the sight of Gore standing at the Rhinebeck station as I got off the train on Friday evening had the effect of instantly cleansing my palate—like some tart lemon sorbet—of the toxic fury I had ingested all week at the movable feast it was my lot to share with Ken, now drama critic of the New Yorker.

Then would follow evening enlivened by the company of Gore's neighbors, Fred and Andy Dupee, and Richard Rovere, and an assortment of the more interesting professors currently teaching at the nearby college, Bard. Then the guests would depart and leave the world to darkness and to Gore, his companion, Howard Austen, a red-haired and freckle-faced young man, the dogs, and me.

I was, I suppose, in those days, the designated laugher, a role I enjoyed playing to the hilt. As the hours and the drinks progressed, certain sign posts would regularly appear: Howard, who aspired to be a pop star, would try out a few songs on us. Gore would balance a half-full glass on his head which was never referred to and which, miraculously, never spilled. While I, enveloped in this ambiance of warmth and ease and gaiety and, feeling at once both liberated and cozy, would start taking off my clothes. And once, and once only, Gore and I went to bed together. Next day everything was back to normal. Let us say we chose to bathe in the pure, refreshing streams of friendship rather than shoot the perilous rapids of physical love. Which is not to say I wasn't in love with Gore because I was. I saw nothing odd about this. If platonic love is not based on passionate feelings how can it sublimate itself and ascend the heights?

Obviously, I was seriously observing the first law of friendship: no sex (unless betrayed by alcohol) if you want to keep the friend.

AFTER *MESSIAH* FAILED IN 1954, I went into television. Grimly, I vowed that in five years I would make enough money to keep me for the rest of my life. As it turned out, five years became ten. I went from television to MGM as a screenwriter. From there to Broadway, where I had two successful plays in a row. I think it was Samuel Johnson who said that there is nothing so pleasurable for a man as to have produced a play that delights the town. I had also gone into local politics.

For close to a decade I was on the move, fulfilling my plan and enjoying myself enormously. From time to time I had the impression that the teacher-writers in my neighborhood were often ill disposed toward me. As Diana Trilling was to demonstrate in "One Night at Columbia," deportment is more important than talent in academe. Some things are simply not done. Success on Broadway was one of those things, and Mary McCarthy, in a fit of savage envy, the dark side to that otherwise bright intelligent nature, gave the game away when she wrote an attack on Tennessee in *Partisan Review* and called it, unconscious of what she was revealing about herself, "A Streetcar Named Success."

Although Fred had his invidious side, he was also genuinely fascinated by theater and actors. He came to a rehearsal of *The Best Man.* "So ghostly," he said afterward, "to see those famous faces from old movies like Lee Tracy and Melvyn Douglas, alive, and small, so very small on the stage."

Fred was also aware that I was frustrated by not being able to write prose. It might be useful to note here that dramatic writing is not prose writing and those who confuse the two will end up writing, yet again, *Guy Domville.* After Fred read my piece on the Twelve Caesars, he thought that I had the right tone for a good discursive critic, and he encouraged me to write more pieces. I did–for *The Reporter,* a liberal paper of the day, as well as for *The Nation,* tiptoeing in Diana's giant footsteps; then for *Esquire,* on politics. This was not exactly novel writing, which I missed, but it was prose and kept me thinking. By and large, I commented on whatever I was reading, and I was still reading almost as hungrily as I had in youth. It was definitely Samuel Johnson who said that he had read so much in youth that, at eighteen, he had, he feared, known just about as much as he now did in old age. There is something in this, with the proviso that with age one will know the same thing in a different way.

I have never known a good writer to hate the act of writing as much as Fred did. There was no workroom in his house. He compensated by talking, brilliantly. But when *The New York Review of Books* was started by Jason and Barbara Epstein, the former a student of Fred's at Columbia, he was forced, groaning and sighing, to write. After his *envoi*, the Columbia riots of 1968, he stopped altogether; and moved with his wife to California.

Like the rest of us, Fred drank too much; and when, at a certain point in the evening, he would turn ugly, his long upper lip would rise and fall over bared teeth, rather like Humphrey Bogart in films.

One day he was awakened, fully clothed, in a potato field, by an interested farmer. Fred quickly got to his feet. Made some remark about what a pleasant potato field the farmer had created. Yes, he had been most comfortable during the night, thank you very much, and, gossiping brightly, he allowed the farmer to drive him home. Later, a doctor felt his liver and said that enough was now enough. Fred stopped drinking for good and died at a reasonably ripe age.

IN THE SUMMER OF 1955, Nina and Dot came to Edgewater for the summer. Nina brought Tommy, her son by Hughdie, and Dot brought the ever-loyal servant Theresa. Although Dot and Theresa settled in easily, Nina was restless. "Our friend Alice Astor," as Nina would call her acquaintance in a late deposition, showed no sign of interest in the household when I was absent in New York, writing for television. Nina took solace in the bottle, while the boy, Tommy, kept her company, as he was to do, nobly, for the rest of her life. But that summer Nina wanted fun.

The inevitable row took place at the end of the first week. We were on the portico, overlooking gray Hudson, blue Catskills. She began a tirade that ended with a glass of something cold and liquid in my face. At that moment, kindly fate—mine not hers—arrived in the form of an invitation for her to go on the maiden voyage of the *United States,* the last of the great transatlantic liners. She had been invited because she–what else?–*knew* someone; also, she was a good bridge player. Nina packed Tommy off to his father in Newport. Then she stopped drinking, pulled herself together, and set sail for that blinking blue light at pier's end that proved to be her Byzantium. Much relieved, Dot and I settled in to a happy cycle of canasta and reminiscing and Theresa's cooking.

Tennessee came to call, and he and Dot recalled his cousin, whom he had not known but she had–John Sharp Williams, a colorful Mississippi senator.

"How I remember the problems Mrs. Williams had with him," said Dot, with a mischievous smile, black eyes very bright, dewlaps aquiver at the memory. "He was often . . . *not* himself at home . .." Euphemism for drunk. "One day I came to the house to pick them up to go to the Congressional Club and she was ready but he wasn't and she said, 'I must go and help the Senator to get ready.' Well, she was gone quite a time. Then I heard this hollering in the yard and I looked out the window and there was Senator Williams on the ground, with Mrs. Williams sitting on top of him, pulling the braces of his trousers over his shoulders. My, how he roared! But once he was dressed, he was his usual courtly self." The Bird looked very pleased: We were deep in his country.

Nina returned at the end of summer. It was plain that something had gone wrong–Byzantium no country for her? She made abusive calls to Newport: Send Tommy back immediately! But Hughdie made it clear that by dumping him in midsummer she had forfeited her custody unless a court found otherwise. She started to drink again. Dot and Theresa looked after her, and I fled to New York City and another play for television. When I came back, Dot said, "She tried to kill herself."

Through the arched windows of the Green Room I watched the river gliding slowly past the house. That morning Dot had heard harsh breathing from Nina's room; when she went in and failed to wake her, she called the doctor. Nina's stomach was pumped in time: sleeping pills and alcohol. Now she was asleep and Theresa was looking after her.

"Things must have gone wrong on the ship," I said.

"Things always go wrong." Dot was bleak.

"She's already lost custody of Nini for good. Now she's lost Tommy."

"Just as well . . . for them." Dot was unsentimental about the failures of kin, particularly if she regarded their misfortunes as the inevitable consequence of not going to college or marrying too soon or taking to the bottle. Alcoholism was not yet known as an inherited disease—in Nina's case, from Dot's Kays and McLaughlins as well as from the Gores.

We sat in wing chairs on either side of the fireplace. On the wall above Dot's head, a painted plate showed Louise of Prussia and Napoleon meeting at Tilsit. Finally, like someone in a dream, I asked, "Why did you send for the doctor when you did?"

"You have to, you know."

I said nothing. In effect, that was the end of my relations with Nina until the very end, which was to occur a few years later in London when I, far, far too late, told her that I would never see her again and, true to my word, did not.

It is difficult for me to understand why I would ever care to see some-one who was, at best, trouble and, at worst, a highly resourceful enemy. Guilt? But I seem to have been born without guilt of any kind, in which I resembled her and, from what I know, the rest of our clan. Duty, yes; guilt, no.

It would be easy for me to claim compassion for this virago with, admittedly, considerable charm when impressing strangers with her lobbyist know-how. But I suspect that my reasons were more base. For Lao Tse the creation of envy in others is a very great crime. By his pre-cept, in my adult dealings with Nina, I was truly criminal. After all, I had risen far higher in the world than she or our other connections, excepting always Jackie, a master criminal in Lao Tse's sense, and I was not about to let Nina forget my victory over her, which she, of course, turned promptly to her advantage. After T. P. Gore, Gene Vidal, H. D. Auchincloss, and General Olds were forgotten, she had only my card to play as she moved above the fringes of the world from a house in Cuer-navaca to the flats of fag-hags in Mexico City and, finally, sadly, to army hospitals and thieving nurses. Along the way she collected the author of a book called *Auntie Mame;* here, at last, was the son that she had always wanted. "*I* am Auntie Mame," she would tell everyone, even though she had met its author long after publication.

My half brother, Tommy, has just sent me a photograph of Nina toward the end. Rage and confusion in eyes that look to be obsidian-black. Dr. Freud, so often wrong in his analyses of types—and almost always wrong when it came to classical labels—might have had some fun with a Medea type, who killed her children as a revenge upon their father. The ever-inventive Freud might also have been sufficiently inspired to invent a Medea son, who escaped and went on to torment the would-be murderess by simply surviving his fate–the Kid from Colchis. I did torture her with heartless kindness; and today I feel nothing other than curiosity that I should have remained on the case for as long as I did in actual time and now in surprised retrospect.

My researcher has found Christine White and–a definite nonse-quitur–Marlon Brando is, according to the newspaper, seventy years old today. At least celluloid has preserved that iconic presence.

A YEAR HAS PASSED since I wrote the above. I am at La Costa, a spa north of San Diego, losing weight and undergoing a medical checkup. I have been told that I have a basal-cell carcinoma on the tip of my nose. In two days I am to be operated on; a plastic surgeon will be standing by in case the cancer turns out to be larger than expected. Meanwhile, Marlon has now published *his* memoirs while, simultaneously, some-one else has published a thousand-page biography of him. Last night Marlon was interviewed on television for ninety minutes. He is bare-foot, showing off tiny delicate feet to go with his tiny delicate hands. The rest of him is enormous, although the face has been neatly lifted and there are angles, especially when he flashes his ten-year-old bad boy's grin, from which he looks like his original self. We have known each other slightly for almost half a century. He now talks a sort of New Age psychobabble, but when he relaxes, one is charmed by his sly defensive amiability. Suddenly, he talks about fear–"You know of death, or maybe–like–uh, getting cancer of the nose."

He looks into the camera *at me*. This is alarming.

I'm reading the biography of Marlon–more interesting than his showbiz-gossip memoirs. The biographer has talked to a thousand peo-ple I once knew in the theater and movies and he does bring back, for me at least, that wonderful lost world of Stella Adler and Harold Clur-man and Gadg Kazan and, of course, the Glorious Bird. Much is made, as always nowadays, of Marlon's "bisexuality." But anyone with a great deal of sexual energy and animal charm is going to try everything. In youth he touched base with a different girl a day, so much so that he had two abortionists on retainer to deal with the results of his activity–safe sex was not for any of us in those days. Next, I read "rumors linked him with," among others, "Leonard Bernstein and Gore Vidal." I must ring Lenny, I thought; then remembered that there is no longer a Lenny left to talk to. Anyway, in gossip-land, such names are par for the course, as garnish.

I read that later, in the sixties, when Marlon was in London, making a disastrous film with Chaplin, he went–rather drunk–to a party at the Tynans' "to celebrate the Labour party electoral victory earlier in the day. Other guests included such literary and film heavyweights as Gore Vidal, Richard Harris, and Michelangelo Antonioni . . . Marlon loudly dared his drama-critic host to accompany him into the bathroom for a full-on-the-mouth kiss 'as proof of their friendship.' Rumors later circulated that Brando and Vidal had a brief affair." I sometimes think that there is a secret committee (headed by Poddy and Midge?) that decides who is to be linked with whom: "What about Marlon and Tennessee? No? Too obvious? Well, Marlon and Gore. They're the same age and . . ."

I do recall that night in London vividly. I scratched my forehead as Marlon and I chatted. "Why are you scratching your forehead *like that*?" This was an old trick to put you on the defensive. I was quick to reply: "Would you rather I scratched *your* forehead?"

The evening made such an impression on Antonioni that he made a film of it, *Blow-Up*.

Last night, Marlon ended his television appearance by kissing the interviewer, Larry King, full on the mouth–like Kerouac, he's a great come-on-er, get it?

I should note here that over the years, I have read and heard about the love affair between me and Paul Newman. Unlike Marlon Brando, whom I hardly know, Paul has been a friend for close to half a century, proof, in my psychology, that nothing could ever have happened.

Paul did tell me that when he was a young sailor, on a troopship in the Pacific, "I went up on deck with a copy of Nietzsche to improve my mind." While he was improving his mind, a kindly chaplain engaged him in a conversation, then made a pass. Paul shook his head. "Now *that* really put me off."

"Off Christianity or homosexuality?"

"Neither. Nietzsche."

To Do Well
What Should Not
Be Done at All

O N FEBRUARY 14, 1954, I spent the day at the CBS television studio on New York City's Tenth Avenue. The studio had once been
a legitimate theater; now its gutted interior is a complex of
cables, wires, hanging lights, crude bulky cameras on go-carts. High up,
where the first gallery was, there is the control room. Through plate-
glass windows the director and his crew can survey not only the entire
floor to the theater, divided up into realistic sets for tonight's play, but
they can see, on a row of monitors, what each of the three cameras is
recording down below. A central monitor will show the program; images
quickly switched from camera to camera will edit the play, my first for
"live" television, and as the play is being acted, it is also being transmit-
ted. In effect, photographed theater. The program, *Studio One*, sponsored
by Westinghouse, presented a new play every Monday evening.

Air-day began early with a technical run-through. For the first time,
the actors saw the sets and the cameras saw the actors. We had been
rehearsing for a week on Second Avenue, across from the kosher
restaurant Ratner's. The rehearsal hall was in a building owned by a
Ukrainian organization that rented its hall to companies like us for
rehearsals. The sets are marked by tape on the floor. A gap in the tape
is a door, a fireplace, a window. A long table is placed against the street
side of the room. Here we sat for the first reading and I heard for the
first time my words spoken by actors.

*Charlton (or "Chuck," as we called him)
Heston acting most powerfully in* Ben Hur,
*for which I wrote a script at Cinecittà in
Rome, down the hall from Fellini, who was
working on* La Dolce Vita. *Plainly, there is
nothing in the acting line that Chuck cannot
do. Note the expression on his face as he
holds the gourd with phallus attached, a
weapon of choice in Roman times. The whip
in the background is a bit of S&M calculated
to delight those audiences that revel in films
about our Lord.*

As I had seen a great many movies, three members of the cast were well known to me. There was the aging Bramwell Fletcher: In *The Mummy,* he had played the archaeologist who first sees the mummy come to life, and dies laughing hysterically. *The Mummy*'s leading man was David Manners, whose father was the editor at E. P. Dutton who had assured me that my reputation would not survive *The City and the Pillar.* As of 1954, he was right. I had been obliged to retreat to television. But, like General MacArthur, I knew that I would return. Of course, no one believed me, because once a serious writer had sold out . . . Look at Clifford Odets, they would say. I did. I thought he'd found himself in Hollywood. But in those days there was much solemn talk of selling out, of commercialism versus art.

Actually, there was not much in the way of art in the American literary world, then or now, while even a commercialite found it hard to make a living in television, where I was paid something like seven hundred dollars for an hour-long play that had, admittedly, taken me only four days to write, after first having watched two plays on a borrowed television set. But then I had had the good luck to meet one Harold Franklin at the William Morris office, a saintly, scholarly man. Harold was born to be a rabbi, and I never understood how he had ended up as a writer's agent. But, luckily for me, he had a good eye for the terrain, and he guided me to Florence Britton, a striking blond woman who had been a minor film star ("Moisten your lips, suck in your cheeks, and think of men" was the only direction that she had ever got in the movies). She was now story editor for *Studio One,* working closely with the producer, Felix Jackson, a refugee from Nazi Germany who had been married to Deanna Durbin, a child soprano and competitor of Judy Garland, whose imitations of her rival were marvelously cruel, involving a crooked arm and a radiant mad smile to match luminous crossed eyes. But Garland could be equally mordant about herself. When she had made her triumphant comeback at the Palladium in London, inspired by merry schadenfreude, she rang her now-forgotten rival. After many delays and false starts, Garland got the sleepy, ill-tempered Durbin at home in the French countryside. "Tonight I had the greatest audience of my life!" At length, Judy recounted her triumph. Finally, out of breath, she stopped. There was a long silence. Then a pitying voice said: "Are you *still* in that asshole business?"

Now I was in it. I had come across one of the earliest recorded stories of dual personality in turn-of-the-century New England. Geraldine Fitzgerald was the lady possessed in *Dark Possession,* the somewhat hokey title of the piece. Barbara O'Neil, Scarlett O'Hara's mother in *Gone With the Wind,* played Geraldine's sister, and the part of a young doctor was played by Leslie Nielsen, now my favorite actor in the Zucker brothers' crowded masterpieces. At the time, Leslie's youthful Nordic beauty was only somewhat flawed by bowed legs, a possible hint of the comedian that lurked within.

I usually rewrote down to air-day. This was hard on the actors, but it did improve the play. Later, when I worked in films, I was astonished to find that the writer was not allowed to attend the first reading or, in any way ever again, see to his script. Yet only when the writer hears the actors say what he has written can he tell what is wrong. He can also adjust dialogue to fit an actor's particular talent, the way a composer writes for a specific musical instrument.

I spent the entire day at the studio. Franklin Schaffner was a good workmanlike director; later he would direct my film (not *his,* as I told the shocked French at Cannes) *The Best Man.* I remember Barbara O'Neil, in costume, sitting very straight on the set of the gloomy Victorian dining room next to a bowl of yellow mimosa. "If I couldn't sit here quietly smelling the mimosa, I would start to scream." For actors on live television, normal stage fright was exaggerated by the knowledge that 8 million people would be watching them and that should they go up on their lines, learned in less than a week, no more television work. There were many terrible stories of actors who had gone berserk on camera. I watched one ethereal blond girl, in the course of a tender love scene, soundlessly vomit onto her swain.

As a detective about to reveal the identity of a murderer, Anna May Wong, plainly in another continuum, walked slowly past the line of suspects, assuring each, in measured tones, that "Nationalist China will fight to the end." Harrowing as all this was, the forced flow of adrenaline made for highly concentrated performances, and it is no surprise that our generation of actors, writers, and directors went on to dominate the movies for forty years. Live soon switched to tape or film, and production was moved from New York, with its then-abundant theater, to Hollywood and its film schools, which, for better or worse, are now the training ground for contemporary moviemakers.

I have just watched a kinescope, as the tape of a live program is called, of *Dark Possession*. The play still seems curiously spontaneous, but one can see, up close, that Canadian-cool Leslie is sweating like a prizefighter in the New England winter, while Barbara's lips quiver as she suffers mimosa withdrawal. The play went smoothly until the first commercial, which was also done live. In a dramatically—even reverently—lit corner of the studio theater there was a special chapel for the Westinghouse refrigerator, for which we toiled. The high priestess-saleswoman Betty Furness was absent that evening, and her place had been taken by a young actress, who briskly described the virtues of the refrigerator. "And it all works so easily. You just *press* the *magic* button..." She pressed the button. Nothing happened. Close shot of actress's panicky face. Then, as she gabbled incoherently, the sound of a crowbar prying open the door. On cue now, she turned, pressed the button and, like a lover come home from who knows what crusade, the door fell into her waiting arms. The next day the story made the front page of most newspapers: There was no mention of the night's play.

I wrote this yesterday. Today I receive in the mail the obituary of Betty Furness. Freezing April day. Rain and wind. The vet has announced that the white cat has skin cancer, both ears. General gloom. Tomorrow would have been my father's ninety-ninth birthday.

I now take refuge in that Tenth Avenue studio. It is exactly forty years ago. Betty usually arrives an hour and a half before dress rehearsal. She is small, elegant, assertive. In later years she will become a defender of the consumer against shoddy manufacturers. She goes into her dressing room and shuts the door.

"Now, watch," said a man from the advertising agency that handled Westinghouse. I did. A handsome cameraman approaches her dressing room; casually, he opens the door and slips inside. "They do that every Monday at this time."

"What about the rest of the week?"

"I don't think they see each other anywhere else except here." In due course, when she ended the affair, the cameraman sent her a gift, glamorously packaged. I am told that there were a number of people in her dressing room when she opened the box to reveal his gift to her, a pair of exquisite crystal balls.

Some years later, a group of us tried to get Betty to run for senator from New York, but she felt that an actress would be handicapped, particularly a liberal one. As I write about her, I *see* her and so feel better, certainly more content, in the past at this moment than I am in the present. But how mystifying all this must seem to someone who knows none of these once *known* names.

A friend, lecturing last month in England at a "good" school, was amazed to learn that none of the adolescents in his audience had heard of John Wayne. Last month in Hollywood I was told that a TV documentary on the life and times of Bette Davis had been killed as "no one knows who she is." This would seem to me impossible since, at any given moment, several movies of hers are playing in every country. Or do later generations somehow block out dead players? Do they watch the story with no sense that the actors were ever anything other than interchangeable shadows in black-and-white or fading color? This also goes for nonfiction. In 1957 Eleanor Roosevelt complained, "There are people that I meet now who have no idea that there ever was a Great Depression." On this April day in 1994, how many, I wonder, know who she is.

Dark Possession was counted a success, and I wrote a couple of dozen plays over the next two years. For the first time I had the money to fix up Edgewater. I was also being written off as any sort of novelist. There might have been a certain sad prestige had I failed in television, but to have been successful was a sign of fundamental flaw. A newspaper story on my sudden rise was titled "Veni, Vidi, Vidal." Geraldine Fitzgerald reported that the onetime literary critic and self-described "book man" Burton Rascoe, now reduced to writing a column about television, had told her how sad he found it that a gifted young novelist like myself had sold out to television. When she told him that it was her impression that I'd be back one day, he said, "No, they *never* come back."

Over the next two years, among my television plays were *Visit to a Small Planet,* which was promptly optioned for Broadway, and *The Death of Billy the Kid,* with Paul Newman, destined, I believed, to be *my* first film—that is, a movie done my way, just as television and stage plays are done as the writer wants them done.

Along with original plays, I adapted Henry James's *The Turn of the Screw* as well as Royall Tyler's *The Contrast* (produced in 1787, the first American comedy), from which I eliminated the tedious comic servant Jonathan—tedious but important in the annals of American literature as the shocked Henry Steele Commager explained to me in the studio as he desperately changed his introductory notes. I had an easier time with two Faulkner short stories, "Barn Burning" and "Smoke." I knew Faulkner slightly. After one of the plays, we ran into each other at the corner of Fifth Avenue and Forty-seventh Street. A dapper little man in a tweed jacket, he enjoyed talking kin with me as the Gores lived just north of his hometown, Oxford. Apparently, my great-aunt Mary Gore Wyatt had taught—or tried to teach—him Latin.

"I don't have the television," he said, in his courtly way, "but some of the family do, and they told me they liked the play very much. I wrote one for the television too, not long ago, but I don't think it was very good, or so they say. I never watch." When I said that I was going out to Hollywood, under contract to MGM, he frowned. "Well of course, the money is very good and we have to live, but I would advise you never to take the movies seriously. It's not worth it. Scott Fitzgerald made that mistake, and it did him a lot of harm. Just go. Do the work. And then go home and write what you should be writing." For a man famous for taciturnity, Faulkner was always very talkative with me on the few occasions that we met.

Unfortunately, I did take the movies seriously, and if it did me no harm, it certainly tested my temper. In television and on Broadway the writer was, as he always is, the *auteur*, to use the French word for what the *Cahiers du Cinema* has assured us that the—any—movie director is. But for me, in those days, a director was simply a technician hired to serve the play and its writer while even in the Hollywood of forty years ago, the writer and director were both secondary to the producer.

"There was a time," William Wyler used to say, "when we got no credit at all. Then we got a very small one, like a makeup man now. It took years for us to come close to the stars in billing. It was nothing but producers then. Sam Goldwyn . . ." Willy started to wheeze at the name. "The *Goldwyn* touch. That's what his publicity people called his pictures. *His* pictures? Finally, I said to him, 'Sam, has there ever been a picture with the Goldwyn touch that I didn't direct?' " But Willy lived long enough to see the producers fade away, to be replaced by directors. Meanwhile writers, unless they became directors or producers, were of little consequence, at least publicly. Within the business, they were—and are—highly regarded (no script, no movie) and very highly paid, or as Isherwood put it grimly, "They pay us well for our anonymity."

First trip to Hollywood as a scriptwriter. I stayed at the Chateau Marmont hotel, where I met Paul Newman and Joanne Woodward. Paul had just acted in my *Death of Billy the Kid* in New York, the only play of mine that I had not seen through to air-day as I was busy writing my first film at MGM, *The Catered Affair*, with Bette Davis.

We would meet by the small oval pool at the side of the hotel. "Like a navel filled with sweat," Walter Slezak, a rotund German actor, says that I said. There were several bungalows around the pool. Nick Ray lived in one, preparing *Rebel Without a Cause* and rather openly having an affair with the adolescent Sal Mineo, while the sallow Jimmy Dean skulked in and out, unrecognizable behind thick glasses that distorted myopic eyes. He too had come from television, from what was already being called "the golden age," which puts me in mind of Randall Jarrell's comment that no matter how golden an age is, there will always be someone who complains that everything looks too yellow. Anyway, we all worked in it. At first my writer-writer friends were disdainful; then, one by one, they asked me, furtively, could I get them in touch with an agent or a producer? Even Jimmy Baldwin got me to introduce him to Florence Britton. Meanwhile, as my plays appeared in quick succession, Latouche said, rather sourly, "Whoever suspected that you would be the Lope de Vega of television?"

Paul had already made one film, as had Joanne. He was still married to his first wife, by whom he had had three children. Joanne was now waiting for him to free himself and marry her. They had met in a play, by William Inge, called *Picnic*. Bill was a "recovering" alcoholic newspaperman who had had a brief affair with Tennessee. As a result of observing the Bird at work, Bill decided that playwriting was obviously a very easy thing to do. He then wrote five successful plays in a row, something of a record, enraging the Bird. "La Belle," as he called him, "cannot fail." The Bird was not too pleased when I wrote two successful plays in a row: "This seems to be Gore's year," he wrote sadly to our friend Maria St. Just in 1960.

In today's Italian newspaper, I read that there is a new biography of James Dean; apparently, he "hated women, loved men, was seduced as a boy by a priest." As Dean was not a Catholic, I rather doubt the last part. There is a strange compulsion for journalists to reveal that stars of every sort and in every field are either homosexual or anti-Semitic or both. Most young men, particularly attractive ones, have sexual relations with their own kind. I suppose this is still news to those who believe in the two teams: straight, which is good and unalterable; queer, which is bad and unalterable unless it proves to be only a Preference, which must then, somehow, be reversed, if necessary by force.

Paul was under contract to Warner Bros., where he and I wanted to make a film of *Billy the Kid*. Joanne was under contract to Twentieth Century–Fox, where presently she would make *Three Faces of Eve*, a story rather like *Dark Possession*. They were a handsome couple, and forty years later they are still together and still working. Recently, Paul was asked the secret of their successful marriage. "It's because," he said, "we have absolutely nothing in common. I race cars. She goes to the ballet." But they also work well together, particularly when he directs her, or as she says, "He keeps me from crying." After watching a retrospective of her films, Joanne observed, with some alarm, "When I'm happy I cry, when I'm sad I cry; no matter what I am, I cry." I asked her how she did it. Most actors find it hard to "drop a tear," as they say in the trade. Did she think of the death of a loved one, as Garbo did until one day she told her director that she had run out of people to kill off and so must remain dry. "No," Joanne said. "There's a place inside my head which I press with this imaginary finger, and then it just starts to rain."

Anthony Perkins joins us at the pool. We all came out more or less at the same time from New York to conquer Hollywood. Tony is droll, quirky; he hitchhikes to MGM, where he is starring in *Friendly Persuasion*. All in all, it was very agreeable to be young and involved in the movie business at this time; that is, it was agreeable for us, the last contract players and writers, less agreeable for the studios. Within a decade the whole system would break down and the once all-powerful studios would simply rent space to the now-independent producers, who made fewer and fewer movies. So, as it turned out, we were the generation that came in with the dawn of television–a bright yellow if not precisely golden age–and then moved on to the sunset of the Hollywood studios, hastened not only by the audience's defection to television but by the federally supervised separation of theater chains from studios. Where once an entire movie could be quickly and efficiently made at one studio, with everything from stars to electricians to costumes at hand, and then released in a studio-owned theater, now movies are made everywhere, often on location, as it is called, and the regiments of researchers, makeup technicians, and carpenters were all let go. Since then, only stars, lawyers, and agents have prospered.

At the pool Joanne's hair is blond again. Fox is trying to package her as a blond bombshell, but although she can play one, she isn't one and the camera betrays her intelligence. She is an actress–the Dixie Duse, I call her–not a star like Paul, who only later will turn into an actor. Tony is having his problems trying to play the boy next door, problems that the director Alfred Hitchcock would finally solve by making him the boy next door who slices up a girl in a shower. But all in all, our prospects were bright that day.

As soon as Jimmie Trimble's mother told me about his engagement to Chris White, I rang Joanne to ask her what had become of her old rival. She was astonished at the connection. It had been years since she had seen Christine. Should she check with the various actors' guilds? But I had already done that. No trace of her; unless the guilds were being uncommonly coy. I told her some of the Jimmie story. We agreed that for such a large country, the lines keep crossing, as if the United States were only a village, like Hollywood.

LUCKILY–INEVITABLY? (my sometime researcher lives in Washington, D.C., as does Jimmie's mother and as did Chris White)–Chris was found in that ultimate repository of secrets, the telephone book. They met. Chris had given up acting and come home to nurse an ailing mother, who had only just died. The researcher recorded their conversation.

Christine is writing a book; she is concerned about the state of the union. She also writes and sometimes works for politicians like Jesse Helms and Dan Quayle. But when Jimmie wrote her what he had written his mother about how the lives of the marines were being thrown away so that politicians back home might make money, she says that although she had not understood him at the time, now she does.

At first, Chris says that she had not wanted to meet Jimmie. He had, as pitcher for St. Albans, defeated her high school's team. Then there was the sharp social division between those in the high schools and those in the private schools, particularly St. Albans, which was considered a snobbish place and, worse, an all-boys' school, and so frowned upon by the sexually integrated public school students.

But one of Chris's girlfriends sang Jimmie's praises: " 'He's just terrific. He knows jazz,' you know, in those days, jazz was so important. 'And he goes dancing, and he has a fantastic personality and a smile that

would just knock the birds out of the trees.' You know, stuff like that."
They ended up at a basketball game with Jimmie and a friend ("They're
all, like, six-foot tall"). She was charmed; he fell in love. Since they knew
each other only three months before he left for good, this must have
been the winter of 1943. "After the first meeting, I invited him to my New
Year's Eve party . . ." So it was only a week before her party that Jimmie
and I had our farewell encounter at the Sulgrave Club. Since I told him
about Rosalind, he must have told me about Chris.

"So there's Jimmie. He's always holding the floor. Talking shop . . . and
then he's, like, 'Mix me another bourbon while we're at it.' Anything he
did, he'd say, 'Listen, I believe in living life to the hilt. If you're gonna
talk, talk. If you're gonna drink, drink. If you're gonna dance, dance,' that
kind of thing, *doing*–he was a doer. He was also kind of poetic." Walt
Whitman again. Guam. Who?

They were definitely going to be married, she says. Would he have
objected to her being an actress? She thinks not.

I think that this might have been wishful thinking. He was, it seems,
fiercely jealous. Someone wrote him to say that Chris had been dating
another boy. "He wrote me a stinging letter: 'If you are really stringing
me along, you'd better let me know right now. Do you think I'm having
fun over here?' I mean, it was really loaded. And so he spoke bullets in
that letter." Convinced, finally, that the story was not true, he apolo-
gized, adding rather balefully, "But be careful in the future."

From Guam, Jimmie wrote: "I want you to resign yourself. I'm going
to be a professional baseball player. No two ways about it. And then if I
have to teach English in my old age, well then, all right." He said, "I also
want to write." A tribute to his one and always other self–when his
bright day was done, he would be me, too. Certainly, one thing that we
had in common was the conviction that the bleakest old age would be
to teach English.

Ruth Sewell gave Chris the diamond ring that Jimmie had wanted her
to have. "I remember her handing it to me the day she was notified. She
was in bed. She couldn't move. I thought, 'I am marked.' " Later, Ruth
"gave me two pictures that were in Jimmie's effects and two letters that
had mud all over them from Iwo Jima that he had had in his pocket for
me. They had just picked them up out of his uniform and the two pictures of me he had carried with him everywhere. So there it is, and so
there they are." It is just as well that she did not know what I now know

about his end and that what she took to be mud was volcanic dust mixed with his blood. Someone told her that he had taken communion before his death, but that does not seem in character. For one thing, he was not Catholic, or religious at all, as far as I knew. Though if we were really to complement each other . . .

Chris mentions Jimmie's friend Carter, who had come to St. Albans after I left. "But the thing about Carter is that he missed him so much, that he really basically went off his rocker . . . I was at Chapel Hill and he was at Chapel Hill, so I began to rebound with Carter and Carter was rebounding with me. He was a really delightful guy. I appreciated him. He had a terrific sense of humor, good athlete, he was probably Jimmie's basketball partner . . . All of a sudden Carter's fraternity brother came down out of the house and said, 'Something happened to Carter . . . he's been lying in his bed for three days and hasn't moved.' So he had to be removed from college. They diagnosed it as acute depression." Thus Jimmie's death hit another survivor, but "he weathered it and got all right and then he married . . ." But "when I think of that violent reaction—which is probably what Gore is after, in terms of the effect and the impact—that a quote-unquote Greek god can have on a group of people within his nucleus . . ." She means nimbus. Yes, he was a sort of god to us.

I LOOK OUT MY WINDOW at the Tyrrhenian Sea. Our part of Magna Graecia was once sacred to the great god Pan, a nature deity, a goatish shepherd who played the saxophone—pipe, that is. As Christianity began to obscure our bright world, it was from this wild country that the cry was heard, resonating across wide and sea: "The great god Pan is dead!" In another age, Marvell came up with a nice double meaning: "And Pan did after Syrinx speed, Not as a nymph, but for a reed." Or Calamus, another sort of reed.

Sirocco today. Wisteria drooping. Judas trees in full bloom. One tulip has opened. My researcher dines with Ruth Sewell and Christine White next month. The search continues. But I still don't know for what. I am struck by just how much living to the hilt Jimmie did before the hilt's blade was in his back. I hadn't heard of Billie Holiday until I knew Latouche. Also, despite an alcoholic father, Jimmie is drinking bourbon at seventeen. Because of an alcoholic mother, I drank very little until I was close to thirty. The lines diverge.

Chris says that there was no affair, as girls from a family like hers did not do that sort of thing. When I told Joanne this, she was dubious; "I came from the same sort of family in Georgia, and we certainly did that sort of thing if we were in love or thought we were." I can't think that an experienced boy like Jimmie would *not* have made love to her. Most southerners in that latitude were sexually mature at an early age. On the other hand, sex was not as easy then as it was to be after the war and before AIDS. The back of the car was still the favored venue should the family not be out of the house, while if there were full-time servants, then al fresco was in order; or that airless game room in the cellar. Early maturity also made sex between boys a natural business, though there were certain rules that "straight" boys generally observed (this weird adjective was unknown to us, by the way; if we had thought that a word was necessary, it would have been *normal* versus *queer*, which we were not–we were just messing around). Rules: Boys did not kiss each other, only girls, and many of us thought that kissing had been invented by girls in the first place, because it was not always pleasant for us when the increased estrogen flow made their saliva's taste unpleasant; cock-sucking and buggery were unthinkable. Didn't it hurt? Wasn't it dirty? Otherwise, we were true pagans who knew nothing about categories. Obviously, there were sissies, whom we made cruel fun of, and there were dangerous older men, like the one who sat next to me in Keith's Theater and put his hand on my crotch. I fled. Every boy I knew had had a similar experience. What we were all up to was a perfectly natural homoeroticism, which some continued for the rest of their lives without lapsing into the physically more complex homosexuality or, for whatever reason, into *serious* heterosexuality, an "avoidance" that was the one true heresy which so bewildered and chagrined Anaïs, goddess of love therapy and astrologist divine.

Jimmie was both homoerotic and heteroerotic. I suppose I am curious about the balance between the two in his nature. But then when one lover goes into shock at the news of his death and another mourns him to the end of his life, we have moved far beyond sex or eroticism and on to the wilder shores of love, and shipwreck.

. . .

LAST NIGHT we played a short newsreel clip of Jack, Jackie, and me at a Washington horse show in 1961. This morning, as now happens whenever I mention anyone in this text, Jackie is reported to be back in the hospital, hemmhoraging internally. A few months ago, after she was diagnosed with lymphoma, she transferred her houses and apartments to the children. Now she is dying. Do I feel anything at all? No, nothing beyond a certain glumness. At a certain age, death is the rule rather than the vivid exception. Since my row with Bobby (coming up), we no longer saw each other; nevertheless, she has always been a part of my family life. Aunt Jackie. Of our three nephews in common, she chose to befriend the manliest, despite his character, while pointedly, indeed cruelly, ignoring the brilliant painter with AIDS and the struggling actor. Selfish and self-aggrandizing beyond the usual, Jackie was still a slyly humorous presence when she was in my life, and I . . . now I write of her in the past tense.

We first met in 1949, at the house of a friend in Washington. I knew that Hughdie had acquired two stepdaughters, but I had forgotten their names. Jackie was very curious about me. "After all, I moved into your room." That night I took the train to New Orleans and started to write *Dark Green, Bright Red,* which fixed the time of our meeting in my memory.

In 1956, we saw each other regularly. We'd lunch together at the Plaza. Once, after lunch, I went out into the street just as Eleanor Roosevelt walked by. I took this as an omen.

Since Jackie was fascinated by Hollywood and movie stars, I took her to a rehearsal of what would be my next to last play for television, *Honor.* She watched as the assistant director, Dominick Dunne, on hands and knees, put down tapes to denote the sets. She was much taken with Dick York, the youthful star; also with Ralph Bellamy, the elderly star.

"I'd love to act," she said suddenly as we drank coffee from Styrofoam cups and watched the actors rehearsing at the far end of the hall. "Do you think it's too late?"

"Isn't what's happening to you now a lot more interesting?"

"For Jack it is." She frowned. "Not for me. I never see him. He's so busy with . . ." She seldom complained about Jack himself, but she was irritated by the family's rules and regulations. "I wanted this small car, a Thunderbird. I mean, what could be more *American*?" The mischievous smile. "But Mr. Kennedy said, 'Kennedys drive Buicks.' So I drive a Buick. How do you go about getting a job acting?"

I was amused. "You mean how do *you* go about it? Well, just for the novelty of it, I'm sure any of the studios would cast you. At least once. What would Jack say?"

"Oh, he loves actors . . ." She was vague. "It's Mr. Kennedy who would be the problem. He used to own a movie studio and he hates actors."

"Except for Gloria Swanson and . . ." I named a number of actresses he was known to have had affairs with. She shrugged that off. Would I show her around the New York theater world?

We went, with Howard, to Downey's, a place on Eighth Avenue frequented by actors. She was much stared at. She was easily the most glamorous woman in the restaurant, though hardly the prettiest. This was the era of the Actors Studio and the celebration not only of the Freudian inner life but also of the lower middle class, who, in the age of Eisenhower, dominated the television screen. Although these supposedly simple folk were sometimes sad when kitchen appliances or other consumer goods were not affordable, they were, all in all, very happy to be humble and, above all, American. Paddy Chayefsky was their television interpreter and he had a perfect ear for proletarian speech. I was content to be, in those days, Trigorin to his Chekhov. Also, I was literally eccentric in that I never wrote about the "little people." I'd go from Civil War to the New Mexico territory to mock–science fiction. I did not write about the people Paddy knew until I went to MGM and, as my first picture, I adapted one of his pieces, *The Catered Affair*. In later years he was always annoyed when the British would refer reverently to his masterpiece *Wedding Breakfast* (the English title), and he would give me full bitter credit for it. In time we became friends, but at first he was–pointlessly, I thought–resentful of my presence on the scene. Recently, I asked the director Sidney Lumet why. Sidney grinned his Halloween-pumpkin smile: "You weren't Jewish, and this was our game."

At Downey's, when actors asked who Jackie was, I'd say, "It's the new girl at Warner's." This seemed to satisfy them.

Next stop was the apartment of Zachary and Ruth Scott. Ruth was an interesting actress from Mississippi and the lifelong beloved of William Faulkner, who wrote the play *Requiem for a Nun* for her, while Zachary appeared in the film *The Southerner*, screenplay by Faulkner, who, somewhat out of character, not only liked the picture but wanted credit for his work. But Jean Renoir, like the true *auteur* that he was, took sole credit for the script. He could barely speak much less write a word of English, but then an *auteur* is a transcendental being, beyond mere words.

New York's High Bohemia was all assembled at the Scotts'. A few recognized Jackie from photographs in *Vogue*. But Senator Kennedy had made no impression as yet on them, as opposed to their Hollywood counterparts, among whom he had already begun a collection of beddable stars that would, in time, outdo that of his father, the object of the exercise. Jack was Big–to Joe's Little–Dipper.

IN THE now-relentless tradition of this text, Ralph Ellison, mentioned here, has died. I hope I haven't done in Allen Ginsberg. Am I marked, as Chris White thought herself to be? Or are we all simply marked by time, and I'm writing this at sundown.

I recall now that even in the idlest conversation, the amiable Ralph would introduce the "Negro situation." Fred Dupee rang me one day. "I've just been over to Saul and Ralph's house." Whenever Fred said the two names together, he would speak in careful italics, as if they were a couple of the sort whose name none dared more than whisper in those furtive days. "Ralph was planting flowers out front. I made the mistake of asking him what they were. He gave me a withering look. '*African daisies*,' he said."

I was awakened early this morning by BBC radio: Richard Nixon died in the night (I am *not* responsible for his death); he was in the same hospital where Jackie still lives. The thirty-seventh president had just been extolled, I was quickly warned on the air, as "a towering figure" by both former prime minister Edward Heath and Henry (never to be former, alas) Kissinger. I said to the program's host that the first would have had a fellow feeling for another leader driven from office, while Kissinger's only claim to our attention were his years as Nixon's foreign policy valet. Otherwise, Henry would now be just another retired Harvard professor, glumly at work on *Son of Metternich*.

So Jack and Nixon (Congress, class of '47) are now both gone–paladin and goblin, each put back in the theatrical box of discarded puppets and, to a future eye (or puppet-master), interchangeable. Why not a new drama starring Jack Goblin and Dick Paladin? In their political actions they were more alike than not if one takes the longest view and regards the national history of their day as simply a classic example of entropy doing its very chilly thing.

The years have passed like Dah's snowflakes on the river since 1947, when two naval officers came to Congress and I, instead of joining them, published *Williwaw*. Would–*could?*–any of us have played his part differently? The sudden image of a chest full of puppets may be more apt than I suspected when it emerged from wherever it is that images–well, words–do. Although there is no puppeteer, I have come to believe that our natures are so predetermined that Nixon could do no other than be his uneasy self, committed to mischief, acting and talking like a sleepwalker in a surreal dream: "American troops have just entered Cambodia. This is not an invasion." More to the point, the fact that so few Americans ever noted the chasm between his words and deeds was always proof to me that he was, in a curious way, the quintessential American, indifferent to–when aware of–cause and effect, acting only to further his own career, which meant that he was sometimes capable of doing the right thing for the wrong reason. Murray Kempton has been writing some lovely pieces in the newspapers about our ancient antagonist; he has just noted that I was the first to write, "We are Nixon; he is us." Text–context–is all. I never met Nixon. But I did hear him say that the auditorium in his library should be used to enact "great debates like–oh, Vidal and Buckley." Also, on his first visit to New York after his defeat by Jack, he said, "I'm here to see *The Best Man*," my play, in which he darkly figures.

Much is now being made, among the tears, of Nixon's foreign policy triumphs. He went to Moscow and then détente. He went to Beijing and then, later, saw the Great Wall. Other presidents could have done what he did, but none dared because of–Nixon. One could hear that solemn hollow baritone: "I am not saying that President Johnson is a *card*-carrying Communist. No. I am not even saying that his presence on that wall in China means that he *is* a Communist. No. But I question . . ." As Nixon had been assigned the part of *the* Nixon, there was no other Nixon to keep him from those two nice excursions, ostensibly in search of peace.

After I heard the trumpets and the drums and watched our remaining Librarians–the high emeritus rank that we bestow on former presidents (a witty one, because now no one does much of any book reading)—I played a film clip of Nixon from his vice-presidential days. The soundtrack is gone, so it is a silent movie. An official banquet of some sort. Nixon remembers to smile the way people do. Then a waiter approaches him with a large, sticky dessert. At that moment, Nixon leans over to speak to his partner on the left, frustrating the waiter's effort to serve him. Waiter moves on. Nixon sits back; realizes that his dessert has been given to the man on his right. Nixon waves to the waiter, who does not see him. Now the Nixon face is beginning to resemble that of the third English king of his name. Eyes—yes, merest slits—dart first left, then right. Coast is clear. Ruthless Plantagenet king, using his fork as a broadsword, scoops up half the dessert on his neighbor's plate and dumps it on his own. As he takes his first taste of the dessert, there is a radiance in his eyes that I have never seen before or since. Nixon is happy. Pie in the sky on the plate at last.

I THINK I WAS the last contract writer at MGM (five years instead of the usual seven), a job that I had taken not for the money, more easily made playwriting for television and theater, so much as to see how the last great studio operated in what proved to be its last days.

A kindly good-hearted politically liberal man of endless sentimentality named Dore Schary had got the studio away from its aging founder, Louis B. Mayer, who preferred his string of horses to movies.

Dore hired me. I had an office in the Thalberg Building, on the second floor, close to the suite occupied by my producer, Sam Zimbalist. Sam had first come to Hollywood in the entourage of Alla Nazimova, a somber actress of almost unendurable power who reigned over Hollywood's lesbian world, which included, I have been assured, just about every woman star or star's wife. In Jean Howard's picture book of Hollywood in the thirties and forties, all is plain, for those with eyes to see. The men are ascotted and blazered and somewhat store-mannequinish in looks while the ladies are vigorous and alert as they cluster around a Dietrich or Garbo in slacks upon immaculate lawns.

In the film *Queen Christina*, a young woman curtsies to Garbo, who gives her a swift sly grin, of the sort that a knowing teenage boy bestows on a girl. This grin summed it all up for me.

I wrote three films for Zimbalist. Despite disagreements, there was never a harsh word between us. He was as pleased as I when my first play was a success on Broadway; he was also touched that I had come back to the studio to finish a script that I had begun for him. Proudly, he took me up to the executive dining room, presided over by a quiet little man called Benny Thaw, who had succeeded Dore Schary in a palace coup. The Broadway producer Mike Todd was also at lunch. Although he had a loud insistent voice, it proved to be no match for the bellow of Richard Brooks, who had directed my first film. I sat next to José Ferrer who was about to direct and star in an ill-fated version of the Dreyfus case, written by me and produced by Sam.

As we left the table of the gods, José said of Todd and Brooks, "Those two sound as if they had just been blackballed from a very good but imaginary club."

"The blackball," I noted, "was not imaginary."

Despite my affection for Zimbalist, I deeply disliked the studio system. Producer picks writer and works with him on the script. Writer then goes on to another project while the producer picks a director, who is allowed to change nothing. Once the film is made (cast chosen by the producer, usually from contract studio players), the producer then selects an editor, who often re-creates the film, particularly if the producer had once been an editor like Zimbalist. Ironically, the *auteur* theory was just beginning to break over Hollywood, much to the amusement of the closest thing most movies had ever had to a single creator, the producer, and to the bemusement of directors, who were, for the most part, simply hired hands who did what they were told. There were, of course, rare exceptions, like Preston Sturges and Orson Welles, but the system always managed to extrude them.

Outside political Washington, I have never known a world so completely obsessed with itself as Hollywood, making the marriage between movies and politics inevitable. The engagement started during World War One when President Wilson, as himself, appeared in a flag-waving film or two while his chief propagandist, George Creel, prodded Hollywood into churning out patriotic product so that all Americans (particularly such troublesome "hyphenates" as German-Americans) would unite in the war against the godless Hun, later to be replaced by the godless Russian Communist, now being replaced by the God-full Islamic terrorist.

Over the years, I have tried to get the sort of control over a film that my colleague Paddy Chayefsky was able to get for a time when he shifted from television to movies, but, except for *The Best Man,* I always failed. For one thing, the money that one is paid for the "property"–accurate word–effectively removes the creator from any control over how the money is spent. The only way to win is to turn director-producer like Brooks or Mankiewicz. But that meant devoting your life mostly to business, not art, if that last noun can honestly be used to describe what a number of people cobble together on a strip of celluloid.

Theater was–is–always more rewarding for a writer, but even there (I speak of old Broadway, long since lost as a venue for the playwright) investors were always a weight on one's back, as I was to learn five times with five plays.

I became hugely commercial on the morning of May 9, 1955. *Visit to a Small Planet* had been televised "live" the previous night. After the program, I took the midnight plane to Los Angeles, where I was to write the first television play to come out of Hollywood, the beginning, as it proved, of the end of live television. The networks had assured us that in Hollywood we would have access to all the great stars: This meant, in my case, Guy Madison as Lieutenant Henry in *A Farewell to Arms;* on the other hand, Catherine was played by Diana Lynn, a child star and pianist now turned engaging grown-up actress with whom, off and on, I kept loving company for several years with no thought, on either side, of Marriage, the central god in the American pantheon during the age of Eisenhower.

After the airing of the play and before the flight to Los Angeles, the producer, Martin Manulis, gave a party, where I met John Steinbeck. He was amiable and reasonably curious about a novelist of the generation after his own. But when I told him that I was now writing television, not novels, he was shocked. Why? I blamed it on the house that I could not furnish. This struck a massive chord. "The dynasty? Yes. Roots deep in native earth. Oh, I know. I know! So many times I've bought that house and put down those roots in order to raise three generations on the spot and then, in no time at all, I've sold the place and moved on. We're nomads." I had liked *In Dubious Battle* when I had read it at Exeter. But I was particularly struck by his 1961 novel *The Winter of Our Discontent.* So was Saul Bellow. In kingmaking mood, we lobbied, each in his own way, for Steinbeck to get the Nobel Prize, an award that some writers crave more than others. Certainly, Steinbeck was cheered when he got it. As for myself, I agree with Flaubert, who wrote, in a letter to George

Sand after Dumas fils had finally crawled on his belly into the Académie Française: "How modest he must be to be honored by Honors."

On May 9, the sort of honor that I do lust for, the attention of the great audience, came my way. The play had given surprising pleasure, something hard to do considering the censorship that we worked under. I had actually got away with a satiric comedy celebrating war, as "it is the only thing you people do really well down here," notes the visitor to our small planet.

As I walked along a Beverly Hills street, I heard people talk about the play. My agents were ecstatic. I was offered movies to write, while a successful playwright in New York wanted me to expand the play so that he could produce it on Broadway. In three years I had gone from television to movies to theater. I have never enjoyed myself more. But I always went home to the Hudson.

Lately, I read a statement of Saul Bellow's: "I come of a generation, now largely vanished, that was passionate about literature." He taught school to make a living. I turned dramatist for the same reason. But– literature or not–I couldn't keep on doing the same thing, nor indeed could he, despite our shared passion for the great thing. When Saul wrote a play, I got *The Best Man*'s director for him and did what I could to help him with a production that effectively killed what had begun as a darkly funny play called *The Upper Depths*. It opened and closed as *The Last Analysis*. Although some plays are literature, the theater, because of its collective nature–not to mention its collusiveness with an audience–simply cannot compete with the sole intelligence of the novelist, who, no matter how great his mimetic gifts, never speaks in any voice but his own. In the theater, Stanislavsky could make Chekhov tragic; while Chekhov could make the same Chekhov comic. What reader of *War and Peace* can take it as farce? Rhetorical question to which the sly rhetorical answer is that Tolstoy did, when he felt obliged to give us his views on history. Although each reader filters and distorts in his own way the text, it is always, like our proud flag in the national anthem, still *there*.

LE NOUVEL OBSERVATEUR has resurrected Maxim Gorky's 1934 notion to ask "*des plus grands écrivains de raconter une journée ordinaire de leurs vies.*" The ordinary day we have been asked to record is April 29, 1994, today. Thus far, I cannot think of a day that has been more ordinary. Last night we watched a videocassette of *Dark Victory*, with Bette Davis and Geraldine Fitzgerald. For the first time I noticed the lesbian subtext. The two ladies are in love with each other. Although the terminally ill Bette marries her doctor, it is Geraldine who sees her through the pearly gates. Ronald Reagan is most convincing as a drunken youth of the horsey set. The sharp-tongued Bette used to refer to him, particularly during his presidential days, as "*little* Ronnie Reagan." Contrary to legend, he was a first-rate actor, and before the war he starred in first-rate movies. When asked for the thousandth time how an actor could be president, he said, most sensibly, "I don't see how anyone who is *not* an actor could get through this job."

I should note that April 29 is the day that a film in which I co-star, *With Honors*, opened in the United States. I am told that it is not good. But like so much of show business, it is usually more fun to do these things than to watch them. Incidentally, this was also the day that I got letters from two first cousins and a half brother whom I've not seen in thirty years.

NO ONE THOUGHT that *Visit to a Small Planet* would be a success; but the producer persevered. Cyril Ritchard, the visitor from outer space, though charming for audiences, was a trial for the rest of us as he could not learn lines. A product of musical comedy in Australia, he learned dialogue as if it were musical lyrics. This meant that whenever he got a line wrong, he would come up with something that neatly, if madly, rhymed with what he had lost. Eddie Mayehoff played a Pentagon general whose passion was laundry. He was more nightclub performer than actor but, in his serene pomposity, a delight onstage. He, too, was hard to work with. Small eyes, aglitter with paranoia, set in a great slab-like face. Whenever he wanted a line changed, he would begin a monologue. "They take out their quarter, see?" He would pantomime a phantom quarter being removed from his pocket. "They put it in the slot, see? They get on the subway." He'd sway back and forth, on the train. "They come downtown. To the Booth Theater. Then they . . ." He would describe minutely the state of mind of "they"–the Mayehoff fans– who would be outraged or shortchanged if he were to say "and" rather than "but."

We opened in New Haven. Cyril had forgot most of the play and lapsed at times into what I took to be a nonmusical version of *The Merry Widow.* The man from the trade paper *Variety* reported, "*Visit to a Small Planet* will visit very small audiences." I was also visited by a delegation from the Yale Drama Department. Helpfully, they gave me their notes on why the play was so bad and so . . . so *liberal.* That word had already been demonized at the university that had earlier given us the CIA.

Boston was better than New Haven. Cyril remembered, in a hazy way, the play's plot and the odd line. Meanwhile, the producer, short of money, went to a friend who was nephew to the actress Marion Davies, companion, but never wife, to William Randolph Hearst. Nephew got aunt, in her cups, to write a check for ten thousand dollars. Needless to say, Ms. Davies and her nephew were both praying that she make back her investment before the chief discovered the hole in her accounts.

In a peculiarly defensive preface to the published play, I wrote:

"On January 16, 1956, the play opened in New Haven. From that moment until the New York opening on February 7 I was more dentist than writer, extracting the sharper (but not always carious) teeth. The heart of the play's argument was a scene in the second act between the visitor and the Secretary-General of the United Nations. At each performance the audience, which had been charmed by the precedent fooling, grew deathly cold as the debate began: this was not what they had anticipated . . . and their confidence in the play was never entirely regained. A few days before we left Boston, I replaced the scene with a lighter one, involving the principals and our subtlest player, a cat. The substitute was engaging; the play moved amiably; no one was shocked (some observers in New Haven had declared the entire conception unwholesomely menacing). And so by deliberately dulling the edge of the satire, the farce flourished."

I should note that McCarthyism was still very much in bloom, and every text was scrutinized for heresy, ranging from bright red to pinko. Subtexts were also carefully examined for the even more sinister, if possible, evil of homosexuality.

"A number of reviewers described the play as a vaudeville, a very apt description, and one in which I concur, recalling a letter from Bernard Shaw to Granville Barker: 'I have given you a series of first-rate music hall entertainments thinly disguised as plays, but really offering the public a unique string of turns by comics and serio-comics of every popular type.' That, of course, is only half the truth, but it is the charming half. In the case of *Visit*, the comedic approach to the theme tended to dictate the form. Having no real commitment to the theater, no profound convictions about the well-made or the ill-made play, I tend to write as an audience, an easily bored audience. I wrote the sort of piece I should like to go to a theater to see; one in which people say and do things that make me laugh. And though vague monsters lurk beneath the surface, their presence is sensed rather than dramatically revealed. My view of reality is not sanguine and the play for all its blitheness turns resolutely toward a cold night."

This strikes me now as a bit much. Rather less portentous is my recollection of the play's opening night as recalled in a review of Dawn Powell's work:

"Once upon a time, New York City was as delightful a place to live in as to visit. There were many amenities, as they say in brochures. One was something called Broadway, where dozens of plays opened each season, and thousands of people came to see them in an area which today resembles downtown Calcutta without, alas, that subcontinental city's deltine charm and intellectual rigor.

"One evening back there in once upon a time my first play opened at the Booth Theater. Traditionally, the playwright was invisible to the audience. He hid out in a nearby bar, listening to the sweet nasalities of Pat Boone's rendering of 'Love Letters in the Sand' from a glowing jukebox. But when the curtain fell on this particular night, I went into the crowded lobby to collect someone. Overcoat collar high about my face, I moved invisibly through the crowd, or so I thought. Suddenly a voice boomed–no–tolled across the lobby. 'Gore!' I stopped; everyone stopped. From the cloakroom, a small round figure, rather like a Civil War cannon ball, hurtled toward me and collided. As I looked down into that familiar round face with its snub nose and shining bloodshot eyes, I heard, the entire crowded lobby heard: '*How could you do this*? How could you *sell out* like this? To *Broadway*! To *Commercialism*! How could you give up *The Novel*? Give up the *security*? The security of knowing that every two years there will be–like clockwork–*that five-hundred-dollar advance*!' Thirty years later, the voice still echoes in my mind, and I think fondly of its owner, our best comic novelist. 'The field,' I can hear Dawn Powell snarl, 'is not exactly overcrowded.' "

To my surprise, Anaïs was at the opening, as a guest of the couple who had been responsible for the sound effects. Although fearful that the play might succeed, she did her best to disguise her terror. Also present, separately, were Gene and Nina. In principle, Nina too would have preferred for me to fail, but as she was a true heavyweight when it came to reflecting glory, she was quick to see that a Broadway success would light her up for quite some time. Gene was less nervous, he told me, than he was the night that he had watched my first play on television.

I have often wondered what it would have been like to have been born into a family that read books or liked any of the arts. Certainly, it might have given us more to talk about, but perhaps ordinary family matters are more useful for a writer to deal with than, let us say, Louis Auchincloss's sharp-eyed bookish mother, by no means, I should think, an easy critic to have so keenly at hand.

The play ran for two seasons; over the next decade, there were many touring companies, and most of the country's comic actors played one or the other of the two leads. For twenty years the play was often done in summer stock and by amateur groups. Then it vanished. "Old hat," a friend said, more accurately than he knew. The film of the play had starred Jerry Lewis at his awesome worst, and as he had only kept the title, the text was promptly cannibalized by other writers. A highly popular television series, *My Favorite Martian,* so closely resembled the play that even *The New York Times* felt obliged to note the fact; this series, in turn, gave birth to *Mork and Mindy,* extending the play's afterlife. Meanwhile, my ending was borrowed for the film of *Superman,* and one of the nicest jokes was lifted by Carl Foreman for his film *The Mouse That Roared.* Whole scenes appeared in so many films that although the original text has never been—and never will be—produced on screen, moviegoers are by now so familiar with the whole notion of a comic visit to our small planet that the original seems like a worn copy. The final coup was the inclusion of the television play in a tenth-grade textbook; thus the story passed into the subconscious of an entire generation, a number of whom now make movies, and in their works, I enjoy, wistfully, bits of my old play. When the wit Elaine May was told that I had written *Visit to a Small Planet,* she said, "No. No. That's not possible. That's too famous a play to have an author."

For reasons not clear to me, whenever I have scored a success—or failure, for that matter—I vanish from the scene. Right after the opening, I took the train to Los Angeles in order to see to my film version of *Billy the Kid*, which Paul Newman and I had set up at Warner Bros. Paul and I had selected a television producer in need of a job to oversee the production. Immediately, our employee replaced our original director with his own, who in turn brought in a friend to "improve" the script of what was supposedly my film. Paul, no tower of strength in these matters, allowed the hijacking to take place.

The result was *The Left-Handed Gun,* a film that only someone French could like. Thirty-five years after the original television play, I finally got my script made as a movie for television, with Val Kilmer as Billy. Was the final result worth all the trouble over all those years? Of course not. But I had finally exorcised Billy from my psyche—Los Alamos, too, because it was at that school, dreaming of shooting dead A. J. Connell, the pederastic headmaster, that I began to identify with Billy, who had lived and died not so far to the south of the school.

William Burroughs, who had been at the school before me, exorcised "A. J." in *Naked Lunch,* turning him into a sort of merry pan-sexualist who livens up the text from time to time. On the few occasions when Burroughs and I have met, I keep forgetting to ask him about Los Alamos. But Allen says he talks quite a lot about the school, and it is my impression that A. J. was more cautious in Burroughs's day than mine.

THAT WINTER Paul and Joanne and Howard and I took a house together in the Malibu Beach colony. Each had a small car. Paul left for Warners at dawn, as that studio was in the far, faraway San Fernando Valley. I left second, to drive to MGM in Culver City. Finally, Joanne made her leisurely way to Twentieth Century–Fox in nearby Beverly Hills. Weekends, the house was full of people that, often, none of us knew. I would think that they were friends of Paul or Joanne, and they thought that they were friends of mine. Christopher Isherwood and Don Bachardy were often there, as were Romain Gary and his wife, Leslie Blanche, and . . .

I am at the point that I have been dreading: lists of names of once-famous people who mean nothing, by and large, to people now and will require endless footnotes for future historians. One might just pull it off if one had something truly intriguing to say about each name or if I had had, like so many contemporary autobiographers, tempestuous love affairs, bitter marriages, autistic children, breakdowns, drugs, therapy, a standard literary life. But I was to have no love affairs or marriages, while casual sex is, by its very nature, not memorable. I have never "broken down," as opposed to slowly crumbling, and I've steered clear of psychoanalysts, nutritionists, and contract-bridge players. Joanne Woodward and I were nearly married, but that was at her insistence and based entirely on her passion not for me but Paul Newman. Paul was taking his time about divorcing his first wife, and Joanne calculated, shrewdly as it proved, that the possibility of our marriage would give him the needed push. It did.

In 1958 they were married at last and we all lived happily ever after. Their honeymoon was spent with Howard and me in London, where, in great secrecy, she promptly miscarried. Had it been known that she was pregnant on the honeymoon, her career might have ended—hard to believe today. It was about then that they made a calculated choice to present themselves as a folksy lower-middle-class all-American couple when, in actual fact, he came from a wealthy Ohio family that had sent him to Kenyon College and Yale, while Joanne was the daughter of a vice president of the publisher Scribner's.

At the beach. The Pacific is lead-gray or bright silver. Sand is brown. Each morning, at dawn, a beagle, who lives to the north of the colony, starts his long march to the south, collecting all the other dogs on the way. The beagle is an inspired and inspiring leader, and our black spaniel always rushes out to join his legion. The dogs vanish for the day. We never knew where they went. But then, at sundown, exhausted, each came home.

DOGS. Our first spaniel was split in two at Edgewater, on the tracks, by a New York Central train. Then Joanne gave us two puppies, one black and one blond. The blond was a hermaphrodite who died early. The male lived on for many gluttonous years, ending his days when, late one night, eating bones on the balcony of the Grand Hotel in Florence, he fell to the Lungarno, where we found him the next morning. Harold Acton liked to pretend that we then went to his villa, La Pietra, at the edge of Florence. "And of course you know how Gore is," he would hum in his Chinese-Italian mandarin English. "He asked did I mind if he buried his dog on the property."

Anthony Powell told me this story in Sofia, Bulgaria, at the only literary conference I—and perhaps he—was ever to attend, a "spirit of Helsinki" East-West affair laid on by Moscow. By then, the story had been much improved in the telling, and suitably mystified the international writers present at the bar.

When I asked Powell why he had come to such a conference—representing England with C. P. Snow—Powell smiled his great gray houndstooth smile and said, "It would have been frightfully *wet* not to have come." Later, the highly political Snow and I commented on the incongruity of this upper-class version of the dread Evelyn Waugh surrounded by Communist apparatchiks.

"Can't think why he came." Snow puffed and wheezed in a cloud of self-made smoke; my answer was bleakly *non*-English: "Ambition."

Snow's eyes became very wide indeed. A look of mock horror on that round Pickwickian face. *"Ambition?"* He actually said the word, the word that no Englishman dares speak, much less be thought guilty of. "How astonishing! You mean . . . You mean . . . ? Publishers in the East and all that?"

I was grim. I nodded, and repeated the ominous: *"And all that.* There is no darkness of the auctorial heart that I cannot lay bare." I will not say that Snow dropped to his knees at this, but I did notice a new respect once he had realized to what extent I was indeed a true authentic, brazen representative of the hard, crass empire of the West.

I last saw Powell with his translator, a pretty girl with whom he went to see the "too shocking" film *The Romantic Englishwoman.* He was short-legged, gnomelike, and moved like Groucho Marx. In the hotel lobby, we would indulge in thirties gossip about L. P. Hartley and others.

Suddenly, he said, "Who was that man sitting next to you in the hall, the one with a turban?" I said that I had no idea, "But," I was all business, "if you want to be on the front page of any newspaper anywhere," I played craftily to his towering ambition, "you must *always* sit next to a man with a turban as *he* is bound to be photographed."

Again, awe in an English face; also, once again, American literature had won. Then I told him that we had buried the black spaniel not at Harold's villa but in the woods back of the good Vernon Bartlett's house near Lucca. As I write, Powell is said to be unwell. I have never been able to finish a book by him, while I have never even tried to read the excellent Snow. But I have read with pleasure all of Waugh, a man I found singularly detestable, as did most of those friends of his who were also friends of mine. Avoid admirable writers. Avoid writers.

The Newmans presented us with a third dog in 1973. Rat lived for thirteen years, a slightly lopsided Australian terrier of great intelligence. He died of cancer of the gums, a disease that terriers are prone to but no veterinarian had ever bothered to warn us about. Rat was at his peak during the five winters that we spent in Klosters, Switzerland. He enchanted our neighbor Greta Garbo, and she would come by the flat each morning to walk me and Rat (she called him Ratzski, as "Rat is so brutal a name").

At sixty-five, Garbo was still very beautiful–that is, she still looked like Garbo. She had two voices. One, she used when she spoke Swedish or German, a somewhat high voice with an odd two-syllable cry for emphasis: *Aie-ee!* The other was her low, "manly" voice, the one that she used on the screen. She always referred to herself as "he." She liked dressing up in my clothes. I think she saw herself as a boy with another boy. She also had an eye for girls and once, on a walk beside the Silvretta River, she asked Irwin Shaw's girlfriend to show her her breasts, which she did. Garbo praised them but no more. Garbo's own hung very low. "I never wore a bra. I was the original women's liberation."

One winter morning I went with her to the magazine stand at the railroad station, where she would buy all the movie-gossip magazines. Debra Paget and Fabian were familiar names to her. But on this occasion she, not they, was cover girl. Cecil Beaton had written about the "love affair" between him and Garbo. With frozen face, she bought all the magazines and, without a word, went quickly home, leaving me and Ratzski to read the Italian version of the love affair that, she assured me later, never took place. "And people think I am *pair*-annoyed," she observed with a scowl. Beaton did tell one story that sounded like her. He was complaining how, with age, his genitals were growing smaller. She had replied, sadly, "I wish that I could say the same."

Once, as we walked in the woods beside the swift river, she began to declaim, in perfect Comédie Française French, an aria from *Phèdre*– "*Ce n'est plus une ardeur dans mes veines cachées: / C'est Vénus toute entière à sa proie attachée.*" I was astounded; then said, "Now, there's something for you to do, on the stage, in Paris." She repeated her usual line, "I am too old."

I said that age made no difference onstage. I told her that Cedric Hardwicke, in his youth, had seen and marveled at the one-legged sexagenarian Sarah Bernhardt playing Joan of Arc in Paris.

At curtain rise, Bernhardt is on a stool, center stage, back to the audience. In front of her, three judges. First judge: "What is your name?" "My name is Joan." Second: "Where are you from?" "Domrémy." Third: "How old are you?" "Eighteen." Then Bernhardt turned and faced the audience and the house exploded with applause. Garbo sighed. "How stupid she must have been." I asked her if she had ever heard the recording of Bernhardt's voice, particularly the death scene from *L'Aiglon.* "Yes, I have. It is so . . . so corny."

Garbo was romantic but not sentimental. One day she told me that she had got a message from Stockholm. The king was dying. When he was crown prince, he had come for lunch at the commissary at MGM and she, as the Swedish queen of the movies, sat next to him. "They made me wear a hat like a plate that kept slipping off. That's the only time I ever saw him. Now they say he has always been in love with me and will I come see him before he dies."

This was MGM dialogue at its greatest. It was also Garbo at her most characteristic.

"You must go."

"So far to go, and for what? He'll die anyway."

That night I produced caviar and vodka for her. We were joined by Irwin Shaw, who asked if he could bring Martha Gellhorn, a journalist I admired. Gellhorn talked nonstop for several hours as Garbo grew more and more withdrawn. Suddenly, Gellhorn left. "How she hates me," said Garbo, now wearing Howard's blazer, which, come to think of it, she forgot to return. Irwin and I assured her that Gellhorn did not hate her, but Garbo was not convinced. The next day, in the street, Gellhorn came up to me. "I want to apologize for last night. I couldn't stop rattling. But what else do you do when you finally meet Helen of Troy?"

I repeated this to Garbo, who rewarded me with one of her most beautiful expressions, head flung back, the long swanlike curve of the neck still beautiful, ice-gray eyes, hooded, downturned lips painted a luminous pale pink, which "Perc Westmore invented just for me." Garbo was pleased. "That was nice of her to say. But of course, I never played Helen of Troy."

Now you have just read a free-association attempt at writing a theatrical memoir. Easier to do than I thought, though I have no idea how it will read to others or if they can find interesting what used to be known as "greenroom gossip." On the other hand, I've enjoyed conjuring up Garbo. For five years we saw her every winter when she came to Klosters to be with Salka Viertel, her closest friend. Then Salka died. I tried to get Garbo to come to Ravello, but she feared the paparazzi. I told her how to get rid of them forever. "Hold a press conference. Everyone will be there. From every country. Then announce that you are producing and starring in a television series. About a Swedish maid who holds together an American family. Then, a year later, hold another press conference. There will be fewer journalists. Hold a third . . . and no one will bother you again."

"I don't think," said Queen Christina, "that that is very funny."

But she was very funny about her visit to the White House. Early on, Jackie had told me, "One of the few nice things about being here is we can get to meet everyone we've ever wanted to meet." So, inevitably, Garbo came to dinner. "The president took me into his bedroom. So romantic. Then he gave me a whale's tooth and we went back to Mrs. *Jah*-kee, who said, 'He never gave *me* a whale's tooth.' "

SO MUCH FOR dogs and gossip. By the spring of 1958, MGM was in bad shape financially. Between the popularity of television and a general falling off of the movie audience, the studios were like so many dinosaurs faced with a dramatic change in the weather.

Zimbalist called me to his office. He was a tall man with a wen on the side of his neck. He had a trick of suddenly opening wide and then half shutting his eyes. Joe Mankiewicz used to do the same thing. It was a trick, I finally learned, that they had all picked up from the legendary macho Vic Fleming, one of the many directors of *Gone With the Wind*. Sam smoked large cigars. Drank milk filled with cream every day. He was devoted to his wife, Mary. "The studio wants me to make *Ben Hur* right away." I groaned. I had gone on suspension the year before, when I was asked to write yet another version of what had been, in the silent era, the studio's most successful film. Since then, there were at least a dozen scripts for a talking version. The last two had been written, respectively, by Maxwell Anderson and S. N. Behrman, two popular playwrights of the day. "I've got Willy Wyler. He'll join us soon as he fin-ishes that western of his." Eyes widen, then narrow. "We're thinking about your friend Paul Newman for Ben Hur." Cigar smoke between us.

"You'll never get him." Thanks to a man called Turnupseed who had run into James Dean's Porsche and killed him, Paul had replaced Dean as the lead in *Somebody up There Likes Me* and was now a star.

"Why not? It's the biggest role there is in town."

I explained that after Paul's first movie, a disastrous Roman affair called *The Silver Chalice*, he had sworn never to act in a cocktail dress again.

"Will you write it?" Sam's powers of persuasion were great. My resis-tance to this story was equally great. I was also becoming restless in Hollywood. I wanted to write a novel about the fourth-century emperor Julian. In a casual way, I had been reading up on the period for several years. I had also begun to lose any hope of making my own film after the trouble that I'd gone through with *The Left-Handed Gun*. Although the theater was still attractive to me, a playwright's career is a short one, as the Bird used ominously to say.

Eventually, Sam and I came to an agreement. I would go to Rome with him and Willy. I would stay three months, in which time I could, he knew, give him a draft. In exchange for this, the studio would let me out of my contract. This suited me perfectly. I had done what I'd originally wanted to do, which was watch the last days of MGM. Now it was time to go. A revised contract was sent to my office. I signed it and gave it back to the messenger, a good-looking boy, smart as paint, as they used to say. Years later Jack Nicholson reminded me of our first encounter.

Sam and Mary Zimbalist, William Wyler, and I took the overnight SAS flight from New York to Rome. Wyler had finally read the script, a com-pilation of Anderson and Behrman, written mostly in Anderson's ele-vated poetic style. "This is awful." Willy presented me with his nondeaf ear, always a sign that he was alert and troubled.

"You hadn't read it before?"

"Never. My God." He was silent. Sam and Mary were at the other end of the lounge. There were, in those gracious times, overhead beds that came down when one wanted to sleep, rather like the Pullman trains of long ago. Hard to imagine that commercial flying could ever have been pleasurable.

"What," said Willy at last, "does a Roman unbuckle when he sits down?" Then he quizzed me at length about ancient Rome. Although I was able to answer a number of his questions, my answers only pointed up his unease about the whole project. He had been given a million dollars to direct the film, the highest price, as of that date, for a director. Casting had been a nightmare. Universal would not lend out Rock Hudson, second choice after Newman. Then there was actually a genuine search for an unknown, which yielded no one. In desperation, Sam suggested Charlton Heston, who had worked in Willy's last film. Although Chuck had all the charm of a wooden Indian, Wyler had somehow got a good performance out of him as a villain in a western. Willy liked to say, "I can't make a bad actor good, but I can keep a good actor from looking bad." But how was he to animate an entire lumberyard?

Glumly, MGM had hired Heston and, as Willy and I flew the Atlantic, the telephone-book-size script between us, Chuck was being costumed and Jerusalem was being built on the back lot of Rome's Cinecittà. What we had on our hands was, essentially, a silent movie with miles of windy dialogue.

Once in Rome, I started to write the script in an office next to Zimbalist's. While I wrote and Sam fretted, our *auteur* was watching every Roman movie ever made, not a good idea, I thought, but it was Willy's only way of getting the feel of the period–from other directors who had watched the work of other directors, all the way back to the *auteur* of *auteurs*, Cecil B. DeMille, who knew nothing about Rome either. The only "accurate" Roman film that I've ever seen–in appearance, that is–was *The Decline and Fall of the Roman Empire*, perfect junk, but with a great set designer, who knew what the city had looked like at the time of Marcus Aurelius, played by Alec Guinness, "in all these flowing robes," as he put it, "and swirling clichés."

I was swirling quite a few clichés myself. The storyline is confusing, to say the least. Two boyhood friends meet as adults. One is a Zionist Jew; the other, a Roman officer. Their reunion is affectionate; then they quarrel over politics; then they hate each other until one kills the other in a chariot race an eternity of movie-time later. "There is," I said to Sam and Willy, "no motivation for all this fury."

"That," said Sam, "is why you are here." We agreed that a political difference of opinion in one short scene was not enough to justify so great an enmity. Ben Hur was no Zionist terrorist and Messala was no foreign oppressor. More to the point, audiences were less simple in the age of Freud than they had been in the age of the original author, General Lew Wallace, or even of the original *Ben Hur* film, with Ramon Novarro.

Down the corridor from my office at Cinecittà was Federico Fellini, preparing *La Dolce Vita*. Fred, as I called him (he called me Gorino), was fascinated to be next door, as it were, to an Epical Colossal Hollywood Film. Neither Sam nor Willy was willing to meet him, so I showed him around the back lot, where the great stadium of Antioch had been built, as well as attractive downtown Jerusalem, with its numerous anachronistic domes, according to an archaeologist friend. "The domes arrived with the Muslims five hundred years later."

When one of the set designers asked what first-century Jerusalem really looked like, my friend said, "Miles and miles of cement block garages." The domes remained, though I was able, on a visit to Mrs. Ben Hur Sr.'s spacious kitchen, to remove a number of pre-Colombian tomatoes from the kitchen table.

Fred quizzed me about *Ben Hur*. I quizzed him about *La Dolce Vita*. I remember thinking what freedom he had acquired as a moviemaker in Italy at a good time in the country's post-Fascist period, when all the arts were in bright revival. I also envied him—in film, that is—his freedom to show people as they are, unfiltered by American superstitions about family, not to mention the oppressive censorship that the Catholic Legion of Decency and other unholy offices imposed on us. As we strolled alongside the spina of the stadium where Ben Hur and Messala would have their final contest, Fred spoke of the sort of thing that he wanted to show about the "sweet life" of postwar Rome. Of course, he was essentially a Puritan and I a pagan. Even so, talking to him about grown-up matters, I got an idea that might just motivate the infantile story that I had been stuck with.

Sam was behind his desk; eyes narrowing and enlarging as he puffed on a large cigar, his normally ruddy face was now an olive color: his heart was preparing to shut off. Willy, a small gray gnome, sat in a chair with his back to the window, the good ear turned disapprovingly in my direction. I had just told them that Ben Hur and Messala had been boyhood lovers. But Ben Hur, under the fierce Palestinian sun and its jealous god, had turned straight as a die while Messala, the decadent gentile, had remained in love with Ben and wanted to take up where they had left off.

Yes, it was *The City and the Pillar* all over again; fortunately, neither Sam nor Willy had read it. When Ben Hur rebuffs Messala's advances, a deep and abiding hatred fills Messala to the brim. If not love (Rome spelled backward is "Amor"), then death. I would break the single inherited scene of the meeting and the quarrel in two parts. First, a sort of cryptic love scene; second, the rebuff, ostensibly over politics but actually over unreciprocated love. I doubt if two Hollywood magnates, their studio faced with financial ruin, had ever been so confounded by what they took to be one writer's mad perversity. When I finished, there was a long silence.

Finally, Willy: "Gore, this is *Ben Hur. Ben Hur!* 'A tale of the Christ' or whatever that subtitle is. You can't do this with *Ben Hur* . . ."

Sam's eyes were now shut. He had worked with me on two other pictures; he was used to my "shockingness"; he also appreciated the fact that I had a hit play running on Broadway even as I pitched the story, no small thing in the land of the commercialites. "How do you *show* this . . . uh, love affair?"

"By never mentioning it. There won't be a line of dialogue anyone can object to. It will all be in their reactions." We'd inherited a javelin-throwing contest between Ben Hur and Messala. This was supposed to symbolize the contest between Zionists and Roman overlords. It could also, as easily, represent male sexuality either in contest or in collusion. I had learned from my days in heavily censored television how to make dialogue that sounded one thing to mean quite another *if* the actors were able to play counterpoint to the usually obligatory dull point. I explained how, when Ben Hur refuses to join Messala in supporting the Roman occupation, one could see in Messala's face that the issue was not politics but thwarted love.

Sam was nodding, as if in his sleep. Willy was looking a bit wild-eyed.

"Imagine the scene with Messala saying something like, 'Remember, I *asked* you,' in such a way that the appeal will register at an unconscious level in most of the audiences. They won't really know that this is the love that dare not screech its name, but they *will* grasp the fact that proud Messala is abasing himself before his old buddy."

Willy moaned; stood up; gave me his deaf ear. "Well, try it. I don't think it's possible, but anything is better than what we've got."

The next day I came in with the two scenes. Willy and I read as Sam listened. True to my word, the scene is still about politics, but as we were required to do at MGM, no matter who the director was, I had written in all the "reaction shots"–expressions on each actor's face as he hears the other's dialogue. Willy said, "Tone down the offstage directions. I'll talk to Chuck. You talk to Boyd. But don't *you* say a word to Chuck or he'll fall apart." The thought of so much wood crashing to the ground committed us all to *omertà*. I did tell Boyd. The bright blue eyes glittered happily. Yes, he knew exactly what to do. "I think there's a dog in the scene," he said. "I can be patting it while I'm getting turned down by old Ben."

In the published diaries of Charlton Heston, I found the entry for May 15 (1958):

Today we rehearsed Vidal's rewrite of the crucial scene with Mes-sala. Indeed, the crucial scene of the whole first half of the story, since it contains the seed of so much that follows. This version is much better than the script scene [Chuck does not seem to know that I had nothing to do with that inherited scene]*, and Willy brought its virtues out in his usual manner as we worked: picking, carping, cutting, finding a reading here and a gesture there till you're smothered by his concept, which then proves to be excellent.*

We never shot this scene of Gore's, nor indeed any of the attempts he made on other sequences. I stress the point because Vidal has gone extravagantly and disdainfully (qualities, I fear, he cannot avoid) on record about his authorship of the BEN-HUR screenplay as well as writer-director relationships in general. As I said, he's a clever man, but not about these things.

May 16: Steve Boyd and I read both versions of the scene through again, to convince Sam, I imagine, that the second one was better.

The second scene, like the first, was mine, and I was present for the reading. Chuck was now imitating Francis X. Bushman in the silent-film version, tossing his head, chin held high, oblivious of what was going on. Boyd, at one point winked at me. *He* was in character.

After the boys left, Sam, Willy and I said nothing for a long time. We were, to say the least, depressed. Finally, I said, "Chuck hasn't got much charm, has he?"

"No," said Willy, "and you can direct your ass off and he still won't have any."

But the scene was duly shot, as written by me. Years later, after I had presented prizes to two writers at the Academy Awards, I ran into Willy backstage. "I loved that cover story on you in *Newsweek*," he said. "But why don't you ever mention *Ben Hur*?"

"Because I didn't get credit." Willy had appealed to the Writers' Guild that credit be given to Christopher Fry, who had stayed with him all through the shooting, a wretched business. The studio had wanted to shut down the production; then Sam died, and there was nothing but trouble to the end. Christopher reminded Willy that as I had written half or more of the script, I should be credited, too. But the Guild, with its secret arbiters, has always been famous for denying credit to those who actually write the scripts, preferring to assign credit to one of its own. In our case, this proved to be a former president of the Guild, who claimed that he had been mailing Sam pages from Hollywood. As Sam was dead, the Guild told Willy to mind his own business. Fry and I were both eliminated. Thirty years later, when the Guild did the same thing to me a second time, I took it into court and won. Now any writer can penetrate the secrecy of its arbitration system and discover why he has been denied credit for his work.

Backstage at the Dorothy Chandler Pavilion, Willy and I again discussed the love scene that opens the picture. Willy denied that we had ever discussed–much less made–anything so radical. Over the next few years, whenever we met, we quarreled amiably over what I had put in the scene and what Steven Boyd is clearly playing. But, finally, annoyed at Willy's party line, I said, "Let's watch the scene together and I'll show you what's going on up there on the screen."

Willy affected not to hear. "Funny about that picture. I was a great favorite of the *Cahiers du Cinema* until *Ben Hur*. After that, they never mentioned my name again." He gave me his twisted grin, a most ambivalent one, indicating that it might have been my secret sabotage that had undone him.

I was soothing. "You did the best with what you had."

I never knew what he really thought of the picture, which, despite its financial success and numerous prizes, should never have been made. Certainly, I would never have laid claim to any of it had my own union not so exuberantly cheated me. In any case, I was now free of my MGM contract. I had also, inadvertently, been reinfected with Roman fever– love of the old city, which only time can cure.

I left Rome in May for the Hudson.

IT IS NOW ANOTHER MAY, thirty-seven years later, and Jackie has just died. On the day after her death I was in Rock Creek Cemetery, standing over a small strip of gray stone that says: JAMES TRIMBLE III, 1925–1945, IWO. I am filming yet another documentary; this time, the subject is Washington, D.C. The day is suitably gray and unseasonably cold. I stand for a long time, looking down at the inscription, while the camera circles me like a buzzard. I keep my mind fairly blank: find it hard to believe that Jimmie has been just bones in a box for half a century.

The cemetery is hilly and full of tall trees. There is well-tended grass between the graves. If memory is a theater not a film, my actors, though they still come when summoned, need pictures and new anecdotes to get them through the old plays, already performed so many times by so many companies in my head. My current Jimmie is blue-eyed and grinning, unlike most of his sad photographs. I stare at the grass–leaves of grass?–that covers whatever is left of him. Then, just as the camera cuts away from me to a huge copper beech back of which is Henry Adams's monument to his wife, a wind starts toward me and the grass at my feet bends toward me, always the same wind effect when I revive this play. Quickly, I bring down the curtain in my head.

As I walk toward the Adams memorial, I do an act or two of the Jackie play. From family, I hear that the cancer had gone to her brain and that she had had a hole drilled in her skull so that radium–or whatever–could be put in. Then the liver was attacked and she left the hospital to die at home. During her last hours, the day before my cemetery scene, as I stood on the lawn in front of the White House, playing tour guide for the camera, I was told that she was almost at the end, and I suddenly remembered that the last time that I had set foot on this lawn, just below the north portico, was the night that I came in from Ann Arbor, Michigan, for a private dinner upstairs in the family's living quarters. I changed clothes in the guardhouse on Pennsylvania Avenue; then crossed the section of lawn to the door . . .

Now I cross the grass to the copper beech and approach the monument, the work of Henry Adams's friend Saint-Gaudens. The monument is a semicircular seat of polished pink-gray stone suitable for meditation as one faces a life-size figure with a shroud over its head and closed eyes. I say "its" because there has always been an argument concerning gender: Is it a young man or a young woman? On Henry Adams's last visit to the White House of Theodore Roosevelt, "the embodiment of noise" as Henry James called TR, the president lectured Adams on the figure. "Of course, it's a young woman," and so on. Adams fled the presence. "Of course, it's a young *man*," Adams said when he got home, "and only our Dutch-American Napoleon could have got it all wrong."

Eleanor Roosevelt liked to come and commune with her old friend's memorial to his wife, whose suicide he never discussed, if indeed he ever understood it. In one of Clover's last letters, she cries out, "If only I were real!" As the camera cuts between the bronze youth and me, I let my actors do some scenes from the Jackie play in my head. She was none too real, either, at least in the performance that she gave to any camera that happened to be trained on her. As she lay dying, the family reports that she was watching herself being memorialized on television. "A fitting end," said one of them, "for a woman who loved publicity more than anything else."

Even as a girl, Jackie liked to be photographed in various roles and moods. Jack, in the interest of advancing his career, created hers by warning her never to talk in public and never to write letters, at least to strangers. Ruefully, she told me how "I write the most brilliant letters, to these dreadful journalists, and I show them to Jack, and he says, 'Oh, that's really great. Now, go tear it up.' "

Actually, to be fair, she loved money even more than publicity and her life was dedicated to acquiring it through marriage, just as her mother had done before her and my mother before her mother, to the same rich man. She had lost her virginity to a friend of mine in a lift that he had stalled in a *pension* on Paris's Left Bank. They had discussed marriage. He came from a better family than hers, as we used, quaintly, to say, but he had no money. He was also Protestant. Then, suddenly, a fellow Roman Catholic, also on the make for glory if not money, came her way. Jack had the income from a $10 million trust fund. Adequate income at the time, but hardly the amount that she would later need to live like her role model, Bunny Mellon. Jack needed a Catholic bride because of his political career; also, even better, thanks to the Auchincloss association, Jackie, was, in the eyes of the Kennedys, a member of the old Protestant patriciate that they intended to erase.

When she told her lift-lover that she was going to marry Jack, he was appalled and said, "You can't marry that . . . that *mick!*" She was coolly to the point: "He has money and you don't." When he asked her how she would like to be married to a *politician* (she had grown up in Washington and had no illusions about the breed), she said, "Of course, I don't like politics and he's a lot older than I am, but life will always be interesting with him, and then there's the money."

"What on earth is going to become of you in that awful world?"

"Read," she said, "the newspapers."

Although the Kennedys would never have allowed her to act in the movies as she wanted to do in 1956, she finessed them all by becoming the equivalent of a movie star–and, best of all, a silent star of unmade films, her face on every magazine cover almost to the end. The later marriage to Aristotle Onassis was cold-blooded but necessary. Actually, Ari was more charming and witty than she, and in the glittering European circus where, to her credit, she did not particularly want to shine, the word was, "What on earth does he see in her?"

To Jackie's credit, she lived up to their encyclopedic prenuptial agreement, but he did not. After his son's death in a plane crash, he became obsessed–he thought that she had *malòcchio,* the evil eye–and tried to eliminate her from the agreed-on will. She was obliged to use the Kennedys to threaten his daughter, Christina. Finally, Christina was told that if she didn't pay off Jackie, no Onassis ship could ever again dock in a U.S. port. In Zurich, Christina wrote out a check for more than $20 million. Before the ink was dry, Jackie reached over and pulled the check out of her hand. In revenge, Christina alerted the Internal Revenue Service, just in case Jackie had forgotten to report the money. Serenely, Jackie then obliged Christina to give her the money that she would need to pay American tax.

Another picture from the now fast-moving play in my head (unlike the Jimmie play, I don't much care for this one). I am at Hyannisport. Summer, late fifties. I'm in Jack and Jackie's house. Jack is away, and if there are other Kennedys about in the other houses, I don't recall them. I had been at Provincetown, losing weight and writing *The Best Man.* I came over to spend a night at Hyannisport. Jackie took me out in a boat to learn waterskiing. We sat side by side in the dinghy attached to a speedboat. Jackie's body was like that of a boy–broad shoulders, long legs, large hands and feet. The hairs on my right ankle tickle as our legs make contact. For an instant, an erotic shock. But then she had always said to me that her aim in life was "to be attractive to men"; this was later modified to being a successful mother as well. No, nothing happened.

In *Newsweek*, Louis Auchincloss has just noted that Jackie had always known exactly what she wanted and how to get it. Certainly, she was a good deal tougher than any of the Kennedys, particularly "those toothy girls," as she mockingly referred to her sisters-in-law. She had had the good sense to make her one alliance within the family to old Joe, the autocrat with the money, who doted on her. I think that eventually she became fond of Jack. Certainly, she had always accepted his promiscuity as perfectly normal, as indeed it was, in the high-powered world.

One evening at a charity ball in the Plaza Hotel, Jackie said, "I've put you at Jack's table. There's a new import from England, wonderfully stupid but very beautiful, and she'll sit between you and Jack and you two can talk across her." In the current sick wave of hypocrisy about sex in politics and the absolute necessity for perfect monogamy, Jackie was a throwback to the eighteenth century. My sister and I often argue if she was at all erotic, or did money rule her passions to the exclusion of all else? She had had her share of affairs with the famous, among them the actor William Holden. But I always suspected that some of these couplings were motivated by revenge on Jack, not to mention just plain stamp collecting. Celebrities are invariably celebrity-mad, just as liars always believe liars. Yet I did get the impression that she was very interested in sex. On the other hand, Louis Auchincloss thinks that she was more *voyeuse* than practitioner, while my sister likes to quote Jackie's advice to her on the occasion of her first marriage: "The great thing about marriage is you can have lunch with men." Clearly, food was not on her mind. In any case, my erotic response that day on the sea soon passed, along with waterskiing, and we discussed what would happen when–not if–Jack was elected. "I've kept a book. With names." She beamed. "Who was it who said, 'Revenge is more sweet than love'?"

"Well, you just did."

"So I did. I think it was someone French." As I let the drama idle away in my mind, I suspect that the one person she ever loved, if indeed she was capable of such an emotion, was Bobby Kennedy. As Lee had gone to bed with Jack, symmetry required her to do so with Bobby. But there was always something oddly intense in her voice when she mentioned him to me, and as it turned out, our mutual dislike ended the Jackie play for me, a good thing, all in all, as I was not designed to play attendant lord.

I now make an addition to the Jackie play. George McGovern and his wife were just here. He told me that when he first knew Jackie–just before or just after the presidency–she told him how, shortly after her marriage, she had overheard old Joe, Jack, and Bobby discussing Jack's career, "and they spoke of me as if I weren't a person, just a thing, just a sort of asset, like Rhode Island." George thought she sounded bitter. But how could she not have known that was all she could ever be in the Great Exchange Market where she had deliberately put herself, as they say, in play?

THE JIMMIE NARRATIVE is more to my liking and I go back to it from time to time, though now there will probably be nothing new ever to add to it.

I had dinner with Christine White in Washington the night after I had been to the cemetery. She still has some of the old beauty that I recalled from television. She showed me snapshots of Jimmie. In one he is in marine uniform, standing in front of the National Cathedral (begun by Theodore Roosevelt and completed by George Bush–the rise and fall of the American empire dramatized in a single fake-Gothic building). Jimmie is smiling for once. "A year later," she said, "he would lie in state inside." I can't think how a nineteen-year-old marine private would merit a "state" burial; on the other hand, he was much loved by Washington sports fans.

"They found this photograph of me in his wallet." She showed me a picture of her youthful self. The photograph has been bent into a curve. "It still follows," she said, "the shape of his body." There, on the dining room table in Willard's hotel, was the outline of the curve made by Jimmie's buttock. I don't know why I found this somehow shocking.

Two other photographs are taken in what looks to be the head–or bathroom–of a troopship. Another boy stands back of him at a washbasin. Jimmie's expression is sad. A final photograph of him with what I take to be his fellow scouts on Iwo Jima. He is unsmiling; he stares straight at the camera, at me. Christine had only known him three months before he went overseas. "But he cannot be forgotten," she said.

"*Will* not be forgotten," I amend, thinking of the cemetery and the sudden soft wind rippling May-green grass.

Although Edgewater, my house on the Hudson, cost only $16,000 in 1950, I soon realized that I had acquired a white elephant and would have to go into television and movies to maintain it. So I went into television, etc., and survived.

Howard Auster at Edgewater in the fifties. He was born in the Bronx, worked at
Walgreen's drugstore to put himself through New York University, tried to get a
job in advertising: Jews not allowed. I said change the *r* at the end of his name
to an *n*. He did and was immediately hired by an advertising agency.
Anti-Semitism was amazingly pervasive in advertising as late as the sixties.

John Latouche, lyricist and wit, preparing for another Christmas. He wrote *Cabin in the Sky, Ballet Ballads,* and *The Golden Apple,* an astonishingly good musical in urgent need of revival. I introduced him to Alice Astor Bouverie, below, who had introduced me to Edgewater when I was staying with her at Rhinecliff. They would stay up all night together, playing Chinese checkers in the country or going from one smokey club to another in the city.

May 8, 1955: *Visit to a Small Planet* (my satiric play for television celebrating war as "the only thing you do really well down there," according to a visitor from another planet), was broadcast live, and I became "famous." That night I flew to Los Angeles to write an adaptation of *A Farewell to Arms* for CBS. May 9, I met Diana Lynn, our star and, as my expression betrays, an amorous friendship of some duration began.

I acted as narrator in my last live TV play, *The Indestructible Mr. Gore*, the story of the scandal surrounding my grandfather's supposed seduction of a young blind girl in Corsicana, Texas, in 1895. One hour before air time, the autocue broke down. I hadn't learned my lines. Eight million people are now waiting to see my shame. I blundered through. Inger Stevens was my grandmother in youth. Mr. Gore was Bill Shatner.

Visit to a Small Planet opened at the Booth Theatre, February 7, 1957. It ran for nearly a year on Broadway while various companies toured the United States, starring everyone from Bert Lahr to Eddie Bracken. I sold the film rights to Paramount for David Niven to play, only to find that it had been bought by Jerry Lewis; his film killed the play just as the film of *Myra Breckinridge* would later kill the novel on which it was based–by others, not me. This rarely happens once; to happen twice . . .

The first screenplay I wrote was *The Catered Affair* for MGM. Based on a Paddy Chayefsky TV play, it was Bette Davis's favorite movie of her middle period, and easily Debbie Reynolds's best picture. Currently, this old movie (1956) is showing life on videocassette.

Alec Guinness in *The Scapegoat* (1959), for which I wrote the screenplay. This was made the Ealing Studios outside London. Robert Hamer, a marvelous director, was too drunk do much directing, and so his old friend Alec more or less took over.

The New York opening of *Suddenly Last Summer.* Joanne Woodward and I being received by the producer, Sam Spiegel, and wife. Sam was spontaneously dishonest at every level; he was also splendid company for anyone who enjoys con men, as I do.

Director William Wyler, co-writer Christopher Fry, myself, and Charlton Heston at Cinecittà in Rome (1959) during the filming of *Ben Hur*.

Henry Fonda in the only film to be made my way, *The Best Man* (1964), based on a play of mine. I was so pleased with the result that I quit Hollywood film writing and went back to the novel.

The wedding of my half sister, Nina, at Merrywood, June 8, 1957. The matron of honor, to her left, is her stepsister Jackie Kennedy.

The lawn at Merrywood during the reception. As I watched the guests, they began to turn into the characters in *Washington, D.C.*, a novel I was to write some years later. At right, Jack Kennedy is with the Peruvian ambassador, mastering foreign affairs.

Joanne Woodward and I have decided not to get married, while Paul Newman has decided, finally, to divorce his first wife and make an honest woman of Joanne. This is the moment of truth on the porch at Edgewater, summer 1958.

Palm Beach, 1958. Tennessee and I drove up from Miami for lunch with Jack and Jackie, both eager to meet him. Jack was already running for president, but Tenn wasn't buying this: "Far too attractive for the American people."

Jack was shooting at a target when we arrived at the Kennedy house. Absently, Tenn took the rifle and shot three bull's-eyes, to Jack's consternation. "And that," said the Bird, "was with my blind eye."

My father and his mother-in-law, Dot, at Edgewater in the late fifties. They always got on well with each other, though neither cared for her daughter.

In 1960, I was running for Congress in upstate New York on the Democratic ticket. Harry Truman came to Poughkeepsie to campaign for us. "Hope I haven't done you any harm," he said as he left.

My 1960 campaign. No one could figure out what there would be "more" of, but since after a dozen years in Congress the incumbent representative was unknown to his constituents, more of anything would have been an improvement.

Milk marketing orders were an urgent local issue. Here you see me getting to the root of the matter.

Politicking from the Green Room at Edgewater.

After a small dinner at the White House in 1961, Jackie dragged Jack and me to a horse show where, "Jack will only have to stay for a few minutes." We were there for an hour while Jack, seething, and I gossiped behind her back.

Bobby Kennedy in a thoughtful mood. It has been reported that the two men he most hated were Jimmy Hoffa and me.

Hell's angels: Lee Radziwill and Truman Capote, having just received instructions from the Lord of the Flies, gleefully surface to do his work.

In 1964, when Lyndon Johnson decided to run for president without Bobby Kennedy as his vice president, Bobby, at a loose end, decided to leave Massachusetts and run for the Senate in New York state against the incumbent Republican, Kenneth Keating. I liked Keating and so, with journalist Lisa Howard, we formed the Democrats for Keating committee. One million seven hundred thousand Democrats voted against Bobby, and he would have been defeated had Johnson not swept the nation and, in the process, elected Bobby.

Our house in Ravello was built in 1925 by the daughter of one Lord Grimthorpe, creator of the neighboring Villa Cimbrone. We got the place in 1972. Set among a dozen acres of olive, lemon, and chestnut trees, it is nicely–literally–at the end of the road. "A paradise," as the Italian press called it when "Lady Clinton" came to call in July 1994.

London, Nina

J ULY THE FIRST and a heat wave; there seems to be not much air to breathe; one moves slowly. Apocalyptic mood in the village, where everyone talks of an irreversible worsening of the climate. Plants that should be in flower this month flowered in March.

I am rereading Elaine Dundy's chapter about me from the memoir that she is writing. I am reminded what a good comic writer she is; she also has a biographer's sharp eye. For instance, she writes that while my clothes are never noticeable, Ken wears deep purple suits and Tom Wolfe's white planter outfits are very showy indeed. They dressed to be noticed. I dressed to be invisible. But perhaps that is the difference between journalists, obliged to make a vivid daily effect, and those of us who write over the long, long haul, revealing, even in our clothes, the slow, dull, bovine temperament of the novelist.

I first met the Tynans at the London flat of Lee and Mike Canfield. Mike was much liked in London. Lee was not. But as we were all friends in those days, I did what little I could to help her social climb, which proved to be not much, since she had, in Judy Montagu's brisk phrase, "Not enough jokes"; of course, in her single-minded way, she had become something of a joke herself and there were many "Lee stories" in circulation, but I don't think that was much consolation.

Elaine was uncommonly pretty, with a quick wit. She was American. She had been an actress. She had family money. She had just written a

Daughter of Former Senator Gore
Weds Army Officer at Washington

Mrs. Eugene Luther Vidal.

Mrs. Eugene Luther Vidal, in wedding gown, who before her marriage last week in Washington, D. C., to Lieutenant Vidal, of the army engineering corps, was Miss Nina Gore, daughter of former Senator and Mrs. Thomas P. Gore of Oklahoma. The ceremony was held in St. Margaret's Episcopal church, Washington.

My mother, Nina Gore (1903–1978), married
Eugene Luther Vidal in 1921. An army flier,
he was instructor in aeronautics as well as
football coach at West Point, where I was
born in the cadet hospital some four years
later, as shepherds quaked.

first novel–everyone was writing novels then, just as today they "work" on screenplays. The Tynan parties were the best of that time and place. Ken was tall and languid, very much an Oxonian queen who preferred women to men; hence, Ken was fondly regarded by us all as one of nature's innate and unalterable lesbians. Like so many of his country-men, he was addicted to the "English vice"–spanking–as he would reveal to all the world a dozen years later, when he made his fortune with a sex revue called *Oh! Calcutta!* Although essentially apolitical, Ken was a committed Marxist of a sort that had died out a generation earlier in the United States. In 1960, when he came to *The New Yorker* as drama critic, he was much feted by the town. At one party, the editor of the *Partisan Review* listened patiently to Ken's discourse on how *money should not breed money*. When Ken, who stammered, finally stopped in mid-tirade to gasp, the editor said, "Mr. Tynan, your argu-ments are so old that I've forgotten all the answers to them."

I had come over on the *Queen Mary* under my MGM contract to work for Sam Zimbalist on a film about Captain Dreyfus. Sam was at the Eal-ing studio (recently bought by MGM), where he was making a seri-ously unneeded new version of *The Barretts of Wimpole Street*, with the ancient director Sidney Franklin, a man so fearful of germs that he was always begloved.

I dined alone in the first-class grill of the *Queen Mary*, easily the best cooking that I have ever known. Only the Atlantic Ocean misplayed its part, and one afternoon, during a storm, as I made my careful way across a vast salon where ropes had been set up parallel to one another for the passengers to hold on to as the ship pitched, I noticed that an ancient lady had started to cross from the other end. Suddenly, a *Titanic*-sinking wave hit amidships, and the lady, now free of man's best friend, gravity, went flying through the upper air. As her arc of trajectory settled on me, she shouted during the descent, "Hold fast, sir, I pray you!"

Fast I held and we were as one between those ropes.

I moved into Claridge's Hotel. I went out to Ealing almost every day, to work with Sam. The Elstree Studios resembled so many airplane hangars set in a large green field where lambs frolicked until ominous shepherds came and put them in sacks, a sight that always disturbed tenderhearted Sam and me.

Shortly after my arrival, I met the Tynans. Elaine reports on our first meeting.

It was in December of 1957 that I met Gore. It was in London one Saturday evening and we were at a cocktail party given by a mutual friend.

Gore came up to me and introduced himself. He was in London to write a film for MGM about Captain Dreyfus. He had learned that Ken was a script editor there. He would like to meet him. Gore was staying at Claridge's. I said we lived right next door in Mount Street. He asked for our telephone number. He called me the next morning. "What are you doing?" he wanted to know. I said I was reading the Sunday papers. What was he doing? "Just had a satisfactory bowel movement," he said, "and now I'm staring at the ceiling." "What's it look like?" I asked. "Tidy," he replied. A chauffeur-driven car was to take him to Ealing tomorrow. Why didn't he pick up Ken [Balcon's story editor] *in the morning and they can go out together? Plans were made.*

Monday evening Ken came home from the studio still bemused about his morning drive. Although it was the crack of dawn, Gore had opened the conversation with a dissertation on Somerset Maugham's latest book which contained the latter's views on the world's greatest writers. "Wait a minute," interrupted Ken after a bit. "It's seven o'clock in the morning and you're talking in whole sentences. Say that last part again." Gore repeated: "Observe how cleverly Maugham, while arranging the statues of the writers he has chosen to grace his special Pantheon, will chop off a head here, a pair of legs there, a couple of feet, or arms, as suits his purpose so that finally only a certain short, wizened man of letters, Maugham himself, is left standing erect; whole and complete, towering over them all."

Memory: I've just arrived from New York. I go to Mount Street. Ken, Elaine, and several friends are all lying on the floor listening to the first recording of *West Side Story* to arrive in the town. Ken put finger to lips; whispered, "Listen! Superb. The repetition of that musical phrase."

"The needle's stuck," I announced, displaying consummate musicianship.

The winters of 1957 and 1958 are now something of a blur to me. I do know that my second visit was due to Ken. He had proposed that I write, under my MGM contract, the script to a Daphne du Maurier novel called *The Scapegoat.* "The novel's dreadful, but we could have fun in London." That winter Howard came with me and we took a splendid flat in Chesham Place, the property of an old lady descended from Gouverneur Morris. One of our founding fathers, Morris had been minister in Paris at the time of the Revolution. When the mob attacked the Tuileries, the minister hired several porters to carry away Marie Antoinette's furniture as it was heaved out the windows, and so the drawing room of the flat was filled with the decapitated lady's magnificence; as a result no one, including our landlady, ever spent any time in that room unless there was a sufficiently large party to make the furniture seem invisible.

For *The Scapegoat,* MGM had wanted Cary Grant, but Daphne wanted Alec Guinness because he so much resembled, she claimed, her father, Gerald du Maurier, a debonair actor of the previous century. She had considerable control over the production, which I certainly envied. She was a tall, handsome woman with short gray hair. She had the equally enviable supreme confidence of the born best-seller writer who has no notion that there is something out there–with terrible sharp teeth and capacious stomach–called literature. Maugham, unhappily for him, did know quite a lot about literature and fretted that he might not be up to the likes of Hardy, much less James. Daphne could not have cared less. Why should she? Her fans were devoted no matter what. When I was fifteen I thought the novel and subsequent movie of *Rebecca* ravishing. I also read several of her other novels with pleasure, though I knew even then what that gray circling Leviathan Time had in mind for her works.

Daphne was unconsciously condescending to me, and so I came to know what an experienced butler must feel in a stately home. I was, she would say to others, "the hack from Hollywood," which was not too far off the mark, and she was *la belle maîtresse sans merci.* With Alec, she was adoring, even, horribly, kittenish. Alec was her father yet again, but also . . . also . . . *incest,* anyone? Alec treated her with ineffable charm during their interviews. He also managed to keep at least one large piece of furniture between them. If he could, I think he would have brought Merula, his wife, to our meetings and let her play sofa to the romantic lady from Cornwall.

Daphne had written a version of *The Prisoner of Zenda,* which she somehow mistook for the passion of Joan of Arc. The born best-seller writer is like Columbus sailing for India and forever discovering American gold. I exercised much tact and patience with her while Alec, a very literary man, was not only patiently tactful but treated her with all the skill of a slightly edgy psychiatrist soothing a potential werewolf at dusk. Certainly, she was in absolute heaven with Alec, and he reported to me that she had told him, several times, the entire story of her life and how she felt guilty that she had so let down her military hero-husband, "Boy" Browning, some sort of royal courtier, recently dead. "He would do everything for me, I nothing for him in his palace life." She lived for her art.

Daphne talked to me of her fascinating family, whose ancestors had been glassblowers in northern France. I affected awe at the thought of all that blue glass awash in her veins. She had set *The Scapegoat* in the same region—near Le Mans—where her family came from. In the story, there are two lookalikes: one a French aristocrat and—I forget, blessedly, the other one. Each was played by Alec.

"What would the aristocrat *wear*?" Alec mused. Alec begins with the clothes and then works to the heart of the character, unlike our method actors, who work from the gut and, with luck, get as far as the belt buckle.

"Tweed?" I had no idea what a French noble in the country wore. "Anglophile, of course," I added, remembering Huysmans.

"Tweed? Mmm. Yes. But boiled first. Yes. Yes. *Boiled* tweed."

Alec had insisted that Balcon let him use Robert Hamer as director. This was not only out of loyalty to an old friend, who had turned alcoholic of late, but also good sense: It was Hamer who had written and directed that perfect comedy *Kind Hearts and Coronets*.

Robert and I got on beautifully. He was droll and cynical and hopelessly in love with the actress Joan Greenwood, easily the best comedienne of the time but not, she had told him solemnly, made for love. "I am too small ever to be entered." Robert actually believed her. But then he was on something like methadone, which he would absently spray down his throat from time to time. Daphne's ears must have heated up whenever Robert and I got on the subject of her novel. We invented scenes of such obscenity that not even the theater at Charenton would have put them on. We also spent a lot of time reading her prose aloud, savoring the rich tautologies, the gleaming oxymorons, the surreal syntax.

In the first version of the script I had written a picnic scene, anything to get us out of doors. "The French," said Daphne contemptuously, "hate picnics." Robert and I blushed as upper servants do when caught out.

"I never knew," I said in a humble voice.

"We were misled," said Robert, tugging his forelock, "by Manet's *Déjeuner sur l'herbe*."

As neither name nor title registered, the picnic was cut. Robert then suggested that he and I go on location to France. I asked Maria St. Just to join us. She was always game for an eating tour. In freezing weather we crossed the Channel, and hired a car. Hamer sat in the back, staring at the snow and ice. "A winter wonderland." He suddenly sneered and pulled a flask from his pocket.

It was a fine trip and, drunk, Robert was much happier than sober. Later, I said nothing to Alec or Balcon. I did tell Alec of our visit to a glassblowing establishment, where all the blowers—a half-dozen elderly men—were drunk and Robert kept shrieking, "Inhale! Inhale!"

In due course, the picture was made. As I had failed to get Bette Davis the part that Katharine Hepburn played in *Suddenly, Last Summer,* I got her a good part in *The Scapegoat,* which was then cut to nothing. Bette was ill pleased, but I was long gone by then. In the end, Alec took over the direction as Robert was too far gone in drink. He did make one more picture that I never saw. I see from a film encyclopedia that he also got co-credit, with me, for *The Scapegoat.* Actually, if it was changed (I never noticed much of anything when I finally saw the film), it would have been Alec's work.

I am a poor guest and dislike staying in other people's houses. But in my early days in England, out of curiosity, I did sometimes go for weekends at the stately homes, of which the one with the most amiable occupants was the Queen Anne house of Jakie Astor and his Argentine wife, Chiquita. Jakie was—is—a splendid wit, not to mention man of conscience: He left Parliament after the Suez debacle for country life and the duties of a justice of the peace, "Which takes far more intelligence than being a member of Parliament."

It was at Jakie's that I met his mother, Nancy Astor. A Virginian who still spoke with a southern accent, she had married an Astor who had become English and bought a title, "back in the days when," as she said to me, "it really meant something to buy one." She then became the first woman to be elected to Parliament, where her eccentric wit gave joy to the world.

At table, she and Jakie would constantly address parliamentary insults to one another; he generally outwitted her, but she was the more startling. Furiously temperance—she would take long sips from everyone's glass, making a terrible face with each gulp. "It is beyond me how people can destroy their systems with this vile stuff." She was against divorce—and had, of course, been divorced from a first husband in order to marry Astor.

Our first dinner at Hatley, I sat on her right. There were only five at table. Suddenly, Lady Astor was seized with missionary zeal—to convert us all to Christian Science. She thundered away as the rest of us ate and drank and spoke under, as it were, her tirade. Then she turned on her daughter-in-law, the pale, ethereal Chiquita. "Look at *you*! Sickly, always sickly. Yet it's all in the mind, I tell you. All in the mind. Change your thoughts."

Jakie murmured something soothing—Chiquita had had a hard time in childbirth . . .

That did it. The game was now afoot. "All those doctors, those unhealthy medicines. Why, when I had my three sons by my beautiful Waldorf—" (discouraged glance at Jakie) "—all three ended up looking like rabbits—even so, I had them without medicine or chloroform or anything at all and all three were born *without* pain . . ."

"Yes, Mother," murmured Jakie. Disraeli now to his mother's Gladstone: "We were born without pain and conceived without pleasure."

Like a jack-in-the-box, Nancy was on her feet; raced to the head of the table; cracked Jakie across the face; returned to her seat beside me and drained the glass of brandy beside my plate. "I can't think how you let yourself be poisoned by this."

Next morning in the garden. Nancy in benign mood. The ancient head gardener from Cliveden was in charge of Jakie's gardens. He moaned about his comedown in the world. Nancy was brisk. "Cheer up. World's changed." She turned to me, "Well, here's the ring-tailed wonder." An allusion to my having just turned down a Senate nomination. "Let's walk." I noted that she was carrying a golf club with which she'd practice whenever we paused. "The English are the best people in the world. I mean, what other people could've put up with me all these years? Marshal Stalin asked me the same thing. Doesn't that sound fine? Marshal Stalin and me! But there we were together in his office. Bernard Shaw and I had made this trip to the Soviet, and there was Shaw on the train, busy reading a book, never once looking out the window because he knew, of course, everything in the world and so never looked at anything. Anyway, Marshal Stalin, after listening to Shaw for a while, gets up and goes to a map and points to England and then to all that pink which was our empire back then and says, 'How did this little island manage to take over so much of the world?' Well, I was inspired. I said, 'Because, Marshal Stalin, we had given the world the King James translation of the Bible.' "

"What," I asked, "did he say?"

"Well, he just changed the subject. Anyway, as we were leaving, I said, 'Marshal Stalin, when are you gonna stop killing people?' And he said directly to me, 'Lady Astor, the undesirable classes do not liquidate themselves.' "

"What did you say?"

"As I had run out of small talk, we got out of there fast."

A WELCOME INTERRUPTION to the upcoming story of Nina. Just before noon, when the temperature was 105°F, a half-dozen Secret Service men, White House, and embassy people arrive to see the place. Mrs. Clinton is to come to Ravello next Friday. She will cross our property to get to the Villa Cimbrone, on the hill just above us, and then I will accompany her and her mother to the concert in the gardens of the Villa Ruffolo. I have never met either Clinton. Also, a potentially delicate matter: In the early primaries, most of the substance of Jerry Brown's speeches was my work, and Clinton hated Brown, though not enough for him to refrain from taking over some of Jerry's—my—best lines. Later, ecumenically, I sent Clinton material for his debates with Bush.

One of the Secret Service men had spent six years at the White House during the Reagans; as he had had the night watch, he read a good many books, among them *Burr* and *Lincoln;* he was pleased, he said, to see the room where those books were written.

Then Howard and I were given numerous calling cards with names and cellular telephone numbers to keep us in close touch with our new friends. The president will be staying in Naples with the rest of the potentates, and Yeltsin. Hillary will have her day off on our coast. I feel somewhat paternal about the Clintons: They really have had the most savage press of any administration this century. Clinton himself said as much last week. Today a columnist chided him; apparently, Clinton had no idea what Roosevelt had gone through with the press. Plainly, the journalist had no idea, but I do. I was reading newspapers at the time and it is true that Roosevelt was attacked for his Communist-Fascist policies, but no hookers were ever given prime time on television (even if it had been invented then) to discuss his cock. Private lives were private, including pre-presidential business arrangements. It is true that Mrs. Roosevelt inspired a good deal of "personal" hatred thanks to our good white folks' ongoing, seemingly eternal, loathing of the Niggers, whom she did her best to befriend.

The Clintons are now under attack because they would improve a society that is a heaven for, perhaps, one tenth of the people and a hell, of varying degrees, for the rest. I doubt if he will survive his first term. He will experience either the bullet or a sudden resignation, and then cousin Albert, the Cromwell of Washington's Fairfax Hotel, will be Lord Protector. Naturally, I hope that I am mistaken as of summer 1994.

"THE ONLY REASON I was born was that rats had chewed on Mother's douche bag, or so she told me." This was an essential starting point to the Nina Story. As it was established very early in her saga, there was probably some truth to it. Dot's time was fully occupied looking after— and reading to—her blind husband. Should they ever fall on hard times, a constant fear, children would have been a nuisance or worse. So, thanks to the torn douche bag, Nina was born in the summer of 1903, in Lawton, Indian territory. Dah and his friends did not make the territory a state until 1907, when, at thirty-eight, he was elected to the U. S. Senate.

They moved to Washington, to Mintwood Place, high above Rock Creek Park. Nina was sent to Holton Arms, a good girls' school. She was dark, with hazel eyes, high arched brows, thin lips, and a propensity for alcohol, which did not become out of control until she was in her thirties. Over the years, she would stop drinking for a month or two and work with Marty Mann, a founder of Alcoholics Anonymous. I note in the biography of Marlon Brando that his mother, equally alcoholic, also worked, when sober, with Miss Mann. Sober, Nina was candid. "I first thought something might be wrong when I was still married to Gene and after a party I'd go around and finish whatever was left in all the glasses."

Dot and Dah, true southerners, worshiped at the shrine of Education, the only way that they knew of for a southerner to rise during Reconstruction. They were not worldly enough to know that in Washington a handsome, well-placed, if penniless, young woman like Nina–and, later, like Jackie and Lee–was expected to marry money, which made useless a degree in accounting or Western civilization.

Nina met Gene Vidal after a football game in 1921. They were at different tables in a Child's restaurant in Manhattan. He was a football coach at the United States Military Academy as well as sole instructor in aeronautics. He was twenty-six; she was eighteen. Someone introduced them. Love at first sight, on her side anyway. He called her Pup. They were married in 1923 at St. Margaret's Church, Washington, in the presence of the disapproving Senator and Mrs. Gore. Nina was still a virgin.

On the honeymoon train, he said, "There's something very important I want you to know."

"Oh, I was so excited," she said to me years later, during one of our truces. "He's going to tell me he loves me!" But he didn't. Instead, he said, "I have three balls!" Apparently, he was in all the medical books. I never dared look–you don't look at parents–but it is recorded that they were all of equal size. On the town, with football buddies, they used to bet other tables of athletes who had the most balls. West Point always won.

From Nina's long deposition to *Time* magazine: "When Gore was six weeks old I took him to my parents' home in Washington, and we lived there until he was nine." Actually, when Gene joined Roosevelt's administration, he took a house for us on Bancroft Place, where Nina entertained as royally as they could afford, drinking up the leftovers, while Gene would go out for chocolate ice cream, which he'd then share with me. They also had a black manservant, Louis, who was very effeminate, with a lisp. I liked him. Years later, when I came to know Jimmy Baldwin, I thought he was Louis born again, but without the lisp.

When my uncle, Tom Gore, left his watch on the washbasin, I stole it. There was a great fuss. I have no idea why I took the watch. I had no interest in watches then or now. But when I realized the gravity of what I had done, I knew that it would take some ingenuity to undo the crime.

So I hid the watch under a bush in a nearby playground; then, when Louis and I passed the bush on the way to market, I pretended to find the watch. "Look!" I exclaimed, with true acting flair, or so I thought. "A watch." I was distressed when everyone saw through what I took to be a superbly executed stratagem.

I was, for a time, being bullied by a larger boy named Tommy Hopkins. Nina gave me a metal dog's leash. "Hit him with this." I did, and nearly knocked out his left eye. That dog leash still haunts me, like Cocteau's lethal snowball. Another boy, caught masturbating, told his mother that I had taught him. Nina took this very seriously. I had no idea what she was talking about. Then, one day, I set fire to a pile of cardboard boxes on the sidewalk in front of the house. The police came; then went away. What was my sudden–promptly extinguished–pyromania all about? A signal, I now think: Send me home to the Gores. Life was unbearable with Nina raging at Gene, who would, smiling, simply vanish, leaving me for her to rage at.

From the deposition: "Gore's father, a charming man, Eugene Vidal . . . was not equipped for civilian life. He had graduated from the University of South Dakota and was proselytized for West Point because of his athletic abilities at football and track." This was true, but he also graduated in the top 5 percent of his class at the Academy. "His first civilian position was with Transcontinental Air Transport, which I got for him through a friend of mine, Burdette Wright of Curtiss Wright in Buffalo. Gene was fired from this." As always, it's not what you know, it's who you know. But Wright had nothing to do with TAT.

In 1929, one C. M. Keys combined a couple of airlines and started TAT. For a quarter-million dollars cash, Keys hired, as consultant, Charles Lindbergh; he also gave the Lone Eagle shrewd advice on how to avoid income tax. Thus, TAT was dubbed "The Lindbergh Line." Keys was perhaps the first true hustler or robber baron in American aviation. TAT also acquired ex-airmail flyer Paul Collins and army flyer Gene Vidal.

Like most of the early airlines, TAT was a combined air-rail service. Passenger planes did not fly at night or over the turbulent Alleghenys. On a TAT transcontinental flight, the passengers left New York by rail in the evening; then, in Columbus, Ohio, the eight passengers boarded a Ford trimotor and flew to Waynoka, Oklahoma. Here they transferred to the Santa Fe railroad for an overnight haul to Clovis, New Mexico, where another plane flew them into Los Angeles–or Burbank, to be precise. It is a tribute to the faith of these pioneers that they truly believed this grueling two-day journey would, in time, be preferable to the comforts of a Pullman railroad car.

Paul Collins describes the end of TAT in *Tales of an Old Air-Faring Man:*

> *About Christmastime 1929 all the St. Louis executives were called to a meeting in New York...We were introduced in Mr. Keyes's [sic] office to one Jack Maddux, President of Maddux Airlines, an operation that flew from Los Angeles to San Francisco...Mr. Keyes [sic] stated that a merger had been effected between TAT and Maddux.*

The ineffable Keys then waited until the assembled management of TAT had returned to St. Louis, where they were all fired.

MORE SECRET SERVICE at the gate. "They'll be coming up from Amalfi around four-thirty. Could you greet Mrs. Clinton at this first gate here and then walk the party on to your place and up to the Villa Cimbrone?"

"How many are there?"

"Forty, fifty." I had been asked to offer them a drink in our cypress alley, but I decided that there were now too many. Meanwhile, the ever-alert, ever-confused Italian press keeps ringing the house. Hillary-mania is sweeping the peninsula. They are intrigued that she is "snubbing" the wife of the prime minister, Berlusconi, to come to the Amalfi coast to see me. Politically, she has every reason to keep her distance from the new prime minister. A nonpolitician "media-mogul," as they call Berlusconi, he owns three television networks, newspapers, publishing houses. "Two hundred and fifty businesses," he told the secretary of the treasury, Lloyd Bentsen. Although the idea of conflict of interest does not exist in Italian law or life, everyone is suddenly acutely aware of what it means when someone who controls the media sets himself up as the country's political chief. The fact that Berlusconi has made an alliance with the neo-Fascists (they like to be called post-Fascists) has not allayed suspicions. Clinton is obliged to stay in Naples with the other chiefs of state; but wives are allowed to pursue culture in the hinterland.

At the insistence of our mayor, I gave several print interviews. In principle, I stopped talking to "the print media" years ago. Also, few Italian journalists speak English–the language that I sternly use with them–and few know about the world outside Italy. Research, even of the most primitive sort, like looking into *Who's Who,* is unknown, and so I am eternally famous hereabouts for having written Visconti's "classic" film *Senso.* I not only did not write it, I never saw it; but that makes no difference.

The press, however, does seem mystified that Hillary would want to see me, or any mere writer. I try to explain to them that many Americans are interested in the novels that I have written, particularly those placed within American history. When I said that there has not been a presidential contender or president in the last dozen years who has not read or claimed to have read *Lincoln,* they think I am making a joke. Yet even Ronald Reagan affected a knowledge of *Lincoln,* and told *Time* magazine that I had got everything wrong because I had described Lincoln watching the dawn from the Oval Office "when you can't see the dawn from there." Of course, there is no such scene in the book and, of course, the Oval Office where Ron so eagerly greeted each dawn was not added on to the White House until 1905.

Hillary arrived with mother and daughter and a large entourage of Secret Service, local police, embassy walkers, and the elegant wife of Lloyd Bentsen. Hillary is small, stocky, with large round blue eyes, a beautiful smile, and an easy manner with the folks, who were quite keyed up.

The last *presidentessa*–the only one, in fact–to visit Ravello was Jackie, in 1963. Italian newspapers report that Hillary is modeling herself on Jackie–God forbid–and so she has come to lunch with me, just as Jackie did thirty-two years ago, only Jackie didn't, as I wasn't in the house then, and in any case, we were no longer on speaking terms.

As we walked along the road that looks down on the Gulf of Salerno, Hillary talked of Jackie and the recent funeral. She finds her fascinating. "Jackie was in wonderful shape last summer when we saw her in Martha's Vineyard. And even when she fell off that horse and they gave her all those tests, they found nothing wrong." I thought the fall might have been a sign of something gone wrong. I also said that I had been at the White House recently, where I'd autographed two green plastic

Easter eggs for the annual egg roll for children, my first visit since my last dinner with the Kennedys. "Give us warning next time," she said. "Come back." This was polite.

I then steered the conversation into an area where we would be as one, the media—a word that I hate as much as I do *agenda*, the last because it is the plural of *agendum*, a perfectly good word now mangled, and the first because it is interchangeably singular or plural; in honor, I suppose, of McLuhan's famous nostrum—why not *nostra*?—"the medium is the message."

Hillary's eyes glittered as we recounted—competing monologues, I fear—our similar views. "It's so pervasive now, everywhere and all the time, day after day, stories that never conclude. Look at O. J. Simpson—there's nothing else on television all day long. Live." I confessed that I had become addicted to the pretrial hearings, and she confessed to some lawyerly interest in the case. "But there is *other* news in the day. What we get now—what it all is—is simply entertainment to boost ratings." I said that I'd not given a print interview in English for five years; and planned never to do so again. (I don't count "Questions and Answers" delivered by chaste fax.) "Don't you wish you could do the same?"

"Oh!" This was sharp; then exhalation, "Oh . . . yes. Yes. But for now . . ."

Beneath century-old tall cypresses acreak with the sound of cicadas, we said farewell until the evening concert. "Meeting you has been the high point of this trip"—radiant blue eyes looked up into mine. Yes, I thought, I am now ready to replace Warren Christopher as secretary of state; then the deflationary coda—"for my mother."

I wonder if her interest in Jackie might not be genuine bewilderment at how a woman so selfish could be so beloved and Hillary, who wants actually to do something useful for others, is currently hated. Some obscure law of public relations is busily working overtime.

The concert was held in the gardens of the Villa Ruffolo. The crowds were ecstatic and Ravello was, once again, historic.

In the interval, the mayor made Hillary an honorary citizen, like me. "I was ten years old when Mrs. Kennedy was made an honorary citizen, and I danced the tarantella with the other children. Now I am mayor . . ."

I USED TO WONDER just how Nina went about revising the scenarios of her life. Certainly, she thought incessantly about herself and her hard times. She played the same tapes over and over again, and I suppose, by sheer repetition, she was able to make subtle changes—particularly with a new acquaintance, to whom she could tell the whole glamorous, doomed story. As a liar, she was Homeric, unlike Capote, who was all rapid intuition and showy improvisation, while Nina was more like an ancient bard who repeated essentially the same story over and over again with, every now and then, a small but significant variation in the sacred text.

In *The Drowned and the Saved,* Primo Levi describes most elegantly the process that I have only sketched: "There are . . . those who lie consciously, coldly falsifying reality itself, but more numerous are those who weigh anchor, move off, momentarily or forever, from genuine memories, and fabricate for themselves a convenient reality . . . The silent transition from falsehood to sly deception is useful: anyone who lies in good faith is better off, he recites his part better, he is more easily believed . . ."

Occasionally, a truth is registered: she says I was "insufferable" to my stepbrother. "It was a nerve-strainer for me to try to keep things agreeable for my stepson, who was a darling, and in no way did I want him upset . . ." This is vintage Nina, with only one flaw: She is right. I *was* insufferable to the poor tot. On the other hand, Nina was insufferable to everyone. Nina's frenzied attempts to find the right school for someone who was plainly not like other boys is noted, but then, "when he was quite young, I realized his problem." Apparently, my boredom with athletics and addiction to reading and writing were the unmistakable sign of an urning-to-be. Later, facing my "problem" head-on, she did what she could to break up Rosalind and me.

Meanwhile, it was necessary for her to keep me as far away as possible. In addition to her drinking, she was now a morphine addict. She was also becoming reckless. One afternoon, the children's nurse, Mrs. Goodman, caught her smuggling a black cabdriver into her bedroom. It was the "black" that upset Goody, a southerner, not his profession or Nina's idle lust. I think what Nina instinctively most feared was an intelligent witness.

Now Nina will tell the truth about our estrangement. Apparently, after *Visit to a Small Planet* closed, I had gone to London to write a film and, "I kept getting calls, cables and letters from Gore asking me to come over. At that time I knew many people in London including our own Ambassador (Jock Whitney), the Cuban ambassador and many others." Ever on the make, I needed Nina to throw open the gates to her glittering world. As it was, between Annie Fleming and Judy Montagu, I was seeing quite enough of "our own Ambassador."

Annie to Jock, "Do you enjoy being an ambassador?"

Jock to the room, "No. I'm a cross between a butler and a pimp for senators."

I had taken a flat with three servants, and as Nina enjoyed that sort of thing, I asked her–once–to visit. Why? I don't know. Of course, she had assured me that she was not drinking, and . . .

When Nina got to London, the flat wasn't ready, so I put her in a hotel suite next to mine. There was a connecting door between the suites.

One afternoon the actor Robert Morley came to call. He was interested in playing the lead in *Visit* in London. "But, dear boy, we must place the story in England." I tried to explain that the point to the comedy was American imperialism and our love for war–an avant-garde notion in 1957, in fact so avant-garde that if any of the reviewers had understood what the play was really about, it would not have run a week.

Morley was not to be budged. "I know English audiences. They don't like American plays." Morley proposed, in his most winning way, that for "Englishing" the play he'd take half the royalties and share my billing. I said, no, and so there was never a West End production.

I came to know Morley, slightly, over the years; he was splendid company. As Rex Harrison said of him, toward the end of their lives, "Here you are, after all these years, with the same house, the same wife and, if I may say so, the same performance." As I showed him out, I heard heavy breathing from the next room. I opened the door. There was Nina, glass of vodka in one hand, ear to the door.

When we moved into the flat on Chesham Place, Nina put in a call to "our own Ambassador." He never returned the call. She then took seriously to drink.

The flat was on two floors, with a backstairs. Dressed in a silk wrapper, Nina would sit on the steps with the housemaid, telling tales of her pansy son and his Jew-boy friend because of whom she was not able to see her dearest friends like "our own Ambassador."

As Nina redid the scenario of her life ("polishing and retouching here and there the details which are least credible or incongruous..."– Levi), she made poor Howard, who liked her, the reason for our "estrangement" in London. Apparently, she could not endure the shame his presence caused her. Actually, it was her nonstop drinking that made it impossible for us to have anyone come to the house. Also, by the second week, two of the three servants were gone. Only Miss Austen, the cook, remained loyally to the end.

Finally, I packed Nina off. In due course, she wrote me an unusually savage letter, which I burned. I then wrote to tell her that I would never see her again, and I never did during the remaining twenty years of her life.

Nina grows reflective at the end of her deposition. "I think many times of John Latouche's saying, 'I have never seen such a sense of competition as Gore has with you.'" Aside from the fact that Latouche would never have made so pointless a remark, I cannot see how even Nina's muddled mind could ever have thought that there was any field of competition between us. Curiously, my father alludes to *her* competitiveness in a letter to me shortly after his second child by his second wife is born: "Nina will probably have another now since she won't want to be tied." Plainly, we all had *her* number. Even so ...

Howard has just asked me why I bothered with her at all. I don't really know. But I am beginning to think that she knew how to play on a sadistic streak in me that would, once awakened, impel me to detonate the Queen Lear of the Lobby in order to revel in her howlings. If true, that would be a victory for her.

Twenty years later, when Nina died of cancer, my half brother, Tommy Auchincloss, was with her. Our sister was not; she too was as "estranged" as I, because when she got her divorce from her first husband and sought custody of her three sons, Nina blithely appeared from nowhere to testify in court that her daughter, whom she hardly knew, was an unfit mother.

This summer Tommy gave me a report of a trip he had taken through the American heartland: Nina had told him that she would like to be scattered on the San Francisco Mountains as that had been where her last husband, General Robert Olds, had been scattered.

...Mom died at the Sloan Kettering Institute in New York. I arranged for her cremation in New Jersey and bought a bus ticket in her name from Paramus, New Jersey, to Arlington, Vermont. You are not allowed to ship remains by parcel post. That was the last I heard about her for three days as she wandered around Vermont, courtesy of the Green Mountain Bus Line... She finally showed up with much apology from the various agencies involved and lived in my attic for ten years until I had a chance to take her out West. I did arrange a stone to be placed alongside her parents in Oklahoma City...

In due course, Tommy

discovered a neat little forest road that wound through the San Francisco Mountains... and traveled out to the end, where there were some distant mountains. It was the perfect spot to spread Mom's ashes and I did so as I slowly drove back to the highway. The forest road was a little rough and it was disconcerting to have the bone dust blowing back on me and trying to make sure the surgical screws did not land in the road where they might end up in a tire. I scattered all but a third of the ashes, as I wanted to place some with her parents in Oklahoma City.

The next day I discovered I had scattered Mom on the wrong mountains. I had been about four hundred miles off. It took a while, but some of Mom got on the right mountains. Strangely, it was not some filial angst or chagrin I felt but an ironic humor, which I am sure she would have shared... Knowing her restless nature, she is still blowing in the wind.

Tommy also wrote me that three days before Nina died, she said that I had come to apologize to her in the hospital and that she had forgiven me. She was so convincing that he checked the hospital records to see if I had actually been there.

So on that "amiable"(?) note, the story of Nina ends for good.

*November 1960. Eleanor Roosevelt has just
voted for me in Hyde Park. I was the
Democratic candidate for the House of
Representatives for New York's 29th District.
She was wonderful to campaign with. "If you
explain yourself clearly, people might be
inclined to vote for their own interests."
Then, she noted sadly, "Jack Kennedy
talks far, far too fast."*

The Twenty-ninth New York Congressional District

REE OF MGM AND HOLLYWOOD, I settled in at Edgewater. Howard was living there now, and I was slowly, very slowly, approaching financial independence. Slowly because anyone who earned more than $100,000 a year was obliged to pay 90 percent income tax–presumably, for that surge of pride which one could not help but feel as our CIA overthrew the democratically elected president of Guatemala and removed the popular Iranian leader, Mossadegh, so that the Shah might continue as American proconsul. It is hard now to think how supinely we put up with so much taxation with nothing to show for it at home. Of course, we still have nothing to show for our tax money, but at least the tax rate was significantly lowered, for a time, so that those with inherited money (or their foundations and companies) might free themselves of taxes, thus, inadvertently, helping us wage earners. In 1958, after the success of *Visit to a Small Planet*, I bought a small brownstone house in New York City. A year later, after I had paid my taxes, I was obliged to slink back to Hollywood and write, under another name, a mystery series for television.

This confiscation of one's hard-earned money did not drive me into the right wing, as it did Ronald Reagan, who was as indignant as I but chose to blame it all on a vague nemesis called "big government." I started to turn left. If the government was going to take so much of our money, then let the government give us health care, education, and all those other things first-world countries provide their taxpayers. Of course, in those days, to favor federal aid to education was to be a Communist. Thanks to Harry Truman's National Security State, the good news about other societies is either kept from us or carefully distorted: Swedes have free education, health care, and so on, *but* they also practice "free love," get drunk, and commit suicide, because they lack the excitement of living in a society where the untrained have the freedom to starve. My real political education began when I made money only to have it confiscated by a military machine. As the age of McCarthy dawned, I would soon be taking a crash course in "radical" politics.

Every week, each television network would secretly produce a list of names of actors, writers, and directors who could not be hired. The list was arbitrary, to say the least. There was, however, a means of expiation for someone excluded. A grocery-store owner in Schenectady had made himself the acknowledged authority on Communism by refusing to sell anything advertised on those programs that hired Communists. Simply, a threat from him could deprive you of work; however, if the proscribed actor or writer proved to be genuinely repentant, he could go to Schenectady, much as a sick Catholic might go to Lourdes, and there the Butcher, as we called him, would absolve him if he swore to sin no more.

All this humiliating business was made worse by the rise of Senator Joe McCarthy. Yet, to be fair, McCarthy could never have flourished had it not been for Harry S Truman's mandatory loyalty oaths for all government workers because the Russians were coming, and we must root out their agents wherever they might be and a crypto-Commie, if he swore falsely, would, everyone knew, crumble to ashes. Earlier, the Republican senator Vandenberg had told Truman that if he wanted his party's help in totally militarizing the economy, "You will have to scare the hell out of the American people." Scared they were, but more of their own government and its "star chamber" procedures than ever they were of a weak second-world country like Russia, rattling its bars halfway around the world.

For me, politics had been the family business and I regarded it more as a process than as a matter of theory, much less ideology. But the radical populist base of the Gores had made me an instinctive noninterventionist, while the personal cost to me of the Second War had been sharp. Although I was now writing for *The Nation* and *Partisan Review,* I stayed out of all their symposia on theoretical politics. I thought the fierce contest between Trotskyites and Stalinists irrelevant to a country where the true historic division is between Hamilton and Jefferson, and I was on Jefferson's side.

My first overtly political play appeared on television on February 6, 1955: *A Sense of Justice.* A returned veteran, out of a sense of justice, decides to kill the corrupt boss of a state. Since he does not know the man, only his works, this is a disinterested rather than a gratuitous act. I suppose that I had been influenced, as most of us were at the time, by Sartre's existentialism (as well as Gide's *l'acte gratuite*). Certainly, *La Nausée* had made an impression on me. The play caused a few tremors when it was done on *Philco-Goodyear TV Playhouse.* The following summer a new version with a different cast was scheduled, then mysteriously canceled.

Visit to a Small Planet, both on television and on the stage, was a satire on the military and our National Security State's terror of Otherness of any kind. As it was a comedy, I got away with it. Then, sometime in 1956, Jack and Jackie Kennedy reentered my life, and I was intrigued to watch firsthand a near contemporary doing what I had wanted to do before *The City and the Pillar* cut me off from that other road through the yellow wood.

In 1958 I went down to Miami to meet Tennessee and the film producer Sam Spiegel. Would I write the screenplay for *Suddenly, Last Summer?* The Bird was manic that season and Sam more than usually devious. I agreed to write the script if Tennessee would have no hand in it. Later, Sam would talk him into taking co-credit for my screenplay on the ground, "Baby, it will win the Academy Award." As the Bird was ravenous for prizes, he put his name alongside mine on the script. Happily, the reviews were so bad that he immediately regretted what he had done; later, he was less disturbed as the press proved to be so bad that the public was driven to see what *The New York Times* shrieked was a celebration of sodomy, incest, cannibalism, and Elizabeth Taylor at her most voluptuous.

When Jackie heard that we were in Miami, she asked us up to Palm Beach for lunch. The Bird had no idea who they were but took my word for it that Jack was running for president. We arrived an hour late. Jack was firing a rifle at a target on the lawn. He was not a very good shot; and I was as bad as he. The Bird casually took the rifle from him and shot three bull's-eyes, "Using only my blind eye," he cackled.

Jackie said how much she had envied her stepbrother (my half brother) Tommy, whom the Bird had once taken out to Coney Island. "I was so jealous you hadn't taken me." The Bird graciously gave her a rain check.

Jack knew exactly how to flatter authors. Always say you admire their least successful work. He praised *Summer and Smoke,* and the Bird began to find him presidential. He also found him sexually attractive. "Look at that ass," he said thoughtfully as Jack led us into the damp, moldy-smelling house.

"You can't cruise our next president." I was stern.

"Don't be ridiculous. The American people will never elect those two. They're far too attractive."

It was a pleasant lunch, and I began to feel the political tug in myself. I had made a speech or two in the congressional district where I lived. One was against capital punishment, an unpopular position, but the roof had not fallen in. Was it still possible? I wondered, gazing thoughtfully at Jack. He always charmed me; yet I thought him something of a lightweight politically, since he was pretty much what the sheltered and unadventurous son of a rich right-winger would be. But then, at the time, so was I. The only difference–small but compelling: I had to earn a living and he didn't. I knew firsthand about taxes. He hadn't a clue. Otherwise, we were both unadventurous conservatives, interested in personal glory. If we had ever had an honest discussion of what each actually thought, I suspect that the only division between us would have been my growing hatred of the empire and his unquestioning love for it. In due course, he wanted us to win the cold war with a hot war. I think, even then, I suspected that the cold war was a fraud.

As we left, I told Jack that the Bird had found his ass attractive.

"That's very exciting." Jack grinned.

ANYONE WHO has ever had a successful play on Broadway (at least in those days) is under constant pressure to write a new play. For one thing, the writer's name makes it possible for producers to raise money. Roger L. Stevens, a real estate tycoon and sometime play producer, wanted a play from me. But what? My interests, partly due to Jack's activities, were more than ever political. Unfortunately, political plays do very badly with the American public, while satire does even worse. Most plays of that era were about women undergoing analysis and finding their true identity through love. Only the Bird could be counted on to liven things up with a castration here, a lobotomy there.

Finally, a play started in my head. I wrote *The Best Man* in three weeks at Provincetown.

I was intrigued by the contrast between a politician's private life and public life. So I set the play at the convention of one of the two parties. The high-minded, "good" candidate is highly promiscuous in private life. The Nixonesque scoundrel is a model of domestic virtue. Who will prevail–and how?

Roger Stevens sent the play to Adlai Stevenson, who said that if the character Cantwell was "Richard the Black-hearted" (Nixon) he was amused, but if the noble but waffling Russell was meant to be him, he was not pleased. At the time of the play's opening, March 31, 1960, Adlai Stevenson was the choice of the Democratic party's liberals and Jack Kennedy was viewed darkly as his father's son. My neighbor to the south at Hyde Park, Eleanor Roosevelt, was fiercely opposed to any Kennedy and entirely devoted to Adlai Stevenson.

I sent the script to Jack. When he came to the part about Russell's philandering, he asked Jackie, "Is Gore writing about me?" She said no. He liked what I had done with his two rivals. He gave me two bits of advice. "You know, in a campaign, we don't have all that much time to talk about the meaning of it all." I agreed but said that no audience would understand the shorthand that politicians talk in. He laughed; then said, "Oh, here's something you can use. When a politician says to you, 'Jack, if there's anything I can do for you, just let me know,' that mean's you're dead."

I like to say that, had it not been for me, Ronald Reagan would never have been president. We were having a difficult time trying to cast a Stevensonian sort of politician. Most middle-aged American actors start out as folksy all-American boys, which means that, even in age, irony and self-deprecation are not to be found in their repertoires. When Reagan's agents proposed him to me for Russell, I said that although he was a good actor, I didn't think that the audience would accept him as a politician in the Stevenson mode. In later tellings, the Stevenson modifier was dropped. In any case, Melvyn Douglas played the part; won prizes; and his career was hugely revived, while the rejected Reagan, at a loose end, became governor of California.

The play was a success, and I was getting close to the fulfillment of my five-year–in the end, ten-year–plan. All at once, I had *The Best Man* on Broadway, a road company of *Visit to a Small Planet*, a botched movie version of *Visit* with Jerry Lewis, and the film *Suddenly, Last Summer* puzzling the public. I was driving over the speed limit on the Taconic Parkway when a state trooper stopped me. He recognized me from television; gave me a warning instead of a summons; then asked, "That guy in *Suddenly, Last Summer*, he was a queer, wasn't he?" I said yes, and had it not been for the all-powerful Roman Catholic Legion of Decency, the audience would have been let in on the secret.

I was now looking forward to the 1960 campaign. I was also getting restless. I wanted to make the film of *The Best Man*, but aside from that, I was through with Hollywood. Live television was sputtering out, and I had just done what was to be my last play for television, *The Indestructible Mr. Gore*, about the courtship of Dot and Dah and the shotgun wedding that almost took place.

Time now to go to Washington; or to go away and write.

IN THE LATE FIFTIES, I had begun to see a good deal of a cheerful Irish politician, Joe Hawkins, an attorney in Poughkeepsie who was also Democratic leader of Dutchess County. In due course, he asked me if I would like to be the Democratic candidate for the House of Representatives from the Twenty-ninth District, the mid-Hudson area that included not only Dutchess but Ulster, Greene, Columbia, and Scoharie counties. The incumbent was unknown to the district, which, as I tactlessly put it, every four years automatically cast its majority vote for President McKinley. Thanks to a decade of television appearances (where I preferred to talk not of my work but of the state of the union), I was far better known than the congressman, whose career had been devoted to enriching the great insurance companies, not one, curiously enough, located in the area. Dutchess County had not gone Democratic since 1910, when Franklin Roosevelt won a seat in the state Senate because most of the voters thought that they were voting for their Republican hero, Theodore Roosevelt. One could not, apparently, win.

But as Joe and I studied the voting pattern, we saw that a shift to the Democrats had begun in the last few years. The veterans of World War Two were not as predictable as their parents. Also, the most important employer in the district, IBM, was headed by Thomas J. Watson, Jr., who, to everyone's surprise, would support Jack at the last moment, causing his many loyal, even slavish, employees to have second thoughts on election day. What I began as a modest showing of the flag started to become serious as I crossed and recrossed the five counties.

I had been born in Orange County, once a part of the district, while the Republican incumbent had been born elsewhere, thus countering any charges that I was a carpetbagger. Even so, Governor Nelson Rockefeller came to Poughkeepsie to urge voters to "Send Wharton back to Washington and Gore Vidal back to Broadway." My Vassar supporters finely heckled him.

At first, Mrs. Roosevelt was wary of my candidacy. She had not liked *The Best Man*. "Private lives do *not* play an important part in political campaigns," she lectured me firmly in front of the Morosco Theater, where she had just seen the play. I was polite; and she was wrong. Her cousin Joe Alsop used to go on about Eleanor's sapphic tendencies, and later, I could see that she had been affected in her public life by these rumors while, as she herself once said to me, forgetting her own words at the theater: "They used to say that Franklin did not have polio but something else, the sort of disease that one gets from not leading the proper sort of life." Today, of course, as actual politics have been entirely excluded from public life, private lives are all that we are allowed to talk about.

In the fall of 1959, I got a summons to visit Eleanor at Hyde Park. Word was spreading that I was going to be the Democratic candidate. It was time for us to have a serious talk. I drove down to Val-Kill cottage. With some difficulty, I found the house. The front door was open. I went inside. "Anybody home?" No answer. I opened the nearest door. A bathroom. Eleanor Roosevelt was standing in front of the toilet bowl. She gave a startled squeak. "Oh *dear*!" Then, resignedly, "Well, now you know *everything*." She stepped aside, revealing a dozen gladiolas she had been arranging in the toilet bowl. "It keeps them fresh." So began our political and personal acquaintance.

I found her remarkably candid about herself and others. So much so that I occasionally made notes, proud that I alone knew the truth about this or that. Needless to say, just about every one of these "confidences" has appeared in someone else's memoirs. But I like to recall her presence, very tall, stout, with that odd fluting yet precise voice with its careful emphases, its nervous glissade of giggles, the great smile, which was calculated not only to avert wrath but warn potential enemies that here was a lioness quite capable of making a meal of anyone.

Then there were those shrewd, gray-blue eyes, which stared at you when you were not looking at her. When you did catch her at it, she would blush—even in her seventies, her delicate gray skin would grow pink—giggle, and look away. When she was not interested in someone, she would ask a polite question, remove her glasses, which contained a hearing aid, and nod pleasantly—assuming that she did not drop into one of her thirty-second catnaps.

Mrs. Roosevelt endorsed me. I saw quite a lot of her, each of us usually on the run. I was at Val-Kill the day the news broke that her son Elliott had married yet again. While we were talking, he rang her and she smiled and murmured, over and over, "Yes, dear . . . yes, I'm very happy." Then when she hung up, she frowned. "You would think that he might have told his mother before he told the press." But this was a rare weakness. Her usual line was "people are what they are and you can't change them." Since she had obviously begun life as the sort of Puritan who thought people not only could but must be changed, her later tolerance was doubtless achieved at some cost.

As the campaign got going and I began to move up in the polls, it suddenly looked as if, wonder of wonders, Dutchess County might go Democratic in a congressional election for the first time in fifty years. Eleanor became more and more excited. She joined me at a number of meetings. She gave a tea at Val-Kill for the women workers in the campaign. Just as the women were leaving, the telephone rang—yet again. She spoke a few minutes in a low voice, hung up, said goodbye to the last of the ladies, took me aside for some political counsel, was exactly as always except that tears were streaming down her face. Driving home, I heard on the radio that her favorite granddaughter had just been killed.

In the course of the campaign, Eleanor found me a "brilliant" young man to help out. Allard Lowenstein was then deeply "closeted," as they used to say; he was certainly brilliant politically. He slept in the back of an old car, piled high with laundry, books, papers. He was accompanied by a daughter of Hale Boggs, a power in the House of Representatives. But, as always happens with zealot political volunteers, I soon proved to be a disappointment. Although I had attacked J. Edgar Hoover in *The New York Herald-Tribune* some months earlier, I evaded a question about him on the campaign trail and so failed as white knight in Al's eyes. He moved on; nevertheless, we remained on amiable terms over the years, during which he got himself elected to the House for one term and then got himself murdered by a demented young man, presumably a lover.

WHAT DID ELEANOR FEEL about Franklin? That is an enigma, and perhaps she herself never sorted it out. He was complex and cold and cruel (so many of her stories of life with him would end, "And then I *fled* from the table in tears!"). He liked telling her the latest "Eleanor stories"; his sense of fun was heavy. A romantic biographer thinks that she kept right on loving him to the end (a favorite poem of the two was E. B. Browning's "Unless you can swear, 'For life, for death,'/Oh, fear to call it loving!"). But I wonder. Certainly, he hurt her mortally in their private relationship; worse, he often let her down in their public partnership. Yet she respected his cunning even when she deplored his tactics.

I wonder, too, how well she understood him. One day she told me about something in his will that had puzzled her. He wanted one side of his coffin to be left open. "Well, we hadn't seen the will when he was buried, and of course it was too late when we did read it. But what *could* he have meant?" I knew and told her: "He wanted to get back into circulation as quickly as possible, in the rose garden. After all, the Dutch word for rose garden is *roosevelt*." She looked at me as if this were the maddest thing that she had ever heard.

The best years of Eleanor's life were the widowhood. She was on her own, no longer an adjunct to his career. Through her newspaper column "My Day," she continued to exert her influence. Just before the Democratic convention, I had dinner with her at Alice Dows's house. We were four at table: Mrs. Dows, Mrs. Roosevelt, her uncle David Gray (our wartime ambassador to Ireland), and myself. Eleanor began: "When Mr. Joe Kennedy came back from London, during the war . . ." David Gray interrupted her. "Damn coward, Joe Kennedy! Terrified they were going to drop a bomb on him." Eleanor merely grinned and continued. "Anyway, he came back to Boston and gave that *unfortunate* interview in which he was . . . well, somewhat *critical* of us."

She gave me her schoolteacher's smile, and an aside. "You see, it's a very funny thing, but whatever people say about us we almost always hear. I don't know *how* this happens, but it does." I felt uncomfortable, as I meant to convey all this to Jack. David Gray scowled. "Unpleasant fellow, that Joe. Thought he knew everything. Damn coward."

"Well, *my* Franklin said, 'We better have him down here'–we were at Hyde Park–'and see what he has to say.' So Mr. Kennedy arrived at Rhinecliff on the train and I met him and took him straight to Franklin. Well, ten minutes later, one of the aides came and said, 'The president wants to see you right away.' This was unheard of. So I *rushed* into the office and there was Franklin, white as a sheet. He asked Mr. Kennedy to step outside and then he said, and his voice was *shaking,* 'I never want to see that man again as long as I live.' "

David Gray nodded: "Wanted us to make a deal with Hitler." But Mrs. Roosevelt was not going to get into that. "Whatever it was, it was *very* bad. Then Franklin said, 'Get him out of here,' and I said, 'But, dear, you've invited him for the weekend, and we've got guests for lunch and the train doesn't leave until two,' and Franklin said, 'Then you drive him around Hyde Park and put him on that train,' and I did, and it was the most dreadful four hours of my life!" She laughed. Then, seriously: "I wonder if the *true* story of Joe Kennedy will ever be known."

Frank Roosevelt, Jr., was openly for Jack, as was Eleanor's favorite labor leader, Walter Reuther. So the three of us converged on Val-Kill cottage for a dinner of Rooseveltian horror–all bread, from fried to boiled. Reuther said that Kennedy could be elected and Adlai could not. Frank, rather maliciously, reminded his mother that Adlai had still not responded to her recent plea that he enter the race: "Doesn't sound like such decisive leadership to me."

I made my contribution: Whatever Jack's failures in the Senate (he was a friend of Joe McCarthy, while Bobby had worked for the rogue senator), old Joe Kennedy would certainly have no influence over his administration. She listened to each of us politely. Then she opened her handbag and read a position paper on the subject–actually, it was her next day's column. It was an even stronger endorsement of Stevenson than before, and a dismissal of Jack.

The telephone rang, as it always did at her house, like the messenger in a Greek tragedy, with bad news. A wire service. She listened a moment, then said, "No, I have no comment." She put down the receiver. "Adlai has said—*they* say—that he will not be a candidate."

"Ma, give him up," said Frank.

"There's still a chance. Once we're at the convention . . ."

Frank groaned. "This Hamlet routine of his!"

"Well, dear, you must take people as they are. He is what he is . . ."

"And that," said Reuther, "is why we don't want him as the candidate."

Then we talked of who Jack's vice presidential candidate might be. I have a distinct memory that Reuther said it would be Lyndon Johnson, a name that no one had mentioned so far, even though the Senate majority leader was running hard for the nomination. Eleanor thought that Johnson would be an unfortunate choice. What, I wonder now, did Reuther know then that no one close to Jack even suspected? An interesting mystery.

Early in 1960, I had had a long talk with Dick Rovere. "Your friend isn't going to be—can't be—nominated." Dick had a large round half-bald head, thick glasses, and a mottled-red complexion from some sort of eczema. He liked to know more than anyone else; and this time he did know something that I did not. He said he was writing a piece for *Esquire*, already advertised as "Kennedy's Last Chance to be President." I had assumed that this would be one of Dick's either-or pieces about Jack's then-troubling Catholicism. Dick enlightened me with his usual No!

"The wife of a friend of mine has Addison's disease." He then nicely explained that this disease breaks down the adrenal system and ends, more soon than late, in death. "Anyway, they sent her to the Leahey Clinic in Boston, to the doctor who looked after Kennedy when he was close to dying from Addison's. Apparently, the doctor had invented a new treatment for Kennedy, some kind of pellet under the skin that creates adrenaline, but only for so long, which means that he's not apt to live through the next four years." I found all this hard to believe, but Dick was punctilious in such matters.

The story was confirmed a few days later, when Jack rang me from Washington. The one and only telephone call that I was ever to get from him began with no greeting. "Tell your friend Rovere that I don't have Addison's disease. How could I and keep the schedule I do? I did have malaria and was treated for it in Boston." Data—most of it false—was then provided me in staccato bursts. Plainly, as I was connected with

Jackie through a common stepfather, I was expected to serve the Kennedys without question. In this case, I did.

I spoke to Dick not only of the busyness of Jack's political schedule but of the intensity of his heroic–and then little known–promiscuity, no easy thing without a certain amount of adrenaline. In any event, Dick did not want Nixon to be president, did he? No, but . . . Finally, I convinced him that Jack was going to be nominated for president in June and that I was absolutely certain–for no reason at all–that he would be elected president, which of course he was, in a close and no more than usually tainted election. Rovere did not mention Addison's disease in his piece. I have heard that Rovere's good friend and occasional collaborator Arthur ("It all began in the cold") Schlesinger, Jr., influenced him. But Arthur was not aboard the Kennedy bandwagon at this time. Not until later in the spring of 1960 did Arthur abandon our lost leader Adlai Stevenson in order to carry a spear for Jack. "The greatest betrayal since Judas Iscariot," proclaimed Marilyn Monroe–or was it Mrs. Thomas K. Finletter?

My next memory–after a collage of speaking trips from one end of the district to the other–is the convention in Los Angeles. I was an alternate delegate, chosen by the head of Tammany Hall, Carmine di Sapio, in a complex and entirely undemocratic process that I have never understood. Di Sapio himself was a charming southern Italian who very much wanted to be respectable; instead, two years later, he went to prison when Tammany Hall was wasted by the forces of reform, led by Eleanor Roosevelt.

We celebrated *that* famous victory at Val-Kill cottage. Frank Roosevelt was amiably drunk. Eleanor was radiant. Frank had wanted to run for governor and Carmine had said no, that it wasn't his turn. Frank ran anyway, as a Liberal, and lost, with considerable help from Tammany. Eleanor had then stormed the barricades of corruption, with which she and the president had lived so comfortably for so many years, and amazingly, at a wave of her hand, Tammany crashed. We toasted her great victory, in the name of reform and civic virtue.

Eleanor responded, gleefully. "When Mr. di Sapio did what he did to my Franklin, I vowed that I would bide my time and then–one day–I would *get* him. And I have!" Thus the voice of pure power at its most essential.

·   ·   ·

I FOUND THE 1960 convention depressing, possibly because there was no longer any real contest. It was clear that Jack would win. Even so, Eleanor was a gallant figure. She appeared on the platform and shook her finger at the delegates for not supporting Stevenson. She was received politely, but no more. Meanwhile, the candidates were making the rounds of the various delegations. I recall Jack, looking a bit dazed, coming to our New York delegation. He had a prepared spiel, which he rushed through. After all, Carmine had already delivered him New York.

Lyndon Johnson was more interesting than Jack. He worked us over thoroughly. He assured us that his recent heart attack had not been all that serious, but he did confess that, at one point in the hospital, he and Lady Bird had debated whether or not to go ahead and buy a blue suit that he had picked out just before the attack. "We decided to buy it because, one way or the other, I'd get some wear out of it." He made some guarded allusions to Jack's health.

I decided that I would make a contribution to history by taking over Romanoff's restaurant so that the New York delegation could meet Hollywood, as well as those candidates who wanted to drop by. Several hundred movie people and politicians came together. Norman Mailer sat, morosely, at the bar. "What's wrong?" I asked. "You're too successful," he said. Then the voice-to-be of the National Rifle Association, Chuck Heston, and I greeted each other with extreme unction. Gary Cooper wanted to meet Tammany Hall. My only conversation with Lyndon Johnson took place in front of Romanoff's, and though I am six feet tall, it was a most unpleasant experience to have his huge head leaning down into my face as he again explained why he was the only one who could defeat Nixon in the fall.

On the day that Jack was nominated, I had "ambulatory pneumonia"; that is, I was feeling odd and didn't know what was wrong. Before I consulted a doctor, I dropped in on Oscar Levant, the greatest hypochondriac I knew. In pajamas, Oscar was practicing at the piano. He wanted to know everything about the convention. The day before, he had finally got dressed in order to meet Jack at a reception.

"Jack said that he had heard a lot about me from old Joe, which is true—we used to have lunch together in New York—but when I told Jack that his father had always said that I was the only Jew he could stand, he jumped two feet in the air and bolted across the room, saying, 'I don't want to hear another word.' "

I went back to the convention hall just after the final vote. I stood with Arthur Schlesinger and Ken Galbraith as the applause and shouting kept on and on. Jack's ghostwriter, Ted Sorensen, passed us and made the bull's-eye sign with thumb and forefinger. It was over. Or begun.

Whatever the candidate was doing that night, we had not been invited to share the victory with him, and so I took Arthur and Ken to the Luau in Beverly Hills, a Polynesian restaurant with a huge ship's wheel in front. "This is the ship of state!" shouted Ken, and tried to turn the wheel (to the right, let me say, for the symbolically inclined), but as the wheel was permanently moored, he broke off several spokes.

Later, awash in rum, we spoke of great matters. Among them, which of us would tell Jack to stop saying "between you and I." We were all expected to write acceptance speeches. But I was too ill to come up with anything, so I took my pneumonia home to the Hudson Valley, where I had a lot of explaining to do about the immoral Hollywood party that I had given.

As I made the rounds of the district, I was staking out a number of positions that, I had been warned, would be unpopular, but they proved not to be. Mrs. Roosevelt always said that if you take the time to explain yourself, people might be persuaded to vote for their own interests. But when I spoke for the admission of Red China to the United Nations, Eleanor was alarmed. "If you say that, always add that they must *first* live up to the UN charter."

I worked out a plan so that those who did not want to be drafted into the armed forces could work for a year or two around the country in whatever capacity might be useful. This idea was very attractive, and later in the campaign, Jack took it over as his own. Eventually, it became the Peace Corps, a useful secret arm of the National Security State, the last thing that I had had in mind.

I also came out for federal aid to education, a sign that I was a pro- or crypto-Red. The incumbent made much of this. He finally debated me in his county of Scoharie. The dairy interests were powerful in that section, and I had to learn, rather quickly, all about milk marketing orders, a subject far from my heart. As the milk producers were few though passionate—and rich—I responded to threats that they would do me in if milk was not properly subsidized by saying that I was essentially the consumers' candidate and consumers outnumber dairymen by a vast number. Then, innocently, I wondered aloud whether or not these subsidies were—well, *socialist*? If so, we had achieved socialism for the rich and free enterprise for the poor. I lost Scoharie, but I carried all the cities, where most if not a majority of the votes were.

Jack came to Hyde Park to make his peace with Mrs. Roosevelt. The advance man, Richard Goodwin, introduced himself to me and I put him up at the house. As I later observed of Goodwin, he is an Iago in permanent pursuit of an Othello. When Jackie complained to me that there was no one on Jack's staff that she could talk to, I said she should get to know Goodwin. "But he's so ugly!" I said that those great Byzantine eyes might grow on her and that he was very bright. I was duly punished by fate for bringing him to her attention.

I had written Jack at length on what to expect from Mrs. Roosevelt. She was by no means happy with his nomination, but she would soldier on. I think I explained the influence on her of an odd couple called Gurevich. He was some sort of doctor, with a Rasputin complex. Just before Jack arrived at the Hyde Park airport, Gurevich said, portentously, "This meeting for Mr. Kennedy is the most important meeting of his life. I hope he understands that." I said that I thought he could rise to the occasion.

As Jack's plane landed, the flower of Dutchess County's Democratic party was on hand. The plane door opened and a lovely stewardess looked out; an instant later, a long arm pulled her back inside and the nominee appeared, beaming and brisk. I met him at the foot of the steps. Gave him a quick briefing on Val-Kill cottage. He asked me for any speeches I might have lying around. "We're getting short of words." Then, at great risk to his back, we helped him onto a fuel barrel so that he could address the crowd. Later, into a microphone, he endorsed me for Congress as "a relation of my wife" who had "vigor," the key word that year. As it proved, the first polls showed that I was running ahead of Jack; this meant that the more I identified with him, the fewer votes I would get. I downplayed any connection with the national campaign, which led to my first row with Jack's brother Bobby.

Jack's lunch with Eleanor went well. Neither ever liked the other, but politicians make arrangements with each other that transcend personal feelings. Jack thought she was envious of his father because his children had turned out so supremely well and hers had not, to say the least. I told him that was not the way her mind worked; unfortunately, that was the way *his* mind always worked. Everyone must envy the Kennedys, who had everything, because, as he too famously put it, "life is unfair."

I thought even then that, excepting him, the family was pretty deplorable, while the father belonged in jail, along with his close friend Frank Costello. In fact once a week, until Joe's stroke, the boss of the mob and the president's father had dinner together in the Central Park South Kennedy apartment. An ancient Teamster would give each a massage first, and sometimes he would stay on to dinner; once, he reported their conversation to the producer Ray Stark, who told me (but now denies the story). Of course, Joe made no secret of his underworld connections, unavoidable for a man who had cornered the Scotch whiskey market.

Predictably, because of *The City and the Pillar,* journalists were amazed that I dared run for office. They did not realize that their sort of inside gossip was almost impossible to transmit to the public in those days. If one had not been in a courtroom, there was nothing to talk about. More to the point, I had been visible to the public for years on national television and the people were comfortable with me, if not with my politics. Nonetheless, *The New York Times* was becoming deeply alarmed at what looked, as of August, to be a victory for me. Earlier in the year, the Sunday *Times* editor Lester Markel ordered an all-out attack on *The Best Man,* which was still playing to full houses. He canvassed five writers. One was Dick Rovere, who warned me about the putative ax job. Finally, Douglass Cater wrote a mild attack on the novel *Advise and Consent* and my play. But this was not enough for the *Times.* More drastic action was needed. The thought that I might be elected was sufficient cause for a jihad.

Ordinarily, the *Times* did not cover congressional elections so far north of the city, but an exception was now made in the case of the Twenty-ninth District, and a Mr. Ira Freeman was sent to interview me. "I don't know anything about politics." He giggled. He did a good deal of giggling. Although he had no interest in politics, he knew that he had been sent to wield the ax. He describes my blue eyes–they are brown. My chain-smoking–I have never smoked. How the dog licked the Château d'Yquem off my fingers–a baroque touch, since the dog did no licking and I don't drink Château d'Yquem. It was a pretty good smear job, in the best *Times* tradition. Although he steered clear of any politics, he did describe, disapprovingly, the way that I made audiences laugh, and he compared me, not unfavorably, with a stand-up comic of the day, Mort Sahl. Smudged photocopies of this piece were spread thinly about the district, inspiring a local attack.

A super-patriot father and son put out a gossipy weekly. They were ever alert to the twin (and allied) sins of Communism and sodomy. The vigorous father was also conducting an affair with his son's handsome wife. After a couple of their attacks on me, I took to the radio in their county. When asked if I had got any ideas for a novel or play during my campaign, I said, "Yes, as a matter of fact I do have an idea. Oh, it's a bit on the fantastic side, but I'm drawn to fantasy. Let's imagine there's an old scoundrel posing as a super-patriot who seduces his son's wife and . . ." There was a wave of delighted laughter across the county, and my name appeared no more in that weekly paper.

Harry S Truman came to Poughkeepsie to endorse the ticket, and I introduced him to a cheering audience. "Hope I haven't done you any harm" was his last remark to me as I helped him into his car. He was larger in life than in photographs, with a big, unfinished-looking sort of head. As of 1960, none of us knew anything about the National Security State that he had inaugurated; he was still a hero to many, myself included. Jack had worked him over beautifully, and he was now coming to the aid of the party. Four years later, however, when Truman was asked to support Bobby for the presidency, on the ground that Bobby had "really changed" from the old McCarthyite Torquemada, Truman said, "You know, you always get told in politics how some son of a bitch has really changed, but I've found in life that no one ever changes, except maybe for the worse."

On All Hallow's Eve at Saugerties Landing in Ulster County, the director of Jack's New York campaign, Bobby Kennedy, arrived two hours late for a rally. The audience had gone home, except for a few children in Halloween costumes, blowing horns. Bobby rattled his way through a speech that consisted mostly of the word *brother.* The children dispersed. He turned to me and snarled, "Why don't you ever mention the ticket?"

"I don't mention the ticket," I said, annoyed as always by his tone, "because I want to win." Thus an enemy was made. I have since read that the two people Bobby most hated (a rare distinction, because he hated so many people) were the head of the Teamsters union, Jimmy Hoffa, and me.

Gene spent election night with me in Poughkeepsie. Elaine Dundy was also on hand. We heard the returns in Joe Hawkins's Poughkeepsie office. At first, as the city vote came in, I was ahead. But then the countryside was heard from. I lost by twenty thousand votes, while Kennedy got twenty thousand votes fewer than I did. I later liked to remind him that had *he* not been at the head of the ticket, I would have won. As it was, I carried the cities of Poughkeepsie, Beacon, Kingston, Hudson, and Catskill. This made me, after the Democratic congressman from Schenectady, the biggest Democratic vote-getter in the Republican north of the state. Two years later, I was offered the nomination for Senate by the city bosses of Albany and Buffalo and the new head of Tammany, Mike Prendergast. Joe Hawkins was eager for me to take the nomination, and Prendergast even came up to Edgewater to ask me to run. But I didn't see how I could beat the incumbent, Jack Javits, a very smooth operator indeed, who appealed as much to Democrats as to Republicans. I wrote Eleanor. What did she think I should do? I received a wan note: "I have not the wisdom to tell you . . ." Shortly after, she was dead of tuberculosis of the blood, a lifelong condition, never properly diagnosed. I declined the nomination. The party lost again.

Earlier, Eleanor had wondered if we might persuade Ed Murrow, a popular television figure, to run. Murrow sent back word, no. I did not get to talk to him until the day of Eleanor's funeral at St. James's Church in Hyde Park, where I was asked to take in Agnes Meyer, wife of Eugene, who had bought and re-created *The Washington Post.* As we sat in our pew, the thirty-third, the thirty-fourth, the thirty-fifth, and the thirty-sixth presidents of the United States passed by us, not to mention all the remaining figures of the Roosevelt era, who had assembled for her funeral. Unlike the golden figures in Proust's last chapter, they all looked, if not smaller than life, smaller than legend—so many shrunken *March of Time* dolls, soon to be put away.

After the service, outside the church, I found myself standing next to Ed Murrow. He had a constant cough, which made the cold air steam. I turned to him. "Mrs. R. and I always wondered why you said no to the Senate race. You could have won."

Murrow gave me a gray, hard look. "You must understand. I don't like people."

"Neither did my grandfather, and he was very useful to them, in politics."

"But I really don't like them." Thus spake the Coriolanus of the Columbia Broadcasting System.

The four Roosevelt sons then passed us, supporting their mother's coffin. The smell of alcohol was overwhelming. I suddenly thought of Rilke's line "You must change your life." I must, I vowed. I would go to Rome–or to Athens–and write *Julian*.

*Jack and Jackie leaving mass around the
time of my visit to Hyannisport in August
1961. "Mass every Sunday," Jack would
moan, "for four years."*

Thirteen
Green Pages
with
Hindsight Added

FOR OVER THIRTY YEARS I have kept, unread, some notes that I made in the late summer of 1961. They are typed on pale green flimsy paper that Howard borrowed from his employers, Lever Brothers. I used the same paper for the first draft of *The Best Man*. There are still some sheets left. I sometimes fantasize that if I were to write on them today, I would be transported from now to then.

At the top of page one: "*JFK August 27, 1961, Hyannisport.*" What was I doing up there? Losing weight at nearby Provincetown. In those days, I used to sequester myself in some unappealing place in order to diet, see no one, work. Pre-cocaine Miami was a favorite retreat.

I checked into a Provincetown motel called the Moors. A week or two before, Khrushchev had put up the Berlin Wall. There was talk of war. I assumed that Jack and Jackie would be in Washington during the crisis. To my surprise, they both arrived for the weekend. I sent them a souvenir plate with their portraits luridly rendered, and a note addressed to "Lancer" and "Lace," their not inappropriate code names. I promptly got an alarmed call from the head of the Secret Service, an amiable man whom I had met before at the White House. He was relieved that I was the sender. Then Jackie rang with an invitation to dinner.

I drove a rented car to their house. Since my last visit, the area had been fenced in; there were guardhouses at intervals. A police car stopped me. What was I doing there? I said that I was on my way to dinner. This was considered hilarious. Several telephone calls (Did they use walkie-talkies then? As I write I have the sense that I could just as well be describing a call on the Garfields). Then I was admitted to the imperial redoubt.

The first line of the first green page: *Arrived 7:30 for dinner. House unchanged since before election. Jackie at bar in a pair of capri pants and windbreaker from waterskiing. She was making daiquiris. Embrace. Into living room from porch bar.* This, by the way, is standard screenplay exposition, waiting to be magically dramatized by—what else?—a director's art.

It is always a delicate matter when a friend or acquaintance becomes president. Ease must be maintained, yet one may not call him by his first name or walk ahead of him into a room. There is also the transformation of a familiar politician into an acronym—in this case, JFK, which always sounded to me like an effort on Jack's part to become instant history by putting everyone in mind of FDR, the enduring nemesis of his astonishing father. One must earn one's acronym, I remember thinking sternly. Or have a name so long—D. D. Eisenhower, F. D. Roosevelt—that the press is obliged to shorten it to FDR or Ike.

Jack was overconscious of his relative youth. Although in America forty-three is considered young for a president, it is early middle age for a man. Certainly, to me, seven years younger, Jack seemed—and indeed was—mildly decrepit. He moved stiffly when he did not limp painfully from a bad back: war wound was the official line; touch football, the reality. "Curious," mused the sardonic Eugene McCarthy, "it was always *touch* football with the Kennedys, never the real thing."

Jack's skin was a curious bronze color that at first looked to be the result of a suntan, but then, when one caught the odd yellow glint, it looked like makeup. Actually, the color was a manifestation of Addison's disease.

I now begin to feel a slight stirring of memory as I try to flesh out and color this scene that lies so flat on the page, all black-and-white, like an old newsreel.

Color? The light at Hyannisport in August is more white than summer-gold or winter-silver. At least I can recall the light of thirty years ago, but who are these people? What are they doing? Who was wearing what? When I see photographs of all of us as we were, I am struck—yes, yes—by how young we are. Also at how–unconvincing?–we are in our roles. Or is that excessive hindsight?

Hyannis living room: *JFK in chinos, blue shirt, looking trim: "172 pounds before I got here and started eating Jackie's meals."* Well, *there* is a bit of specific description. Blue shirt. And his weight; the same as mine.

Since one tends to recall only pictures of pictures of pictures of the long dead, let me show him as I saw him up close in April of that year. I wrote for an English paper:

> *Kennedy looks older than his photographs. The outline is slender and youthful, but the face is heavily lined for his age. On the upper lip are those tiny vertical lines characteristic of a more advanced age. He is usually tanned from the sun, while his hair is what lady novelists call "chestnut": beginning to go gray. His eyes are very odd. They are, I think, a murky, opaque blue, "interested," as Gertrude Stein once said of Hemingway's eyes, "not interesting"; they give an impression of flatness, while long blond eyelashes screen expression at will. His stubby boy fingers tend to drum nervously on tables, on cups and glasses. He is immaculately dressed; although occasional white chest hairs curl over his collar.*

Warm brief greeting, returned to his chair. Usually, a rocking chair to relieve his aching back. *He was reading a letter from De Gaulle to Mrs. Chuck Spalding.* That is my shorthand, of course. The general had written the president, not Mrs. Spalding, and Jack was reading her a translation of the letter. I have little recollection of the Chuck Spaldings. I do recall that they were family friends, not courtiers or employees, two groups to be avoided at Camelot unless one was on the make.

The first play that Jack saw after his election was *The Best Man.* He went with Spalding. From stage left, just back of the proscenium arch, I watched Jack's face as he watched the play from first-row-center. The sexual indiscretions of one of the presidential candidates caused him to blink and glance quickly at Chuck. The audience laughed; the president-elect–or "-erect," as we privately called him–grinned. Although his promiscuity was known to court and press, the public was excluded from such irrelevancies in those civilized days. After all, he would soon be exhorting them "to bear any burden" so that freedom, or something, might prevail in a "twilight time." I wonder who thought up that last phrase. I do know that he liked it far too much. But then his own fragile health was itself a kind of premature twilight. So why not share it? Cuba, Laos, Berlin, Vietnam—he would keep us in permanent crisis. Better night than twilight?

Jack continued to read De Gaulle's letter. *As he read, his hand started to saw the air and the voice started to fall into the rhythmic cadence of stump-speaking. He was delighting in the rhetoric, especially a triad: . . . "negotiations on what field? to what end? to what further provocation?"*

De Gaulle was referring to a possible meeting with Khrushchev over what Jack had proclaimed was not so much a "Berlin crisis" as "a world crisis." In response to Jack's escalation of anti-Soviet rhetoric, combined with the reconstitution of Germany as a military power, Khrushchev had put up the Berlin Wall, thus, as we now know, carefully avoiding war. In any case, Jack's Cuban debacle of April—how close together all these crises were!—was being erased by the "Berlin crisis" of July. We also now know that Jack had secretly decided to go to war with the Soviet Union if access to Berlin was denied us. Hence the somber tone of De Gaulle's letter. When Jackie and I talked on the telephone before I came to dinner, I had joked that if war was to start now, the president would be the first to get blown up, so why not meet in neutral nearby Provincetown—far, far from the spectacular nuclear fallout at the compound? "We can all go together," she said serenely; then, not so serenely, "It's a terrible thing to realize that all the children will be dead, too." I thought her overacting. But Jack was indeed bringing us to the brink. He wanted to win—not play at—the cold war.

Jack repeated the triad, aesthetically pleased. Wondered what the French word for field *was, in this case.* He did not remark on the content of the letter, warning him not to meet Khrushchev during the present crisis. Earlier in the year, De Gaulle had predicted that Jack's June meeting with Khrushchev at Vienna would be a disaster. He had been right. Later, De Gaulle remarked to a friend that Jack's general demeanor on the international stage was rather like that of an elegant hairdresser combing his way through a lady's hair.

Joined by Jackie and Chuck Spalding. Discussion of De Gaulle. Much admiration, noncommittal, however, on the effect of the letter. Bobby K.

entered in a vivid orange shirt, looking very slender, very young. The usual cold greeting.

Jack and I talk in political code. As always, the politician's message is not in the words spoken but what is unsaid.

JACK: *"What did you think of Rockefeller's reverse on foreign aid?" It had happened the day before, and I hadn't seen it. Jack remarked on Rockefeller's waffling, cowardice. I guessed that he was trying to get some Goldwater votes. Jack wished I would do my long-promised piece on Rockefeller.*

When I finally did get around to Nelson Rockefeller, it was in a piece proposed by *Esquire*, called "The Best Man: 1968." The assumption was that Jack would serve two terms; then it would probably be Rockefeller versus Bobby. This was published in 1963, when the family's dynastic plan was unknown to the public. Although I was supposed to have written the piece out of pique at Bobby, the idea was not mine but the editor's. As it turned out, I found nothing to praise in either candidate. Later, during the Vietnam War, Bobby uncharacteristically approved of the International Red Cross's plan to send blood to our mortal enemy the Viet Cong. When attacked for this, Bobby replied, "I didn't say send blood to the Viet Cong, I said send Gore." At the end, he had clever writers.

Jack was obsessed with Rockefeller as a rival: "People who knew him around Washington always say he's a fine guy but muddle-headed." "Stupid," I said, more precisely. "Stupid," said Jack. Talked of New York.

I had just been offered the Democratic nomination for Senate in 1962. I told Jack that I had turned it down.

What did I think of Congressman Sam Stratton for the Senate race? I said, "A lightweight, unknown outside Schenectady." I proposed Thomas J. Watson, Jr., president of IBM and a surprise Kennedy supporter. "Great," said Jack, "only he's from Connecticut." Even so, Jack conceded that he was a possibility, or could've been with enough preparation. "No," said Jack, "what we need is a silk-stocking Jew. Like Orville Dryfoos." As it turned out the party lost, yet again, with a wool-sock Irish Catholic named Donovan.

Bobby wanted to see the McCloy note.

What could that have been? A Republican, John J. McCloy, was the president's disarmament adviser. A year or so later, Richard Rovere wrote a spoof called "The American Establishment," a production of the "Edgewater Institute." Rovere sent up those who think, mistakenly in his own mistaken view, that the United States has a ruling class; and he placed John J. McCloy at the head of what was to him a mythical establishment.

I now read that McCloy was pretty much a dove in the White House aviary of hawks. In April he had been appalled by the Bay of Pigs. In June, Jack had had his unpleasant meeting with Khrushchev at Vienna. Khrushchev wanted total disarmament, as opposed to Kennedy's meager ban on nuclear testing, so devised that each side could cheat. It seems clear now that the Russians wanted to settle their accounts with us and move from war to peace. But Jack was not about to let twilight turn to peaceful evening if it meant that, in the process, he would be reduced from potential warrior-god to mere Chester A. Arthur.

McCloy was with Khrushchev in Russia at the time of Jack's July "Berlin crisis" speech. Khrushchev was furious; the speech, he said, was "a preliminary declaration of war."

On the face of it, Jack was sounding tough largely to make American voters forget the Bay of Pigs. He rattled the nuclear saber loudly and proposed something that even Eisenhower had not dreamed of: nuclear bomb shelters for civilians. According to a recent biography, McCloy was secretly pleased when the Berlin Wall went up, because it meant that Khrushchev was in retreat and that he had tacitly accepted the principle of two Germanys. Even so, I am still trying to figure out what the "McCloy note" of August 21 might have contained.

Bobby took the letter from Jack and *went off into a corner and read it.* I have a vivid memory of the two furry heads together, a lamp back of them, as they murmured to each other in silhouette. It is chilling to think that all our lives were in their callow hands.

Then joined by Pat and Peter Lawford. They were staying in one of the other houses. Since Joe Kennedy had exiled the singer Frank Sinatra from the Holy Family (Sinatra was alleged to have met those underworld figures that Joe had done business with all his life), Peter was Jack's Plenipotentiary to the Girls of Hollywood. But then all Jack's Hollywood connections were put to use. Jack would ask me endless questions about the "availability" of this or that star, availability not in the emotional but the logistical sense. Since my own approach to sex was not unlike Jack's, I have never been as shocked as people still appear to be by his promiscuity. But I have had the occasional impression that Jack's sexual success might possibly have been a source of envy in others. Certainly, Jack himself always blamed any attack on him or his family as being motivated by envy. Remote as he was from the lives of ordinary Americans, he may have grasped this aspect of the national character all too well.

Jack turned to Caroline, who was passing around canapés: "Buttons, you want to dance for us?" Jack snapped his fingers and wriggled in his chair. She giggled and shook her head. I looked at his hands and noticed, as always, how young they are: the hands of an adolescent. No veins, no discoloring, pink stubby smooth fingers. He is also given to shaking trousers and self in a provocative way.

General talk. I gave JFK the Commentary *piece on the John Birch Society.* That I would give *Commentary* to anyone now seems positively mythical. *He wondered how anybody could believe the nonsense the Birchers put out. When I said that 10 percent of the American people did, he said, with weary expertise, "When it comes to polls, 10 percent will favor* anything *they're asked."*

He glanced at the piece professionally, skipped to the end, and said, "Well, I don't agree with this*"; and quoted a severe criticism of the Kennedy administration as not liberal, dispirited. Went into a hot tirade against the liberals, especially in economics. "I just wish they'd tell me what they want me to do. We're limited by resources and also by Congress . . ." Then he answered his own question: "Of course, I know what they want: a deficit of $7 billion. Well, they should be happy. Berlin is going to cost us $3.5 billion and that will just do the trick, all the pump-priming they want."*

Jack asked directly about my political future. I said it was in abeyance, though I still kept an eye on the district.

As a professional politician, Jack knew exactly who had got how many votes in every district in the country. "The most humiliating experience of the election," he would say, "was Gore running 20,000 ahead of me in upstate New York and," true recollected pain, "Claiborne Pell, running for the Senate, one *million* ahead of me in Rhode Island." Years later, I told Pell this story. He smiled demurely and said that, yes, he knew that Jack never could understand how someone like himself could so outdo a regular fellow like Jack. Pell had come from the diplomatic service; from the New England aristocracy; from the more discreet watering holes of Sodom. Although Jack had acquired a number of fag friends, as Bobby called them, the subject always made the hearty family giggle. Jack and Bobby used to argue over which of them had first thought to call James Baldwin "Martin Luther Queen."

The artist-warrior Bill Walton (he liberated Paris, while his friend Hemingway freed the bar of the Ritz) was easily the best of the many influences on Jack and Jackie. A rollicking roughneck with aesthetic tastes, he wanted nothing for himself other than to be amused, which he was, by court life. Occasionally, he would assert himself. When builders threatened to tear down most of the houses around Lafayette Park, he hustled the president into declaring the houses national monuments. "Probably the only thing," said Jack dryly, "that this administration will be remembered for."

Bill told me that when "perennial bachelor" columnist Joe Alsop got married at mid-administration—a supposed sacrifice to his idol Jack—the president had said, "Now, if we can only get Bill and Gore married off . . ."

Jack and Spalding both impressed by my reduction of the Republican plurality. Ought to run again. I said '62 would be bad. Jack agreed. He had given up on New York. Bloodbath ahead for the Democrats, with Rockefeller as governor and the unbeatable Senator Javits. Although Jack is referring to the midterm congressional election, his pessimism also reflected his own worries about his reelection in 1964. As it turned out, I was offered the congressional nomination that year in what we had made a "safe seat." But I turned it down. I was a novelist again and had no desire to go to what Jack used to call that "can of worms," the House of Representatives. Also, by 1964, Jack was dead. *Non sequitur.*

"I can beat Goldwater," he told me, "but Nelson's something else." Rockefeller had not yet ended his political career by exchanging an old wife for a new one who was not only Catholic, with children, but married to one of his employees. The American Woman never forgave Rockefeller, to his surprise. Mine, too. If only Jack had lived another year in order to witness Nelson Rockefeller being booed at the Cow Palace in San Francisco by the Republican delegates. I was there and heard the leathery Bacchae scream, "Lover, lover!"

"There but for the grace of God," I can hear Jack mutter from beyond the grave, "go I."

But Jack did point out that "individual candidates are a law unto themselves." Particularly when well financed by family money like the Rockefellers'; Kennedys', too. *Cited examples of bucking trends. Spalding made a reference to a television program on left versus right that I had done with John Crosby. To my surprise, Jack had seen it, too.* All I remember now is that I was faced with a hot-eyed true believer. But then there were so many television programs in those days, and I moved like a blur through the lot, remembering nothing, including myself on those rare occasions when someone shows me an ancient kinescope or tape.

We discussed the frenzy of the far right, which he took a lot less seriously than I. *I teased Jack that I might have won if only I had come out for Nixon. He was not sure how to take this. He did note that I had not supported him in the race.* This was doubtless Bobby's version of what I'd said to him the previous Halloween.

Jack was delighted by my June piece in *Life*, written in the form of a conversation between myself, a liberal, and the conservative senator Barry Goldwater. The far right had been so outraged by the piece that after the publisher, Harry Luce, complimented the editor, he said, "I also never want to see anything like that again in *Life*."

I told Jack about my piece on the future of conservatism to balance Buckley, Jr.'s piece on the future of liberalism. I said that I wanted to change the terms, making Kennedy a conservative and Goldwater a reactionary. A sharp retort from Jack: He *was liberal. He would only accept the conservative label in the sense that FDR might have used it. Very touchy about this. "Just talk to Eisenhower if you want to meet a real conservative. You feel it in him right to the core." Then he complained that Eisenhower was still a sacred cow; no one could touch him. Jack looked at me hopefully: "Maybe you could."*

When Senator Kennedy first met Eisenhower, the general kept addressing him crisply as Kennedy. "As if I was a junior officer or something." On the other hand, Eisenhower was the first president Jackie had met. "I was so overcome, I felt I should curtsy."

Bobby returned from his corner with the McCloy report. Cryptic exchange. JACK: *Nice?* BOBBY: *Yes, but too nice. Why to him? (Possible reference to a letter that Jackie had told me about?–from Khrushchev, suddenly temperate.)*

As I write these lines thirty years later, I realize that only the smallest tip of that vast glacier, the National Security State, was ever on view even to the interested press. Also, when I check these old notes with later revelations, I realize how little understanding any of us had of what was actually going on at the time.

We had been carefully conditioned to believe that the gallant, lonely USA was, on every side, beleaguered by the Soviet Union, a monolithic Omnipotency; we now know that they were weak and reactive while we were strong and provocative. Once Jack had inherited the make-believe war against Communism in general and the Soviet in particular, he proceeded, unknown to all but a few, to change the rules of the game. He was about to turn Truman's pseudo-war into a real war. He was going to fight, somewhere, anywhere. Cuba had gone wrong. At Vienna, Laos had been marginalized as a place of no essential interest to us or to the Soviet. Yet in June and July of 1961, Jack had called for a $3.5 billion military appropriation to deal with what he termed the "Berlin crisis."

As we gossiped in that spare white beach house, Jack had just acquired the powers to call up 250,000 reservists; he could also mobilize two army divisions, as well as fifty-four air squadrons. During Jack's brief reign, military spending rose $17 billion above that of the Eisenhower years, "constituting," according to the historian C. N. Degler, "one of the largest and swiftest build-ups of military power in history." Although Jack had claimed in the campaign that there was a "missile gap" between the United States and the Soviet Union, the gap proved to be in our favor, as he later admitted. So the build-up was simply to get us ready for a serious war somewhere or other. The venue was of minor importance; glory all-important—but glory for whom?

Since politicians say what their auditor wants to hear, Jack made the $3.5 billion military build-up sound to me like so much "pump-priming for liberals," a group he deeply despised. "No one can be liberal enough for the *New York Post*," he used to say. But then the speed with which so many liberals abandoned Stevenson to join him was a source of his amused contempt as he himself went about courting conservatives like John J. McCloy.

I am looking at all this in retrospect, that is, in history, where the agreed-upon facts are not as numerous as professional historians like to think, obliging them to fictionalize anew those official fictions that have been agreed upon by altogether too many too-interested parties, each with his own thousand days in which to set up his own misleading pyramids and obelisks that purport to tell sun time.

Reminiscing of the campaign. Jack asked if I had read Teddy White's book The Making of the President. *Jack talked about how good White was on the Wisconsin primary. Jack and Spalding discussed the horror of Wisconsin. Jackie chimed in: a hateful place. Apparently, the people were rude and apathetic. Jack wondered why. Jackie told of going into supermarkets with cameras following in her wake, and how she'd stalk a desperate woman who would do anything to escape shaking hands. Same treatment outside factories. No interest in the election. Schoolkids even worse. Spalding described how Bobby had spoken at one high school. Got no response. He asked if anyone could name the state's governor; no one could; the representative? the senator? Nothing. Much wriggling about. Finally, Bobby could take it no longer: "This is the worst school I ever saw. You don't know, you don't care . . . and it's also the first school where I've seen boys holding hands with boys."*

We all laughed. Jack asked, "He said what?" *Spalding repeated the story. Jack shook his head, "I'll be damned." Spalding then told how, as Bobby was leaving, one cretinous boy came up to him and said, "Your brother* really *running for president?"*

Between Bobby's primitive religion and his family's ardent struggle ever upward from Irish bog, he was more than usually skewed, not least by his own homosexual impulses, which, Nureyev once told me, were very much in the air on at least one occasion when they were together. "Nothing happen," said Rudi. "But we did share young soldier once. *American* soldier. Boy not lie . . . *maybe.*" Rudi gave his Tatar grin, very much aware, firsthand, of the swirls of gossip that envelop the conspicuous. Yet anyone who has eleven children must be trying to prove–disprove?–something other than the ability to surpass his father as incontinent breeder.

Once Jackie, Bill Walton, and I were contemplating the phenomenon of Bobby's fecundity. "Catholicism?" I proposed.

Jackie sighed. "Ethel used to have a bleeding heart of Jesus on nearly every wall."

"But," said Bill, trying to be fair, "they do fit so well together, like two very small end tables."

Anyway, the Spalding story was yet another bit of evidence in the case that I was, quite unconsciously at the time, making against Bobby. Now I am aware of another side to him as I contemplate all that family pressure brought to bear on what must have been a delicate psyche; and pressure right to the end–and after. As Bobby was dying in Los Angeles, a sister rang their mother to report on his condition. Rose's response was swift: "Now, Teddy must run." For crude Rose, this world is just a staging area for that great touch-football field in the sky, where all the lads will be reunited forever. Although, according to the strict ground rules of Rose's faith, if father Joe was going to be in on the game, the playing field would have to be located somewhere below rather than above.

Jack pondered the mystery of Wisconsin. Home to the La Follettes and to his ex-friend–and Bobby's mentor–Joe McCarthy. In Massachusetts *Jack could tell one school group from another without being warned. "There would be these awful kids, picking their faces and holding hands with their girls, and then there'd be a group from a school a mile away and they'd be full of zip." I brought up minimum academic standards. He thought that impossible: states' rights argument.*

Much joking about Lawford's weight. He is off to do a picture about D-Day. He's to play Lord Somebody, a friend of Jack's. "You're too fat," said Jack. The Lawfords left.

We go into dinner–four. Spalding and I remain standing while Jack is outside saying goodbye to sister Pat. When he comes into the dining room, Mrs. Spalding stands, too; very informal, but the Fact is acknowledged. Cold Spanish soup, lobster, mousse. As always, Jack is curious about theater, movies. How much do I make for writing a picture? How do I get to keep it from the government? I don't. Jack would bring down the 90 percent maximum tax to 60 percent.

Will my new play be a success–a sudden jolting remark, reminding me that in the world of power the only criterion is: Will it work now?

Jackie asks Jack to tell me the plot he had thought of for a movie. He says he has only the beginning. He gets into the White House elevator in the morning [the one that takes the president down from the private apartment to the main floor]. *The camera cuts to his office "and there is Lyndon. Where is the president? No one knows." He grins: "It's just Lyndon and Sam [Rayburn] then."*

I must say these lines certainly come as a shock. But then I have never looked at them since the day they were typed. Obviously, Jack had a coup on his mind–a Texas coup. Vice President Lyndon Johnson and Speaker of the House Rayburn were both Texans.

Assassination was often on Jack's mind. He was fatalistic. "If the assassin is willing to die, it couldn't be simpler." Once, at a horse show where we were obliged to sit together for an hour because Jackie had promised her horsey friends that she would deliver the president, I said how easy it would be for someone to shoot him in that vast indoor track. "Except," I added, "they'll probably miss you and hit me."

"No great loss," he said; then he asked me if I had read Edgar Wallace's *Twenty-four Hours.* I had not. He told me the plot. A British prime minister has been warned that he has exactly twenty-four hours to live. He is locked inside Downing Street and surrounded by guards. Midnight, the hour of his death comes; nothing happens. "See?" He is delighted. "All that fuss for nothing." The phone rings; he answers it. "And," said Jack with quiet satisfaction, "he is electrocuted."

Was it the knowledge that he was probably not going to live very long in any case that made him preoccupied with assassination? Since he had been ill so much of his life, I suspect that if he had been forced to choose between a bullet in Dallas and a long, painful death in bed, he would have taken the first exit. In the British *Sunday Telegraph,* April 9, 1961, I wrote "despite his youth, Kennedy may very well not survive. A matter, one suspects, of no great concern to him. He is fatalistic about himself. His father recalls with a certain awe that when his son nearly died during the course of a spinal operation, he maintained a complete serenity: if he was meant to die at that moment, he would die and complaint was useless."

I am no believer in dreams as portents, but not long after this conversation I dreamed, in color, of Jackie, all in pink, weeping and saying, "What will become of me now?" That dream was still on my mind when I was ordered by the White House to take Rose "I am the president's mother" Kennedy to the opening of the Metropolitan Opera House. In the entr'acte, I wondered if too much good fortune might not entail some sort of nemesis. She was cold. "Let them enjoy it while they can." Onassis, on the other hand, believed in the old gods. As we stared from his ship in Venice ("Why not buy this place," he mused, "and save it? And make money, too?"), he suddenly said, "Those two are in for bad luck."

Talk immediately shifted to the recent resignation of President Quadros in Brazil. Quadros had been a reform civilian candidate in a military-dominated country. Shortly after his election, he resigned. On a visit to Brazil a few years ago, I was told why: The military wanted to rule through him and he had said no, and that was that. But we–I, that is– had no idea of any of this in August 1961.

Jack irritated: "He had no right to go just because it got tough." Jack also resented Quadros's reference to "outside influences," helping to pressure him—meaning, some thought, the United States. "That's absolutely wrong. If there was any place we ever played it . . . uh . . . straight it was Brazil. The loan. Buttering him up. No complaints about his foreign policy. Then he does this and now there'll be a military dictatorship." Jack scowled.

I have often played this speech back in my head, one of the few bits of dialogue that I was never to forget—a glimpse, as it were, of the rest of the iceberg: ". . . any place we ever played it . . . uh . . . straight . . ."

Since Jack constantly complained about enemies real and imagined in government and press, *I suggested that he might be the first president to say, "Sorry, it's just too much. Goodbye." He laughed: It was tempting, but one did not do that—like Quadros.*

Talk of Fellini's new movie La Dolce Vita. *Jack liked the scene of the aristocrats in the house at night, and also the scene where a woman talks to her lover (whispering into a corner) as a man comes and takes her away. I made the point that Fellini had created a realistic mosaic but, slyly exploiting Anglo-Saxon Puritanism, he pretended that this was decadence when it was only life as it is lived. Jack responded enthusiastically to my exegesis. Jackie mentioned how all the movies that she likes are on the Index, a fact Mother-in-Law Rose continually reminds her of.*

For a season I liked to use *La Dolce Vita* as a sort of Rorschach test. I would ask someone if he had seen the film—who had not? And then, What was your favorite scene? The answers were satisfyingly revealing. I was not surprised that Jack liked the whispered seduction scene. But I was surprised when he said that he had also liked the scene where the drunken father collapses on his son's bed.

Noël Coward had been to lunch that day and played piano; they are delighted. In the summer of 1948, Noël invited Tennessee Williams and me to dinner in London's Gerald Road. We sat at a small table in the living room: nearby, on a dais, was a piano. We were served kidneys, which neither of us ate. Coward, whom we had just met, then proceeded to enact for us the entire story of his professional life, often springing up from the table to assault the piano as he brayed briskly the lyrics of past triumphs—to my delight and Tennessee's disgust. "He thinks," said the Bird as we vanished into the night, "that we don't know who he is." The Bird was generally amiable with other theater people, but Noël always got on his nerves, particularly during the filming of the appropriately named *Boom*. I always liked Noël, possibly because each of us had been brought up on the books of E. Nesbit.

Talk of high taxes. Jack: "It annoys me the way they [the Pentagon] *throw money around." No sense, however, that* he *might control the waste.* But then most presidents complain of "they"; presidents also tend to feel insufficiently admired by the nation, whose good luck it is to have so fine and selfless a leader. Although Jack was one of the least pompous of politicians, even he, as early as 1958, began to refer to himself as "Kennedy" rather than mere "I." To be, in one's own time, a third person as well as a first is plainly ravishing; imperial, too.

Jack liked talking about Jefferson; noted Jefferson's shifty eyes—*something he said he had read somewhere. I reminded him that he had read it in my piece on Goldwater for* Life *magazine.*

Jackie was delighted: "Isn't it wonderful to be quoted!" Jack wanted to know who my authority was. I said Claude G. Bowers. Jack had met Bowers in 1940, when he was ambassador to Chile. He had a low opinion of Bowers—no doubt inherited from Joe. Thought the matter should be checked out. Remarked that Jefferson was "one of the two geniuses that the United States had produced at the beginning of the republic; the other was Ben Franklin." Then we all wondered why the eighteenth-century personages were so much more accomplished than we—more languages, more learning. Too many modern distractions? Poorer education? Or just accident? General discussion of the eighteenth century. Jack very much admired Duff Cooper's Talleyrand. *Discussed Palmerston. I told him I'd lend him* Palmerston Versus Regina, *which I had just read.* A book that I have now totally forgotten.

Recently, an old friend of all of us remarked that Jack, alone of the Kennedys, had been "civilized" by his stay in England during Joe's embassy. Jack had been transformed from preppish Boston Irish to Whig nobleman: "He always knew more about English history and social life than he ever did about America." This was another connection between him and me. We knew the same English, stayed in the same houses, shared the same gossip. Jack was taken up by the lot; except for his sister Kick, the others were not.

Much high spirits for us on vin rosé. Jack on beer. Jack thought a good study might be written on the difference between us and our eighteenth-century counterparts. Why are we so fragmented, so specialized? Jack thinks continually in historic and literary terms. One gets the feeling he is a writer manqué. *Yet, politically, in action, the eager sportsman merges with the other self; he also has the coarse energetic quality that wins battles.*

What an actor he was! What a gullible audience I was! I was tempted to write over this–palimpsest it–but I must show us as we were then, no matter how idiotic I sound. In any case, the strain of appearing vigorous with no natural adrenaline function must have been unremitting. But here he is projecting fierce energy, and I am taking it all in. Yet when I replay him in my memory, I tend to see him in a rocking chair, unable to lean over to pick up a brass box beside his foot. "Easily," he said when I retrieved the box and gave it to him–a present from Khrushchev at Vienna, "the cheesiest gift ever presented by one head of state to another."

Dinner was over now; he was on his feet and out the door first. Spalding and I united to play backgammon against him. We won two games; he won the third. Much chortling, high whinnies at wins and groans at losses.

Since the interview with me in Look *magazine–on the subject of Jackie–his new word, he said, was* ambience. *I had referred to prewar Merrywood's "golden ambience." He started to talk about Merrywood. Said I had badly misrepresented it. "The place was like . . . like* The Little Foxes." *One by one he described Hughdie's children and stepchildren; each a disaster. Tactfully, he omitted Jackie and me. When she said, "Well?" He said, "Well, you know what I mean."*

I said that much of the atmosphere–ambience!–had to do with the fact that each of us had a mother who had married Hugh Dudley Auchincloss, Jr., for his money. Jack seemed startled at my bluntness and muttered something about "security," but Jackie agreed with me. Jack puffed on his cigar over the board and looked at me thoughtfully. I puzzle him, I suspect.

Talk of Berlin, Khrushchev. Jack had given up on talking reason to him–not possible. "We've got to start looking out for our interest. No more worrying about the world. We're in a spot in Berlin and something will eventually have to give. But the issue is the neutralization of West Germany. Khrushchev's aim." Jack said he had written a letter to Galbraith, Kennan, all the ambassadors to neutralist countries, to ask one question: Why is it that they are always against us, against any action we

take in the world? Why can the Soviet do brutal acts like invading Hun-
gary or closing off East Berlin and the neutralists are serene, but if we so
much as protest, they are down on us. Jack answered his question: the
fascination that the bully-boy has for people, "just like Hoffa-r." During
the Senate hearings, he said he used to watch how reporters and visitors always hovered around Hoffa. "They like power, evil. Same thing
with Che Guevara in Montevideo. Everyone hanging around him. Even
Dick Goodwin has to go visit him. They're all fascinated."

This is interesting psychologically: Milton's vivid Lucifer versus
dull God. But Jack was–deliberately?–manipulating the psychology.
Because Khrushchev opposed our military and economic restoration of
West Germany, he must be depicted as a demon, which, perversely in
Jack's view, made him a figure of fascination for those neutralist countries that Jack felt were insufficiently grateful to the United States as the
lonely bearer of the nuclear shield in a Hobbesian world. Yet a neutralist like India's Prime Minister Nehru felt that there was not much to
choose between the paranoia of the American imperium and that of a
perennial victim like Russia, three and a half times invaded in 150
years–the half was the American-led military expedition of 1919, to
overthrow the Bolshevik Revolution.

As I was now beating Jack at backgammon, the war that had been
designed to be permanently chilly was heating up. In addition to the
current games over Berlin, Jack was busying himself in Southeast Asia,
while Bobby's Operation Mongoose was in place to murder Castro. So
stimulated and alarmed were the Russians by our busyness that they
brought in nuclear missiles to Cuba to defend the island from what, not
unnaturally, they suspected would be a second invasion. A recent television documentary–with recorded conversations–reveals Jack starting to get cold feet even as his warlords, mostly professors trained in the
murderous maquis of Academe, wanted an air strike against Cuba.
Finally, a secret deal was struck; we would remove our missiles from
Turkey if they would remove theirs from Cuba, which we would not
invade–maybe. As one historian put it, this was surely the most reckless
American act since the end of World War Two.

Talked of neutralist complaints of his saber-rattling. Then, unexpect-
edly, Jack said, "Well, I'm almost a-peace-at-any-price man." Jackie said,
"Yes, it would be better to be Red than dead, not maybe for oneself, but for
the children."

Talked then of starting a national newspaper. I said, "On the lines of The Observer *in England." That got Jack off the track immediately. He attacked* The Observer *and* The New Statesman *(I wrote occasionally for both); thought them profoundly soft-headed. He turned to Jackie: "What time is the helio called for?" Jackie said, "7:15." As tribute to our debauchery, "Make it 8:10." Then he went up to bed.*

Earlier, when I had proposed that she and Bill Walton come have dinner with me in Provincetown, she was delighted. "Can I, Jack? Can I?" He finally agreed, "But in disguise." She checks everything that she does with him.

Then the Spaldings went to Bobby's house to see The Young Savages. (*Halliwell's Film Guide:* "tough, realistic melodrama of the N.Y. slums . . . and a political conscience. Directed by John Frankenheimer." Bobby was to stay at Frankenheimer's house in Malibu the night before he was killed.)

Jackie and I drank a good deal of wine and talked of family matters. She was willing to see Nini. After the election and the almost simultaneous birth of Jackie's son, Nini went to see Jackie at the hospital. Teasingly, Jackie asked Nini whom she had voted for, and Nini said, "Nixon." The girls fell out with a crash. Later, Jack said that if *he* didn't mind how Nini had voted, why should Jackie? Now she was beginning to see the comedy in the situation, though it hadn't seemed so humorous after a difficult birth, not to mention an election that, zealots like to tell us, Nixon had actually won.

Jackie reached for the bottle of vin rosé. "And they talked about Mrs. Eisenhower!" She had not been amused when she had paid her duty call on Mrs. Eisenhower after the election. *"Not even a cup of tea did she offer. But the upstairs sitting room, the oval one, was worth the whole tour. They had two TV sets, his and hers, with little tables in front of them, where they had their TV dinners, he watching his Westerns and she her soap operas."*

As it turned out, my sister never did make up with Jackie until the night that Jack's body had been installed in the East Room and Jackie and her sister, Lee, put messages in the coffin, presumably for Jack to deliver on the other side. Jackie also put her wedding ring inside the coffin; then, on second thought, retrieved it. "Very creepy," was the general impression. Jack's head was so swathed in a huge turbanlike bandage that he didn't resemble much of anybody.

Jackie spoke of how much she liked Bobby, how sensitive he was. My dislike of him must have been apparent even then. *She said that Bobby had scolded her for having been so hard on Nini. She said that Miss Hennessey, governess to the Kennedy children, had told her what a sad time Bobby had had, too old for the last two children, too young for the others, scrawny and wistful, but philosophic and not embittered.* Plainly, Jackie did *not* sell him to me.

Jackie on the subject of "life in the White House": "Never alone. You sit in a room and try to write a letter and someone comes in." She wondered about holding cultural gatherings. *Tennessee, she loved. Faulkner, too. "But I'd like to spend an evening with just a few people. I'm terrible at crowds, and everyone gets so precious in the White House, they'd all clam up."* This explained the powerful drinks served. According to Robert Craft, Stravinsky, after just one, exclaimed "I am dronk!"

"I feel like such a philistine," Jackie went on, *"because I don't really know enough."* Earlier, I had mentioned the critic Eric Bentley as someone to invite for a theater affair—she had laughed, *"You see? Until just now I never heard of Eric Bentley."* I now wonder why on earth I was trying to make the world safe for Eric Bentley, admirable figure that he is. *She did look forward to getting Malraux to the White House. She had found him impressive. At De Gaulle's reception for the Kennedys in Paris, Malraux had appeared with his wife, whose face was bloated from weeping . . . their son had just been killed in an auto crash. But he had taken Jackie around museums and theaters and completely captured her imagination.*

Jackie was particularly pleased that the thank-you letter that she had written De Gaulle had been answered promptly and at length by him, while Jack's letter to the general had gone unanswered. I commented on this to Romain Gary, a colleague of De Gaulle's, who said, "That's typical of the old-guard army officer. If one general wants to communicate with another, he writes not to the general but to his wife, out of what appears to be supreme politeness."

After the state visit to Paris, the Kennedys had stopped off in London for a private visit to sister Lee and her husband, Stas Radziwill. The British government decided that, private occasion or not, the queen must give dinner to president and wife. The Palace wanted to know whom they would like to invite. Jackie proposed her host and hostess, Prince and Princess Radziwill. She would also like to meet Princess Margaret, while Jack would like to see Princess Marina of Kent, the only member of the royal family that he knew from the old days. The Palace sent a delicately phrased reply to the effect that *Mr.* and *Mrs.* Radziwill, as divorced people, were not invitable.

Stas was a man of great charm, though not, perhaps, of fanatical probity. According to Auberon Herbert, Stas had walked off with the entire capital of the Polish Red Cross, leaving an ancient Polish general to take the blame. Stas made money with the money; then, as prison doors began, creakily, to swing open, he restored what he had stolen, without interest. In the 1960 election Stas canvassed Polish-American voters for Jack, who then wanted to give him some sort of an appointment. The usual FBI report was presented to the president. It is said to have weighed many pounds. Jack was plaintive: "Should I read all this?"

"No, sir," he was told. "Just don't make the appointment." He did not.

Jack told the Palace "not to bother about us, we're here unofficially." But then, to Lee's delight, the Palace backed down. "Anyway, the queen had her revenge," said Jackie. "No Margaret, no Marina, no one except every Commonwealth minister of agriculture that they could find. The queen was pretty heavy-going." (Years later, I repeated this to Princess Margaret, who said, "But that's what she's there for.")

"I think the queen resented me. Philip was nice, but nervous. One felt absolutely no relationship between them. The queen was human only once." Jackie had been telling her about the Kennedy state visit to Canada and the rigors of being on view at all hours. ("I greeted Jack every day with a tear-stained face.") *The queen looked rather conspiratorial and said, "One gets crafty after a while and learns how to save oneself." Then she said, "You like pictures." And she marched Jackie down a long gallery, stopping at a Van Dyke to say, "That's a good horse."*

Discussing Hughdie, trying to recall some of his sayings: He speaks almost entirely in platitudes, often just a little off, or else in set stories. Jackie said that one of his favorite adages had cropped up after Jack and she got back from Vienna: "You can always trust an Englishman because his word is as good as his bond, but you can never trust a Russian." One should note that the first of Hughdie's three high-powered wives was Russian, the second my mother, the third Jackie's mother, Janet, born Lee or, as my mother used to observe thoughtfully, Levy. Apparently, Janet's father had changed his name in order to become the first Jew to be a vice president of the Morgan bank. My mother wondered how Hughdie, a quiet but sincere anti-Semite, would respond when he found out.

Hughdie's stories never varied in detail; the effect was bardic. A favorite number was the slow but relentless revelation of the original Jewish names of movie stars, starting, inexorably, with Kirk Douglas. The director Mike Nichols told me that when Jackie introduced him to her stepfather, Hughdie immediately asked him if he knew what Kirk Douglas's real name was . . . Jackie cut him off, as it were, at the pass. In any case, my lifelong passion for bores began with Hughdie.

Gleefully, Jackie and I recalled his sayings. " 'All good cooks are fat. The ultimate test of a cook is, Can she make codfish cakes?' " Jackie, referring to my "golden ambience" description of Merrywood, said, "Poor Jack really suffered a lot in that house over the years." I am told that during Jack's thousand days as president, he discussed his mother-in-law almost as much as he did Khrushchev, and in much the same manner. At her best Janet—rather like Nina—had no conscious mind, but her unconscious jet stream was more than usually turbulent. I am told (on not entirely reliable authority) that in her last years, no matter where she was she thought that she was at the Argentine embassy, where she was obliged to apologize for the Falklands war. On the other hand, although she had married poor Hughdie for his money, when he finally managed to lose his fortune, she bailed him out with money inherited from her father.

Jackie was amused at Grace Kelly and Rainier, who had moved heaven and earth to get invited to the White House. Finally, they came to lunch with Fred Coe and Frank Roosevelt. Grace was as nervous and dull as ever, terrified of Jack. All easy conversation was addressed around her. Jackie remembered that she had been just the same when she was companion to Cassini.

This is all a bit unfair. Grace was a passionate conservative, and she and I used to argue politics when I was a writer at MGM and she was preparing to quit acting to marry Prince Rainier. "Why," I asked her, "after having worked so hard to be a movie star, do you want to give it all up to live over a French gambling casino?"

She was droll. "You know what a makeup call is?"

I said yes: It is the hour when the actors are called in to be made up before the shooting starts at nine or ten or whatever time it was at Metro. The place was run like a factory, everything on the dot.

"Well, I'm still fairly young, but I have a tendency to gain weight. So my makeup call is at a proper hour—let's say eight. But if I'm heavy, I have to come in at seven-thirty, and there I'll find Joan Crawford, who has been there since six, and Loretta Young, since five, and some of the others look as if they've spent the night there. No, thanks. I'm quitting before I get moved back to seven o'clock."

I think Jackie's dislike of Grace began when she and Jack were looking at the press coverage of the wedding in Monaco. Jack studied the pictures intently; then frowned and said, "*I* could have married her!" Jackie's face was again tear-stained.

AUGUST 31, 1961–PROVINCETOWN

Jackie and Bill Walton arrive at the Moors Motel at 5:30. That morning Jackie had been pondering over the phone to me—should she wear a blond wig "with braids" in order not to be recognized? Instead, she wears a silk bandanna, a jacket, capri pants, and looks dazzling. Bill wears a dark blue sports shirt; and the usual lopsided grin.

Several years earlier I had introduced Jackie to dark glasses, partly as disguise as practiced in Hollywood, but mostly as a means of looking at people without their knowing it. For a *voyeuse*, this was the perfect mask. As it proved, our best disguise was Bill's old Chevrolet with the top down: that should give no one any ideas.

They came into my room at the motel. No one about. Jackie flung herself on the bed–free! Bill described the effect of Jackie's blond wig with her dark complexion and eyes—people would have come from miles around to see the freak. We then left for the Chrysler Museum. The recognition began in one of the rooms where the Hawthorne collection was being shown. "Are you Mrs. Kennedy?" Jackie gave a brilliant smile and shook her head. "You travel in disguise . . . beautifully," said the woman.

Talking of pictures, friends, gossip, we looked at several galleries. The crowd began at the second gallery. Ten, twenty, thirty people–newcomers kept joining the pack that followed us at a two-yard distance. I asked where the Secret Service were. "Right behind us." Jackie was amused that I hadn't seen Mr. Jeffrey at the motel. He had been right in front of me. Much banter about the cold naturalistic novelist eye that missed nothing. She was not particularly keen on Mr. Jeffrey. He was a bit heavy-going;

enjoyed talking to HQ on his walkie-talkie. Each of the Secret Service men has a code name—"Dapper," etc . . . She thought that the names they chose for themselves very revealing. Only recently have I learned that their code name for Lee Radziwill was "Rancidass."

We had dinner on the sea at a large restaurant called the Flagship. Again the recognition, though we sat in a dark corner. Happily, no one came over. At this point, I decided that despite demurs, Jackie was delighted by the attention. She noted that today was not bad at all, that the worst part was the apprehension, particularly in cities where the crowds could be demoralizing. After two Acapulcos for me, a tourist drink, two Pimm's Cups for her, and gin for Bill, we left in a gala mood— as we did, the waiter shook our hands and said that he was going to keep Jackie's glass as a souvenir.

We went to the Provincetown Playhouse to see Mrs. Warren's Profes- sion. *I had bought the tickets the day before and no one knew that even I would be on hand. We entered after the curtain was up. The boy taking tickets was so overcome that he gave us all his programs. In the inter- mission he brought us tea. By this time the street outside the theater was full of people. The box office phone was ringing. Is she there? Meanwhile, we had, somehow, lost the Secret Service man. We debated whether or not to send a word back to headquarters: "Lace" torn; "Lace" missing. We decided that he had gone back to the motel to wait (he had). The performance was good and the management got us out by way of the stage.*

We drove down the street (by then unobserved) and went to a dive called the Ace of Spades—young couples, dirty songs. A man with a badge asked for our identification as the place is a "club." We decided to move on to the bar of the Moors. Next day all Provincetown would be dis- cussing how Jackie was not allowed to enter the Ace of Spades.

As we were about to get into Bill's car, a mildly drunk, rather sardonic man recognized Jackie and said, "So the stories are all true. Why don't you come on in?" We fled. Then wondered what stories? Bill suggested a lesbian cell at the White House, Tish, Pam—Jackie. I suggested heterosex- ual orgies—one man and three girls.

At the Moors we sat downstairs in a cellar bar with candles and kegs set around for color. Upstairs was another bar, frequented by lesbians. Jackie was fascinated but dared not look in.

Conversation: Eisenhower. An old acquaintance of my father's from West Point. Ike's coldness, bad temper, and general phoniness were duly noted. *Jackie described how mechanically he puts on his smile; otherwise, he sits, empty and remote.* According to my father he was seldom seen smiling when he was MacArthur's chief of staff–"a sourpuss." Only in England, as Supreme Allied Commander, did he develop "charm."

Unpleasant lunch with the Japanese. I don't know what this refers to. *Also, the Pakistani dinner, where Eisenhower went up to the prime minister, all teeth and tonsils showing; threw his arm around him and then walked away when the photographers were gone. At table, when the wandering marine band would play certain songs, Ike would suddenly look warmly at Mamie across the table, lift his glass, and remind her how this was one of their songs.*

Sometime after the Inauguration, the Eisenhowers came to lunch at the White House. Mamie still suffering from power withdrawal. "The worse part is not having the switchboard. For twenty years, I've had a switchboard. It's really awful because *I can't dial.*" There is something Firbankian about all this.

Jackie said how much she and Jack liked Galbraith's letters from India, which are numbered. I said that later he would supply chapter headings. Double duty: currying favor with the president and writing a book. She also loves Arthur Schlesinger. When Bill mentions Arthur, she says, "Look, I just start smiling at the mention of his name." We were all Arthur fans. She said he writes her at least once a week, informative letters.

In due course, thanks to history's relentless surge, I became less of an Arthur fan when I became the target of one of his famous disinformation campaigns about That Night at the White House. I think, eventually, the party line was that I had never actually met the Kennedys and that photographs of me with them, when not doctored, were simply accidental affairs, as I am a known habitué of horse shows and the like.

To Arthur's credit, he served his masters loyally in life and then, prodigiously, after death as one thousand days followed upon the next like so many demented leap years. Unfortunately, history was not so well served by Arthur. As Allen Nevins said to me in 1964, "He's too partisan, too polemical. One can never believe him. This is fatal for a historian."

Arthur did make a good point when I asked him what it was like to be inside an administration rather than writing about one years later from the outside. He scowled. "The press, those famous primary sources. Between partisanship and incompetence, they're hopeless. So how can you reconstruct what happened if all you have to go on is, let's say, *The New York Times?*" When one considers the lies that Arthur felt obliged to tell the *Times,* like "our cover story" for the Bay of Pigs, he certainly spoke at absolute first hand. Years later, I had Arthur in mind when I coined the phrase "agreed-upon facts," which so dismays those simple historians, particularly the Lincoln priesthood, who think that absolute truth exists not in Plato's attic but in some dusty yellowing newspaper cutting, to be squirreled from an archive.

Jackie and I return to the ever-delightful subject of our common step-father. He liked food when I was stepchild; now food is his reigning passion. Jackie remarks on how wonderful it is *"just to watch his face as the last Triscuit on the plate is about to be taken away."* The novel about *Washington, D.C., that I've started to brood on again gets another character.* Six years later *Washington, D.C.* was published and in it there was, indeed, a character obsessed not with madeleines but with the poignant passing of Triscuits from a room. Until I read this note, I had not realized that in addition to the novel *Julian,* other works were crowding my head, and my days in politics and Hollywood were coming to an end.

Concern over the story in Look *about the Secret Service chief: how in Miami a madman was all set to blow up Jack, but when he saw that Jack was with Jackie and the children at the door to the Palm Beach house, he couldn't go through with it. Jackie was most alarmed by the SS chief's admission that they had no idea the man was in Palm Beach. "They should always pretend they know!"*

In the bathroom at the Moors Motel, Jackie found some paper bathroom slippers with MOORS MOTEL *printed on the tops. Bill insisted that she wear them next weekend when Jack was back in Hyannis.*

JACKIE: *"When Mr. Kennedy talks about all the people in his time–like FDR–though he himself wasn't as important maybe as . . . (a delicate pause, delighted smile) people now, they all seemed like such extraordinary figures: larger than life, Hopkins and Ickes and Hull . . . now this week* Larry O'Brien's *on the cover of* Time*! Bill, you remember him? Blundering along, back in Massachusetts." To which Bill replied, "If he stays in office awhile and the administration's a success, he'll be more famous than Hopkins." What has happened is that each of us, in his own way, has been put into the first rank at least a decade ahead of time.*

Against my better judgment, I have saved this inanity from brutal palimpsest. Certainly, for "first rank" I should have written "public eye."

I recall, now, something that Jack had observed about the great of this world. "In this . . . uh . . . job you get to meet just about everybody. You get to know all the big movers and shakers, and the thing that most strikes me about them is how second-rate they really are." He said this with some wonder, even wistfulness—as if he had really wanted to be impressed and wasn't.

SEPTEMBER 3, 1961: TRURO–A. SCHLESINGER

Ran into Arthur at Gilbert Seldes. A busy arts commentator of the day (and father of a schoolmate of mine at Exeter), Seldes lectured me on the failings of Live Television Drama, something that I had not only abandoned for the theater three years earlier but that, as an "art form," had already been supplanted by the quiz show. Apparently, word had not yet spread to Truro.

For the first time, Arthur was worried. The last forty-eight hours have alarmed the government. Possibility of war near. I check the records now. On September 4, the day after Arthur's intimations of war, Jack signed the Foreign Assistance Act, authorizing more than $4 billion for use in military and economic programs abroad. So the forces of freedom and democracy everywhere were indeed working themselves into a lather. No doubt a CIA report had landed on Jack's desk, assuring him that a Soviet invasion of Mexico was only hours away.

Jack's analysis of the great presidents: "It really hasn't much to do with them or their characters so much as when they lived. What would Lincoln have been with no Civil War?" How much, I wondered, was he consciously or unconsciously willing a war that would put an end, one way or another, to the "twilight time," and ensure for Jack the sort of glory that, ironically, he was about to achieve anyway by falling victim to a gangland plot? The ultimate irony is that the elements that did him in—the Marcello mob in New Orleans and so on—were the kind of people that his father had comfortably done business with all his life.

It was the genius of Proust to take for granted that every appearance is either a deception or subject to misinterpretation and that the only gift the killer Time bestows is to allow us to see, on later viewings, what it was that we missed first time around.

Arthur discussed Jack's mood; finds him tired and peremptory. I described his mood as lively but given to not entirely humorous tirades, all coming from frustration. Schlesinger described a major conference on the Berlin crisis. Tough policy people like McCloy, et al. (They resumed nuclear testing, so we'll show them that we are as tough as they are, we'll resume testing) versus the slyer advisers, who prefer to milk our world advantage as long as possible (Bundy, Arthur, et al.). Arthur notes that Jack is finishing everyone's sentences; his mind works so quickly. He is impatient.

Or bored, I would think, at being told things that he already knows, the great burden of the presidency as expressed by Woodrow Wilson to my grandfather. At the end, neither the tough nor the sly line was adopted. " 'But I wish,' said Arthur, 'he had listened a bit longer.' " Actually, just as Jack was advocating a world nuclear ban on testing, we were secretly building tunnels so that we could cheat undetected. Did Arthur know this? I doubt it. He was never on the inside.

Arthur talked of Rusk's loathing for Galbraith. Apparently, Galbraith, in addition to writing directly to the president over Rusk's head, also writes sardonic letters to the State Department, expressing contempt. When Rusk sent out a memo on our relations with Red China and Chiang, all piety and China lobby propaganda, Galbraith replied, May I respectfully submit that the case given is not accurate but merely reflects domestic political considerations and is of no practical use outside the country. Rusk was furious. Arthur is not an admirer of Rusk. He also finds McCloy one of the most overrated of figures. Even Jack had said, after one of McCloy's reports, "A bit Republican, isn't it?"

SEPTEMBER 5: PROVINCETOWN–BILL WALTON

Ran into Bill cruising the Atlantic House, very relaxed. He told of a girl, "an art critic now on a Washington paper who used to sleep with Jack and she said that he always insisted on a second girl, to alternate with her during the night." Jack knows about Joe Alsop, who recently had police trouble. Bill thinks that Jack's flirtatiousness with men is a part of his sexual drive and vanity.

I have often wondered about Jack's relationship with LeMoyne Billings, his Choate roommate and lifelong slave. I have just read a curious passage from a letter Jack wrote Billings when he was in the navy at Charleston (1942): "After you hear someone call you a fairy and discuss it for two solid hours, and argue whether you did or did not go down on Worthington Johnson, you don't write a letter saying you think that fellow is a great guy—even if it's true [re: Worthington Johnson] which it was." A few years later Billings picked up a friend of mine, anonymously, in Times Square. While Billings was in the hotel bathroom, my friend noted his unusual name on a tag sewed to a sock. One night at the White House, I was tempted to remind Lem of that encounter; but refrained.

Walton says Jack is now rigorously dieting, exasperated by newspaper accounts that he has aged in office. The problem is lack of exercise since the last back ailment.

Bill said that Arthur had been complaining that Bill saw more of Jack than of him. Bill told Jack this, who grinned and said: "Well, Arthur's been given a couple of big things now. He's doing better." Very dry, amused. We both agreed that Jack is the best-informed man in America. Partly natural curiosity, partly the resources of information available to a president; also, he reads everything and invites confidences.

"Do you tell him everything?" asked Bill, lopsided grin turned my way. I said, "Well, almost."

Jack is particularly fascinated by sex lives. "But he's rather sad these days," says Bill. "Nothing happening except Jackie, maybe twice a week." I pointed out that their marriage had revived—or perhaps really begun—when he started to see her face in every newspaper; he's now taken to calling her "the sex symbol." Not till he saw the world's response to her did he find her interesting.

Bill said, "He used to be brutal to her in public, but now it's the other way around; she needles him too much. I find myself saying, Come on, you can't say that to him. After all he's the president, give him a break."

Bill talked about Joe Kennedy; he felt that he exerted no influence: "He knows his place." But occasionally Joe gets a bug: At the moment he is violently against newspaper proprietors owning TV stations. "Wrong sort of capitalism."

I said that one could occasionally hear the voice of Joe in Jack. The other night at Hyannis, Jack got on the subject of what he called "that old drunk Churchill. What was so marvelous about him? Nobody could've mishandled that war. He didn't have a chance of going down, because we would never have allowed it."

There the green pages end.

The convention floor in the film of
The Best Man, *1964. When I wrote the screen-
play I had in mind the 1960 Democratic
Convention at Los Angeles, where I was a
Kennedy delegate.*

Getting Out

I T IS MUCH HARDER to get out of worlds than to get into them, or so I have found. I got into television, then the movies, then theater, then conventional politics. Ten years had passed since I had published my last novel, *Messiah*, in 1954. During that decade I had accomplished my original mission: I could now afford to do only what I wanted to do, which was to write novels, even though it had been clear to me for quite some time that the novel as an art form—much less diversion—was of no great interest to the public at large and of too great an interest to academics in pursuit of theory. But this did not seem to me any reason not to go on doing what I liked to do.

Fortunately—or unfortunately—I had experienced far more of the world than most writers. This did not mean increased wisdom on my part, but it certainly meant a broad knowledge of the complexities of a life in one's time and of the numerous and often dangerous opportunities to be taken or avoided. What Frost had thought of as two roads diverging in a yellow wood had become, for me, a sort of cloverleaf in what is known currently, oddly, as "the information highway." Faced with multiple choices, I checked many wrong ones, but thanks to a short attention span, once I had got the point to a world, I moved on. Upstairs in the White House, I got the point to the presidency as I stood in the doorway waiting for Jack to precede me into the family dining room. He stopped beside me. "So, will you run for the Senate?" I said no. I couldn't win: No Democrat could that year.

Jackie had just finished redoing the dining room with an eighteenth-century wallpaper of soldiers with rifles, a bit too martial, Jack had observed while complaining of the smell of cooking from the nearby kitchen. At that moment I thought—well, this is what it's like to be president. The smell of cooking. Alice Longworth, Bill Walton, and Oatsie Leiter at table. A bad back. A bad press. Possibility of nuclear war. And gossip, endless gossip, which then congeals into history. My curiosity was satisfied.

As we sat down, Jackie said, "We're old-fashioned *observant* Catholics, and it's Friday." Then we were served not fish but a tub of beluga caviar from the "21" Club. I asked Alice what this room had been in her father's day. "My bedroom. Oh, I couldn't wait to get out of this house!" Gray eyes shone; gray snaggley teeth all exposed in a Roosevelt grin.

THIS MORNING, Jackie's will was described in the Italian press. Lee was left out of it on the grounds that Jackie had done quite enough for her in life, which was certainly true. I wonder if, at the end, Jackie had come to dislike Lee as much as everyone else did. Happily, Lee's malice is mitigated by her slowness of mind. Now, from the grave, Jackie inserts the knife. I think, for Jackie, revenge must really have been as sweet as love, even posthumously. I had always thought that she was joking about keeping a little book filled with the names of enemies. Now I suspect that she was not. But her life in the world had been a good deal harder than she ever let on.

There was never much money for either girl. Certainly, Hughdie's fortune—when he had it—was insufficient to launch two ambitious girls in society. Janet (just described by *Newsweek* as "an icy social climber, trying to disguise her Irish [*sic?*] roots") had no money until she reconciled, late in life, with her father, who had objected—I wonder why—to her marriage with Jack Bouvier. So Jackie, constantly presented as a wealthy debutante of the highest society was, like me, a poor connection of the Auchinclosses. Had it not been for Nina's exasperation with Hughdie, Nina's candidate for her replacement, Janet, could never have taken her place at Merrywood and Newport, Rhode Island. I have often wondered what would have become of Jackie had Nina stayed with Hughdie. Jackie would certainly have married money. That is to be taken for granted. But she would never have got Jack. One shudders to think that there would never have been a Jacqueline Kennedy Onassis if Hughdie could have had a satisfactory erection.

MY DECISION to change my life was not all that easy to act upon. One does not just step away from politics. It is necessary to go away, physically, at least for a time. Elaine Dundy recalls that late at night after my 1960 defeat, I was on the phone to my agent in Hollywood. "Get me a picture fast," I said. He did.

Esquire asked me to write a column on anything. I did. Mostly about politics. A television magnate of the day asked me to preside over the first television program where people could ring in. It was called *Hot Line,* and was shown six nights a week in the New York City area.

The program was so popular that Fred Dupee could bear it no longer. If I was changing my life, it was plainly for the worse. "I never thought I'd see a friend of mine talking to gossip-writers like Dorothy Kilgallen and Ed Sullivan *on television.*" That did it. I told the producer that I was quitting. A look of deep pain: the ratings . . . No, I said; that was that.

I accepted an invitation to tour the Mediterranean on the *Leonardo da Vinci.* Howard would join the ship at Palermo. In New York harbor, Paul Newman and Joanne Woodward came to see me off. I was feeling grim. I had started to write *Julian,* but I had no idea if I could pull off so complex a book after such a long time out in the world.

That night at dinner I sat alone at a table for four. Then I was joined by the Newmans. "You didn't make it ashore?"

"No. We're coming too." They had joined the cruise. Ship of Fools, we called it.

I watched the dawn come up over the Piraeus and thought, "This is the morning of the world." Howard and I skipped ship at Athens. It was my first trip to Greece, and I could not get enough of what was left of the world that Pausanias had described. I spent hours at Eleusis, trying to figure out what the mystery cult had been like, and I brooded in the agora on Julian's days as a student at Athens before he was sent by Constantius as caesar to Paris. We got to know an ancient World War One aviator who lived in a dusty house crowded with soldiers and eccentric objects, all nicely described by the English novelist Francis King in *The Fire Walker*. Again, I note that only the novel can ever be true.

The critic Leslie Fiedler was also living in the city, and we would concoct stories for future literary historians in order to prove that the Athens of the early sixties was far more exciting than the Paris of the twenties. He was–is?–a lively critic with rather too many ideas about literature, if that is possible. Perhaps I mean too many wrong ideas.

Over the years, I have made several pilgrimages to Delphi. Today, the place is ruined for me–everything fenced in, so one cannot wander through the Sacred Enclosure at night and brood on the eagle-shaped mountain that rises above the Castalian Spring. During the day golden eagles used to be a common sight in the sky above the theater of Apollo, where, the year before my first visit, a famous actor played Prometheus in the ancient theater. At the play's end, Prometheus is bound to his rock, liver gnawed at by a vulture. Then, just as Prometheus curses Zeus and pronounces an anathema upon the gods, three golden eagles suddenly appeared in the sky above the actor's head and circled him slowly as he shouted to heaven, "I am wronged!"

Was Kimon Friar in residence that season? I think so. He had set himself up as link between modern American and Greek literature. He translated Kazantzakis's *Last Temptation of Christ*, a marvelously dead landscape of a book in which not even a weed could grow. But Kimon thought it magnificent. I also saw a good deal of Nikos Gatsos, a poet who produced very little, but what he did gave me almost as much pleasure as Cavafy, especially the long poem "Amorgos." Nikos was tall and bulky and pale of face, with weak squinting eyes. He would hold court at a table in Floka's, a sort of tearoom around the corner from Syntagma Square, where we were staying. He could only go to Floka's. He had phobias about all the other places in the area. Certain streets were simply not negotiable for him. He supported himself by translating plays for the National Theater. One afternoon we sat with him while a small revolution took place in the streets. Nikos was very cool. After all, Papandreou, the head of the Socialist party, was sitting near us, and it was his forces that were attacking the government–or was it the other way around?

As tear gas swirled into Floka's, we continued to eat yogurt with honey and sesame seeds and watch through plate-glass windows men waving placards and firing guns, mostly in the air.

"It's a bit like when the Italians came," he observed. "The Italians got nowhere, of course, when they invaded us. The Greeks, all in unison for once, said no! And in the Morea, where my family came from, every man got down his rifle and headed north. We had won, we thought. But then Hitler came to the aid of the Italians, and there wasn't much we could do but starve to death. Terrible to watch the children. Out there in the streets." Nikos could eat a pound of pistachio nuts at a sitting.

I HAVE JUST COME BACK from Rome, where the American Academy has celebrated its centennial. Since I wrote *Julian* and *Creation* in its library, I try to be helpful when asked. The Agnellis had taken over the newly restored Sistine Chapel for an evening; then dinner for 150 in the Hall of the Statues, a brilliant long room with statues in niches like front-line troops poised to defend Olympus from Titans.

Among the crude Titans was Henry Kissinger. In the next few days he and I attended a half-dozen functions together. I have no idea what he was doing memorializing the American Academy; but the people who give money for such causes have made something of a pet of him, rather as they had made one of Capote in an earlier time. Although Kissinger and I were careful to keep some distance apart, I could hear the ceaseless rumbling voice in every corner of the chapel. The German accent is more pronounced in Europe than on television at home. He has a brother who came to America when he did. Recently, the brother was asked why he had no German accent but Henry did. "Because," said the brother, "Henry never listens." As I left him gazing thoughtfully at the hell section of *The Last Judgment* (as pretty and bright now as Tiepolo), I said to the lady with me, "Look, he's apartment hunting."

I sat with Roberto Calasso, whose *The Marriage of Cadmus and Harmony* I had greatly praised. He is a quick, witty little man. Nicely, he thanked me. "I've just come from Sweden. Even there, they use your quote."

I am now reading his earlier book, *The Ruin of Kasch*, reflections on Talleyrand and everything else. He is wonderfully reactionary. Between Creation and Chaos, he would have chosen Chaos.

I return to Ravello with what I take to be lumbago, the result, I think, of walking several miles backstage in the Vatican, a place more vast than I ever suspected. I had the feeling, once again, that I was trapped inside Proust's last chapter, where the characters all meet again, each aged in the extreme (though if one works out the chronology, they cannot be half as old as he depicts them). Roman nobles hold up pretty well, while the Americans look decrepit. Marella Agnelli is Oriane, and little different from what she was when we first met at the White House thirty-three years earlier. Exotic venues become her.

In old age Dot complained of her dreams. "They're so awful, and so tiring. In one I was obliged to wash a pile of laundry—sheets and all in this huge tub, and I've never really done any laundry." Cocteau said of his later dreams that they were like long bad movies in desperate need of editing. The latest theory tells us that dreams are the brain's way of sorting out memories—some to be kept on file, others let go. I must be holding a bonfire. They go on and on, ending usually with frustration and anxiety that wake me up. I then take a beta-blocker to keep down blood pressure, which normally rises before awakening but, in my case, rises much too high, causing the unpleasant dreams. Beside my bed there are two varieties of beta-blocker, as well as Synthroid to stimulate an inactive thyroid, and pills to sleep, and pills to control a chronic allergy that has affected my sinus ever since the north wind brought us the fallout from Chernobyl and the Italian government, alarmed for the first time ever for the public good, forbade the population to eat that season's fresh vegetables and, for once, farmers and consumers obeyed. There is still cesium-137 in the soil, but the press is silent on the subject.

Morning's dream: I am with Prokosch and two others. We are escaping from something unnamed. Long dead-end passages. Intricate Piranese ups-and-downs where at every point one is frustrated. Then a hotel where I have no key to my room and no money to book a new room. Suddenly, I am in a doctor's office. I show my leg to the doctor: Thick, gummy blood is making a small red badge of distress (the cat scratched me last night). "In such an extreme case as yours," the doctor says gravely, "the blood pressure is now being triggered by the marrow of the bone, causing the blood to come through the skin." As this was the best medical advice that I have had so far, I wake up.

AFTER ATHENS, we moved on to Rome and looked about for an apartment. The Rome of thirty years ago was at the start of an economic boom, and the people, sad and confused in 1948, were coming to life.

Every evening hundreds of boys converged on the Pincio in order to make arrangements with interested parties. Drugs were still the province of the few, mostly artists; there was thievery, but no violence; there was no AIDS, and sex was spontaneous and untroubled. If one knew two or three girls who enjoyed sex for its own sake, splendid orgies were possible, usually between eight and twelve in the evening, with no drinking permitted, or desired, as every fantasy was acted out in flesh. One girl, so pleased with a party that we gave, went to sleep bolt upright in a nearby trattoria where we had gone to review the evening. Eventually, she opened her eyes to say that she had never before been entirely satisfied.

But I don't want to raise false hopes for today's jittery sexual athletes as I did for Burroughs in the fifties, when I told him of the Roman baths, which promptly shut down before he got there. Today's Rome is sullen, with mephitic air, and full of crime of every sort. Currently, the Poles are thought to be the most murderous of the recent arrivals, while prostitution is either very expensive and antiseptic or, between AIDS and knives, too dangerous to be bothered with. But in 1961, when we decided to take a flat near the Tiber, Rome was, in its gravely discreet way, a sexual paradise.

MEANWHILE, I was slowly disengaging myself from Hollywood and politics. Slowly, because there were loose ends, and attractive prospects. Frank Capra had got United Artists to buy him the rights to *The Best Man.* He would produce and direct and–prepare, I suppose, is the verb–the script. Although I had wanted to quit Hollywood with a final picture that would be mine, I accepted the fact that the project would now be Capra's. I had enjoyed some of his translations to the screen of Broadway plays, hits like *Arsenic and Old Lace;* although I hoped that he would do as well with my play, I was not optimistic. Washingtonians, jaded as we were by politics, had thought his films about Messrs. Smith and Deeds pretty ludicrous, and those pictures had been made in a far simpler time than the sixties. Would Capra, who had just made the cloying *Pocketful of Miracles,* and the even-worse *A Hole in the Head,* be up to the sort of realism that had made *The Best Man* a success? As is usual in these matters, the creator of the play whose success had attracted Capra and United Artists had nothing at all to say about what would be made. When United Artists paid me $400,000 for the screen rights, Capra, not I, became the *auteur.* I could have made myself the producer and kept some control had there been great interest in "the property," but political films—not to mention any form of satire—are known to fail more often than not, and so I accepted the relatively small amount and surrendered control.

"*Small?*" exclaimed Jackie. "Imagine being paid $400,000 for *anything.*" While Jack said, "Be sure there's a part for my brother-in-law."

Sudden memory: In the White House projection room we are watching the television coverage of the Kennedy state visit to Paris. Jackie sighs when she sees her hair on the screen. "A mistake," she murmurs. Jack watches himself attentively. In one shot, they are getting out of an open car. The black-and-white film is of poor quality and looks to be very old. When the lights came on, I hear myself say, "It all looks so long ago, like the archduke arrives in Sarajevo."

Back on the Hudson, with Fred Dupee's blessing, I assembled my first book of essays, *Rocking the Boat.* I wanted to include an interview I had given *Playboy* magazine. Fred was severe. "*No interviews.* That's the first rule."

"But Mailer did almost nothing but interviews in *Advertisements for Myself.*"

"You are not Mailer. Don't advertise yourself. Address your subjects. Leave yourself out." Excellent advice for any essayist, should anyone want to practice so archaic a form. Later, I would write of myself if I thought that it was relevant to the subject at hand, but by and large, if one wants people to read Thomas Love Peacock, put the light on him, not on the electrician.

In the summer and fall of 1961, I was at first delighted and then somewhat dismayed at being a part of the Kennedy court. Howard started to complain, "It's the White House again." Their switchboard was one of the wonders of the earth. They always found you. "Would I take Rose Kennedy to the opening of the Metropolitan Opera?" The next day there I was on the front page of *The Journal-American,* in white tie, Rose beaming on my arm.

I remember that when I picked her up, she promptly gave me a lecture on the night's opera, *Andrea Chénier,* which I'd never heard. She had done her homework. As we pulled up in front of the opera house, the manager, Mr. Bing, greeted us and cameras flashed. I second-fiddled Rose into the lobby. A crowd got in our way. She raised her arm.

"I am the president's mother," she proclaimed. Like the Red Sea, the crowd parted. A woman reporter shouted, "Where did you get *that* dress?"

"Klein's," she replied. "A little something off the rack." The dress, I later read, was a masterpiece by Balenciaga. In the car Rose complained about old age: "There's still so much you want to do but can't."

"Surely there's nothing *you* can't do," I said, dropping to featured player.

"I'm not talking about *me*." She was icy. "I'm talking about my mother."

As in the election, my Kennedy connection was doing me no good as a freelance who wrote about politics and appeared on television. I was becoming known as an unrewarded Kennedy apologist. At one point during my discomfort, Bill Walton said, "Why don't you ask Jack for something. You'll probably get it." This would be, of course, a payoff for stopping Rovere from writing about Jack's health. But I said that I couldn't think of anything that I wanted other than Jack's job, plainly not destined for me. Then, without being asked, I was put on the President's Advisory Counsel on the Arts. At least, I made it a point never to attend a meeting or reply to a letter because I didn't believe that government–particularly one as philistine and corrupt as ours–should involve itself in the arts in any way. I am Darwinian in such matters: What cannot adapt dies out.

In November 1961, the Kennedys gave their first private party in the White House. The guests of honor were Gianni and Marella Agnelli; this was a sort of political payoff to Frank Roosevelt, who represented the Agnelli family business, Fiat, in the United States. I arrived with Arthur Schlesinger and his wife, Marion. By then Arthur was court jester. "I've been here three times this week," he announced, preparing to sing yet again for his supper. He had been given some ill-defined job by Bobby, not Jack, with the understanding that one day he be court historian. "I can see the book now," said Jack, *"Kennedy, the Only Years."* In the happily unforeseen future were those one thousand days and yet another thousand days: works of hagiography that Arthur would be obliged to write.

I note today that Arthur is still busy modifying history in order to serve his Holy Family. For *The Times* of London he has written an obituary of Jackie. Since the only agreed-upon mistake that the Madonna might ever have committed was the marriage to Onassis, Arthur boldly declares that it was only after the murder of Bobby that Jackie, fearful for the lives of her children, fled America to marry Onassis. Actually, as he knows, she had been planning for a year to marry Onassis (brother-in-law Steve Smith was at work on the prenuptial agreement) much to the consternation of Bobby. The marriage, he said, could cost him five or six states and he tried to get her to delay the great apostasy till after the election. Then came his death . . .

The party was fashionable rather than political. In the crowded Red Room I found myself face to face with Hughdie and Janet. Hughdie looked dazed and very happy now that he was stepfather-in-law to an honest-to-God president. "To think," he said, "here I am, a Republican who hates publicity." He reveled, however, in reflected glory. But then most people do, except those who are themselves generators of that lovely, dangerous stuff.

Almost sincerely, I complimented Janet for how well she had acted as a surrogate mother to my sister, who had fled at an early age from Nina to her father and his wife. Eager for a quarrel, Janet said, "How dare you attack your mother?"

"I thought that I was praising *you*." She began a tirade, the great beak of a nose like some furious parrot-beak, moving from side to side a foot below my chin. "Nina will be happy to know that you admire her," I said gently. "But then you should. She did everything for you." I pushed her carefully to one side as I headed toward the Blue Room.

Then I was face-to-face with yet another non-fan, Lem Billings. "Why don't you ever go to the meetings of the Council on the Arts?" I thought this none of his business, but I answered, gently, that I had never wanted to be on the council and that I didn't believe the government should involve itself in the arts. "Then why did you go on the council?" I said that I thought it would have been rude to have turned down something once it had been given me. He, too, was eager to quarrel. Also, as the principal fag at court, Lem felt that he should eliminate any potentially controversial figure from the scene. My temper—no gentle affair at best—was certainly being tested, I thought, and I took it as Apollo's revenge on me for not yet having changed my life as I had vowed to do. I have never liked parties of any kind, and the grander they are, the less I like them. Also, a court affair—if one is not a courtier—has a certain nightmarish

quality as everyone tries to get the attention of the sovereign. It is far better to read Saint-Simon than actually to stand about and watch a Sun
King flare.

A number of round tables had been set in the State Dining Room. I
was to sit at the one presided over by Ethel Kennedy. No doubt Jackie
thought that I would use the occasion to charm the wife of Bobby,
whom I had recently criticized in an *Esquire* column (August 1961). I
had described how the police attacked two nonviolent men in front of
the YMCA (I was in a taxicab en route to the airport after dinner at the
nearby White House). I asked the cabdriver if he would be a witness
when I reported the police's brutality. "No, sir, I don't dare. This is one
dirty town."

I got back to New York to read that a southern editor had written an
editorial attacking the John Birch Society. In the course of his editorial,
he quoted the FBI as saying that the Birchers were "irresponsible."
Some hours *before* the editorial was published, two men from the FBI
arrived at the editor's office and asked him on what authority he meant
to quote the FBI. The editor's sources were not, as it turned out, reliable.
But then the editor, quite naturally, asked how it was that the FBI knew
the contents of his editorial *before* it was published. He got no answer.

I described these two misuses of power, then concluded: "Now the
point of these two stories is that here is something we *can* do: guard our
own liberties. We may not be able to save Laos; but we can, as individ-
uals, keep an eye on local police forces, even if it means, as some have
proposed, setting up permanent committees of appeal in every city to
hear cases of police brutality or to consider infractions of our freedom
to speak out in pursuit of what our founders termed happiness—two
rights always in danger, not only at the local but at the Federal level."

I sent a copy of this to Bobby, who, as attorney general, was in charge
of the FBI. I got a terse acknowledgment for reply. Had I known to what
extent J. Edgar Hoover was blackmailing the Kennedy brothers, I might
have been more understanding, if no less irritable.

In the Blue Room I found a friendly face. Jackie was seated in a
straight, armless chair. There was a good deal of noise, and as there was
no other chair near her, I squatted down beside her. We chatted. Then I
started to stand up. To steady myself, I put my hand on her shoulder; the
other option was her knee, hardly a decorous thing to do. As I started to

rise, a hand pulled my hand off her shoulder. I looked up. There was Bobby. Jackie was now talking to someone else and she had not seen– no one had seen–this intervention. Bobby walked over to the door of the Red Room. I followed, blood, as they say, in my eye.

I have read so many invented versions of our conversation that I can no longer recall exactly what was said, but the whole encounter lasted about two minutes, rather less time than Ben Hur's chat with Messala. In my best Augustan manner, I said something like, What the fuck do you think you're doing? The White House brings out the macho in guests as well as residents, witness the manly dialogue of Richard Nixon as taped.

Bobby looked startled: "What's wrong, buddy boy?" An expression that I have never heard used outside a thirties movie.

I told him it was dangerous to behave as he did–the blood of genera- tions of honor-minded crazed southerners was flowing, along with the adrenaline, through my veins. Then, while I had his attention, I reminded him of the FBI caper with the southern editor. He said it was none of my business. I said that I could make it, or anything else, my business and in the most public way. "You . . . a *writer*?" He was scorn- ful. Kennedys *bought* writers. I was now cooling off. Later, he would say that I had said, "I'll get you." But macho as our chat was, I was not into thirties dialogue, even though my political role model, Eleanor Roo- sevelt, sometimes was. Now myself again, I summed up, "Writers, since they have so many words, often have the last one."

This infamous exchange was heard by no one except the two of us. A year or two later, at the request of Harold Hayes, the editor of *Esquire,* I wrote "The Best Man 1968," where I gave away the family game plan. *Esquire*'s cover was brilliant, a row of Kennedys–Jack, Bobby, Teddy, John-John, each in the president's rocking chair. The story was fea- tured on the television evening news, and much was written about it, pro and con. Years later I learned that, although the family intended for Bobby to succeed Jack in 1968, there was a plan afoot to replace Lyndon Johnson with Bobby in *1964*–a Kennedy-Kennedy ticket, undone by Dallas and, perhaps, mildly skewed by my too-sharp glimpse of Bobby's dynastic ambitions.

Arthur was the case officer in charge of disinformation, with a great deal of help from other Kennedy loyalists. Capote said that Lee, always eager to bear false witness, told him that I had been physically thrown out of the White House; Capote embellished the tale. Actually, I left, what seemed an eternity later, with Arthur, Ken Galbraith, and George Plimpton. I was, I confess, in a rage by then, which champagne had not soothed. The next morning I rang the historian, Arthur, to tell him exactly what had happened. This was naive. I had always thought that the historian was someone who, in a sense, has sworn an oath to get things right. I was wrong.

Years later Capote, in an interview–his principal art form, as it proved–repeated, yet again, the story, and I sued him for libel. On oath, Lee refused to admit ever having talked to him about that night. I settled with Capote for a signed statement that he had knowingly lied, and so on. He then went on television, drunk, and denounced not me but Lee, and then she... The squalor never ends once one gets involved with people for whom truth is no criterion. I should have known better. I stayed among them for too long.

I now think that I was the one spoiling, unconsciously, for a row of some sort in order to break the Kennedy connection. This was certainly a glorious opportunity. In a single evening, all in a row, Janet, Lem Billings, Bobby; like Macbeth's witches, their presence alone reminded me that I had not the temperament to belong to any group, much less a court where Jack's coven of little foxes was busy spoiling not only a nation's grapes but, in the end, its own, too.

One curious detail: In the case against Capote, my lawyers came across a letter from Jackie to me *after* that night, asking me to come up to Hyannisport. I can't think what that was about. I never went. I had now lit out for another country, in every sense. Life changed.

THREE MONTHS before my last White House engagement, I was told that United Artists was unhappy with Capra's approach to *The Best Man.* Would I consider doing the screenplay?

I met Capra in Hollywood; he was a lively little man with eyes like bright black olives. We would meet in his office–at Columbia, I think it was. Unknown to me, he had already prepared a script with one Myles Connolly, a dedicated Catholic who wanted to convert the masses through popular movies of the sort that Capra used to make.

I sat on the top of a low bookcase while Capra did his best to charm me. Of course he loved the play but... One great "but" was the scene where the "good" presidential candidate and the former president, who is dying, agree that there is no afterlife, which is why we must make the best of this one, and so on. Naturally, "bad" candidate admits to being "a very religious kind of guy, in a sort of way." Capra thought that even one presidential figure who was an atheist was too many.

We had several meetings (August 9–16, 1961, according to Joseph McBride's biography of Capra), which means that the following week I was in Provincetown, writing my thirteen green pages. The more I talked with Capra, the more alarmed I became. He was deeply reactionary in his politics. Communism was triumphing everywhere and only Nixon could have stemmed the Red tide, but since he had lost, "our" best man–the movie's best man, that is–must offer the nation hope *under God*. I tried to explain to Capra that there are very few practicing Christians in the foxholes of the electoral college; and no Communists. Although Stevenson and Nixon and Truman–my archetypes–differed markedly from each other in temperament and class, each was a Protestant of the American ruling establishment and quite unlike a superstitious, authority-loving Sicilian peasant like Capra–and I mean those adjectives, as Nixon once said of *sly* and *devious* in reference to Eisenhower, in the very best sense of those words.

Capra never mentioned the Connolly script. He had had a few ideas, he said vaguely, and Max Youngstein at United Artists had thought that I should be called in so that he could try them out on me.

"You know," said Capra, "I was at that convention where you were a delegate. It was great, really great. I thought Kennedy wonderful. I thought the atmosphere wonderful for a movie. The delegates . . . the . . . the . . ." Suddenly he stopped. Smiled. Eyes blazed. *An idea had come!* Script conferences are all the same. There is always one visionary who suddenly glimpses the blazing bush. "I got it. Listen. The good guy–maybe Fonda–he dresses up as Abraham Lincoln and he comes down on the floor just when the vote is going against him and he talks to the delegates and turns them around. Yes." Capra applauded his own vision. "*Yes!*" he added, with what he took to be a contagious hoorah.

I did not fall off the bookcase, but I believe that my face was masklike as I tried to disguise my horror. "So, what does . . . well, yes–but what does he *say*, dressed up as Lincoln?"

"Oh, you know. Some fourscore and seven years ago stuff . . ."

For a moment, I thought that one of us had gone mad. I began to make agreeable noises and small demurs like, "Candidates never come down on the floor of a convention, or even onto the stage, unless maybe they happen to be the governor of the state they're in, or something, and the Secret Service would never allow . . ."

Airily, he dismissed my objections. "It's a great scene," he said. "Want to take a crack at it?"

Capra was nothing if not duplicitous. We would not have met at all if I had known what Mr. McBride tells us had been going on before I was called in.

The Capra who made Mr. Smith *might have made another great film out of* The Best Man, *but the Capra who made* A Hole in the Head *took on the property only to muddy it up, to sidestep the theme of McCarthyism, which tempted him but cut too close to the bone. He and Myles Connolly set about rewriting the play for United Artists to purge it of what Capra felt were un-American overtones in its criticisms of political hypocrisy.*

Capra was on the floor of the Democratic convention in Los Angeles that July when Kennedy won the nomination, soaking up atmosphere for The Best Man. *He was not immune to the Kennedy mystique, telling Lulu (a Harvard graduate student then a Kennedy supporter) that Kennedy was sounder on communism than Stevenson and praising his precocious political skills. But Capra remained a Republican, and he warned her about the vicious tactics Communists, Communist sympathizers and liberals would be using against his man Nixon during the campaign . . .*

The Capra-Connolly script for The Best Man *invents a new protagonist: the hero is no longer the man who refuses to blackmail his opponent because "one by one, these compromises, these small corruptions destroy character" but the dark horse of the title, who receives the nomination when the two leading candidates cancel each other out–*The Best Man, *in their grotesquely sentimentalized version, is the guileless young mixed race governor of Hawaii, their muddled notion of a John Doe for the 1960s. After reading the script, UA's Max Youngstein wrote Capra on January 24, 1961, that he was "laying it on too thick to make the point . . . [The Hawaiian governor] is far from being my concept of someone to root for. He is*

*a schnook Boy Scout... He spouts clichés at the rate of one a
minute, and while many of those clichés have great truths behind
them, no one can take that many, back-to-back, without vomiting."*

I, too, was duplicitous: Yes, I would take a crack at it. Instead, I went
to Max Youngstein and said, "There is no way that Capra can make *The
Best Man.*" I told the Lincoln story. Youngstein sighed. I said, "It's better
not to make it than let him wreck it."

"Who could direct it?"

I suggested Franklin Schaffner, who had directed my first television
play, then gone on to movies. Capra was replaced. McBride reports that
in Capra's memoir, *The Name Above the Title,* "Vidal was portrayed as
the 'gay blade' who made Capra flee *The Best Man* in a fit of righteous
timidity, although not, as one might have suspected, for political or
homophobic reasons but because of what Capra claimed was Vidal's
desire to propagandize for atheism." This is a somewhat tortuous way of
saying that he was fired not because of me, as I had no contractual
power at that time, but because his approach to the story had made Max
Youngstein, a man of stout stomach, want to vomit.

Capra made no more films, and I got to make *The Best Man* my way.
Despite the fact that it was made in black-and-white, not much favored by
today's television, it goes on and on. Schaffner was a thoroughly decent,
workmanlike director and the only cloud upon our relationship occurred
when we arrived in Cannes, where I was to collect the film festival's Critics' Prize. In front of our hotel there was a large sign with the French title
of the picture and under that a "*un film de Franklin Schaffner.*" I then proceeded to lecture an auditorium full of French *cinéastes* on what the word
auteur meant in their dictionary and what they had so weirdly made it to
mean. But it did no good. Recently, when I was president of the jury of the
Venice Film Festival, a member of my jury was the cultivated head of the
Cannes Film Festival. He asked me what was the best moment that I had
had in my checkered film career, and I said, "Firing Frank Capra!" He
nearly fainted. He staggered; clutched with nerveless hand at a passing
table. "Oh, no! It is not possible."

For many, cinema is now a high religion and–well, why not? Certainly, it is better to worship a false image of the likes of Capra than that
sky-god religion, which did him and his work so much harm.

WHILE I WAS MAKING the film of *The Best Man*, Lenny Bernstein was staying in the other half of the bungalow that I had taken at the Beverly Hills Hotel. As Lenny was eager for sex, I arranged for two would-be actors to join us one evening. Lenny vanished into his section of the bungalow, wearing only a towel and a happy smile. In due course, my companion departed. But Lenny did not reappear, nor did his friend for the evening. I began to worry. Could the maestro have had a stroke? Been murdered? I opened the door between the two suites. Lenny was seated on a bed, where lay the youth, mesmerized, as Lenny lectured him on his career, character, future–and the act of performing. Lenny was a born pedant with a powerful need to explain–everything.

"I could've listened to him all night," the boy said to me next day, to which the only response was, "Well, as it turned out, that's what you did."

When Senator Cranston, a California liberal, rang Lenny to ask for money (this is what senators do even if they have never met the investor-to-be), Lenny listened impatiently as Cranston explained his positions on war and peace. Finally, Lenny said, "Well, all that sounds fine, but I really don't know you or where you stand on . . . Well, on a really *important* issue like . . . like . . ."

"Like what?"

Lenny took the plunge. "Like what would your position be on doubling the strings in the fourth movement of Beethoven's Ninth?"

The senator was calm. "I'll get back to you." Later that day, he rang again. "Before I give you my position, how big is the auditorium?"

LAST NIGHT we watched *Suddenly, Last Summer* in Italian on television. I had forgotten how beautiful Elizabeth Taylor was, how shattered Montgomery Clift. One side of his face was paralyzed from an automobile accident. Even so, Taylor had insisted he play the part. Between drink and painkillers, he could only work mornings. Before the picture started, Clift and I went to Norman Mailer's apartment, where we read aloud a play that Norman had made of *The Deer Park*. In due course, Monty got drunk. When asked the next day by the producer if Monty was all right, I said yes. After all, even under the influence, he was better than most actors. Unfortunately, the director, Joe Mankiewicz, hated him. All one day, he made Monty repeat, over and over again, a scene where he must hold a document in a shaking hand. The result sounded like a forest fire on the audiotape.

Katharine Hepburn, in turn, tortured Joe. She had helped him rise in the world when she hired him to produce *The Philadelphia Story*. Now he was ignoring her, she felt, and playing up to the star, Taylor. "You are treating me like an *old* actress!" she shouted. Then she denounced the whole project. "I'm far too healthy a person to be in something like this. Who are these people?" But she knew exactly who they were, and she gave easily her best performance. She also awed Sam Spiegel, the producer, by spitting in his face.

LAST NIGHT I also played a tape of the commencement address I gave at the University of South Dakota a month or so ago. Several thousand people. Hot auditorium. Students in bright vermilion robes. I speak briefly. Talk of my father, who had graduated in 1916; then went on to West Point. He was from nearby Madison, a town that I had visited for one day exactly fifty years earlier.

The students filed by to get their degrees. It had been years since I'd seen so many white people at a school. Most chewed gum. The head of the English Department, a lively Jewish woman from New York, said, "When I first got here, I had two John Andersons in my class. 'How am I going to tell you apart?' I asked. They were indignant: 'Because we're two different people.' I said 'But you also look alike.' They were really puzzled. 'What did you do in New York?' one asked. I told them that about a quarter of my students would be black, another Asian, another Hispanic, with a wide variety of names."

The next day I drove with two officials of the university to Madison. There had been a lot of rain lately, and the state is bright green and hot, and quite unlike the dry prairie land that I had remembered. It is also so flat that the sky seems to start below the normal horizon, giving one the sense of being airborne in a limitless sky. It was no accident that Gene and so many others from the flat mid-continental states were attracted to flying.

The house where he was born is a three-story wooden box whose veranda has been taken away. There are three brick steps to the front door. As the present owners were away, I stood on the steps and tried to imagine him young; and failed. Pictures of him as an athlete at South Dakota show an uncommonly handsome Italianate youth with a beautifully proportioned body. He was a star at football, basketball, track. I went around to the backyard, where his father had constructed a jungle gym, to build up his sickly son. I suspect that Gene had been tubercular. He disliked his father but never told me why. He was fond of his mother; he was also ashamed of her because she was fat. "Always with a baby in one arm and a book in the other," said my aunt Margaret last winter, the last of Gene's generation. Gene asked neither parent to his graduation from West Point or to Washington, D.C., when he was in office.

I have never known anyone as vague as Gene about his past or that of the family. He lived in a constant present, with boyish dreams of pirate gold in the future. There was always a scheme afoot to raise a sunken Spanish galleon off the Florida coast or to invest in a silent toilet and make millions. When he came to register my birth in Orange County, New York—I was to be "Junior"—he couldn't remember if his own middle name was Luther or Louis. So my birth certificate says "Eugene Louis Vidal": this was changed to Eugene Luther Vidal, Jr.; then Gore was added at my christening; then at fourteen I got rid of the first two names.

Gene was equally vague about his dislike of his father. He thought that his paternal grandfather had come from somewhere in Switzerland. But that was his grandmother Emma de Traxler von Hartmann, from Lucerne. Eugene Fidel Vidal was from Feldkirch in Vorarlberg, Austria, of Romansch origin. Some years ago, I went to Feldkirch and saw Vidalhaus, built around 1300. Then, from the 1580s to 1799, the family had moved south into the Alps of Friuli. Gene did manage not to lose a stained-glass medallion that has been handed down from eldest son to eldest son: It shows a bearded apothecary behind a counter; inscribed at the bottom, "Caspar Vidall, 1589."

In an autobiography, Victor Weybright quotes Norman Mailer as saying that Gore Vidal is far too "sophisticated" [*sic?*] to be a gentile. Norman may have been on to something. The researcher that I sent to Forni à Voltri, the village in Friuli where we spent two centuries under Venetian rule, studied the remaining church records and got to know a priest who had interested himself in our family history. "They were," said the priest, "thought to be of Jewish origin." My researcher was a mild Italian intellectual with a passion for old documents. I wanted to know how, if the family had been Roman Catholic since 1300, could anyone know what they might have been before that?

"You must understand," he said, with a happy sigh, "that in the villages of Italy, such rumors are eternal."

I got interested in the case. I asked Gene if he knew anything about our supposed Jewish origin. He thought this was very funny; and told me that "there was only one Jewish family in Madison, and we were all told to be very nice to their daughter because she felt so out of place." But what about *our* family? He thought it impossible. The only dark secret that the Vidals had ever felt obliged to keep was the fact that they were originally Roman Catholics of Italian descent, and all Italians were looked down upon in his youth. At West Point, in the yearbook, Gene was known as "Tony the Wop," while Eisenhower was known as "Ike the Swedish Jew." Those boys at the Point had sharp eyes.

In Feldkirch I studied the only surviving parish records—marriages. The births and the deaths had vanished. Twice we had married Romanins. Then one Maria della Valle, and one Maria della Sopra–plainly, women with no family names: Maria of the valley; Maria of up in the hills. We married a Meyer von Baldegg, a Ludwig von Hartmann, a Herzog . . . All the names are a bit ambiguous–that is, names that converted Jews might have taken. I asked my Venetian agent about the Romanins. She knew them. "They are from Padua. A rich Jewish family, like the Rothschilds."

Alain Vidal-Nacquet, a nephew of the French philosopher, said, "Of course we are Jewish."

"The Nacquet part?"

"No. The Vidal part." Vidal is a common name in every Latin country as it derives from *vitalis,* the genitive of the word for life; it made sense that a converted Jew would be more apt to take a neutral, common name rather than one that might draw attention to itself.

In the seventies, an ancient scholar in Feldkirch published a paper on Vidalhaus and the family. This only caused more confusion. There had been two Vidal families. Each had died out or gone away; one had been of Jewish origin, the other Romansch. Which were we? I had always assumed we were Romansch, a race peculiar only to the Alps, with a language full of triple diphthongs, which gave spectacular rise to the yodel. But what about all those people that we had married? With those . . . well, *suggestive* names?

When I came to make the television documentary *Vidal in Venice,* I spent some time in the ghetto, talking to an old rabbi. The Venetian republic had usually been friendly to the Jews, and warmly welcoming to Jewish converts. But should a convert ever again appear in the ghetto to attend a Jewish rite, he would be executed for having mocked Christianity. "They were very careful not to be caught," said the old rabbi.

"You mean that they would go on being Jews *secretly,* in the ghetto?"

"Only if they were suicidal. No. What they did do was to keep marrying each other."

"So they took Christian names, practiced the religion, but kept on marrying other Jewish converts?"

"Exactly." That explained all those Romanins and Herzogs. Like a witches' coven, these converted Jews, known as *marranos,* perpetuated themselves, disguised as Christians.

"Was Vidal a name they took?"

The old man shrugged. "I'm not an expert. But there have been great rabbis with that name. On the other hand, there are Christians who have the same name. Do you know the Hebrew word for 'life'?"

I said that I did not.

"*Chaim.* Life. *Vita. Vitalis.* Vidal."

This should give pleasure to the likes of Norman Podhoretz, who once drew up a list of important American intellectuals and showed it to Victor Navasky, now editor of *The Nation.* Victor said, "You've got practically no gentiles on the list."

"Because," said Poddy complacently, "we're so much smarter than they are."

Will I play the Reverend Stonehall in a film of *The Scarlet Letter*? They had offered the part to Marlon Brando, but he had wanted too much money. Plainly, I must lose weight. Am I too old to play Shylock?

{ *WHAT PEOPLE ARE READING* }

The list below, based on reports received from leading booksellers around the nation (see below for stores reporting this week), is meant to indicate which books are currently the most popular in the U. S.—not which are the best. Books deemed by Book Week critics to be of special literary, social or historic interest are marked thus (🌸) — The Editors.

Week's Score	*FICTION*	*Weeks Listed*
1 🌸	**Julian, by Gore Vidal** A novel about the Emperor Julian in 4th-century Rome.	*11*
2 🌸	**The Spy Who Came In From the Cold, by John Le Carre** Powerful and moving story of Cold War espionage.	*35*
3	**Armageddon, by Leon Uris** A novel about the beginning of the Cold War in Berlin in the late Forties.	*13*
4 🌸	**The Rector of Justin, by Louis Auchincloss** Picture of the inner workings of a private boys' school.	*7*
5	**This Rough Magic, by Mary Stewart** Suspenseful novel about British residents on a Greek island.	*3*
6	**Candy, by Terry Southern and Mason Hoffenberg** Satirizing the off-color novel.	*14*
7	**You Only Live Twice, by Ian Fleming** James Bond in Japan.	*3*
8	**Convention, by Fletcher Knebel and Charles W. Bailey II** A Presidential candidate runs too candid a campaign.	*25*
9	**The 480, by Eugene Burdick** The "computer boys" master-mind a Presidential nomination.	*9*
10	**Children and Others, by James Gould Cozzens** A collection of short stories.	*1*

Julian *was the number one fiction bestseller in the summer of 1964. Thus, I returned to the novel after ten years as a commercialite.*

Getting Back

AT THE BEGINNING OF 1962, Howard went into New York's Memorial Hospital with a large growth in his neck that looked to be cancer of the thyroid. I was amazed at how difficult it was to get into Memorial, a hospital that specializes in cancer, the ongoing epidemic of our prosperous era. Finally, he got a bed in a room with several other patients. The man in the bed beside him kept his lamp on all night long, "To see the light," he said; soon after, the light was switched off.

I ran into Tennessee in front of the hospital building. Upstairs, on a special floor, Frank Merlo was dying from lung cancer. The Bird would mourn Frank ever after, quite forgetting that he had thrown him out several years earlier. A true romantic, the Bird associated love with death, and having lost to brain cancer what he always said was his first love, a dancer who had left him to get married after a summer at Provincetown, the Bird was now mourning Frank, with whom he had lived from 1948 until about 1960. Frank had tried to bring some order into his life. Unfortunately, the Bird's paranoia was sprouting ever stranger blossoms in those years. He accused Frank of serious drug addiction, which might have been true, while the Bird's drinking and Nembutal addiction was making him more and more difficult to be with. After one row at dinner, Frank heaved a leg of lamb at him.

"When people I care for turn violent," the Bird was solemn as he recounted to me the story of their breakup, "I have no choice but to withdraw from the field. I abhor violence of every kind."

There was no use in saying that Frank had a good case for throwing a lot more than a leg of lamb at the maddening Bird. Eventually, Tennessee's brother put him away for a year. "I played quite a lot of bridge in the bin. And, of course, watched a great deal of television. There are some wonderful actors on the soap operas—unsung, of course, but still admirable."

These were the years when we did not see each other. "Gore no longer receives me," he would announce in the numerous interviews that he was in the habit of giving during the last years. This was partly true, but I always remained fond of the idea of him, and when he published his chaotic memoirs, I wrote a counter-memoir in *The New York Review of Books,* describing our early days traveling in Europe. He wrote to our friend Maria St. Just to say that my piece was "hilarious." But when next we met, a gelid eye was turned my way. "I was number five on the nonfiction best-seller list until your review appeared. Then I dropped entirely off."

We last met in Chicago on a television talk show. A third-rate woman writer went on and on about how blacks had nothing to complain of in the American paradise. Finally, the Bird leaned back in his chair and shut his eyes. Nervously, the host asked: "Tennessee? Are you asleep?"

"No," the Bird responded, eyes still shut. "I am not asleep, but sometimes I shut my eyes when I am bored."

In *A Streetcar Named Desire* Blanche DuBois thought that she would die of an unwashed grape. The Bird, as grotesque as always in detail as he was magnificent in total design, died from inhaling the plastic cap of a nasal spray container: suffocation, the worst possible death for a claustrophobe, or as I put it in a letter to Paul Bowles, recently published, "There is a Bowlesian principle at work; what is most feared fearfully happens."

IN THE WINTER OF 1962, Howard and I rented a ground-floor flat in Rome's Via Giulia; my bedroom window looked onto the Tiber and the Janiculum hill beyond. The owner of the flat was a former British minister to the Holy See. He told me that, with Compton Mackenzie, he had invented the British secret service at the time of the First War. Upon arrival, he took me to lunch at La Carbonara, in the Campo dei Fiori. "Rome is a heavy place, you'll find. Heavy food, people." We ate a very light tortellini with fresh peas.

As it turned out, for the next thirty years, Howard and I were never to live far from the Campo dei Fiori. Each morning, a market is set up in the oblong piazza, with fresh produce from neighboring farms. Then, by noon, all the carts are gone and the piazza is spotless. At its center, there is a statue to Bruno, burned at the stake by the Holy Office, whose grim building is nearby, the work of Michelangelo in somber mood. He also built the Farnese Palace in the next square, using timber from Friuli. I've often wondered if any of my ancestors cut the wood.

During Howard's stay at Memorial–his growth was benign–I developed a duodenal ulcer. A year's diet and regular workouts at a gymnasium got me into fine physical shape. Also, each day, I would walk across the Tiber and climb up the Janiculum hill to the American Academy, whose classical library had everything that I needed for *Julian.*

In those days, a number of Americans and English, more or less connected with the arts, still lived in a city that was relatively cheap. Now, all are gone: High prices and bad air have emptied the city not only of foreigners but of the poor and much of the middle class as well; only the rich and the ubiquitous government live in Vecchia Roma, a somewhat ghostly quarter at night, with only tourists abroad in the street.

Judy Montagu, my old friend from London, lived on the Island in the Tiber with husband and daughter, and everyone from her London days came to stay.

Rudi and Consuelo Crespi, she American, he Italo-Brazilian, did their best to create a salon in Rome, but that has never been possible in a city where nobles stick with nobles, intellectuals with intellectuals, and so on. But the Crespis did maintain an interesting salon where, at one side, stood suspicious Colonnas and, at the other, glowering Moravias. Aesthetically, the palace dinner parties were pleasing and I went out a lot in the first years I spent in the city. Then, one evening, I realized that I was having exactly the same conversation that I had already had a dozen times with a genial bore, and so it was that I slipped off into the Roman night, never to come back. If one is advancing one's career or sex life, there is some point to a social life, but my career is elsewhere while, as far as I can recollect, I have never gone to bed with anyone that I met at a party and, finally, that is what any social world is about. If you take part, you are expected either to marry someone in those circles or at least have an affair with someone's wife or husband. If you don't, move on. I preferred nights at outdoor trattorias, with a few friends, without strain.

Isherwood stayed with us. He had just returned from his first trip to India. The culture shock had been extreme. "There are so many of them," he said. "And how few there are of us, the white race. We must create special reservations for people like the Danes, to protect our exotic blond wildlife." Christopher took the manuscript of *Julian* back to America.

In Rome I was surprised that I did not miss politics or the theater. I was still committed to making the movie of *The Best Man*. But that, I thought, would be that. The rhythm of novel-writing–particularly in longhand, as I do–suits what Victor Pritchett calls the true novelist's "bovine" nature, an endless cud-chewing that does not suit quick-witted sorts like Pritchett, who prefers the short story or essay. As I slowly made sentences at a large table, the Tiber at my back, I felt that I was home at last. I did miss Edgewater, which was rented, but nothing more. But then wherever I live, I seem to know only four or five people who happen to be at hand.

Jack Kennedy made a state visit that spring, and, suddenly, there was Dick Goodwin at lunch, trying to extract enough gossip from me to tell Jackie. Dick Rovere was also there, with the press corps, and he reported on Hudson Valley life. Dick saw a good deal of Arthur Schlesinger, who kept him supplied with stories favorable to the administration, and to my surprise, Dick was never suspicious of Arthur. Fortunately for Dick, his on-the-one-hand-this and on-the-other-hand-that style of writing restrained him from overexcitement as he contemplated Jack's presidency, now moving restlessly toward Asian war.

In those days, one of the pleasures of Italy was driving along empty autostradas to cities that one did not know. I had bought a secondhand Jaguar, and we visited, in due course, every city and town in Italy except Enna, in central Sicily. But we did drive around the island with Maria St. Just. It was March, wildflowers everywhere. Empty roads. Yellow-white Greek ruins. Dark blue unpolluted seas. A shirtless adolescent boy hitched a ride. He got in the back with Maria. "Look," he said, pinching his nipple. To her horror, milk. He was very proud of his uniqueness. When I reported this phenomenon to a doctor, he said, dourly, that a certain kind of cancer made men lactate.

The 1940s platoon of American queens was still drifting in and out of Rome, though Istanbul was now its preferred campsite. They were always full of amusing gossip, some of it true.

Truman Capote came for lunch. With some success, I had avoided him in America, but in a foreign setting he seemed less dangerous. He lied with all his usual inventiveness. At the mention of a famous name, the eyes lit up. The nasal whine would start. "Oh, I see Jackie *all* the time. You two should really make up." I offered him not a word on that subject. "I think she's happier now, with Jack. *Resigned,* I suppose, to all those girls in the White House. Remember how she used to carry on years ago when I first knew her and we'd go to the movies together and she would tell me how unhappy she was?" Capote's biographer, not given to checking any vivid data that might prove to be inconveniently untrue, chose to believe that this had been a long, close friendship. Certainly, Jackie was intrigued. But I had warned her about Capote. "You'll enjoy the awful stories he'll tell you about everyone, but you won't enjoy the ones that he'll tell about you." In late October 1960, she rang me. "Well, I finally met him at C. Z. Guest's. And he did have a lot of very funny, very awful stories about people. After lunch, he asked me if I had a car, and when I said yes, he asked me if I would drop him off. Then he sat back and said, with this great stagy sigh, 'Well, you've just seen me singing for my supper.' "

According to Truman's biographer, he was a regular at White House functions. Years later, I asked Bill Walton if this was true and he said no, he had never been a guest. But he did become intimate with Lee, who fed him gossip, which he would then embellish as his own. After Rome, I saw him only once again, in 1968, when, without my glasses, I mistook him for a small ottoman, and sat on him at Drue Heinz's house in New York. But lack of contact did not stop him from analyzing my character in the numerous interviews that he gave the press—the lowdown on everyone. Apparently, I had set out to be a great success and I had succeeded. "But now he's so cold and so distant that no one is close to him anymore." This is his curious gloss on my ten-year battle to make myself secure financially. Greatness had nothing to do with it: only bleak necessity.

The three stepchildren of Hugh D. Auchincloss ("The first gentleman of the United States," according to the starry-eyed social chronicler Stephen Birmingham), Jackie, Lee, and I, were bought up in a wealthy manner and yet were penniless, unlike the first gentleman's five official children. Of necessity, Jackie married twice for money, with splendid results. Lee married twice, far less splendidly. I went to work.

Capote, as he more and more mastered the art of the astonishing interview, developed a network of gossip columnists who would oblige him by printing unpleasant stories about people he disliked. One of his stories—a blind item, as they say in that world—became the central theme of a piece that Martin Amis wrote about me for the English-Canadian *Sunday Telegraph.* I was said to have said that I am resented because of my genius, my sex, my beauty, or some such nonsensical triad. I pointed out to little Martin that this was not only not my style of conversation but that, more to the point, the item had simply been stuck in a column of the *New York Post,* without attribution, meaning that it was made up. But he had based his whole piece on this one line, which I later learned that Capote had got printed when I was suing him for libel. Thus, fantasies congeal into fact. I am told that Martin is currently aggrieved that what he used to do to others, they now do to him. Oh, what a tangled web we weave, I used to declaim back in the forties whenever Truman had gone even further than usual into deception. It is a mystery that he never used his truly uncanny inventiveness in his attempts at fiction.

During my ten years in the wilderness, a good deal had happened in literature. The Beats had for a time flourished, and many of us were alarmed. Was this what writing was destined to be—an endless report on what one had done the night before while listing the names of the all-alike towns that one sped through on the ever-same road? Although, as writers, Kerouac and Burroughs were not much different from such conventional writers as Philip Roth and John Updike, I feared that their imitators would, like the executors of some inexorable Gresham's law, drive literature itself out the window. All this proved to be a false alarm. Their imitators were few, while the originals either died or did not continue, and literature went out the window anyway.

I have just read in *The New Yorker* an update of a piece that I wrote twenty-one years ago on the top ten fiction best-sellers of that day. As opposed to when I wrote, there are now no "literary" books on the list and, except for the occasional accident, none will ever appear there again. The mechanics of publishing favors a certain kind of pulp fiction that the great chains can sell in volume while, according to one literary agent, the American public that buys good novels is about four thousand people. Gene used to tease my first publisher, Nick Wreden: "How is it possible, in such a large country, to sell as little of *anything* as you do of books?"

But then I seemed to have figured it out in 1956, when I wrote, "After some three hundred years the novel in English has lost the general reader (or rather the general reader has lost the novel) and I propose that he will not again recover his old enthusiasm." This caused outrage at the time. Every book reviewer in the country is, after all, a novelist or a would-be one, and to say that there will be no public for his genius is vile. I am still occasionally denounced for having said that the novel was dead. What I wrote was that the public has gone missing. Television, movies, journalism claim the general audience. Today publishers are reluctant to publish first novels by anyone who has not been, at the very least, a movie star or serial killer.

But if one is meant to be a novelist, then one goes on with or without the general public, never all that large in any case. Henry James's last great novel sold less than two thousand copies at a time when the novel was central to the culture. Although the theater still commands a considerable audience around the world, I more or less walked away from it before I was left behind.

My moment of revelation came in West Berlin, where I had gone to see *The Best Man* at the Schiller Theater. The play was mounted by the intendant himself, Barlog, and acted by Martin Held. It was a success. Then I made the mistake of visiting some other theaters in town. I saw Ionesco, who made me laugh, Brecht, who made me yawn, Saroyan in surreal mood. By the end of the week, I realized that the well-made play, in whose tradition I had grown up, was at an end except in England, where the new playwrights, allegedly angry, were writing the sort of realistic plays that New York had done in the thirties. Plainly, if I were to keep on as a playwright, I would have had to depend more on what the surrealists used to call the night-mind and go Off-Broadway, a nonexistent place in those days. I suppose I might have done for the stage the sort of thing that I would later do in novels like *Myra Breckinridge* and *Duluth,* but as I watched the poor Bird with his endless anxieties—will Kazan direct? will Marlon play the lead?—I retreated to the luxury of the yellow pad and the ballpoint pen. I was not yet through with movies and theater, but they were now only a sideline.

In the summer of 1964 we were again at Edgewater. One Sunday morning I read in *The New York Herald-Tribune* that *Julian* was the most unlikely number one best-seller in the United States. I promptly swam out to the island, much as I had done when I first moved to the Valley. Now the house was up for sale. Even so, that morning I was content. The film of *The Best Man* had just opened to good reviews. Mailer came to the party that United Artists gave. "You would have lost all respect for me," he said, "if I had seen the movie." *The Best Man* went from commercial failure to "classic" without an intervening success.

Joe Hawkins paid a call. The district was certain to go Democratic in November. Did I want to run for the House? "Let this cup pass unto Joe Resnick," I said; and it did; and he was elected in the Johnson landslide, and that was the end of me as a political force in the area. Resnick served two terms; lost a race for the Senate; then, unexpectedly, died. He was a pleasant rich man from Kingston. He told me that when Lyndon Johnson came into the district, Resnick sat in the back of the limousine with him while Johnson's devoted enemy, Bobby Kennedy, sat in the front seat. Bobby was now running for Senate in New York.

Johnson asked Joe how his race was going against my old St. Albans schoolmate Hamilton Fish.

"It's rough," said Joe. "I mean, he's got a lot of money and a famous name and his father was Congressman from here all those years . . ." As he spoke, Johnson chuckled and pointed his finger at the back of Bobby's neck. He, too, had such an adversary.

IN THE FALL, I made a final intervention in New York politics. The incumbent senator was an amiable liberal Republican called Keating. I liked him politically and personally. So I teamed up with Lisa Howard, a television journalist who had reputedly had an affair with Castro; together we started a "Democrats for Keating" committee.

I have a sharp memory of Lisa, Keating, and me standing in the back of the empty store that we were using for headquarters while the press was gathering in the front of the store. Lisa was hectoring Keating on some political point; he was getting flustered. Finally, I said, "Lisa, for

Christ's sake, leave him alone. He *is* a Republican. But at least he's not Bobby, who's been trying to kill your friend Castro all these years." A moment later, we faced the press united. In November 1.7 million New York Democrats voted for Keating. Had Johnson not carried the state so hugely, Bobby would have lost.

A month before the election, I got a telephone call from a man with a thick New Jersey accent. He had some information about Bobby that I might find useful. I said, Come to my apartment. No. Someplace else, he said. Where? We finally agreed on the bar next to the Chelsea Hotel. In a booth sat a stout, bald Italo-American with a large diamond ring. He was, I am certain, a member of the Teamsters union, whose gangster leader Jimmy Hoffa had long been Moby Dick to Bobby's Captain Ahab.

The hood's first useful information was a police report about Bobby's involvement with a minor. "They paid off the girl's parents." As the author of *The Best Man,* I took the lofty line that sex ought not to be involved in any campaign, even one against Bobby. Patiently, the hood then presented me with a set of documents, which proved to be sealed testimony from a New York court.

Although I don't know much about legal procedures, I did know, even then, that once a judge seals testimony, it is a criminal act to unseal it.

The hood opened a folder. "So let's see what's there." What was there was a lawsuit between a notorious young Englishwoman and the members of her late husband's family. After a month or so of marriage, her elderly husband had died and she had inherited his fortune. The family then sued her for their share. I already knew this much of the story from the press. But I did not know that, to prove she was of bad character, there was a sworn deposition to the effect that she had had affairs with both Jack and Bobby Kennedy.

I forget now who settled what with whom, but I do recall she had refused to pay her lawyer what she owed him. The lawyer brought suit against her, with the threat that if she did not pay his fee, the Kennedys would be named. At that point, Bobby, the attorney general, came to New York and told the young woman that if she did not promptly pay her lawyer, he would have her deported as an undesirable alien. This struck me as remarkably high-handed, even for Bobby. She paid the lawyer. The judge then sealed the testimony and that was the end of that until my New Jersey acquaintance and his friends got their hands on the deposition.

"But anyone who publishes this will go to jail." I had grasped this essential point.

"Don't be so sure." There was a dreamy look in the hood's eyes. "You know, all over the country these small weekly papers are up for sale for maybe ten, fifteen thousand dollars apiece. Well, go buy one, anonymously. Publish the testimony. When the wire services pick up on the story, and they will, you fold the paper, and that's the end of it as far as you're concerned. And that's also the end of Bobby."

I discussed the matter with Lisa. She was more knowledgeable than I of crime. She was grim. "It's the mob. Don't touch it. Nothing but trouble." That was the end of that, and so, on this peculiarly bleak black note, my political life in New York State came to an end.

AFTER THE ELECTION OF 1964 we were back in Rome, in a rented penthouse on top of the moldering seventeenth-century Origo Palace at the center of what bureaucratic Romans call the Historic Center and everyone else calls Old Rome. Here we were to live, off and on, for close to thirty years.

The palace is at the northwest corner of a busy square that has all the charm of New York City's Columbus Circle, minus Huntington Hartford's masterpiece but plus, below street level, three classical temples, home to a colony of cats, a perennial–no, millennial–reminder that this precinct was once sacred to the goddess Isis, and the cat was, and is, her creature. In a nearby street there is a large marble foot on a pedestal, all that is left of Isis's cult statue. Cats sun themselves on her toes.

Question I often hear: Why did you spend almost a third of your life in this Roman apartment? I quote Howard Hughes. When asked why he had ended up a long-nailed recluse in a sealed hotel room, he croaked with perfect candor: "I just sort of drifted into it." That's almost always the real answer to everything. But there were, of course, a thousand other reasons. For one thing, I had never had a proper human-scale village life anywhere on earth until I settled into that old Roman street.

Literature? Two blocks to our north, back of the Pantheon, Thomas Mann lived and wrote *Buddenbrooks*. Nearby, George Eliot stayed at the

Minerva Hotel. Ariosto lived in Pantheon Square; Stendhal was also close by. I myself wrote at least a part of several books in this flat, as well as all of *Myra Breckinridge,* in one month, one spring, from new moon to new moon. The last chapters of *Lincoln* were composed on the dining room table.

Italo Calvino lived at the north end of the street, and we used to *cher confrère* each other when we met. Then, one stormy day, I went, with real sadness to his funeral.

The last photograph of Jimmie Trimble (kneeling at left). He is with his squad of scouts, most of them killed, too, at Iwo Jima on March 1, 1945. Midway between his gravestone and Henry Adams's monument to his wife in Washington's Rock Creek Park cemetery, Howard and I have, as we used to say in the army, bought the farmstead.

Section:
E Lot 293½,
Subdivisions 2 and 4

Oct
ber 3, 1994. I am at La Costa, a "spa" north of San Diego, where I often come to lose weight and dry out.

This morning I got up at five-thirty and checked my blood pressure: 129/82. As this is normal for me, I shall take no beta-blockers. Blood sugar is slightly high. I must cut back on fresh orange juice. A few years ago I was told that I was a "senile" diabetic; I have controlled this condition by diet, not pills.

Senile? Yes. I am sixty-nine today, an age that I never expected to reach when I was young. At noon on the East Coast, the time of my birth, I shall enter what in Italy is called, accurately, my seventieth year. I can't say that my cup is exactly overflowing.

Before breakfast, I read Lucretius *On the Nature of Things*. I've been quoting passages from him for years, but until now, I've never read him straight through. I'm now at the end of part two, where he anticipates Darwin by two thousand years. "For it is not true as I think, that the race of mortal creatures [man] were let down from on high by some golden chain . . ." So much for the antique notion of Cadmus sowing dragon's teeth to create human beings or the peculiarly silly story of Adam and Eve believed by so many of my countrymen. Lucretius is aware–how, I wonder?–that we evolved. I've often quoted his law that nothing can come from nothing, but wonder about his corollary that nothing can go to nothing since, if the *it* is transitive–the going, that is–then it must be *some*thing and so, by definition, not *no*thing.

Lucretius had also worked out that we live on a globe and that there are a myriad of other globes in the heavens and that many of them will support "mortal races." Lucretius is also a proto-ecologist, fretting about overpopulation. Nature "of her own accord first made for mortals the bright corn and the luxuriant vineyards of herself; she gave forth sweet fruits and luxuriant pasturage," but now "we exhaust our oxen and the strength of our farmers, we wear out the plowshare, and then are scarce fed by our fields"; man seems congenitally unaware that "all things gradually decay, and go to the reef of destruction, outworn by the ancient lapse of years." Thus he anticipates the second law of thermo-dynamics, not to mention giddy entropy.

While I've been here, I've also been reading through this memoir, adding, subtracting, writing over half-erased texts–"palimpsesting"–all the while looking for clues not so much to me, the subject, if indeed I am the subject, as to what those first thirty-nine years were all about as we grew more and more ingenious in finding new ways of killing off the human race and its support system, the small planet that each of us so briefly visits. No, I haven't found any pattern at all to life itself, but then there is probably none other than birth and growth, decay and death, something we all know from the start. As for who I was then as opposed to now . . .

IN MY THIRTY-NINTH YEAR, where I shall now leave myself in this narrative, a dinner was given for me in Washington. Alice Longworth sat beside me. The gray, flinty eyes are not unlike first cousin Eleanor's. "I loved *Justinian*," she said. She always got the title wrong, but I think that she may have read the book, no commonplace thing in what Henry James called "the city of conversation."

"You know, you were so wise to get out of this town and do what you've done and not stayed on like the rest of us–like Joe over there." Her cousin Joe Alsop is booming across table about "the balance of power." "You've made an interesting life for yourself out there in the world while we just stay on and on here, as fixtures."

But that is doomed to change. I have just bought two small plots for Howard and me in Rock Creek Cemetery; we will be midway between

Jimmie Trimble and Henry Adams—midway between heart and mind, to put it grandly.

Paul Newman just rang. He and Joanne want to come to hear me speak at the National Press Club in Washington. He proposes we have dinner with the Clintons, four days before the midterm elections. Since no one else is talking to them, we will.

So here I am at the end—of this book, that is. I am again a novelist, and I have spent close to thirty years beneath the shield of Apollo, for whom I changed my life when I moved to Rome. Occasionally, I slipped out from under the shield to write theater, movies, television. Unlike grandfather and father, I was not physically shattered in my late forties and so I have been able, if not to complete, to get on with my work in a way that they could not. I was also to become more intensely political than I was in my conventional youth. Will I write about all this? I don't know. A right-wing radio windbag called Rush Limbaugh, after the 1994 Republican sweep of Congress, declared, "The age of Lenin and Gore Vidal is over." I am inclined to dust off my six-shooters: Billy the Kid will ride again—unless he meant Lennon, not Lenin.

I do feel surprisingly serene when I contemplate Subdivisions 2 and 4 of Lot 293½ in Section E. I note that Alice Longworth is nearby, my fellow fixture, while the half of me that never lived to grow up is only a few yards away.

Finally, I seem to have written, for the first and last time, not the ghost story that I feared but a love story, as circular in shape as desire (and its pursuit), ending with us whole at last in the shade of a copper beech.

Meanwhile . . .

Index

Page numbers in *italics* indicate illustrations.

Photo Credits

Antonello Nusca/Gamma Liaison: p. 2; collection of Gore Vidal: pp. 8, 22, 66, 142, 202, 416; U.P.I./Bettmann: pp. 42, 352; Bob Sandberg/*Look* magazine, © May 1943: p. 80; Wisconsin Center for Film and Theater Research: pp. 98, 116; American Heritage Center, University of Wyoming: pp. 134, 314; George Silk, *Life* magazine, © Time, Inc.: p. 158; Allen Ginsberg: p. 210; A.P./Wide World Photos: pp. 236, 332; Photofest: p. 272; Everett Collection: p. 382.

Photographs in section I, following page 152

Page 1, from the collection of Gore Vidal.

Page 2, top, Carl Albert Center Congressional Archives, University of Oklahoma; bottom left, Brown Brothers; bottom right, Carl Albert Center Congressional Archives, University of Oklahoma.

Page 3, top, Wisconsin Center for Film and Theater Research; bottom, collection of Gore Vidal.

Page 4, top left, American Heritage Center, University of Wyoming; top right and bottom left, A.P./Wide World Photos; bottom right, U.P.I./Bettmann.

Page 5, top left, © 1933 Time, Inc.; top right and bottom, collection of Gore Vidal.

Page 6, collection of Gore Vidal.

Page 7, Wisconsin Center for Film and Theater Research.

Page 8, collection of Gore Vidal.

Page 9, Wisconsin Center for Film and Theater Research.

Page 10, from *The Diary of Anaïs Nin, Volume Four, 1944–1947,* © 1971, top, courtesy of the Anaïs Nin Trust, photograph by Maya Deren; bottom left, collection of George Bixby; bottom right, Wisconsin Center for Film and Theater Research.

Page 11, Jerry Cooke, *Life* magazine, © Time, Inc.

Page 12, collection of Gore Vidal.

Page 13, top left and right, collection of Gore Vidal; bottom, Wisconsin Center for Film and Theater Research.

Page 14, photographs by Jo Healy, courtesy of Erin Clermont.

Page 15, top, Dennis Stock/Magnum Photos; bottom, Lisa Larsen, *Life* magazine, © Time, Inc.

Page 16, Karl Bissinger.

Photographs in section II, following page 312

Page 1, Wisconsin Center for Film and Theater Research.

Page 2, collection of Gore Vidal.

Page 3, top, Wisconsin Center for Film and Theater Research; bottom, collection of Gore Vidal.

Page 4, top, Wisconsin Center for Film and Theater Research; bottom, collection of Gore Vidal.

Page 5, Walter Sanders, *Life* magazine, © Time, Inc.

Page 6, top left, Everett Collection; top right and bottom, Photofest.

Page 7, top, collection of Gore Vidal; bottom, Everett Collection.

Page 9, collection of Gore Vidal.

Page 10, collection of Gore Vidal.

Page 11, collection of Gore Vidal.

Page 12, top, John Loengard, *Life* magazine, © Time, Inc.; bottom, A.P./Wide World Photos.

Page 13, Leonard McCombe, *Life* magazine, © Time, Inc.

Page 14, top, A.P./Wide World Photos; bottom left, Globe Photos; bottom right, Archive Photos.

Page 15, U.P.I./Bettmann.

Page 16, collection of Gore Vidal.

ABOUT THE AUTHOR

GORE VIDAL was born in 1925 at the United States Military Academy, West Point, where his father was the first aviation instructor. Vidal's maternal roots are thoroughly political. As a boy, he lived with his grandfather, the legendary blind Senator T. P. Gore, to whom Vidal read. His father, Eugene Vidal, served as director of the Bureau of Air Commerce under Franklin D. Roosevelt. After graduating from Phillips Exeter Academy, Vidal enlisted at seventeen in the United States Army. At nineteen he became a warrant officer (j.g.) and first mate of the army ship *F.S. 35*, which carried supplies and passengers from Chernowski Bay to Dutch Harbor in the Aleutian Islands. While on night watch in port, he wrote his first novel, *Williwaw*, published in 1946, the year he was mustered out.

Vidal's early works include *The City and the Pillar* (1948), the short story collection *A Thirsty Evil* (1956), and two successful Broadway plays, *Visit to a Small Planet* (1957) and the prize-winning *The Best Man* (1960). Vidal also wrote a number of plays for television's "golden age" (*The Death of Billy the Kid*) as well as Hollywood screenplays (*Suddenly, Last Summer*). In the sixties, three widely acclaimed novels established Vidal's international reputation as a best-selling author: *Julian* (1964), a re-creation of the world of the apostate Roman emperor who attempted to restore paganism; *Washington, D.C.* (1967), the first in what was to become a multi-volume fictional "chronicle" of American history; and the classic *Myra Breckinridge* (1968), a comedy of sex change in a highly mythical Hollywood.

Myron (1974), a sequel to *Myra Breckinridge*, continued to mine the vein of fanciful, sometimes apocalyptic humor that informs *Kalki* (1978), *Duluth* (1983), and *Live from Golgotha* (1992), works described by Italo Calvino as "the hyper-novel or the novel elevated to the square or to the cube." Vidal also continued to explore the ancient world in the wide-ranging *Creation* (1981). The *Boston Globe* noted, "He is our greatest living man of letters."

Gabriel García Márquez praised "Gore Vidal's magnificent series of historical novels or novelized histories" that deal with American life as viewed by one family from the Revolution to the present: *Burr* (1973), *Lincoln* (1984), *1876* (1976), *Empire* (1987), *Hollywood* (1990), and *Washington, D.C.* Vidal's interest in politics has not been limited to commentary; he ran for Congress in New York in 1960, and in 1982 came in second in the California Democratic senatorial primary.

Vidal's essays, both political and literary, have been collected in such volumes as *Homage to Daniel Shays* (1972), *Matters of Fact and Fiction* (1977), *The Second American Revolution* (1982), and *At Home* (1988). In 1993 his *United States: Essays 1952–1992* won the National Book Award.

Vidal divides his time between Los Angeles, California, and Ravello, Italy.

ABOUT THE TYPE

This book was set in Walbaum, a typeface designed in 1810 by the German punchcutter J. E. Walbaum.